Reading India

Reading India

The *Reading India* series is meant to disseminate a selection of scholarly research work that has been published in the *Economic and Political Weekly* and *The Economic Weekly* over the decades. The three volumes, spanning 1949 to 2017, give an overview of important issues relating to India's economy, politics and society. Each set of readings is compiled by three senior academics, who have also written an introductory chapter for the volume. *EPW* is grateful to M/s Seksaria Sons Pvt. Ltd., Mumbai for the permission to reproduce the articles included in this volume. *EPW* also thankfully acknowledges the contributions made by the authors to the volume. This series has been produced with the help of a grant from the Tata Trusts. *EPW* is grateful to the Tata Trusts for supporting this venture.

Reading India

Selections from *The Economic Weekly*

Volume 1: 1949–1965

Edited by

Pranab Bardhan
Sudipto Mundle
Rohini Somanathan

TATA TRUSTS

EPW

Orient BlackSwan

READING INDIA: SELECTIONS FROM *THE ECONOMIC WEEKLY*: VOLUME 1—1949–1965

ORIENT BLACKSWAN PRIVATE LIMITED

Registered Office
3-6-752 Himayatnagar, Hyderabad 500 029, Telangana, India
e-mail: centraloffice@orientblackswan.com

Other Offices
Bengaluru, Bhopal, Chennai, Guwahati,
Hyderabad, Jaipur, Kolkata, Lucknow, Mumbai,
New Delhi, Noida, Patna, Visakhapatnam

First published 2019

ISBN 978-93-5287-715-7

030174

Typeset in
Adobe Garamond Pro 11/13.5
by Manmohan Kumar, Delhi

Printed in India at
Yash Printographics, Noida

Published by
Orient Blackswan Private Limited
3-6-752, Himayatnagar Hyderabad 500 029, Telangana, India
e-mail: info@orientblackswan.com

Contents

PART III

Identity and Politics

PART IV

Analytical Frameworks

PART V

Development and Planning

PART VI

Policy Debates: Agriculture

PART VII

Policy Debates: Industry

PART VIII

Public Finance and Distribution

PART IX

Culture, Administration and Leadership

Tables and Figures

TABLES

Figures

Note to the Reader

As you begin to read this rich and varied collection of articles and commentaries written over the past half century, please do keep in mind the following points:

1. We have made a sincere effort to correct obvious errors and to fill gaps wherever possible, especially with regard to the captions and sources of figures and tables. However, in some cases where the sources have been mentioned or explained in the body of the text, or in a Note, the sources may not appear in the regular format, that is, immediately below the figure or table.
2. In Chapter 16, each table presents the required change in initial level of consumption, under various conditions. Since these conditions have been explained in the text, only the table numbers for all three tables have been retained.
3. All tables and figures that are included have been reformatted.

Economic Weekly, Selected Articles, 1949–1965

Pranab Bardhan, Sudipto Mundle and Rohini Somanathan

Introduction

The *Economic Weekly* (*EW*) was launched in 1949, shortly after India began its journey as independent nation in 1947. The period covered by this volume was an exciting one in the life of the new democracy—full of hope and expectation, but also questioning and rethinking. These expectations and questions are reflected in the pages of the *EW*. Under the leadership of the illustrious founding editor, Sachin Chaudhuri, the journal soon became a major platform for debates about the way forward. It is reported that Jawaharlal Nehru, prime minister at the time, had left standing instructions that every week a copy of the *EW* should be placed on his table as soon as it was published.

During this period, the *EW* was unique in its range of scholarship, the diversity of author backgrounds, and in its willingness to provide space for differing, and often conflicting, ideological positions. Sachin Chaudhuri gathered around him some of the finest minds of that time, persuading eminent social scientists to reflect on a topical policy issue or provide an article summarising their research. Both Indian and foreign scholars contributed to the debate, and bureaucrats, bankers and industrialists often brought in their expertise and experience. The issues covered in the journal were manifold and of wide-ranging significance. On sensitive issues, we often come across contributions using pseudonyms, presumably from inside the government. A tribute to Sachin Chaudhuri that appeared just after his death in 1966 summed up his view of the journal's mission: "He believed the written word had power … The only criterion [for inclusion] was that the case be intelligently and intelligibly argued."[1]

Deciding upon articles for this volume was extremely difficult. The *EW* came out every week, along with two large special issues a year. We could include only a tiny fraction of the many outstanding pieces published. We have chosen a few landmark studies in sociology, politics and economics that capture major analytical and policy debates. The selection also represents a sample of the many excellent Indian and foreign scholars who had a deep knowledge of local and historical contexts and were committed to a new India. This said, the ultimate outcome is inevitably somewhat idiosyncratic. At another time, we may have chosen a little differently. Our hope is that this volume captures some of the flavour of the kind of debates that animated the social thinkers of the day and that it will inspire the interested reader to delve deeper into the archives.

We have divided the articles into nine broad sections. The first three focus on themes and scholars outside the discipline of economics: family and social structures in Indian villages, newly emerging political alliances, and broader issues of ideology and method in social analysis. The next five are on important policy debates. These are mostly among economists and often quantitative in nature: the role of planning in development, policies to increase agricultural productivity, the advantages of small versus large firms, and public finances and spending. The volume concludes on a more general note, with articles on administration, language and leadership. In this introductory chapter we provide context for the included articles and highlight some of their main contributions.

Social and Political Themes

At the start of this period, India was largely rural and agricultural with four out of every five Indians living in one of its half a million villages. This is reflected in the articles that appeared at the time. We begin the volume with the now classic study of a Mysore village by M. N. Srinivas. Srinivas played a critical role in bridging the gap between what he used to call the "book-view" and the "field-view" of social phenomena such as family structure and caste. The first three sections of the volume include some of these anthropological investigations.

These village studies illustrate the many ways in which village unity is created and maintained through an acknowledgement of a shared background, common interests, and a dense set of vertical and horizontal social ties. This allows the village to function as a unit even in the presence of intense group rivalries and antagonisms. We see from Srinivas's study that government officials were rarely seen even 22 miles from an important capital city, so villagers had to find ways of resolving their disputes amicably. This was facilitated by collective activities. In the Oriya hill village studied by F. G. Bailey, the entire village hunted together, separating into their caste groups only as they approached the main settlement after the hunt. Bailey narrates the case of a Brahmin demanding too much of the villages for conducting their rituals and being ostracised by all, including Brahmin families: "The village unity is a rope of many stands ... [The Brahmin] was unable, by pulling on the one strand of caste, to break the whole rope."

In McKim Marriot's north Indian village in the fertile Gangetic plain of Uttar Pradesh, the changes predicted by Srinivas start to become apparent. Land fragmentation results in most cultivators farming multiple non-contiguous plots. This requires them to maintain good relations with an average of 15 field neighbours. Although they manage this, more broad-based collective action is unsuccessful.

The three articles in the section on rural structures focus on the interaction between family structure, assets and mobility. Srinivas and Shah highlight the many connections between villages, dispelling the myth of isolated, self-sufficient villages. In addition to being connected by marriage ties, farmers often cultivated plots located in different revenue villages, and markets and craftsmen serviced clusters of villages. The articles by Irawati Karve and Bernard Cohn relate to family structure. Cohn explores the relationship between family structure and caste. Chamars tend to live in nuclear families that are relatively mobile and rarely trace their ancestry beyond a couple of generations. Thakur landlords in the same village live in joint families and can rattle off their genealogy for 15 generations. These differences partly result from the uneven distribution of land across the two castes, but Cohn highlights many other interesting influences on family composition. For example, Chamar men who survived infancy typically died between 35 and 45, so three generations were less likely to be present even in the absence of mobility.

Karve makes a case for use of statistical methods in the study of family structure. She uses primary data to show that the likelihood of residing within a joint family varies during the life-cycle and many individuals live in both nuclear and joint families for significant parts of their lives. Statisticians can estimate the duration of these phases and help anthropologists uncover the regularities governing cultural life over large areas and long lifespans. We decided on this article rather than Karve's better-known work on caste because she was making a case for specialised knowledge that she did not possess. Providing a forum for non-specialist voices was one of the unique features of the *EW*.

The fourth section, Identity and Politics, links caste and religious identity to the emerging political landscape. D. V. Kelkar, a close collaborator and admirer of K. B. Hedgewar, the founder of the RSS, published a remarkably candid view of the RSS in the *EW* just a year after it was launched. This is a useful article for those interested in the ideological roots of right-wing politics in India today. Rajni Kothari and Ghanshyam Shah study a legislative assembly constituency in Gujarat and show that there is no simple map between caste and political allegiance. The Baniya community in the area splits into two factions and each finds allies among other caste groups. Nirmal Kumar Bose revisits the age-old question of class and caste, criticises commonly used perceptions of both, and argues for historically grounded categories of social boundaries that are Weberian rather than Marxian in character.

ECONOMIC POLICY DEBATES

As the economy tried to diversify away from agriculture, questions of how to bring about growth and structural change came to dominate the discussion in the journal. Many well-known economists reflected on the appropriate theoretical frameworks for India. A. K. Dasgupta believed that Keynesian economics, with its emphasis on demand deficits and excess capacity was irrelevant for an economy whose main challenge was to increase capital stock and labour productivity. Joan Robinson laments the fact that bright students from India coming to Cambridge spend a disproportionate fraction of their time studying price theory and assuming a relatively equal distribution of a given resource base when the main task at hand is to increase resources and foster growth in a highly unequal society. Daniel Thorner argues that by conceptualising India as a "peasant" rather than a "subsistence" economy, we can better understand the process of transformation taking place and learn from the contemporary and historical experiences of other countries.

Following the Second Five Year Plan, growth and investment occupied centre stage. Decisions had to be made about overall rates of savings and investment as well as their distribution across sectors. We have not included the elaborate planning models that were discussed in the *EW* in that period because our space is limited and their details are not likely to interest the reader. We have instead chosen the 1962 article by Sukhamoy Chakravarty and Richard Eckaus which outlines the basic elements of all such models: initial consumption, the acceptable level of inequality, the target rate of growth and the time horizon. Chakravarty and Eckaus highlight the need for reducing current consumption by the wealthy in order to generate resources and limit the import of consumer goods and their demands on scarce foreign exchange reserves. Their open acknowledgement that planning is a political as well as economic process is refreshing.[2]

Given the shortage of resources for investment and a very low per capita income, it was imperative to focus on sectors that could stimulate others. P. Rosenstein-Rodan draws on his work on underdevelopment in south-eastern Europe and emphasises the role of public spending in catalysing private investment. George Rosen provides an important historical lesson by pointing out that the economy of British India failed to expand in spite of the phenomenal expansion in the railway network because incomes were too low to generate the demand for a consumer goods industry and the colonial government was unwilling to protect it through trade restrictions. Also, a significant share of total income leaked to the metropolitan economy as payments for the services of British personnel. Krishna Bharadwaj and Ashok Rudra both use input-output tables to quantify the strength of forward and backward linkages between sectors. Bharadwaj does this for a range of industrial sectors, while Rudra focuses on connections between agriculture and industry and asks whether agricultural productivity is likely to be an impediment in achieving targeted rates of industrial growth.

The next two sections cover important debates in agricultural and industrial policy. The former is much longer, reflecting the concerns of the period: land reform, irrigation, cooperative farming, rural credit, food security and the relationship between farm size and productivity. W. Arthur Lewis and D. R. Gadgil both focus on the problem of raising farmer incomes. Lewis identifies three main factors that can improve agricultural incomes: the demand for agricultural products, productivity increases and the movement of labour out of agriculture. He did not believe that the export of primary products could help farmer welfare or foster growth because quantity increases are accompanied by unfavourable movements in the terms of trade. Gadgil's article responds by explicitly advocating subsidies and price support to famers to stabilise their incomes.

Debates in agricultural policy centered around the efficiency of various property rights and farm sizes. There was particular interest in cooperative farming following experiments in Russia, China and Poland, and many cooperatives were set up across India. Daniel Thorner narrates his experiences of field visits to 117 of these. He finds them mostly captured by village oligarchs. Amlan Datta draws on Polish data on agricultural output under different farming arrangements and argues against cooperative farming, but he is in favour of service cooperatives which provide agricultural inputs, credit and marketing. M. L. Dantwala uses data from a rural credit survey conducted by the Reserve Bank of India in 12 districts and finds that both large and small farmers lease in and lease out land but smaller cultivators have more limited access to credit because of the composition of their assets. Ranjit Gupta cautions against the government's predilection for large irrigation works, and argues for a careful comparison of benefits and costs of major and minor projects, an approach which has been endorsed by the recent literature on irrigation. Raj Krishna looks into the determinants of marketed surplus of grains in what was still predominantly a subsistence farmer economy. V. M. Dandekar in the context of India's livestock economy calls for an examination of the trade-off between Hindu cultural values against cow slaughter and the principles of efficient management of cattle stock, a problem that has raised its disturbing head in recent years.

We include one of Amartya Sen's several pieces on explaining the observed inverse relation between land size and productivity per acre. One of his arguments is that if families with better land have more children, then quicker subdivision of the fertile farms will result in a correlation between farm size and output, with smaller farms producing more per acre in cross-sectional data. While these sources of endogeneity are now well-recognised in the empirical literature in development economics, this was a novel argument at the time.

The size-productivity debate also dominated industrial policy. K. N. Raj points out that while cottage industries are less capital-intensive and may generate more present output from a given stock of capital, the larger capital-intensive plants may produce a higher volume of surplus to support a higher rate of investment and growth, and therefore higher output in the long run. J. C. Sandesara uses data from the cotton textile industry to demonstrate that, when properly measured, smaller units are in fact neither more employment-intensive nor less capital-intensive. In other words there was no case for protecting small and cottage industries, a lesson that Indian policy makers learned many years later. Jan Tinbergen argues for textile policies based on a social cost-benefit analysis which incorporates shadow prices of labour, foreign exchange and other inputs.

Our penultimate section is on public finance and spending. On fiscal federalism and the role of the Finance Commission, Bhabatosh Datta discusses the principles for the equitable allocation of tax revenues across states. He critiques attempts to establish a fiscal architecture for a new federal polity through patches on a pre-existing system deployed for the centralised functioning of a colonial government. He also suggests making clear distinctions between grants and revenue-sharing arrangements and advocates balanced budgets for the states. Large state deficits and discretionary transfers from the central government are live issues today and we may do well to revisit the arguments made by him at the time.

The *EW* carried many articles on central or state taxes that could be imposed to boost state finances. There was an important debate on the agricultural incomes tax, which has not been introduced to this day. Undoubtedly the most important policy document on taxation during this period was the Kaldor report, a comprehensive set of tax reform proposals. It included many recommendations in addition to the proposed expenditure tax for which it is best known. The included article by Nicholas Kaldor discusses tax proposals in the 1958–59 budget. It makes clear that many of his proposals were either ignored or implemented in a distorted and diluted form. Kaldor had argued for delinking the expenditure tax from the income tax, keeping the maximum income tax rates low, and generating resources from the corporate sector through wealth taxes rather than profit taxes for efficiency reasons. In a generic sense his critique remains valid even today.

In contrast to the many writings on taxation and infrastructural spending, there was very little discussion on public services such as health and education, or on the overall distribution of income. Our final two articles in this section of the volume represent these areas. Nikhilesh Bhattacharya and Banamali Dey discuss the results of surveys on education and health expenditure in Madhyamgram in West Bengal. They find that free primary schools and public hospitals are effective in reducing inequality, while secondary schools are less effective because they serve higher expenditure groups. V. K. R. V. Rao documents the increase in the ratio of urban to rural per capita income over the 1950s and attributes this to the decline in industry, commerce and transport in rural India. He calls for a renewed emphasis on rural development to avoid these disparities emerging as a major political constraint to future growth.

Leadership, Administration, and Language

The volume concludes with articles relating to leadership, administration and language issues in independent India. D. P. Mukerji traces the role of leaders and reform movements in envisioning the new nation. Discussing the influence of Tagore, Gandhi and Nehru among others, he argues for clear thinking on the ways in which Indian educational systems build the values of future citizens. We have included two articles that deal with the question of national and regional languages, a prominent issue in that period. O. L. Chavarria-Aguilar is concerned about the constitutional requirement of Hindi as a national language by the mid-sixties given that India had at least 14 major regional languages. If Hindi was adopted as a national language, it should only be for official use by the Union Government and the selected states whose inhabitants used it as their mother-tongue. If imposed on others for the non-official purposes of "literature, of science and of everyday intercourse," it would threaten to "gobble up" other major languages, and lead to resentment and regional chauvinism. The controversy continued and I. P. Desai, a decade later, argued that Hindi is more likely to gain when it is promoted in parallel with the regional languages.

Rajni Kothari, one of the most distinguished Indian political scientists, published a series of articles in 1961 on the development of democratic institutions and their interconnections. From this set, we include the article focusing on the bureaucracy. As the administrative services expanded, the gulf in quality between the elite top and the other levels widened and tensions between bureaucrats and their new political masters emerged. Kothari cautions against expanding the bureaucracy too quickly and points to the key dimensions of required administrative reform.

Beyond the old colonial administrative system, bureaucrats in independent India had to take on the additional role of fostering socio-economic development. The ability of the administrative machinery to cope with its new role depended in large measure on the capacity of the bureaucrats who ran it. The two-part article by Asoke Mohan Roy argues that the new demands required the skills of the "generalist" as well as the "specialist," with generalists more important at higher levels of management. In his comment Deepak Lal agrees that both types are required, but takes the position that while a specialist can acquire the skills of a generalist, the reverse is not always true. The debate is yet to be settled.

Our last two pieces are tributes to Jawaharlal Nehru. Nehru played a larger-than-life role in building and consolidating the new democracy as its pre-eminent leader. Upon his passing away in 1964, many articles on his vision and his contributions appeared in the pages of the *EW*. Rajni Kothari claims that Nehru's greatest legacy was neither his foreign policy of non-alignment nor his adoption of the path of planned economic development, but the building of durable institutions of democracy and the consolidation of the party system through his consensual style of leadership. M. L. Dantwala portrays Nehru as a pragmatist rather than a doctrinaire socialist. He believed in the socialist goals of equity and poverty reduction but did not necessarily endorse the socialist means of achieving these goals.

The mix of voice and personalities published reflect, perhaps more than anything else, the very high value placed on open, uncensored and well-informed discussion that today seems lost in the mists of time. Our selection of articles hopes to revive it in some small way and create a renewed demand for non-partisan spaces in our democracy.

Notes and References

[1] C. Flibbertigibbet [pseud.], "A Man for All Seasons," *Economic and Political Weekly* 1, no. 19 (24 December 1966).

[2] We direct the interested reader to the better-known but much more space-consuming multi-sector model developed by Sukhamoy Chakravarty and Louis Lefeber ("An Optimizing Planning Model," *Economic Weekly* 17, No. 5-6-7 [31 January 1965]) along with the critique by T. N. Srinivasan.

PART I

Early Villages Studies

1

The Social Structure of a Mysore Village*

M. N. Srinivas

There are about 560,000 villages in what is now the Indian Union, and the bulk of the population of 357 million live in these villages where the traditional mode of life still continues. But the villages have begun to change rapidly nowadays, and the pace of the change is likely to increase rather than decrease in the near future. This makes the field study of typical villages in the different linguistic areas of our country an urgent necessity. Either we collect the facts now, or they are lost forever.

The Indian village community has figured rather prominently in early sociological literature. Sir Henry Maine brought the Indian village community into prominence by making it the basis of his theory of primitive communism of property. Basing his theories on a certain type of village community existing in parts of North India, he argued that originally land, that is property, was owned jointly by kin groups, and that individual ownership of land was a later phenomenon in the history of human societies. Attempts to reconstruct the history of social institutions were fashionable in the latter half of the nineteenth century. Social anthropology or comparative sociology is a more mature subject today, and consequently social anthropologists are more modest than the Victorian predecessors. They either attempt to describe the structural features of a small society which they have studied intensively for two or three years, or compare similar institutions in a few neighbouring societies.

We may note briefly one or two general points about village communities all over India, before proceeding to give an outline of this village community in

* Originally published in *Economic Weekly* 3, nos. 42–43 (30 October 1951), pp. 1051–56.

Mysore. Earlier writers like Maine distinguished between two types of villages in India—the "joint" and the "severalty." The first type prevails in the NWFP, the Punjab, and UP, and the second in peninsular and central India. The latter type existed in Bengal and Bihar before the introduction of the Permanent Settlement in 1793. The "joint" type may further be subdivided into the *pattidari* and the *zamindari* subtypes, in both of which the village lands constitute the joint property of an organised proprietary body. But while in the pattidari system the joint families constituting the proprietary body own separate shares in the cultivable land and hold the waste and pasture lands in common, in the zamindari system all land is held and managed in common, and not divided. In the latter subtype, the tenants, if any, are the tenants of the whole body of proprietors, their rents and other receipts are paid into a common fund from which the common expenses are met, and the annual profits are divided among the co-sharers according to their respective shares. In a joint village, there are two classes of men, one with proprietary rights, the other without them, power resting exclusively with the former.

In the severalty or *ryotwari* village, a type which prevailed over the greater part of India, the unit for land revenue is not the village, but the holding of each cultivator, which is separately assessed, and each cultivator is individually responsible for its payment. There is no waste land held in common which can be divided if required for cultivation, though there may be common rights of use in the waste, e.g., for grazing and collecting fuel.

A feature of the village community all over India is the *panchayat* or council of elders which decides disputes between villagers, and discusses matters of common interest like holding a festival, building a temple or road, etc.

The nature of the village community is much better realised if we disregard for a moment the development of communications and the increase of administrative centralisation of the revenue, police, law courts, etc., of the last 150 years or more. Before this, the village communities were far more isolated than they are today. A man's effective contacts and relations, one imagines, normally stopped a few miles from his natal village. A distant pilgrimage or a journey to a cattle fair were probably the only occasions when an individual ventured beyond the range of his normal contacts. Even then, he was often accompanied by his friends and relatives. Groups of relatives and friends moved a considerable distance only when there were compelling reasons like a famine, war, or religious persecution by a prince professing a different faith.

The overall political authority does not seem to have been much more than a tax-collecting body in its relations to these villages. As long as a village paid its taxes and no great crime was committed in it, it was allowed to go its own way. If we exclude for a moment the hereditary headman of the village and the hereditary accountant who are primarily members of the village community discharging certain duties for the government, officials of the government rarely visited the village. The elders in Kodagahalli told me that even as recently as 50 years ago a policeman was a rare sight in their village, only 22 miles from the capital of the State of Mysore. Formerly every village had its own watch and ward , and this continues in certain villages even today.

Nobody can fail to be impressed by the isolation and stability of these village communities. Some of the early British administrators have left us their impressions of the village community. Sir Charles Metcalfe wrote in 1832:

> The village communities are little republics, having nearly everything they want within themselves, and almost independent of any foreign relations. They seem to last where nothing else lasts. Dynasty after dynasty tumbles down; revolution succeeds revolution ... but the village community remains the same ... This union of village communities, each one forming a separate little state in itself, has, I conceive, contributed more than any other cause to the preservation of the people of India, through all the revolutions and changes which they have suffered, and is in a high degree conducive to their happiness, and to the enjoyment of a great portion of freedom and independence.[1]

All over India, excluding Bengal, Assam and parts of the West Coast of southern India, the village is a cluster of houses and huts with the fields all around. Narrow, uneven, winding streets run between rows of houses, thatched or roofed with tiles made presumably by the local potter. The village occupies a very restricted area—Kodagahalli is a somewhat large village, containing 1,523 inhabitants, and yet one can go round it in about half an hour.

Every villager knows most of the other members of the village. Everyone belongs to a caste, is a member of a joint family, and of the agnatic kin-group which is made up of a few joint families. A man's idiosyncrasies are common property. Adults are aware of the "history" of almost every joint family in the village. A relation between two persons seems to be a continuity from a relationship between their parents, and leads to a relationship between their children. One occasionally comes across instances where past animosity between two joint families acts as a bond between their present representatives.

The headman of the village, commonly called the *Patel*, and the accountant, the *Shanbhog*, are key figures in the community. They both belong to the village and their offices are hereditary. The headman is usually a non-Brahmin, whereas the accountant is invariably a Brahmin. The headman represents the village to the Government and vice versa. His dual position of agent of the Government and representative of his village gives him the respect of all. He is an indispensable go-between. While the Government regards him as one who can be held responsible for the village, to the villagers he is their spokesman. Till recently, the government seems to have been regarded with awe by the villagers. Only the boldest seem to have remained in the village when a high government official visited it—perhaps such a visit was undertaken only when something was seriously wrong in the village. The need for a spokesman is better appreciated when we remember these facts.

The accountant keeps a register of how much land each head of a family or joint family has, and the amount of tax on the land. Just before harvest the accountant reports to the government the state of the crops. He usually sends his report in the form, "The harvest will be 8 as. in the rupee this year." The government's assessment will be adjusted to this estimate, after the accountant's estimate has been checked by a higher official.

The village is a unity in several senses of the term. It is, firstly, a physical unity. If the monsoon fails, it fails for everyone. Formerly, when there was an attack of cholera or plague or smallpox, the entire village acted as one, and moved away to a different place. (The present site of Kodagahalli is only seventy years old, the old site having been abandoned during an epidemic of malaria.) They all joined together to propitiate the deities presiding over these diseases. The disease was ritually driven out of the village—the village boundary had a certain ritual significance.

This ritual unity of the village is important. During the early part of the summer of 1948 there was a long drought and this adversely affected the summer crops, horse gram, black gram, green gram, etc. The villagers felt that they were being punished by God. Some attributed the drought to the fact that the priest of the Basava temple, an old widower, was living with two women to whom he was not married. The rains are liable to fail for other reasons too: burial of a leper's corpse leads to defilement of Mother Earth (*Bhumitai*) and this results in a drought. A leper's corpse has to be cremated or floated down a river.

There was a striking demonstration of village unity during my stay. The government suddenly passed an order that fishing rights in tanks all over the state should be sold by auction. When Kodagahalli people learnt of it, their spontaneous reaction was, "What right has the government to auction fishing rights in *our* tank?" The government was, according to them, encroaching on something that belonged to them. (It must be mentioned here that in Kodagahalli, once every year, during the height of summer, when water is at the lowest, the headman and elders organise a fishing expedition. At night, by moonlight, most of the adults go with fishing baskets to the tank and catch fish. The next day there is a feast in every house.) On the day fixed for auction, the villagers saw to it that nobody in the village or from any of the neighbouring villages was there to bid. The visiting government official had to return without an auction.

This sense of unity is also usually seen when the villagers contrast themselves with others. Kodagahalli people think themselves refined compared to Sihalli people. They concede that Arakere people are more educated than themselves, but they say that they are quarrelsome, and do not cooperate with others for constructive tasks. On the other hand, Arakere people regard themselves as advanced and consider Kodagahalli backward. Pride in one's village is very common, though this does not completely shut out objectivity.

We occasionally find two villages fighting each other. There is a Madeswara (a form of Shiva) temple two furlongs from Kodagahalli, and every year, in the month of Kartik (October–November), there is a festival in honour of this deity. People from within a radius of about twenty miles come to this festival. Parties of devotees from surrounding villages come and carry an image of the deity round the temple. It is customary to allow each party to carry the image three times round the temple. In 1947 a party from Arakere was intercepted by a party from Sihalli soon after the former had completed the second round. Arakere people said they wanted to complete the three rounds. Sihalli people replied that a great many people were waiting, and there was no time for the customary three rounds. A fight ensued, in which an Arakere youth was injured. Soon Arakere people massed up for a fight, and started moving towards Kodagahalli. The police then intervened, fired a few rounds in the air, and were able to prevent the fight from assuming serious proportions.

Sihalli people felt uncomfortable after the festival was over. They knew that Arakere people would try to avenge themselves. So they wanted to come to a settlement (*raji*). They reported their desire for settlement to the headmen of Kodagahalli and Bannur—in the latter is an important panchayat for the settlement of disputes. Arakere people were asked to be present in Bannur on a certain day for the settlement of the dispute. They refused to comply with the request. Arakere has a panchayat of the same standing as Bannur, and Arakere people thought that it was a slight for them to be summoned to Bannur. Finally, it was agreed that the parties concerned should meet in the Madeswara temple itself. They met at last, and the battle took a legal turn. It was finally decided that Sihalli people had committed a wrong, and they reluctantly paid the fine imposed on them. They then went back to their village and fined heavily all the youths who had taken part in the fight. At both Arakere and Sihalli, people were informed of the end of the dispute by the beating of a drum, with a stern warning that anyone who did not heed the decision would be summarily dealt with by the village panchayat.

We have said enough to show that the unity of the village has several aspects. Most members of the village, whatever their caste, consider themselves to be *villagers* in certain contexts. There are 16 sub-castes in Kodagahalli. Each of these sub-castes has a distinctive tradition with strong ties with the same sub-caste in villages nearby. That is, the village is a vertical unity of many castes whereas caste is a horizontal unity, its alliances going beyond the village.

There is one aspect of the caste system which does not receive sufficient emphasis. All the various castes in a village are interdependent. This is seen in day-to-day matters and is prominent on ritual and other important occasions. Any villager will say, for instance, that at the wedding of a peasant all the castes have to cooperate. The Brahmin is priest, the carpenter puts up the pandal, the goldsmith makes the ornaments, the potter makes the pots, the washerman supplies clean cloths for the bridal pair to walk on, the barber shaves the groom, the oil-presser supplies the oil for the lamps and cooking, the shepherd provides wool for the sacred thread which is tied round the wrists of the bridal pair, Banajigas (traders) supply the provisions, the Medas (basket-makers) the baskets, and the Holeva (untouchable) performs menial tasks and makes a pair of sandals for the groom.

The carpenter (he belongs to the caste of carpenters and blacksmiths, it is important to remember) makes the peasant's plough, and it is his duty to see that the peasant's agricultural implements are all in good repair. Each family he serves pays him annually a fixed amount of paddy and straw at the rice harvest. He also gets a share—a very small one—of the grains that are grown during summer. The washerman similarly washes the clothes of every family in the village, except of families belonging to very low castes. The men of the washerman's family wash the men's clothes, while the women wash the women's clothes. A man considers it beneath him to wash a woman's clothes. The washerman also has special duties and privileges on ritual occasions. He is paid annually in paddy and straw by every family he serves. The same holds good for the potter and barber.

The oil-presser does not seem to be included in such traditional arrangements. The Brahmin and Lingayat (non-Brahmin, Shaivite sect of South India) priests of the three important temples in Kodagahalli are also paid a small quantity of paddy and straw annually. It must be mentioned here that each of these temples has been endowed with lands which the priestly families enjoy. The paddy and straw which they are paid in addition is said to be a contribution towards the daily rice-offerings to the deities.

Formerly, in Kodagahalli, it was customary for two families, one belonging to the upper caste and the other to the untouchable caste, to be linked in a master-servant relationship. The servant was called the *halemaga* (old son) of the master. The servant family had certain duties on ritual and social occasions, e.g., at a wedding in the master's family the servant had to present a pair of sandals (*chemmalige*) to the bridegroom. The servant family was paid a quantity of paddy and straw at the harvest. In addition, it had the right to the carcass of any cow or bullock which died in the master's house.

Nowadays, untouchables are beginning to refuse to perform these and other tasks which are considered to be degrading. But the upper castes want them to continue performing them, and there is friction.

Formerly, it seems that entire sub-castes occupying a very low position in the hierarchy were attached as halemagas to certain sub-castes occupying a relatively high position. Thus, we find a man of a high caste saying that "formerly such-and-such a sub-caste were halemagas to us. They are no longer so." Sometimes this relationship seems to have been purely nominal—as when a wandering sub-caste like the Garudigas (caste of acrobats and magicians) are halemagas to a sub-caste in a village. The Garudigas might visit this particular village once a year only. Sometimes a man might claim a sub-caste higher than his own as halemaga in order to boost his own sub-caste.

Servants cultivating their master's lands are paid in paddy or a combination of paddy and money, and tenants pay their landlords a certain share of the crop. Paddy occupies to a large extent the place of money in the economy, and barter is even today common in individual transactions.[2] But money is being used more and more.

The village is even today largely self-sufficient. But nowadays there is a need for goods made or grown outside the village: clothes, salt, sugar, matches, kerosene, soap, tea, coffee, beedis, lanterns, cycles, and safes are some of the goods that come from outside. A self-sufficient economy is possible only if each sub-caste adheres to its traditional occupation. The occupations are complementary. This is true to a great extent in Kodagahalli even today, though every caste has agriculture either as its main occupation or practises agriculture along with its main occupation. The members of the peasant caste practise agriculture, the barber shaves, the washerman washes clothes, the potter makes pots, the Banajiga trades, the Ganga works the oil press and sells oil, the Besthas are fishermen, the Idigas sell toddy, though they no longer tap it, the Medas make baskets and the Koramas are swineherds. The untouchables are labourers and servants.

But most of the Kurahas are agriculturists, though their traditional occupation is keeping sheep and making woollen blankets. The few Muslims in Kodagahalli are recent immigrants, and they are traders and contractors.

A few peasants and a Lingayat have opened grocery shops, and a potter and a fisherman sew clothes on a sewing machine. The priestly castes also cultivate their lands. It is even today considered a proper thing to follow one's traditional occupation. (This view, however, does not obtain among many of the younger people who have been to school and who are urban in their outlook.)

A caste has a ritualist attitude towards the tools, implements, and objects associated with its occupation. Annually, at the festival of Gauri (Parvati, wife of Shiva), each caste worships its tools. Books are identified with Saraswati, the goddess of learning, and everyone has ritual respect for them. The Brahmins worship books during Dassera. It is customary to perform Saraswati puja in the village school.

The entire community, composed of all the Hindu castes, regard the earth as Mother Earth, and the crops and manure are regarded as Lakshmi, the goddess of wealth. The domestic lamp, granary, a heap of grain, a grain-measure, etc., are all objects of ritual respect.

The various sub-castes in a village are interdependent economically and otherwise, and they see themselves as villagers in certain contexts, but these do not prevent intercaste rivalry and even hostility. This is the natural corollary of caste solidarity. Intercaste rivalry expresses itself in joking about the customs and habits of the castes of which one is not a member. Along with a pride in one's own caste, there goes an ignorance of, and often contempt for, the ways and customs of other castes. The upper castes tend to be especially contemptuous of the ways of the lower castes.

Occasionally there are fights between sub-castes. Recently, Besthas and Lingayats fought each other in a village near Kodagahalli. Both Besthas and Lingayats are credited with a great deal of caste solidarity.

There are villages in which stones have been planted to mark the boundary of a caste. A man who finds himself on the wrong side of the boundary might be beaten. It is necessary to mention here—even though it means digressing—that there is another type of solidarity besides those of kinship, caste, and village. The various sub-castes in a village are grouped into two divisions: Nadu and Desha. It is not very easy to discover which sub-castes belong to the Nadu division and which to the Desha. One version is that Brahmins, Kshatriyas and Okkaligas belong to the Nadu division, whereas all the castes which usually have the suffix *-shetti* (from Sanskrit *Sreshti*, elect) belong to the Desha division. Thus, the Banajiga, Agasta (Madivala), Kumbara, Ganiga, Hajama, Bestha, weaving castes, Medas, and Koramas belong to the Desha. It is thus seen that all the trading and artisan castes belong to the Desha division. The Okkaligas certainly belong to the Nadu, but one is not so certain about the Brahmin and Kshatriya. Perhaps the Brahmin was extraneous to the village in this matter, as he certainly is in some others.

It is relevant to introduce another matter here: the smith group of castes are said to have "one colour less" than the others. Formerly, this group suffered from certain civic disabilities. Their weddings could not be performed inside the village. They were excluded from village assemblies, prayer parties, and marriage houses. They were not allowed to wear red slippers. No other caste, not even the Holeya, the right-hand division of the untouchable caste, dined at the house of a smith. It is usual to say that the Holeya is the lowest caste. But there are castes to which the Holeya does point and say that he does not eat food cooked by them, or drink water given by them, or even borrow *chunam* (lime paste for betel leaves).

An attempt by the smiths to assert their equality with the other castes led to a fight between them and others. Fifty years ago the Cheluvadi (untouchable, hereditary servant of the village, belonging to right-hand division) of Arakere village beat a wealthy smith from Mysore who walked into the village wearing red slippers. The smith had lent money to the extent of Rs. 50,000 to the villagers.

Perhaps the grouping of castes into those "with full colours" and those "with one colour less" coincides with the grouping of castes into right-hand and left-hand divisions. The smiths certainly belong to the latter. Of the untouchables, the Holeyas belong to the right-hand, while the Madigas belong to the left-hand division. Formerly, a fight usually arose when a left-hand caste tried to assert a privilege which was denied to it by the right-hand division.

The village has a solidarity even though composed of several different castes. Each caste again has a solidarity cutting across the village. Thirdly, the various castes living in a village can be grouped into Nadu and Desha divisions. This distinction, like the "with full colours" and "one colour less" division, and the right-hand and left-hand division, is a general distinction between castes and is not confined to the castes of one village. In every village one finds castes belonging to the right- and left-hand divisions, "full colours" and "one colour less" divisions, and Nadu and Desha divisions.

We must now mention the existence of caste-courts, which punish people guilty of caste offences. They are even today powerful organisations, though the legal system introduced by the British has well-nigh broken them. For instance, a person who has been excommunicated by a caste-court can sue it in a court of law for defamation. Theoretically, the caste-court has been more or less declared illegal. But it actually functions vigorously. Even as recently as 1945, there was an instance of a woman of the washerman caste who was very nearly thrown out of caste because of alleged inter-dining with a sister who had been thrown out of caste sometime previously for living with an untouchable. Excommunication from caste is the most powerful weapon in the hands of the caste-courts. It can be final and irrevocable, or temporary. The former is for very grave offences like living with a very low caste man, or eating with him. The milder punishment is for smaller offences: the offender expresses regret for his action, pays a fine, undergoes purificatory ritual, after which he gives a feast to the members of his caste. When one is excommunicated for good, he is as good as dead to his caste which stops all social intercourse with him. A notice is often circulated which makes it impossible for the wretched man to settle elsewhere. If the offender is the head of a family, the entire family comes under the ban unless they disown him.

At a wedding, betel leaves and nuts are distributed to all the guests assembled. This distribution has to take place in a certain order. It has to take into account the qualifications of each guest. The wedding guests are very touchy on the question of precedence, and if a guest feels that he has been dishonoured, he creates a scene. The formal distribution of betel leaves is such a hazardous affair, that several years ago the elders of Kodagahalli decided that anybody could drop it if he paid Rs. 8–40 into the village fund. Nowadays most take advantage of this escape.

There are caste-courts for the potters at Keragodu and Ashtagrama. These courts are called *gadi*, which literally means frontier or boundary. Each caste has several caste-courts and they are said to constitute a hierarchy. But the hierarchy does not seem to be clearly defined. For instance, there is a keen rivalry between Keragodu gadi and Mysore gadi. The Mysore people claim precedence over Keragodu on the ground that they represent the gadi of the capital of Mysore State. To this the Keragodu people reply that these gadis came into existence during the time of Hyder Ali, father of Tipu Sultan, and even then Keragodu had precedence over Ashtagrama, the then capital of Mysore State—in other words, that Keragodu has always enjoyed precedence over the capital.

Two years ago, representatives of the potter caste in Mysore started claiming precedence over Keragodu representatives in villages like Arakere, Pura, Kadlagala, etc. In none of the places did they have any success. But in Tagadur gadi they were successful in pressing their claim.

Again, Arakere gadi claims to include under it Keragodu gadi, but the latter considers itself to be a separate gadi and not merely part of Arakere. It is said that formerly potters had 48 gadis, and at a wedding in a potter's house, 48 betels had to be kept aside, irrespective of the fact that only a few of the 48 representatives were present. In Arakere village, this custom was stopped only a few years ago, and nowadays only those actually present receive betel leaves.

The ritual of betel distribution at a wedding reflects the village organisation, and also reveals the existence of a hierarchy of caste-courts. Sometimes the hierarchy is not very clearly defined. One of the reasons for this may be the fact that a caste-court which is supreme in one area tries to assert its authority in a different area. This would reveal that the process of unification had not been carried sufficiently far.

Certain matters fall very clearly within the jurisdiction of a caste-court, for example, dining or living with a member of low caste. Matters like lopping off the branches of someone else's tree, diverting water belonging to another field, stealing grass from a field, setting fire to hayricks, etc., fall within the jurisdiction of village authorities who are armed with powerful sanctions, ranging from fines to boycott of the offender. The offender who has been boycotted (and his family) lose access to the village tank or canal. His cattle will not be allowed to graze on the village pasture. The barber, washerman, etc., will not serve him. No neighbour will offer fire and hot water. Even today in the village it is common to light a stove from the embers taken from a neighbour's stove. Similarly, hot water for bathing or washing is borrowed from a neighhour who has a cauldron full of boiling water.

The village and caste authorities normally work together. Sometimes the former may tell the disputants, "We don't like to interfere in this case. It is much better if you took this matter up to your caste authorities." Again, the caste authorities consult the village authorities when a question of fact is involved—the latter are the men on the spot and know the parties to, and sometimes the facts of, the dispute.

In Kodagahalli, as far as the Okkaligas (peasants, 735 of them) are concerned, there is a caste headman (*nadu gauda*) in the village to whom they can take their disputes. The village headman (*patel*) is also an Okkaliga, and he and the village headman are great friends. Each supports the other in almost all matters. The result is that disputes from Kodagahalli Okkaligas rarely go out of the village. In fact, Kodagahalli people are well-known for their love of peace.

Both the village headman and the headman of the Okkaliga caste are well-to-do and have a reputation for being fair-minded. This normally ensures the settling of disputes within the village. Also, the two headmen refrain from trying to exercise their authority in disputes in which certain people well-known for their quarrelsomeness are involved. The latter take their disputes to the law courts.

The headman of the Okkaliga caste in Kodagahalli is normally called in to settle disputes of non-Okkaligas, disputes which clearly lie within the jurisdiction of respective cast authorities. For instance, the case of a Kuraba (shepherd) girl of Kodagahalli who did not want to join her husband away was taken before the Okkaliga caste headman. The reputation of a leader for fairness often might induce people of other castes to take their disputes to him.

Every political leader and every official who comes into direct contact with villagers, complains about "party politics" in the village. Every village is divided into factions, and each faction headed by a leader. These factions are preventing the working of the village as a unit.

The village is an interdependent unit, economically self-sufficient, having its own village assembly, watch and ward, officials and servants. Inside each village each caste lives its own life, though it is dependent on other castes within and without the village. There is also a division along class lines. The untouchables are never wealthy, and they are usually servants and labourers at the houses of the upper castes. But there are also poor members of the upper castes who act as servants to rich members of their own caste. Thus, a poor Okkaliga often becomes the servant of a rich Okkaliga. An upper-caste man rarely becomes a servant at the house of a man who belongs to a much lower caste.

We have said enough to indicate the kind of ties that bind together the members of the village community. These ties are strong and traditional. But the forces set in motion in the last 150 years have been such as to weaken them, and the arrival of Independence has marked a concentrated effort to snap these ties. What kind of village community will come to exist in the future can only be a matter for speculation.

Notes and References

[1] *Report of the Select Committee of the House of Commons*, 1832, Volume III, Appendix 84, p. 331.

[2] In certain spheres, the role of barter has increased in the post-war years, which have been characterised by acute shortage of rice. Vegetable sellers refuse cash and sell only for rice.

2

Social Structure and Change in a UP Village*

McKim Marriott

The social structure of many Hindu villages raises problems for concerted action which must be squarely faced by all who would speculate upon or plan for the real future of rural India. Kishan Garhi, a village in the Brij division of the upper Ganges-Jamuna Doab, is a fair specimen of the complex village settlements which crowd the most productive agricultural areas of the country. The present situation there and the trends which have created it give pause to thought.

Kishan Garhi, with its 160 mud houses, is half again as large as the average UP village. Its greater size allows it to include a fortress belonging to three one-time landlords, and a large number of specialists (45 houses) and traders (10 houses)—small but vital elements of rural life—as well as the agricultural core of tenant farmers (68 houses) and landless agricultural labourers (34 houses).

Economic Groupings

The rich alluvial plain where Kishan Garhi's 535 acres lie is extremely flat—so flat that a rise or fall of two inches in a field may be worthy of close attention. Two inches, more or less, in the amount of the monsoon rainfall is worth no particular notice to farmers here, for the summer crops of millet and maize provide hardly a quarter of human foodgrains. Most crops and nearly all foodgrains are grown only by dint of sustained irrigation from fifty deep wells. From June through August and from October through March, teams of two men and a pair or two of oxen

* Originally published in *Economic Weekly* 4, no. 34 (23 August 1952), pp. 869–77. The author studied the people of Kishan Garhi as a resident of that village for fourteen months in 1951–52, thanks to a fellowship granted by the Social Science Research Council of Washington, DC, USA.

tread the well ramps hoisting 30-gallon buckets of water. A boy guides the water through raised channels to moisten the squared fields of wheat, barley, oilseeds, peas, and gram. In the spring harvest, there may be some advantage if six or eight men work side by side for a day or two on the fields of one holding, but no other agricultural operation—ploughing, smoothing, weeding, threshing—demands the simultaneous work of more than three persons. The yield of these labours is a sufficiency of fodder for some 400 animals, a moderate quantity of oilseeds for sale, and a slight surplus of foodgrains beyond the appetites of the villagers themselves. The total annual produce of Kishan Garhi, if equally divided among all residents, would amount to about 8 as. per day.

Work groups were always strikingly small, and with subdivision of the average holding from 16 to 12 acres over the past thirty years, work groups even of small size have become less sustained. But the problems of essential cooperation are tremendous and growing. A farmer ordinarily depends on others' wells for half of his irrigation. Since the average holding has now come to be divided into nine non-contiguous plots, the success of one man's crops may depend on his maintaining good relations with the fifteen persons who ordinarily comprise his field neighbours. No more than half of the tiny work groups can consist of fellow members of the same caste and clan. Sixty-eight families of farmers cultivate forty holdings and ultimately distribute the yield of each holding among some twelve sharers. Even the landlord rights have come to be complexly divided, changing from three units eighty years ago to eleven separately managed units at present.

Economic dependencies thirty years ago constituted much larger and much more inclusive groupings. These were focused quite narrowly on a few persons of outstanding wealth and power. For access to land, most cultivators were dependent on short-term, unwritten leases granted by one of three families of a single line of landlords. The landlords in those days kept a third of the village lands in their own control always—one-fifth for their "personal" cultivation through servants, and the rest in forest, pasture, road, and house areas for the enjoyment of their followers. Most persons were borrowers of grain and money, and most had then to turn to two or three wealthier tenants or to the same landlords for credit. Disabled by debt, many of the thirty families of landless labourers worked year after year for one tenant or landlord master. Heavy debtors could never repay fully, nor could they readily shift their debts from one creditor to another. But the depression, followed by rising crop prices together with new tenancy legation helped to unbind most of the older land and debt dependencies. Five families of landlords and two of tenant lenders were themselves bankrupted. The forest and pasture lands were parcelled out to tenants for cultivation. Most of the tenants were made secure, their rents reduced and fixed. The landlord's personal fields were whittled away: today there remains but a single tenant-at-will of one landlord. Sub-tenants and sharecroppers are an increasing class of cultivators; for fear of the 1939 tenancy laws, they are moved about every year or, at the most, every two years. Labourers are rarely kept by an employer for longer than the six-month watering season. Groupings whose form is determined by economic dependency have thus generally become smaller and more diffuse; they no longer clearly organise the village into segments of distinct allegiance.

A similar break-up of larger dependent segments has overtaken the artisans and servants. The third of the village people who live by means other than their own cultivation—priest, wizard, accountant, barber, musician, cobbler, cotton carder, potter, weaver, carpenter, tailor, trader, and so on—find more than half of their clientele in some ten fanning hamlets outside of Kishan Garhi. Until thirty years ago, most of the specialists were aligned as special retainers of one or another of the landlord families of this area, and as servants of that landlord's tenants. These old segmental clienteles have now dissolved into a helter-skelter pattern of many more equal clients. The plots of land granted free of rent in return for special services have mostly been subdivided beyond the point of efficient utility. Half of the artisans and servants now shift masters with each generation.

Paralleling the clear, old hierarchy of economic power thirty years ago was an informal but compelling structure of power. The landlords were the law for all purposes beyond the caste councils. The landlords maintained their own court and record room, and dealt summarily with all offenders through their strong organisations of dependent followers. One landlord always held the office of police headman (*mukhya*) for Kishan Garhi. Village crimes and disputes could reach formal trial in the district courts only with the support of one of the landlords or his tenant allies. But unrivalled economic status has slipped from the hands of the petty landlords of Kishan Garhi, and they have seen their power and influence jolted downward. The village thereby lost old leaders.

Kinship Groupings

The work groups, classes, and dependent clusters whose progressive fragmentation is described above comprise only the economic solidarities of Kishan Garhi society. They are intersected and complicated by two other kinds of social structures, those of kinship and those of rank.

The largest kinship groupings of Kishan Garhi, its 24 castes, has been perfectly stable over many years. The number of persons within any one caste in the village averages 35, or five-and-a-half households. The smaller castes in many instances comprise but a single family. The largest caste, that of the Brahmans, who are here mainly farmers, has forty households, and is followed in order of size by the caste groups of the Chamars, Jats, Kumhars, and Muslim Faqirs, all of which number more than a dozen families. Most castes and some of their clans have particular sacred stones and trees for periodic worship and once had a number of distinctive gods and rituals.

The larger castes in the village contain clans, which are patrilineal and patrilocal groups named or nicknamed according to their traditional origins or ritual duties. The larger clans are further divided into lineages having a known common ancestry. These lineages are known by the names of their most prominent living members and generally comprise two or three families. As far back as the oldest men and the oldest records are able to trace—about 80 years—there were no less than forty lineal groups of kinsmen, entirely separate in descent. But with growth of population, the number of lineages has grown proportionately. Over and beyond this growth, the number of lineages has suddenly increased by 20 per cent in the past thirty years, since nine new lineages have moved into the village to take up cultivation of lands obtained through female inheritance from their relatives by marriage. Such immigrations of new kin groups were much rarer under the customs and laws of landholding which prevailed thirty years ago. Each clan and lineage demands extensive and exclusive loyalty to itself. The multiplication of kin groups to the present number of 55 makes the problem of village organisation much more acute.

Lineages and clans are not simply more numerous than they were 30 years ago, but the members of any one kin group have now come to act together in certain ways less readily than before. Tenant families belonging to the same lineage previously tended to cultivate jointly any lands that any individual among them held on lease from the landlord. The name listed in the accountant's books was felt to stand for the rights of the whole group. As many as six or seven related households often worked together in this way, dividing their investment and profit according to ability and need, and maintaining a common grain store for common ceremonies and joint irregular needs. Beyond the lineage and within the clan there was less intense cooperation, but strong preference was given to clan members in making loans and exchanges, and support could be expected by any member in case of dire financial need. Agrarian legislation over the past thirty years has made holdings stable and has thereby eliminated some of the flexible old arrangements for sharing. Bitter experience with individual treachery based on technicalities of the new land laws has now changed the forms of cooperation materially for many clans and lineages. At each new settlement and recently at the granting of proprietary certificates under the Zamindari Abolition Act, group holdings have been more frequently listed in the separate names of all male members of the group. The cultivators welcome such opportunities to subdivide their lands without the costs of a court fight. Officials advertise the act as such. Even minor children's names are now entered as separate landholders. In this way the popular changes in the agrarian structure are quietly accomplishing some of the effects that are most feared and opposed from the Hindu code bills.

The artisans, menials, and landless labourers have not, of course, lost forms of cooperation dependent upon joint management of lands. But they, like most castes, have seen their caste and clan councils lose force. The loss of force seems to have been occasioned by an increasing differentiation of statuses within the castes, by widened contacts with less constrained ways of life outside the village (hastened by emigration from the crowded lands) and by internal dissension of a kind which has come to be pervasive throughout village social life. The loss of force has also been paralleled and helped by an accelerating loss of distinctive elements of caste culture once associated with particular occupations and ritual duties. The special religions of the lower castes have been fast giving way to ceremonies imitated from the Brahmans and from the generalised neo-Hinduism of the cities.

Only the clan of the landlords has retained some semblance of effective organisation beyond the village and beyond a single generation. But the landlords are a special case: their lineage is a junior comprised several hundreds of villages in the districts of Brij. Their conquest of Kishan Garhi in relatively recent centuries and their continued association with a royal house keeps them aware of a larger area of organisation than that of the settled cultivators or even of the more mobile artisan castes. Over the past 30 years with its changing economic fortunes there have been many dissensions within the landlord lineage. At the same time, the landlords' wider organisation has actually been strengthened by their taking over many government and party jobs which require a background of wealth and education which only their class possessed.

All of the kin groups of Kishan Garhi have vital connections outside the village through marriage. The organisation of marriage, like the organisation of caste which results from it, is one of the most stable of all elements in village society. Since most persons who are born in the village are considered to be related by a kind of fictional common descent, and since most persons address each other—even across caste lines—by kinship terms appropriate to age and descent, a marriage between a boy and a girl of Kishan Garhi would constitute incest. The feeling is extended: no one is married within less than four miles of the village. The average distance of marriage is in fact, twelve miles. The kin groups of Kishan Garhi have living marriage ties with some seventy other villages on all sides; twenty of these other villages which lie toward the heart of Brij account for half of all marriages.

Marriage in Kishan Garhi—strongly patrilocal, as in most of northern India—is oriented to flow in a single direction only. The family and village to which one gives a daughter occupy a "high" relationship; the family and village from which one takes a wife occupy a "low" relationship. There can be no mixing of the two: once high, a village remains high. Additional marriages linking the same two villages and bringing or sending more women in the same direction are desired; exchange, or a reversal of direction is unthinkable. The feeling behind this organisation is that the daughter and sister at marriage becomes the helpless possession of another group. To secure her good treatment, lavish entertainments and gifts must be made to the husband's family. The more the husband's family demonstrates its high position, the more the wife's family must exert to please and to bribe their guests. The economic effects of this patterning of marriage are great. Not only are marriage expenses thus kept high, but quantities of goods follow marriage in later years by the same non-rational path. One third of all milk animals are given and an equally large proportion of cash is lent to marital relatives. Perhaps one quarter of all debt is to fulfil marriage demands. The persistence and vigour of such a structuring of marriage puts limits on the degree to which a village can manage its economic affairs as a local unit.

Rank Groupings

The categories of rank thirty years ago in Kishan Garhi probably corresponded much more neatly than they do today with the kinship groupings of caste, clan, and lineage. By ritual criteria having to do with occupational duty and manner of life, all 24 castes were placed with perfect agreement in five or six ranked groups of castes. These larger ritual ranks of castes may be given the general name "orders." Villagers refer to the orders from top to bottom as "highest" (Brahman), "high" (Kshatriya, Vaisya, and some six others), "low" (most of the other Hindu castes, known to urbanised Hindus as Shudra), "Muslim," "very low" (Chamar, Dhobi), and "untouchable" (sweepers, hunters). The arrangement of castes in orders determines most inter-caste ritual behaviour—forms of greeting, the arrangements for eating, smoking, sitting, etc. Within the orders, ranking of separate castes, clans, households, and individuals was more complex, being affected by diverse criteria which are less permanent and objective. Among these other criteria are power, wealth, position in the service system, familial morality, age, and personal virtue. Thirty years ago there was a closer correspondence in Kishan Garhi between the distribution of power and wealth and the ritual ranking of castes. Almost all land rights and all formal political power were in the hands of the top two orders and the four or five top castes. Thirty years of economic and political changes in the larger society have done much to jostle this old structure and to rearrange wealth and power among different persons and among ritually lower persons. The greater differentiation of economic and of kinship groupings noted above has made it harder for anyone to apply rank attitudes simply to whole castes. Judgements tend to be more individualised and therefore to be less well agreed. Many Brahmans and sweepers would continue to say that all Brahmans are to be respected far above all sweepers; at the same time, most persons in the village would rate one particular sweeper as far more respectable than several particular Brahmans. If such discrepancies are old, they are now commoner.

At present there is rather intense competition for rank between castes and between individuals. Competition is intensified by the current elimination of landlords as tax collectors, and by the election of a few villagers to serve on the village committee and on the rural court. The Brahman tenants, now substantially equal to the old landlords in their rights and possessions, are trying to organise their own effective dominance over the village. But effective dominance is an entirely new problem for them. They constitute one quarter of the population of Kishan Garhi and control half its lands. But they cannot agree on leadership, on who is to take precedence among them, or even on the idea that one person, or a small group of persons might speak impartially for all. By older techniques of organisation, each man spoke for himself and for his own kin group, or else failed to speak and thereby showed his intention to withdraw from cooperation. The tenants and wealthier artisans of eight other castes in the village are trying to consolidate their economic gains by adopting a ritually higher way of life; they are helped in their efforts by older caste-raising movements outside the village. But most castes and clans cannot even agree to rise together, for they are as divided as are the Brahmans by new rivalries which represent intrusions of changing economic situation. Many ritual services and requests for alms which were the special claims of some ten of the castes a generation ago are now tending to be dropped because they clearly imply an insufferable degree of subordination.

"To behave properly" and "to respect" are synonymous in village language. Older villagers look on the new disagreements about rank as evidence for a general loss of respectfulness, as a crumbling of all ordered relationships in their society. There is perhaps some truth in the village idea that the ritual hierarchy and order itself are identical, for the ritual hierarchy was, along with the power blocs forced by economic dependency, one of the few systems by which the multiple, sovereign, and demanding kin groups of the village were fitted into some regular and intelligible general pattern. A more mobile general pattern of socio-economic classes could evolve only by further weakening both the ritual values and the larger kinship units of the old hierarchy.

Convivial Groupings

Association among persons outside of the kinship groupings in Kishan Garhi seems always to have been limited, except for certain mass activities, to very small groupings. These groupings have been strongly shaped by ceremonies. Small, limited, and ritualised as they are, these convivial groupings are nevertheless numerous and important. Their diffuse patterns link together, however tenuously, the ranks and kin groups which are formally set apart.

Men and women live their associational lives in sharply separated spheres. This separation in itself promotes a greater diffusion of contacts, for the associations of husband and wife may take entirely different directions. In the same way children, although admonished by adults as to their associates, rarely conform in their play groups to the adult pattern either of formal groupings or of cliques.

Cliques and friendships are variously determined by neighbourhood, by kinship, by shared work or other similarities of social position, and occasionally by sheer personal attraction or common personal interests in disregard of social differences. A strong positive attachment outside of one's kin group is, however, a potential threat to that group's primary demands for exclusive loyalty. When adults do form such cliques or friendships, they do so secretly and deny that the association exists. Pairs or groups of men who sit together frequently without some formal reason in spite of differences of kinship, rank, and power are likely to be regarded as fools or as trouble makers. To be sure, one common reason for the existence of cross-kin and cross-rank associations is that there are serious troubles within the primary formal groups; splits within those groups require members to seek allies outside, if anywhere. As a result of strong disapproval, very few friendly secular associations do span great differences of social status. There are perhaps a dozen pairs and two or three small cliques of this type, to be compared with numberless warm clusters of persons of similar social position. There are no larger permanent voluntary associations.

Ceremonial patterns provide many approved contexts for briefer convivial associations among all persons. Such ceremonial contexts may be put to varied social uses, but in themselves seem to be old and stable elements of village culture.

Family ceremonies, especially the ceremonies leading up to and following marriage, require the most active and organised group participation. On ten nights, one to four dozen women gather to sing without invitation at the house of the betrothed. Marriage feasts and processions are joined by invitation only according to an explicit formula. The formula gives fullest participation and first claim to the nearest kinsmen, representative participation to other kin groups of the same caste, smaller representative participation to other castes considered as wholes, and individual participation to persons who have been one's hosts in the past, to non-relatives who have made token contributions to marriage expenses, and to other economic associates and servants. Any of these categories may extend beyond the village itself. But if a category of persons is invited, it must be invited consistently, for errors are taken as slights, and may be sternly reciprocated. Still, there are some unstructured opportunities for personal choice within each category. Family ceremonies at birth and death are much more narrowly constrained.

The festivals of the Hindu calendar, which occur in monthly and annual cycles, provide numerous occasions for brief convivial association and give much wider scope to interpersonal choice. Although no festival can be said to be wholly unconnected with family patterns, these calendrical ceremonies are much less completely governed by formal categories of social structure. Primarily for male attendance are sacred recitations and incendiary sacrifices held occasionally at the dark of the moon and in great numbers at Divali and Holi. To these sacrifices, from five to twenty kinsmen and associates may be invited; rarely, a feast is added, which may attain the proportions of a marriage feast. During the month before Holi and on a few other festival days, two or three small male singing societies meet informally but with some frequency. Primarily for female and child gatherings are a dozen annual festival days. These are celebrated in small groups in nearly every household by neighbours, kinswomen, and playmates. Freer, open participation occurs among about half of the younger men on a few annual days of sports, and among most of the women on two annual days of songs. An annual fair at a village shrine and an annual propitiation of one goddess of smallpox are occasions for mass participation by all and by women, respectively. The great annual saturnalia at Holi consists of three days of mob, clique, and individual expressions of love and aggression in forms which represent a general privileged overriding and overturning of ordinary social structure.

The many tiny and frail convivial groupings in Kishan Garhi thus maintain a minimal network of positive connections among people across ordinarily formal lines of economic, rank, and kinship divisions. At no time in the knowable past has there been any more comprehensive organisation of the village than that which they provide. There seems never to have been any form of associational behaviour which regarded the village as a unit in which all groups have a shared equity, or which looked on village problems as the problems of all. The disciplined followings of landlords and lenders had great strength and heterogeneous composition, but never organised the whole village. The councils of the several castes have only rarely had the assistance of non-members of the caste in arbitrating their private solutions. The informal council of the Brahman tenants, potentially the strongest of all associations, has stood only for itself. Villagers voting in the recent election grouped themselves by caste and clan, took their choice among five sets of candidates, all of the local landlord's caste, voting for the candidate whom they felt best represented the interests of their particular class or order.

Present Problems

No one will be surprised if a village whose social relations are structured in the manner of Kishan Garhi does not rapidly develop an active village committee (*gaon panchayat*) or contribute to an effective rural court (*panchayati adalat*) as prescribed in the UP Panchayat Raj Act. The village committee that was officially elected includes a fair sampling of many castes. But that committee never meets. The group that actually considers public issues and uses the new authority granted by the act is none other than the old informal Brahman caste council, representing one quarter of the people and one half of the land rights. The ex-landlords proudly abstain from this body, manoeuvring as best they can through the remnants of their followings or experimenting with alliances among the other disinherited persons. The Brahman council acting as village committee has been unable to establish sufficient trust to collect as much as one half of its small committee tax or to realise a fraction of the fines it has levied over a period of nearly three years. It was able with great difficulty to collect enough straw to repair the roof of the two-room village school. It has been unable to carry through any of the three projects of village improvement which it haltingly undertook. It has achieved punishment of one petty criminal case within the Brahman caste, and of two minor crimes by lower persons against Brahmans. In all other cases there have been dissident opinions which led the committee to appeal to non-official coercive arbitration by the police or by a neighbouring landlord, or to refer the cases to due process of law in higher courts.

The failure of the village committee to dispose of cases of conflict in the village does not mean that conflict has been in any way lessened. Since its official inception, the village committee has formally entered more than 30 cases, an average of a case per month. Of these 30, 25 have passed up to the rural court at Brij Garhi. Cases are trivial in origin; insult, threats, and suspected plotting are common instigations, although the formal charge may be theft, beating or default of payment. The initiating fees and gifts are deceptively small. One vague issue quickly deviates and diffuses into other issues as additional members of the affected groups join in the case as "witnesses." Two or three officially unrelated cases are always in progress; not uncommonly all dissolve at once if crucial advantage is gained by one faction. If the other faction can manage it, three more cases may be fabricated on the next day. An average case runs for two months in the rural court. An average man spends a whole day of each month in litigation, throughout the year.

The rural court at Brij Garhi has superior jurisdiction over the village committee at Kishan Garhi and over four other village committee areas in the region. The members of the rural court were elected just as were the village committees, by public show of hands confirming a panel of nominees which had been previously negotiated among the village factions. Almost all of the 25 members are landlords. But the landlords' own hierarchy of dominance has been much disrupted of late, and they too, like the litigating tenants of Kishan Garhi, are torn by competition and aligned in factions. Unable now to arbitrate conflicts individually, these rustic magistrates do battle among themselves using litigants as pawns. Such a contentious court welcomes new litigation but has little interest in achieving real composition of the cases which come before it. Its "dismissals" often simply represent delays and diversions of process into the higher courts; its inept "decisions" often simply provide the technical bases for higher appeals.

The ex-landlords still have a smattering of the law and enough valuable higher connections to guarantee their control of the rural court for some time to come. Tahsildars and Sub-Divisional Officers, deluged now with the new volume of litigation from the rural courts, regard their villagers as depraved, or look back longingly on the days when there was at least one strong man in each village who could be depended upon to settle petty quarrels with a firm hand. The strong men of the past are the amateur advocates of the present.

Kishan Garhi's internal divisions are not entirely disadvantageous to governmental administration; indeed, factional splits are often temporarily useful to officials who might otherwise have to cope with united opposition against their official acts. The three major crimes of Kishan Garhi in recent years which fell to the police for investigation were all solved by the technique of widening village divisions at promising points, and then extracting mutually incriminating information from both of the two opposed groups. The revenue officials who had to collect landlord abolition payments and the party organisers who had to get out the vote in the elections similarly made use of competition among Kishan Garhi's factions.

Were the national economy moving smoothly towards the goal of improved sustenance, then the problem of concerted action in villages like Kishan Garhi might not arise. But some amount of concerted action is now required by intense and inequitable competition for static resources and static social goods. Most programmes for political, technical, or economic development of rural India require a modicum of classless local cooperation. Officials at the planning level recognise village factionalism as a chief obstacle to all programmes.

The low state of cooperation that presently prevails among the kin groups of Kishan Garhi and the structural features that determine it suggest that greater concerted action will be achieved only by a more severe unsettling of basic structures than has occurred in any age of the past. The energies of the kin groups are devoted to securing their private prestige and prosperity, to advancing and fulfilling the claims of marriage. The inequities that once articulated the kin groups in work and subordinated them one to another in wealth and power are largely levelled. The traditional criteria that once set them in an agreed hierarchy of ranks are now confounded. The kin groups themselves remain as so many sovereign states, loosely linked by a few work relations, by a handful of friendships, and by the ceremonies of an ancient cycle. To ask the fifty-five kin groups of Kishan Garhi to continue to live by shifting alliances is to promote inaction or strife as much as cooperation. To entice them to delegate some of their loyalties for the work of the village as a whole is to lure the old social structure toward its sure destruction.

3

An Oriya Hill Village*

F. G. Bailey

Introduction

Bisipara is a hundred miles east of Cuttack and forty miles south of the Mahanadi River. It lies on the southern edge of an egg-shaped plain, which is two miles from east to west and a mile from north to south. The plain is 1,750 feet above sea level and the hills around rise between 500 and 1,000 feet higher. The Salki River runs from south to north through the plain and the village is built in a crook of land between the Salki and a small tributary. Both these rivers have cut channels between 10 and 20 feet deep. The Salki is about eighty yards from bank to bank. The smaller stream, where it has not been controlled for paddy fields, is about 10 yards wide.

The plain consists of jungle-covered mounds, in height about fifty feet. On one of these Bisipara is built. To the west of the village, the stream is used to water paddy fields. A mile to the north a spring rises and gives water for a wide crescent-shaped belt of fields, which curl along the north-eastern side of the village. On the east side there are levelled "dry" paddy fields, irrigated only in the rains. The edges of the mounds, clearings on other mounds, and the sides of nalas are used for dry cultivation of crops other than rice.

The hills around are jungle-covered and infested by tigers and leopards. Bears make the forest paths dangerous. Cerebral malaria kills many children. The area has a reputation as a place "gloomy and pestilential."

History of the Area

The hills have been occupied, since time unknown, by Kui-speaking peoples. The rajas of the Oriya-speaking lowland states had control over nowhere but the

* Originally published in *Economic Weekly* 5, no. 12 (21 March 1953), pp. 326–28.

foothills. This they achieved by sending warrior chiefs to found colonies. Many Oriya villages were established in this way. The relation of the colonies and the mother state is not clear; but we know that the hill chiefs were rather lords of the Marches, owing allegiance and often refusing it, than proconsuls administering a colony.

The men of Bisipara came originally from Baud in the north, via another hill village, Bolscoopa. The ruling caste are surnamed Bisi, once a title of service under the Orissa kings. Genealogies indicate that they have been in Bisipara for 200 years, but such evidence is approximate. However, at least we know that the Bisis were firmly established here 100 years ago, and provided leaders against the soldiers of the East India Company.

Between 1840 and 1850 there were expeditions every year into the hills, based on Russelkonda in the south, to suppress the rite of human sacrifice. This was performed by the Kui and by the Oriya settlers. In 1850 a tahsildar, one Dinabandu Patnaik, an ex-policeman, began a regular administration from a headquarters which settled eventually at Bisipara. At the end of 25 years he retired with the title of "rai bahadur" and the profits of an administration so conducted with systematic pillage and calculated ferocity that even today I have heard Kui men comment with satisfaction on the extinction of his lineage.

From 1850 onwards Oriyas came from the south to join those who had come many years before from the north. Bisipara became the administrative capital. Policemen and revenue officials settled here. Dinabandu Tahsildar encouraged brahmins to go into the hills, where land could always be found for them. He built a temple. A market was opened. Bisipara continued to expand until in 1904, A. J. Ollenbach, then SDO, moved his headquarters to Phulbani. Now there are no officials in Bisipara; the descendants of some remain; other families have gone to the new capital.

In these years, those who profited most were the Sundis, a caste whose traditional occupation was liquor-making. The story of the moneylender and the toddy-seller among the Adibasi is too familiar; but in this area action was taken as early as 1910 when all liquor shops were abolished. Again, in 1920, a land settlement of Oriya villages was made, and, imperfect though it is, it gives force to the law that no one but an Adibasi may buy land, without special permission.

Composition of the Village

This history is reflected in the siting of the village houses. There are six streets: Kumharsai, Sudosai, Panosai, Sundisai, Khodalsai, and Hatopodera, containing about 750 people.

The street of the potters, Kumharsai, is built in the Kui fashion—two lines of houses, not detached, with gardens behind them. At each end of a Kui street there was usually a fence of tall stakes to protect the village at night from enemies and wild animals. The Kumhars are officially Adibasi, and, although now their assimilation to Hinduism is almost complete, we may conjecture that they are the true Adibasis, the first occupants of the site. Their genealogies all indicate long residence. There are no longer any posts at the end of Kumharsai and the houses have been rebuilt in Oriya fashion; but the siting is typically Kui.[1]

The Bisis and others whose ancestors were in the service of the Baud Raja, are by caste Sudos. Their street, Sudosai, is built of two parallel lines of continuous houses, demonstrating that they were sited in the days when there were wars and a greater need than now for protection against wild animals. Nowadays the Bisis live in the centre of the street. On the fringes are strangers who have come since 1850. They are: a Gauro (herdsman) schoolmaster, whose father came from the south as a constable; a Brahmin household and a barber household; a Christian whose father was head clerk; a Gauro; and a Mahanti shopkeeper who arrived last year.

The street of the outcastes, Panosai, is set apart from the rest of the village. It, too, is sited in the Kui fashion. Genealogies indicate a similar origin and length of residence as the Sudos, and it is likely that the Panos came to the hills with the Sudos from the north.

Sundisai is built on the same plan, although the decline in its prosperity is shown by several gaps in the line, where houses have fallen in. Genealogies indicate that these Sundis arrived at about the same time as the Sudos and Panos.

These four streets—Kumharsai, Sudosai, Panosai, and Sundisai—offer similar characteristics. The siting of the houses and the evidence of the genealogies show that these are old streets. Secondly, they have a clear majority of households of the eponymous caste.

It is not so in the other two streets—Khodalsai and Hatopodera. All the inhabitants of Hatopodera are either immigrants or the sons of immigrants. Their houses are sited irregularly in several short streets and blocks: and the people are of different castes, Sundi and Kuli predominating, but including also Keuto, Brahmin, and Gauro.[2] This, as the name implies, was the street of the market (now closed) and in every case the motive for immigration was either trade or work at the headquarters. Khodalsai is the name given to scattered houses on the west side of the village, where the government buildings, of which no trace now remains, were sited. There are two families of Panos who have come up from the south: a family of sweepers (Ghasi); a Brahmin house which has charge of the big temple founded by Dinabandu Tahsildar; and several Kui families who have come here within the last 10 years in search of labouring work.

There are then, two categories of street: one old and, relatively, peopled by one caste; the other new, and, for political and economic reasons, heterogeneous.

Economic Activities

It is not possible to say with certainty what was the pattern of economic life in Bisipara before the 1850s. We know there were no markets and it is said that each village was self-sufficient economically. If that is so, its income would be derived entirely from the land, and there would be a limited exchange between cultivators and those who practised a traditional occupation—barbering, oil-pressing, etc.—in addition to working on their land. The same goods were produced and consumed within the village. There was, so to say, no foreign trade.

After 1850, some of the village income, in the form of taxes, was expended outside the village. A portion of this was returned as salaries and government expenditure, and consumed within the village. Money circulated more freely and the cultivator exchanged a proportion of his crop with the new class of specialists—policemen, peons, etc.—in return for money, which he used to pay his taxes and to satisfy new needs for manufactures. A market was founded. Shops were established and, by trade, Bisipara began to derive some of its income from outside. In other words, since 1860 Bisipara has been integrated into a larger economic structure, getting income from other villages, and spending on goods and services which came from outside.

The inhabitants of the four old streets—Sudosai, Kumharsai, Panosai, and Sundisai—*tend* to be the producers of primary goods, while those who live in Hatopodera and Khodalsai are either manufacturers or middlemen. Thus, four of the five shops in Bisipara are situated in Hatopodera. One Gauro was a trader, another makes and sells snuff. Three of the Kulis make and sell cloth. The Keuto makes *chura*, a product of rice, and exchanges it with Kui people for paddy. In Khodalsai the Panos are carters, and the Kui are either farm labourers or basket-makers.

However, this economic difference between the old and the new streets is beginning to disappear. On the one hand, those who profited as manufacturers or middlemen—particularly the Sundi shopkeepers—invested their money in land, which they work by sharecropping or with hired labour. On the other hand, when a land-owning family multiplies and land is not sufficient, a man may go in for trading in the Kui villages. With his own money, or money borrowed from a mahajan in Phulbani, the district headquarters, he buys turmeric and mustard and other crops, and sells them in the market at Phulbani or to the mahajan. His wife might make *mudi* (parched rice), or buy dried fish and salt, and trade these around the villages. The proportion of households which regularly derive a larger or a smaller part of their income from sources other than the products of their own land is 91 per cent.

The position nowadays of the village in the larger economic structure is this: Bisipara imports cloth, tea, sugar, salt, metal goods, kerosene, some vegetables, and the services it gets in return for paying taxes; it exports a small quantity of paddy; some manufactured goods, mostly from its looms; and the services of those who go to work as policemen, schoolmasters, or peons away from, or within the village; and it re-exports turmeric, mustard seed, and other crops grown in Kui villages.

Village Unity

From several points of view the population of the villages is heterogeneous. Some are new-comers; some have been here for generations. Some are Adibasis; some are Oriyas. Of the Adibasis, some have Oriya as their main language and have forgotten Kui; others know Oriya and use it when they must, but in their homes speak Kui. Some Oriyas have come from the north; others from the south. There are high castes, low castes, outcastes, and some Adibasi families altogether outside the caste system. There are craftsmen, middlemen and cultivators. Traders and shopkeepers compete both with one another and with their customers. There are rich and poor.

However, in spite of diverse origins, occupations, languages, and interests, the population of the village can be a unity. For example, in the middle of October it was discovered that the ripening paddy was being eaten by an insect. This bug, *Leptocorissa* spp., is not uncommon in Orissa; but this was the first time in living memory that it had attacked the village crops. The village headman sent a report to the Agricultural Department. The people of the village decided to hold a *rugo bolani*—a ceremony to avert the disaster. This ritual was conducted by a *gunia*, an Adibasi Kumhar. It was done in the Hindu fashion with offerings of rice, coconuts, ghee, and mango leaves. No animal was sacrificed, as is the Kui custom. The gunia was closely assisted by a Sundi, by the Sudo headman, and by another Kumhar. Music was provided by a man of the sweeper caste (Ghasi) and three Panos. To the cost of the ceremony every house except the Christian contributed two pice.

Again, at this time of the year, when occasional showers of rain leave the ground soft enough to show tracks, the village goes hunting. Five guns take part, four belonging to the Sudos, and the fifth lent by the Christian. Any man who can spare the time goes out as a beater. On the hunt, men of all castes, clean and unclean, rub shoulders freely; but on the return path, if it should lead near to the outcaste street, Panosai, the high caste Sudos will make a wide detour.

A third example of how the village functions as a unity in certain contexts is provided by the Brahmin who got above himself. There are two temples in the village, in each of which a daily *thakur puja* is performed. One old Sudo also has a thakur puja done each day in his house. The Brahmin family, who officiate at the big temple, received from the grandfather of the present headman the gift of two fields. Another Brahmin family officiated both in the old man's house and in the village temple. About a year ago, this Brahmin demanded four fields, two from the old man and two from the village. The old man gave the fields. The village held a meeting and refused, saying that he must be content with the paddy which each house paid him for making the puja. The village held another meeting; they appointed the third Brahmin family to do the thakur puja; and they withdrew from the offender, not only his thakur payment, but also other "insurance" payments which each household made yearly in return for his help at deaths and other ceremonies. They still speak to him; but no one will employ him as a priest.

The factors which underline such unified actions are these. Firstly, the majority of the villagers have a common background. They have grown up with one another and have a common experience which goes back for generations. This is an imponderable factor, but nonetheless real. Secondly, they have a common interest in their economic life. Everyone's fields were attacked by the bug. Traders are rivals, but they have a common concern in such topics as the price turmeric is fetching, and in the fact that a rich and enterprising Kui man has now begun to market his own turmeric and mustard seed. Thirdly, there is a great multiplicity of ties between persons. For an example, I take the son of the headman. He is nineteen; he left school last year. Having been away in Phulbani at school for the last ten years, he is less integrated than other youths of his age. He is an Oriya, a Sudo descended from those hill chiefs who came from Baud. He is a member of a large and influential family. In other contexts he is a man of the Sudo caste. If visitors come from Gochapara, he is one of a group in this village who owe them hospitality, since his mother came from Gochapara. He has obligations to help and rights to be helped by a small category of individuals whose fathers or mothers pledged ritual friendship with his father or mother. He is especially friendly with four or five young men of his own age, who attended the local school when he did. They are all of different castes. He can read and write, and knows some English, and so is one of those who get together to write petitions or keep accounts when the village feels it is necessary. In this way we may look upon him—and almost every other person in the village—as a link between groups otherwise not connected.

Next to the house of this Sudo boy, there lives a widow with her son. Between these two are the following links: they are of the same caste; she is his classificatory aunt, since her husband was a classificatory elder brother of the boy's father; her daughter has married a man of the village, so that she is also his classificatory mother-in-law and her son is his brother-in-law; the widow is a poor woman and she regularly earns paddy by helping the boy's mother with the threshing; the widow's son and the boy's younger brother are in the same class at school; when he is not at school, the widow's son works as a servant for the boy's uncle. These are only a few of the situations in which these two individuals interact, either directly or indirectly. By tracing out the links between the relatives and friends of the boy and the relatives and friends of the widow, the list could be multiplied almost indefinitely. This case is typical.

The village unity is a rope of many strands. When the village decided to discipline their Brahmin, he was not supported, as one might expect, by his fellow Brahmins. They were tied into the village in too many ways. The metaphor appropriately suggests that he was unable, by pulling on the one strand of caste, to break the whole rope.

The Future

I do not suggest that the village is a utopia of perfect integration. It is a village axiom that the poor are helpless against the rich. Up to the present day, the majority of the rich are tied into the village in the manner I have described above. But one wealthy man, who has fields here and a prosperous business in Phulbani, has for years defied the canons of good behaviour. In particular, he is said to have cheated several people in land transactions. The panchayat is powerless. One victim won a case against him, but the rest are too poor or too ignorant to go to law. He is rich enough not to depend on friends and relatives for help at harvest or transplanting time, and when sickness comes.

The point is not only that this man is without a social conscience, but also that he has interests outside the village. Thus, he is less dependent on his fellow villagers than are other men in Bisipara. This suggests that the more the village becomes integrated in the larger economy, by the private enterprise of men like this, the less of a unity it becomes. There are schemes for development in this area. How far they will cause Bisipara to become part of economic India remains to be seen.

Notes and References

[1] Kui houses are built of wide horizontal planks. Oriya houses are made from vertical planks, plastered over with mud. Both have a double roof: of mud, an air space, and then thatch.

[2] The Sundis are, by tradition, toddy-drawers; the Kulis, weavers; the Keuto, fishermen; and the Gauro, herdsmen.

PART II

Rural Structures

4

The Myth of Self-Sufficiency of the Indian Village*

M. N. Srinivas and A. M. Shah

The idea of the isolation and self-sufficiency of the Indian village was first propounded by Sir Charles Metcalfe in 1830, and since then it has had distinguished supporters—scholars as well as politicians. Sir Henry Maine and Karl Marx supported the idea, and in recent times, Mahatma Gandhi and his followers not only stated that the Indian village was traditionally self-sufficient but also wanted a political programme which would restore to these villages their pristine self-sufficiency. We make no apology for giving below a lengthy quotation from Sir Charles Metcalfe's writing in which he propounds his famous theory of the self-sufficiency and vitality of the Indian village:

> The village communities are little republics, having nearly everything that they want within themselves, and almost independent of any foreign relations. They seem to last where nothing else lasts. Dynasty after dynasty tumbles down; revolution succeeds to revolution; Hindoo, Pathan, Moghul, Mahratta, Sikh, English, are all masters in turn, but the village communities remain the same. In times of trouble they arm and fortify themselves: a hostile army passes through the country: the village communities collect their cattle within their walls and let the enemy pass unprovoked. If plunder and devastation be directed against themselves, and the force employed be irresistible, they flee to friendly villages at a distance; but when the storm has passed over, they return and resume their occupations. If a country remain for a series of years the scene of continued pillage and massacre, so that the villages cannot be inhabited, the scattered villagers nevertheless return whenever the power of peaceable possession revives. A generation may pass away, but the succeeding generation will return. The sons will take the places of their fathers; the

* Originally published in *Economic Weekly* 12, no. 37 (10 September 1960), pp. 1375–78.

> same site for the village, the same positions for the houses, the same lands, will be reoccupied by the descendants of those who were driven out when the village was depopulated; and it is not a trifling matter that will drive them out, for they will often maintain their post through times of disturbance and convulsion, and acquire strength sufficient to resist pillage and oppression with success.[1]

Maine to Marx

About 40 years later, Sir Henry Maine revived the idea of the self-sufficiency of the Indian village:

> For the most part, the Indian village communities have always submitted without resistance to oppression by monarchs surrounded by mercenary armies ... I have several times spoken of them as organised and self-acting. They, in fact, include a nearly complete establishment of occupations and trades for enabling them to continue their collective life without assistance from any person or body external to them.[2]

Karl Marx, from whom one could have expected a departure from the conventional view, also popularised the concept of village self-sufficiency:

> Under this form of municipal government, the inhabitants of the country have lived from time immemorial. The boundaries of the village have been but seldom altered, and though the villages themselves have been sometimes injured and even desolated by war, famine, and disease, the same name, the same limits, the same interests, and even the same families have contributed for ages. The inhabitants gave themselves no trouble about the breaking up and the division of kingdoms; while the village remains entire, they care not to what power it is transferred or to what sovereign it devolves: its internal economy remains unchanged.[3]

Part of a Wider System

When an idea is over a hundred years old and is advocated by thinkers as diverse as Maine and Marx it nearly acquires the status of a dogma. Until recently, most writers on rural India took for granted the idea of village autonomy and autarky. This has resulted in falsifying the true nature of the Indian village community, and has provided a basis for revivalists' and utopians' programme of political action. It is only in the last twenty years or so that trained anthropologists and sociologists have made intensive studies of village communities in different parts of India and in some areas they have been lucky enough to come across historical data. The picture that emerges from these data is that while roads, especially inter-village roads, were very poorly developed, while monetisation of the rural economy was minimal, and while the locally dominant caste could lay down the law on many matters, the village was always a part of a wider economic, political, and religious system. The appearance of isolation, autonomy, and self-sufficiency was only an illusion.

In some parts of the country, like coastal Kerala, Coorg, highland Gujarat, and elsewhere, nucleated villages do not exist. The village in these areas consists of a number of distinct farms with every owner of a farm or his representative living on his farm. The dispersed village is not a clear, architectural entity like the nucleated village. There is no clear boundary between one village and another. The members living in it are served by artisan and servicing castes from several dispersed villages. That is, each artisan caste serves a distinct group of villages, and the village may be represented by a series of partially overlapping circles.[4]

The administrative and "social" villages are not always identical even in areas with nucleated settlements. An administrative village occasionally includes more than one social village while a social village is more rarely divided into more than one administrative village.

AGNATES DISPERSED

A village is a vertical unit composed of sections of various castes while a caste is a horizontal unit made up of different sections living in several neighbouring villages. The members of a caste living in a village are bound by ties of kinship, marriage, economic obligations, and membership of caste panchayat with their caste-fellows in other villages. Even in South India, where cross-cousin and cross-uncle-niece marriages are preferred, the marriage field for a rural caste includes at least twenty to thirty villages. The field is much bigger in North India where relatives are not preferred for marriage. In addition, there is village exogamy and occasionally, village hypergamy. That is, a man may not marry a girl of his own village, and he is not permitted to give his sister or daughter in marriage to the village from which he has obtained a wife. The marriage circle in the north includes 200 or 300 villages.

The members of an agnatic clan are often found dispersed in several villages. This is specially true of some parts of North India where members of the locally dominant caste residing in several neighbouring villages are agnatically related to each other. Close ties exist between such groups. Similarly, close ties also exist between those members of a caste who live in towns and others who live in villages. This is specially true of the "twice-born" castes.

The fact that villages are usually multicaste in composition is pointed out as evidence of self-sufficiency of villages. But even big villages, villages with over a thousand people, do not contain all the necessary castes, whereas nearly two-thirds of India's villages have a strength of less than 500 each.

Weekly Markets

There are also single-caste villages. Where these villages are of artisans, they sell their goods in nearby towns or, more frequently, in the weekly markets. The latter are an eloquent testimony to the Indian village's lack of self-sufficiency. They also imply a certain amount of monetisation of the economy, which in turn means that the village was part of a wider politico-economic system.

Weekly markets again vary in their range. Some are patronised by people living in a few neighbouring villages while others are patronised by people spread over a wide area. Occasionally, there is also a certain amount of specialisation in weekly markets: one market is famous for trade in cattle, another in sheep and poultry, a third in woollen blankets, and so on. Pilgrimages also take the villager beyond the village, and occasionally into a different language area. The periodical festival of a deity attracts devotees and others from nearby villages, and a bazaar springs up around the temples. The prospect of buying and selling at the festival is as strong an attraction as the religious one. There are fairs which are famous for the sale of cattle, and nowadays, cattle are moved by lorry a distance of 200 or 300 miles to reach a fair. Such fairs occur all over the country and they reveal the fact that the peasant's social and economic universe is very much wider than his village.

Pattern of Land Ownership

The pattern of land ownership, tenancy, and labour frequently cuts across the village. The land which is included within the boundary of an official or administrative village is not always owned by those resident in it. Some of the land is usually owned by people in neighbouring villages or towns. During the last hundred years or more, there has come into existence a class of absentee landowners, of people who reside in towns but own land in villages.

Again, members of a village are commonly found to own some land in neighbouring villages. Even tenants and labourers are occasionally found cultivating land lying in another village. In some irrigated areas where the density of population is high, it is not unknown for a tenant to cultivate land lying six or seven miles from where he is staying.

External Trade

It is often assumed that trade and commerce did not touch villages in India. This assumption was perhaps true only of villages in the tribal areas. In the non-tribal areas, however, village economy has for a long time been integrated in varying degree with regional, national, and even international trade and commerce, in certain regions, such as Gujarat, and the Kerala and Coromandel coasts, there was a high degree of integration of village economy with the economy of the wider world. These coastal areas had maritime commerce with overseas countries since at least the beginning of the Christian era.

The exports of Gujarat included, for instance, agricultural and forest produce as well as finished goods. In the former category may be mentioned indigo, cotton, wheat, rice, tobacco, edible oil, ghee, honey, lac, hides, dried ginger, and myrobalan. In the latter category there were goods of three kinds: firstly, goods such as cotton cloth, yarn, cushions, canopies, carpets, and cotton tape, which were manufactured mostly by urban artisans but the raw materials for which were supplied by villagers; secondly, goods such as precious stones which were manufactured by urban artisans from indigenous minerals; and thirdly, goods such as silk cloth and objects of metal and ivory which were manufactured by urban artisans from imported raw materials.[5]

Interregional Trade

The interregional trade of the country also included the exchange of agricultural and forest produce. Gujarat, for instance, received a considerable quantity of wheat and opium from Malwa, rice and coconuts from the Konkan, sugar from Bengal, and groceries and drugs from the Himalayan regions.[6] Within Gujarat itself there was local specialisation in the matter of crops, and there was much exchange of agricultural produce between different areas. While indigo and tobacco were grown in central Gujarat, sugar cane was grown in south Gujarat. The local produce was transported over land as well as water. There was a great deal of trade along the coast of Gujarat, Saurashtra, and Kutch.[7] Finally, even in the same locality villages supplied several consumption goods to towns.

In brief, most villages in Plains Gujarat sent out some commodity or other to the wider market. They received in return various goods such as salt, spices, groceries, certain kinds of cloth, metals, metal objects, household goods, and ornaments. The dependence of the villager on the outside world was visible particularly during the *rites des passage*, the periodical festivals and other ritual occasions. The villager purchased the goods he wanted from the village shopkeeper, from the peripatetic trader or artisan, and at fairs and weekly markets. According to available records there was at least one shopkeeper in every village with a population of 500 or more in central Gujarat at the beginning of the nineteenth century.[8]

Dependence on Towns

The villagers also depended upon towns for certain specialised services. Whenever they wanted to build a brick-and-mortar structure, whether it was a dwelling house, a well, a hospice (*dharmasala*), a village meeting house (*chavadi*), or a pigeon tower (*chabuturi*), they had to call in bricklayers and lime-workers from nearby towns. They also got their gold and silver ornaments made by a town smith. Though mud pots and pans were popular in the house, the few metal vessels which were in use, and the immense metal utensils for cooking community dinners, were bought and repaired in the town. The florist, the tailor, the washerman, the *vahivancha* (genealogist) and the grain-parcher were all to be found only in the towns and very large villages.

In this connection, it is necessary to stress the importance of regional economic history, a field which is as important as it is neglected. The study of economic history on a regional basis will tell us how the village was related to the wider economy—national as well as international—in different parts of India. For instance, the American Civil War resulted in the stoppage of the supply of raw cotton to the factories in Lancashire, and this resulted in India's becoming an exporter of raw cotton to Britain. Cotton brought prosperity to peasants in Gujarat and in the former Central Provinces, which in turn led to several changes in the social and economic life of the people. Some peasants in the Central Provinces used silver in their ploughs and bullock-carts to tell their friends they had "arrived."[9]

Political Structure

The assumption that the Indian village community was not influenced by, and did not in turn influence, the wider political structure, is also facile. This assumption is a result of looking only at the top and not at the base of the political structure, a result of concentrating on the history of kings and generals and not of the people. At the village or slightly higher level, there was usually the dominant caste, the members of which owned a good deal of the available arable land, and also wielded political power in addition. Each such caste had a leader whose position was further strengthened by ties of kinship and affinity, and by his capacity to confer favours on his clients. Such chieftains stood at the base of the political pyramid everywhere in India. Above them was the raja or king, the viceroy of an emperor, and the emperor himself, in ascending order of importance.

The lower-level authority acknowledged the supremacy of the higher authority when he paid tribute, and declared his independence from the latter when he stopped payment. There was a continuum of power relations from the lowest to the highest levels, and changes at each level were followed by changes at the other levels. In "orthodox" histories changes at the higher levels are said to be the cause of change at lower levels, but not the other way about.

RAJPUTS AND MUSLIMS

Before the conquest of Gujarat by the Muslims in the thirteenth century, the Rajputs were a dominant caste over the entire region and Rajput chieftains were to be found everywhere.[10] When the Muslim conquerors removed the sovereign king of Gujarat all the lower chieftains fought the Muslims. The Persian chronicles—*Mirat-i-Sikandari*,[11] *Mirat'i-Ahmadi*,[12] and Ferishta's work[13]—bear eloquent testimony to the relentless fight put up by the local Rajput chieftains (called Girasiyas) and their allies, the Koli chieftains, for over 400 years. It was only in central Gujarat, in the region around the capital city of Ahmedabad, the centre of Muslim power, that the Muslims were able to control the Rajputs. Three-fourths of the landed estate of each Rajput was confiscated and turned into *khalsa* or crown land. This marked the beginning of change in the position of Patidars, the great peasant caste of central Gujarat, *vis-à-vis* the Rajputs.

The decline in the power and wealth of the Rajputs was marked by the rise to wealth of the Patidars. They exported indigo, cotton, and other agricultural commodities, and provided raw materials to urban artisans for the manufacture of such articles as cotton textiles. In course of time the Patidars acquired political power also. It is interesting to note that the Patidars were the principal supporters of the Marathas during the latters' campaign in Gujarat.[14] And gradually the Patidars asserted their ritual superiority to Rajputs. At the present moment, Patidars do not accept water or cooked food from Rajputs.

WINDS FROM WITHOUT

We have already mentioned how pilgrimages and festivals took the villager to places beyond his own village. Apart from this, his religion embraced the whole of India, and at least the more knowledgeable villager had heard of Benaras, the Ganges, and the Himalayas. The Brahmin priest was the visible representative of all-India or Sanskritic Hinduism. The institution of Harikatha, in which the priest read and explained a religious story from the *Ramayana* or *Mahabharata* or *Bhagavata* to the villagers, enabled the latter to absorb all-India Hinduism. This helped in the gradual Sanskritisation of the lower castes and in making villagers everywhere an effective part of all-India Hinduism.

The Indian village was thus always a part of a wider entity, subject to the winds which blew from without. The incredibly bad roads, the heavy monsoon, the growing of food crops and vegetables, the existence of barter, and the powerful sense of membership of the village community have all given students an illusion of self-sufficiency and of isolation. But it is only an illusion and the reality is quite different. It is, of course, true that villages in different parts of India were integrated in different degree with the wider political, economic, kinship, religious, and ethical structure, and this is an important field for comparative research. Further, it is a field in which sociologists and historians have to cooperate.

Notes and References

[1] *Appendix to the Report from the Select Committee of the House of Commons on the Affairs of the East-India Company, III*— Revenue (London: 1833), p. 470.

[2] *Village Communities in the East and West* (London: 1890), pp. 124–25.

[3] *Letters on India*, eds B. P. L. Bedi and Freda Bedi (Lahore: Contemporary India Publication, 1937), pp. 6–7.

[4] See Eric J. Miller, "Caste and Territory in Malabar," *American Anthropologist* 56 (1954): pp. 410–20.

[5] W. H. Schoff (trans. and annotation), *The Periplus of the Erythraean Sea* (New York: 1912), pp. 39–42; *Gazetteer of the Bombay Presidency* 6 (Bombay: 1880), pp. 187–98; Bal Krishna, *Commercial Relations between India and England, 1601–1751* (London: George Routledge & Sons, 1924), pp. 12–17; W. H. Moreland, *India at the Death of Akbar* (London: Macmillan, 1920), pp. 196–245; W. H. Moreland, *From Akbar to Aurangzeb: A Study in Indian Economic History* (London: Macmillan, 1923), pp. 52–136.

[6] Moreland, *India at the Death of Akbar*, p. 244; *Gazetteer of the Bombay Presidency* 6, pp. 187–98.

[7] See chapters on "Trade and Manufacture" and "Places of Interest" in *Gazetteer of the Bombay Presidency* 2 (Bombay: 1877); *Gazetteer of the Bombay Presidency* 3 (Bombay: 1879); *Gazetteer of the Bombay Presidency* 4 (Bombay: 1879); *Gazetteer of the Bombay Presidency* 6 (Bombay: 1880); *Gazetteer of the Bombay Presidency* 7 (Bombay: 1883); *Gazetteer of the Bombay Presidency* 8 (Bombay: 1884). An important source for the study of history of local trade in Gujarat are account books and commercial correspondence preserved by merchant families.

[8] For a description of the records, see A. M. Shah, "Social Anthropology and the Study of Historical Societies," *Economic Weekly*, Special Number (July 1959): pp. 953–62.

[9] Seth Leacock and David C. Mandelbaum, "A Nineteenth Century Development Project in India: The Cotton Improvement Program", *Economic Development and Cultural Change* 3, no. 4 (July 1955), p. 349; Hiralal Tribhuvandas Parekh, *Arvachin Gujaratnun Rekhadarshan*, vol. 2 (Ahmedabad: 1936), pp. 68–74.

[10] A. M. Shah, "The Vahivancha Barots of Gujarat: A Caste of Genealogists and Mythographers" in *Traditional India: Structure and Change*, ed. Milton Singer (Philadelphia: American Folklore Society, 1959), pp. 52–58.

[11] Sikandar ibn Muhammad, *Mirat-i-Sikandari*, trans. Fazlullah Lutfullah Faridi (Bombay: n.d.), p. 239.

[12] Ali Muhammad Khan, *Mirat-i-Ahmadi: Supplement*, trans. Syed Nawab Ali and Charles Norman Sedon (Baroda: 1928), pp. 193–94.

[13] Mahomed Kasim Ferishta, *History of the Rise of the Mahomedan Power in India*, vol. 4, trans. John Briggs (Calcutta and London: 1910), p. 18.

[14] *Gazetteer of the Bombay Presidency*, vol. 7, pp. 169–71, 174, 187; C. V. Joshi, "The Amins of Vaso," *Indian Historical Records Commission, Proceedings of the Meeting of the Silver Jubilee Session*, vol. 15, Part 2 (Delhi: 1949), pp. 177–79.

5

Chamar Family in a North Indian Village

A Structural Contingent*

Bernard S. Cohn

Social scientists working on questions of the nature, distribution, and processes of change affecting the Indian family have generally used simple structural criteria to develop the classifications of family types. Most of these scholars tend to think in terms of nuclear and joint families. In this view the joint family is associated with the rural, pre-modern sector of the society, and the nuclear family is viewed as the result of modern industrial and urban conditions. A few scholars, notably Dr. I. P. Desai, have pointed to the complexities involved in the relationships within even what appear to be nuclear families and have argued that the whole conception of the joint family in urban India is changing, but that the direction of change is not simply from the joint to the nuclear family and there are many intermediary types to be found. Desai has called strongly for the use of cultural criteria as well as structural criteria in the study of the family.

Dr. Irawati Karve's standard definition of the joint family strongly suggests the need for cultural as well as structural criteria:

> A joint family is a group of people who generally live under one roof, who eat food cooked at one hearth, who hold property in common and who participate in common family worship and are related to each other as some particular kind of kindred.

Karve adds that the joint family always has an ancestral seat or locality which is the home for the members of the joint family even though trade or service takes them away from the locality.

* Originally published in *Economic Weekly* 49, no. 34 (July 1961), pp. 1051–56.

It is the argument of this paper that not only do we have to include these cultural phenomena in our discussions of changing family types but that the simple structural criteria used to define family type need to be re-examined to determine the structural preconditions which set the type of family and household given individuals will live in at any given time in their life. Most field workers who talk about family structure in India freeze processes which take place over time. To analyse family types, we have to look at the individual families we are studying at a moment in time. The view taken here differs from this in trying to view the type of family not as a fixed entity but rather as a structural contingent.

In a North Indian village the distribution of family types found is a result of the interaction of cultural traditions, structural necessities, and economic factors. The type of family which can be seen in the village are *nuclear*—"typically consisting of a married man and woman with their offspring, although in individual cases one or more additional persons may reside with them,"[1]—and *extended*—"two or more nuclear families affiliated through an extension of the parent-child relationship."[2] Extended families may be thought of as two subtypes, *unstable* and *stable*; the stable ones are those which are often called *joint*. Extended families, which are the cultural ideal among Hindus in North India, develop in response to specific conditions, among which are a tradition of living jointly, an economic base to support a joint family, sufficient role differentiation within the family, clear lines of authority among the generations, the need for a labour pool, and longevity of members of the family.

To illustrate the importance of the underlying conditions of family types and the actualisation of the structural contingents, I will describe the situation found among the Chamars, a landless agricultural caste found in the village of Senapur in eastern Uttar Pradesh. Senapur is a large multicaste village, which is dominated by the landlord Thakur caste. The total area of the village is a little over 2,000 acres; and the population in 1953 was 2,100, of whom 600 were Chamars and 450 Thakurs. The Chamars, who provide most of the agricultural labour for the Thakurs, live in six hamlets which are located away from the main village site where the Thakurs and the artisan castes reside.

Chamar Family Types

The Chamars themselves have no separate terms to distinguish the types of households they live in; they use one word generally to encompass those who live in one household: *ghar*, which literally means "house." Other words are used for family, but often they encompass more than those who live in one household and refer at times to lineage segments as well as the household. The word ghar, when used in the context of a family, means those who take their food from one *chula* (stove). Those who take food from the chula form the commensal group, which means to a Chamar the sharing of property and rights, a common pocketbook, a common larder, common debts, common labour force, and usually one recognised head. The head of the household is usually the oldest competent male in the household. In affairs of the hamlet, the household is recognised as the basic unit and is easily recognised by the other Chamars, who can name the members of every household and identify the head.

The 122 households of Chamars in Senapur, on the basis of structural criteria, may be divided in the following fashion:

TABLE 5.1: STRUCTURAL COMPOSITION OF CHAMAR FAMILIES

Nuclear	
Single aged adult	8
Man, wife and unmarried offspring; or woman and unmarried offspring	72
Total	80
Extended	
Man, wife, sons, sons' wives and offspring	24
Brothers, wives and offspring	14
Man, wife, daughters, daughters' husbands and offspring	4
Total	42

Source: Author's fieldwork.

Table 5.1 summarises some structural facts about the composition of the families among the Chamars as they were in 1953. It does not tell us anything about the family as a process, and it does not tell us anything about the family over time. The type of household—nuclear, extended and/or joint—in which the Chamars live is determined by a number of complex social, economic, and cultural factors. Family type for the Chamar is not a fixed given, but a structural contingent.

Most Chamars would state that the ideal household should consist of three generations, in which the grandfather, his sons, and their wives and families all lived in one house and ate from the same chula. The Chamars had before them as a model the Thakur family, which was usually the three-generation joint family. Some Chamars thought that the Thakurs got some of their economic, political, and social strength from their family structure.

In Table 5.1, of the 42 families classified as extended, only 14 approximate the cultural ideal type of a joint family in that there were either three generations living together, or if the grand-parental generation had died, the brothers were over the age of 20. Many of those families classified as extended predictably were going to break apart within a few years. In many of the cases there were several sons, one or two of whom may have been married and many families had infant offspring, giving three generations; but when the sons grew older, usually above the age of 20, the households would break apart into their constituent nuclear components. Those fourteen which I call joint households had sons or sons-in-law over 20 with children over five years of age. It should be noted that the age of consummation of marriage among the Chamar males was usually between 15 and 17 with the wives aged 14 to 16.

There are several important factors which make the achievement of the ideal joint family difficult among the Chamars: demography, economics, the role of women and mobility.

Demography

Chamars, especially males, have low life expectancies. Out of 319 Chamar males in Senapur, only 19 were above the age of fifty. Out of 338 females, only 25 were above the age of 50. Clearly a three-generation family is impossible if the third generation is nonexistent. My impression was that those Chamars who survived childhood usually died between the ages of 35 and 45. Among the Thakurs, where the joint family is much more prevalent, my impression is that life expectancy is much higher.

Economics

It was difficult to obtain accurate statistics on land held and cultivated and on other possessions among the Chamars. Before 1952, no Chamar owned land; all land was owned by Thakurs. After the Land Reform Act of 1952, however, a few Chamars had the option of becoming landowners. The key concept in the relation of Chamars to the land is not how much they own, but how much they cultivate and under what types of tenure. In December 1952, by their own estimates, the 122 Chamar households cultivated 124 acres as non-permanent tenants and only 12 acres as permanent tenants. In addition, they cultivated 9 acres on a share-cropping basis. Chamars estimate that 4 acres are needed to support a household of five to six people. Is there any relationship between family type and land holding?

The six hamlets in which Chamars live in the village were classed as rich, middle, and poor, in terms of land held. In every hamlet, extended families have slightly more land per capita than nuclear families.

TABLE 5.2: LAND HOLDING (IN *BISWAS* PER CAPITA)

Poor	
Joint:	3.4
Nuclear:	2.4
Middle	
Joint:	6.2
Nuclear:	5.6
Rich	
Joint:	11.1
Nuclear:	6.9

Source: Author's fieldwork.

The average Chamar household cultivates a little under one acre. The average Thakur family cultivates six times as much. Connected with the amount of land cultivated is a range of other economic factors which affect household types.

A Chamar attaches great importance to the land he cultivates, even though the produce of his cultivation provides food for himself and his family for only about four months of the year. Most of the land which a Chamar cultivates is part of his pay for working as a permanent agricultural labourer for the Thakurs. Acting as a permanent or as a day agricultural labourer is the main source of income for a Chamar; for all but a few, this is the only way to make a living in the village. The peak working period of a Chamar is when he is between 15 and 35 years old; after that he is considered by Thakurs as old. Older Chamars cannot get employment as ploughmen and have a harder job getting daily work than the younger and better workers. Therefore, there is a sharp decline in the economic role of the Chamar male as he grows older and contributes much less to the household. It should be noted that the decrease in economic importance is not so sharp among Chamar women as they grow older. They continue into their fifties and sixties to be economically productive; they may act as servants in Thakur houses, or they may be midwives, or they may release younger Chamar women for held work.

In Thakur households, men do not have a comparable loss of economic role. It is true that these days Thakurs do much the same work as Chamars, except for actual ploughing. Thus, as a Thakur male grows older, he is not able to make as much of a direct physical contribution to the household. But since Thakur holdings are comparatively larger, an older Thakur man may still have a role as a farm manager; because of his knowledge of crops, agricultural technique, and marketing, he can still keep the household managerial role in his hands. He oversees and directs the activities of his younger brothers, sons, and hired labour. He still continues to be head of the household in the economic sphere of the family's activities.

The Chamar man, on the other hand, loses his economic role as he grows older. Once his ability to contribute directly through his labour is lost, his position as the head of the household is weakened. His ability to hold his sons and younger brothers together in a joint family decreases, if it does not altogether disappear.

Another factor connected with their lack of land and their low economic position which presses Chamars to live in nuclear-family households rather than in extended-family households is the bare subsistence level of Chamar life. Most Chamars of Senapur are on a semi-starvation diet for at least two to four months a year. The average Chamar family grows only a four-month supply of food on the land they cultivate. Other income is earned by daily wage work for Thakurs or by outside employment in an industrial centre. During August and January, even by pooling all its sources of income, the average Chamar household gets only a half-pound of coarse grain per head, per day. For those who get jobs in the village, their wages are at their lowest point during these months.

The most frequent explanation given for the splitting up of Chamar joint-family households was squabbling over food. In 12 cases of partition on which I have data, in eight the stated reason for breakup was quarrels over differential contributions of food and income. A brother with one small child does not see why he should share his meagre earnings with a brother who has three small children and hence gets a larger share of the common household food supply. Thus, it appears that a joint-family household requires something above a bare minimum subsistence for its continuation.

The Role of Women

The small amount of land cultivated leads to another factor tending towards nuclear-family households among the Chamars. There is no reason for them to pool their labour to cultivate their small plots. A man and his wife and children are fully capable of performing all agricultural operations, except the sowing of sugar cane. Of the agricultural activities that Chamars engage in on their own plots, this is the only one that requires more than one adult male. For artisan castes, such as Lobars or Kohars, or for Thakur landlords, a pool of labour is an economic asset. For example, several carpenters can work together more efficiently with respect to tools, facilities, and tasks, and thus an extended-family household is an advantage.

After disputes over food sharing, the most common causes for separations among Chamars are disputes between brothers' wives or between a woman and her mother-in-law. A Chamar woman is a full economic partner of her husband.

She does the same agricultural labour that her husband does, except ploughing. She is paid the same rate as a man for agricultural labour. In addition, many Chamar women act as servants in Thakur households, helping Thakur women with all tasks except those which take place in the kitchen. For their work as house servants, they are paid in grain, cloth, and cooked food.

When a Chamar woman gets into a dispute with her mother-in-law, she is in a strong position because of her important economic contribution to the household. Her threat to leave the household is taken seriously, because it would mean considerable economic loss. Chamar women do leave their husbands for short or long periods, and they can divorce their husbands. A woman's father or brothers are not unhappy to see her come home, because she can contribute to their household. For a Thakur woman to return to her father's house on a permanent or semi-permanent basis is almost unheard of. Not only is tradition against it, but a Thakur woman would become to some extent a burden on her father's house. When a Thakur woman is young, she contributes indoor labour and children to the household. But in comparison to a Chamar woman, she does not make such a direct and visible contribution to the income of the household. A Thakur woman is directly under the control of the older women of the house, while a Chamar woman is out working and mixing with men. The Chamar woman has a view of herself as a person apart from her husband. She is a full and active economic contributor to her household, and she may demand separation of the joint-family household if she feels it would be to her benefit. In a joint-family household, there is need for the submission of its members to the authority of a head. Along with this, there should be role differentiation. In most Chamar households, the economic roles of husbands and wives are interchangeable.

Mobility

Traditionally, there should be a locus, in a physical sense, for a joint-family household. The importance of a traditional seat of a joint family is obvious among the Thakurs. They point proudly to their ancestry and to their connection with the village and the local region. A Thakur knows his genealogy for 15 to 17 generations. He remembers the ancestors who lived, farmed, and fought in the village and the region. To a Thakur, land and family are one. Even under modern conditions, the interests of the joint family and its land are always put first, even at the cost of caste solidarity.

A Chamar's roots are not in his land, but he is linked to a Thakur who has provided him with land and the opportunity to gain a livelihood. The primary tie of a Chamar to a village and a locality is through his Thakur by means of the Thakur-Praja tie. Before the enactment of the Land Reform Act of 1952, the Thakurs owned all the land in the village; all non-Thakur households owed a primary allegiance as *praja* (dependent) to that Thakur household on whose land they had built their house. Theoretically, the Thakur protected his praja and supported him in time of need. The praja owed allegiance and assistance to his Thakur. Even Chamars often describe a fellow Chamar not by name, lineage or household—as upper caste men describe their fellow caste members—but by referring to him as the praja of a particular Thakur. The principal reason a Chamar stays in his village is because that is where he can get work. The greatest depth I found in Chamar genealogies was three ascending and three descending generations, compared with seventeen for some Thakurs. The Chamar does not need the genealogical knowledge that the Thakur does as there is little land to be passed to kin.

From a study of Chamar genealogies it was evident that over the last 70 years there has been considerable geographic mobility among Chamars. Out of 48 households found in the largest Chamar hamlet, only eight claimed to be first settlers (that they came with the Thakurs). The other 40 households have migrated to the village from elsewhere during the past 200 years. Fifteen per cent of the living adult males in Senapur were from other villages. As far as I can find out, all adult Thakur males were born in the village.

There are three situations which lead Chamars to move. A serious dispute with his landlord will make a Chamar flee with his stock and few belongings; he usually flees to the village of his wife's family, his mother's family, or his married sister. Secondly, if a Chamar has little land in his natal village, and if his father-in-law has land and no sons, he often goes to his father-in-law's village; he settles in his father-in-law's house and hopes that his son will inherit the father-in-law's cultivating rights or land. In Senapur in 1952, there were four such men living in or near their father-in-law's house. A third reason for leaving is if a Chamar hears of an opportunity to get more land to farm in another village, usually the village of affines or uterine kin; but in one case a Chamar family consisting of a father and two sons and their families left the village because they could buy land in another village.

The mobility of Chamar families tends to break up joint families, as often only part of a household moves, leaving behind a nuclear family. The kin ties among the Chamars who move seem particularly brittle and after one or two generations knowledge of the kin who have moved is lost.

Establishment of Joint-Family Households

As I have already stated, most of the Chamar joint-family households are only temporary. A Chamar household continually changes in response to certain conditions. We freeze process to talk about it; but we should not lose sight of the fact that for Chamars the joint family is a structural contingent and not a fixed form.

What I mean by a structural contingent can be seen in the following example, which shows the effects of extra-village employment on Chamar households in the village. Of the 42 joint-family households, 18 had one or more members working outside the village. Of the 80 nuclear-family households, fourteen had members working outside the village.

Urban employment works in two ways to maintain or bring about temporary joint-family households. First, if a man leaves his family behind while he goes to work in the city, he usually leaves his family with his parents or with his brother. For the period of the man's absence, there is a joint family since the money remitted from the city goes into the common fund and what land the man may have is used jointly. When the man returns, however, he may set up an independent household will not share the money he brings back. I call this type of joint family an unstable joint family: one which has been set up to meet a particular economic situation.

Outside employment may also be a major factor in setting up a stable joint family: a three-generation joint family existing through time. The families of the three Chamar school teachers illustrate this. In each case, the children who became school teachers grew up in joint families. This is not accidental: only a joint family among the Chamars could probably afford to forgo a child's labour so that he could get sufficient education to become a school teacher. Each of the three teachers continued to live in a three-generation joint-family household after getting his education, though none of them is head of his household. In one of these joint families, the oldest generation consists of two brothers and their wives. Whether the joint families will continue after the oldest generation dies, I do not know. I do think, however, that it is the steady cash income combined with the little land they have to work which makes it possible for these joint families to endure. In several other cases industrial labour on the part of a younger son or brother seems to perform the same function.

Another factor which seems to stabilise joint families is tradition; some of the Chamar families have a tradition of living in joint-family households. These families tend to be the relatively wealthy and powerful Chamars and also tend to be the leaders of the Chamars.

My hypothesis is that it is not only land or property which tends to bring about joint-family households among Chamars: rather, a combination of factors may be involved. Land is important but not sufficient; some of the wealthiest Chamar families do not have joint-family households. The combination of factors should include urban employment and literacy. Literacy leads to a drive for Sanskritisation, which in turn is an incentive for joint families.

Notes and References

[1] George Peter Murdock, *Social Structure* (New York: Macmillan, 1949), p. 1.

[2] Ibid., p. 2.

6

Individual Case Study and the Statistical Method in Social Investigation*

Iravati Karve

Among many methods of study, anthropologists have certain preferences and prejudices. There are some who think that the only way to understand a social structure is to study it personally in the field. Each example of a social structure is a unique entity, and when one describes a structure in general terms one abstracts all the time so as to leave out the more individual features and give a general picture. Yet the presence of the individual features is in the consciousness of the investigator and at any time an individual feature or a complex of individualities throws very penetrating light on the structure and its working. A structure is to be interpreted in a particular way because it works in certain ways under certain circumstances. What appears as very unique in certain examples may be an important item in the functioning of a structure under certain circumstances. An anthropologist is, therefore, anxious to see and analyse for himself the structure he studies.

On the other hand, features of social organisation are manifest over wide areas. One wants to know the extent and frequency of certain phenomena. Anthropology is not just a collection of descriptions and analysis of individual structures found at a particular time in a particular space; in anthropology one seeks to know the regularities governing human cultural life and wants to interpret phenomena over large areas and long timespans. This can be done by studying a large number of samples belonging to different times. For this purpose a statistical approach is necessary. It does not suffice to know the different ways in which a structure manifests itself but one wants to know also which ways

* Originally published in *Economic Weekly* 15, no. 17 (27 April 1963), pp. 701–06.

are in vogue and in what proportion in a given society. Also, whether there are factors connecting particular types of a structure to particular stages in life, economic conditions, or the cultural phase through which an individual or a society is passing. Some of these questions occurred to the author in a recent investigation. The author is not conversant with statistical methods but would like to place before the statisticians her needs and problems in order to get the answers as to how to count numerical possibilities of different varieties of a structure in a population.

Jointness and Non-Jointness

Three families were investigated for certain purchases. The history of one could be obtained for six generations. This family, K, was a landed family. The other family R gave a history of four generations and was not based on land but earned its living through service and profession. The family U is an extremely young family owning a little rice land and doing domestic service. All the three families have been alternating between jointness and non-jointness. Jointness and non-jointness also appear to be very much a matter of degree. For some time a family is joint in as much as three of four generations of men with their wives and children live under one roof, eat food cooked in one kitchen, hold property in common, and have common worship and ritual. This is the picture of the classical joint family. This type of family has never kept together for generations. It splits into smaller joint or non-joint units.

A small joint family may be made up of parents and a married son or sons, or two or more married brothers living together. This latter form of a joint family—the collateral joint family—is less frequent and seems to represent a transitory form between the big patrilineal family and its break into several non-joint or smaller patrilineal joint families. In this context, an interesting variation is of a family where only one parent is alive and circulates periodically among the sons. We have examples of a widower father sharing the house of his sons by turns. This happens also in the case of a widowed mother. The father owns property jointly with the sons, but in some cases he is dependent on his sons. The widowed mother generally owns no property but has a certain status, and the neighbourhood expects the young mistress to show proper deference to the widowed mother-in-law. The presence or absence of a parent in a dependent or non-dependent position does constitute a type of jointness, but if the parent circulates, then the different families of the sons would be joint or non-joint by turns. The author has witnessed such cases.

The third type of a position between jointness and non-jointness occurs when one brother (or some brothers) lives on the ancestral land, in the ancestral house and is a farmer, and the other brother(s) migrate(s) to cities like Bombay or Poona or Sholapur, is a wage-earner, and his wife and children stay with him. The city brother sends money for land-improvement or for routine agricultural work to the brother at home, visits himself or sends his wife occasionally to the home. All familial ritual prescribed on certain holy days is performed at the home on the ancestral land. Each of these families is non-joint in residence, food, and household management, but is joint for purposes of religion, property, and mutual help.

CYCLICAL PROCESS

Between 100 per cent jointness and 100 per cent non-jointness, there are a number of families which are "semi-joint" in these ways. In our recent work in rural and urban areas and in census reports, over 60 per cent of the families appeared as non-joint. One would like a statistical measure about the nature of these families. One would also like to know how many families might become joint when the eldest son marries, how many might be non-joint because the parent is with another son, how many are non-joint in residence but joint in property, worship, and mutual help.

Besides these, there are non-joint families which are products of a recent split in a joint family on the death of parents, but which develop into joint families when the sons come of age and marry. This non-jointness represents a phase in the cyclical process of jointness and non-jointness which families seem to be undergoing. Therefore, one would like to know whether it is possible to estimate the age at which a man is likely to be the head of a non-joint family. Our records show that the period after the death of both the parents and before the son is of the age to marry is the period when a man is likely to be the head of a non-joint family. The factors which might disturb this expectation are the living together of the brothers after the death of the father. As stated above, this appears to be a transitory stage, but in some cases, the period is prolonged—the membership of a widowed mother and very young brothers seems to be the factor responsible for such prolongation.

One would also like to have an idea about the jointness and non-jointness likely to occur in urban and rural areas, among the land-based families, among wage-earners and among commercial people.

Jointness and non-jointness are generally mentioned with reference to the headship of a family, but a person may spend parts of his life in joint and non-joint families without being the head of either. For considerations of personality development, communication of cultural items, and feelings of security or non-security, it is very important to know the periods spent by an individual in different types of families. One wants to know the kind and extent of investigation—i.e., the design of experiment—from statisticians to get adequate answers to such questions. The nature of the structure must be

FIGURE 6.1: GENEALOGIES

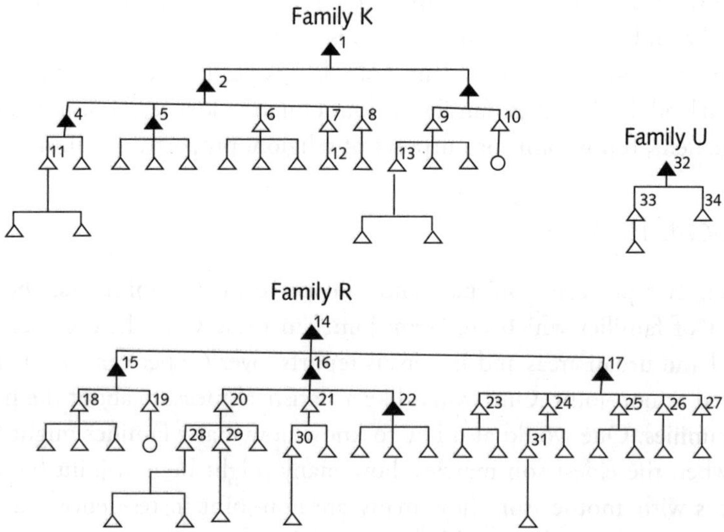

Source: Author's fieldwork.

studied in individual cases, but the questions, like the frequency of occurrence in the total population, can be attempted only through statistics. Statistical experiment, in its turn, sometimes draws attention to features which may have escaped attention in individual studies.

Figure 6.1 and Table 6.1 relate to men whose families have been investigated. The dates of birth and death are given. The total period of life spent in joint and non-joint families, as also the period during which a man was head of a non-joint family, are given. The families in which the mother lived with different sons periodically are given separately. The families which live hundreds of miles apart but are joint in property, etc., are also noted. Studies like this give an idea of the different types but not of the likely frequency of such types.

Figure 6.1 gives the genealogies of the men whose family history is given in the table. Each individual is given a number which is the same in the table and figure. In Table 6.1 in the case of each individual, the actual years of the century spent in each type of family are given.

We have dealt with 34 males in Table 6.1. All of them have lived alternately in joint and non-joint families. The paternal joint family made up of a father, a mother, and one or two married sons, with or without other unmarried sons, seems to be the prevalent pattern of a joint family. The death of the father generally breaks up a joint family. The widowed mother lives with one of the sons or circulates among different sons. This phase is called a 'non-joint' family.

TABLE 6.1: DISTRIBUTION OF INDIVIDUALS ACCORDING TO LIFE LIVED IN DIFFERENT TYPES OF FAMILY

Numbers and Life-Span of the Individual	Paternal and Fraternal Joint	Only Fraternal Joint (with or without Widowed Fa/Mo)	Father's Non-Joint	Widowed Fa/Mo Member of Ego's Non-Joint Family Widowed Ego as Member of Married Son's Non-Joint Family	Ego as Head of Non-Joint Family	Ego as Head of Joint Family with Married Son's	Widwoed Ego as Member of Married Son's Fraternal Joint Family
(1)	(2)	(3)	(4)	(5)	(6)	(7)	(8)
			Family K				
(1) 1828–1900 Marriage – 1842		1843–1900 (15–72) –58–	1828–1842 (0–14) –14–				
(2) 1859–1922 Marriage – 1879 1899	1859–1900 (0–41) –41–	1901–1902 (42–43) –2–			1903–1913 (44–54) –11–	1914–1922 (55–63) –9–	
(4) 1900–1949 Marriage – 1913	1900–1902 (0–2) –2–		1903–1913 (3–13) –11–				
	1914–1922 (14–22) –9–	1923–1949 (23–49) –27–					
5) 1902–1949 Marriage – 1921	1914–1922 (12–20) –9–	1923–1949 (21–47) –27–	1902–1913 (0–11) –11–				

(contd.)

(Table 6.1 contd.)

Numbers and Life-Span of the Individual	Paternal and Fraternal Joint	Only Fraternal Joint (with or without Widowed Fa/Mo)	Father's Non-Joint	Widowed Fa/Mo Member of Ego's Non-Joint Family Widowed Ego as Member of Married Son's Non-Joint Family	Ego as Head of Non-Joint Family	Ego as Head of Joint Family with Married Son's	Widwoed Ego as Member of Married Son's Fraternal Joint Family
(1)	(2)	(3)	(4)	(5)	(6)	(7)	(8)
(6) 1909– Marriage – 1928 1931	1914–1922 (5–13) –9–	1923–1949 (14–40) –27–	1909–1913 (0–4) –4–	1950–1961 (41–52) –12–	1962 (53) –1–		
(7) 1912– Marriage – 1936	1914–1922 (2–10) –9–	1923–1949 (11–37) –27–	1912–1913 (0–1) –1–		1950–1961 (38–49) –12–	1962 (50) –1–	
(8) 1920– Marriage – 1943	1920–1922 (0–2) –2–	1923–1949 (3–29) –27–			1950–1962 (30–42) –13–		
(11) 1928– Marriage – 1945	1928–1949 (0–21) –21–			1950–1962 (22–34) –13–			
(12) 1938– Marriage – 1961	1938–1949 (0–11) –11– 1962 (24) –1–		1950–1961 (12–13) –12–				

(13) 1928– Marriage – 1956	1928–1936 (0–8) –8– 1957–1962 (29–34) –6–		1937–1956 (9–28) –20–				
(10) 1909– Marriage – 1935	1927–1936 (18–27) –10–		1909–1926 (0–17) –17–	1937–1947 (28–38) –11–	1948–1962 (39–53) –15–		

Family R

(15) 1865–1945 Marriage – 1883 1888	1865–1898 (0–33) –33–	1899–1900 (34–35) –2–		1901–1920 (36–55) –20–	1921–1936 (56–71) –16–	1937–1945 (72–80) –9–	
(18) 1907– Marriage – 1938	1937–1945 (30–38) –9–	1946–1962 (39–55) –17–	1907–1936 (0–29) –29–				
(19) 1912– Marriage – 1942	1937–1945 (25–33) –9–	1946–1962 (34–50) –17–	1912–1936 (0–24) –24–				
(16) 1872–1948 Marriage – 1892	1872–1898 (0–26) –26–	1899–1900 (27–28) –2–		1901–19145 (29–43) –15– 1940–1948 (68–76) –9–			1916–1939 (44–67) –24–

(contd.)

(Table 6.1 contd.)

Numbers and Life-Span of the Individual	Paternal and Fraternal Joint	Only Fraternal Joint (with or without Widowed Fa/Mo)	Father's Non-Joint	Widowed Fa/Mo Member of Ego's Non-Joint Family Widowed Ego as Member of Married Son's Non-Joint Family	Ego as Head of Non-Joint Family	Ego as Head of Joint Family with Married Son's	Widwoed Ego as Member of Married Son's Fraternal Joint Family
(1)	(2)	(3)	(4)	(5)	(6)	(7)	(8)
(20) 1895– Marriage – 1915	1895–1900 (0–5) –5–		1901–1915 (6–20) –15–				
	1918 (21) –1–	1917–1939 (22–44) –23–		1940–1948 (45–53) –9–	1949–1952 (54–57) –4–	1953–1962 58–67) –10–	
(28) 1922 Marriage – 1952	1922–1939 (0–17) –17–		1940–1952 (18–30) –13–				
	1953–1962 (31–40) –10–						
(29) 1925– Marriage – 1957	1925–1939 (0–14) –14–		1940–1952 (15–27) –13–				
	1953–62 (28–37) 10						

(21) 1898– Marriage – 1920	1898–1900 (0–2) –2–		1901–1915 (3–17) –15–			
	1916 (18) –1–		1917–1926 (19–28) –10–		1927–1958 (29–60) –32–	1959–1962 (61–64) –4–
(30) 1926– Marriage – 1920	1959–1962 (33–61) –4–		1926–1958 (0–32) –32–			
(22) 1906–1954 Marriage – 1939	1916 (10) –1–	1917–1939 (11–33) –23–	1906–1915 (0–9) –9–		1940–1954 (34–48) –15–	
(17) 1877–1957 Marriage – 1897	1877–1898 (0–21) –21–	1899–1900 (22–23) –2–		1901–1920 (24–43) –20– 1956–1957 (79–80) –2–	1921–1928 (44–51) –8–	1929–1955 (52–78) –27–
(23) 1899– Marriage – 1928	1899–1900 (0–1) –1–		1901–1928 (2–29) –28–			
	1929–1955 (30–56) –27–			1956–1957 (57–58) –2–	1958–1962 (59–63) –5–	

(contd.)

(Table 6.1 contd.)

Numbers and Life-Span of the Individual	Paternal and Fraternal Joint	Only Fraternal Joint (with or without Widowed Fa/Mo)	Father's Non-Joint	Widowed Fa/Mo Member of Ego's Non-Joint Family Widowed Ego as Member of Married Son's Non-Joint Family	Ego as Head of Non-Joint Family	Ego as Head of Joint Family with Married Son's	Widwoed Ego as Member of Married Son's Fraternal Joint Family
(1)	(2)	(3)	(4)	(5)	(6)	(7)	(8)
(24) 1903 Marriage – 1928 1933	1929–1952 (26–49) –24–		1903–1928 (0–25) –25–		1953–1959 (50–55) –7–	1960–1962 (57–59) –3–	
(25) 1912– Marriage – 1935	1929–1943 (17–31) –15–		1914–1926 (0–16) –16–		1944–1962 (32–50) –19–		
(26) 1914– Marriage – 1951	1914–1928 (15–37) –23–		1914–1928 (0–14) –14–		1952–1962 (38–48) –11–		
(27) 1917– Marriage – 1950	1929–1953 (12–35) –25–		1917–1928 (0–11) –11–		1954–1962 (37–45) –9–		
(31) 1935– Marriage – 1959	1935–1952 (0–17) –17– (1960–1962) (25–27) –3–		1953–1959 (18–24) –7–				

			Family U		
(33) 1935–	1954–1957	1958–1959	1935–1953		1960–1962
Marriage – 1953	(19–22)	(23–24)	(0–18)		(25–27)
	–4–	–2–	–18–		–3–
(34) 1936–	1954–1957	1958–1959	1936–1953		1960–1962
Marriage – 1956	(18–21)	(22–23)	(0–17)		(24–26)
	–4–	–2–	–17–		–3–

Source: Author's fieldwork.

Purely fraternal joint family seems to be a longer or shorter phase between the paternal joint family and one's own non-joint family.

Enduring Joint Family

In the following three cases, the fraternal joint family endured for a long time:

(1) Nos. 4, 5, 6, 7, and 8 lived in a fraternal joint family, with the widowed mother, for as long a period as 27 years. This was due to the fact that No. 4 was the only brother who was capable of looking after the property and supporting the younger brothers, sisters, and the mother. His death finally separated the family.
(2) The second case is that of numbers 18 and 19, who have lived in a fraternal joint family for 17 years. This was because No. 19's wife separated from him soon after marriage and his baby girl was brought up by No. 18's wife. So No. 19 and his daughter have made their home with No. 18 and his wife. The presence of the widowed mother has also helped this togetherness.
(3) The third case is that of Nos. 20, 21, and 22. No. 20 is the eldest brother. No. 21 married and separated after staying for six years in the family of No. 20. No. 22 separated immediately after marriage. So, for some time, No. 20 lived with his unmarried brothers, then for some time with one married and one unmarried brother. When one married brother left, he was for some time with the unmarried brother after whose marriage he lived as the head of a non-joint family. All these years the widower father of these brothers lived with the eldest son. In three other cases, the fraternal joint family broke up within two years.

A man is usually supposed to live as the head of a non-joint family until the son or a brother gets married, generally between the ages of 18 and 25. In some cases a son or a younger brother does not marry till after 25 (No. 19 in Table 6.1). The son or the brother earns his living but still goes on living with his father or brother if he happens to be in the same town. Employment outside the town may lead to earlier marriage. Marriage might lead to a separation from the joint family but not always immediately.

Families may appear to be non-joint, as in the case of Nos 33 and 34. The two brothers live about a 100 miles apart, each with his wife and children, but they own property in common. All the familial ritual is done by the brother who lives on the ancestral property and No. 33 sends him money every now and then for the improvement of the ancestral land and property. Thus, though these families are non-joint for daily work and as regards the up-bringing of the children, they are joint in property, worship and mutual help.

Temporary Non-Jointness

The other non-joint families also represent temporary non-jointness of different types. For example, No. 6 is living as head of his non-joint family. His sons are above 22 years of age and might marry any time now, so that his family may change from a non-joint to a paternal joint family.

No. 9 has a married son who serves in another town. The son's wife came for both her deliveries during the last three years for several months at a time to live with her mother-in-law. This therefore, also is not a completely non-joint family. The same is true also in the case of No. 31.

Jointness and non-jointness appear as alternate phases in the family life of persons as depicted above. The ages of men who became heads of non-joint families are between 22 and 59. Most are near 40.

The occasion on which one becomes head of a non-joint family seems to depend not so much on one's marriage or capacity to earn, as on the death of the male parent.

PART III

Identity and Politics

7

The RSS*

D. V. Kelkar

The Rashtriya Swayam Sewak Sangh (RSS) has often been in the news in recent years. It came into the headlines, however, only since the assassination of Mahatma Gandhi. The organisation was banned on 4 February 1948 by the central government and similar action was simultaneously taken by the provincial governments. As the Government of India's communiqué stated, "It has been found that in several parts of the country individual members of the RSS have indulged in acts of violence involving arson, robbery, dacoity and murder, and have collected illicit arms and ammunition. They have been circulating leaflets exhorting people to resort to methods of terrorism, to collect firearms, to create disaffection against the Government and suborn the police and the military." The communiqué added that "the objectionable and harmful activities of the Sangh have continued unabated," and "the cult of violence sponsored and inspired by the activities of the Sangh has claimed many victims. The latest and the most precious to fall was Gandhiji himself."

In reply the Sangh demanded that either the charges be proved or the ban withdrawn. Thousands of members of the RSS were arrested for participating in the Satyagraha which was launched, and later were released on the understanding that the affairs of the Sangh would be run on democratic lines. The Sangh now has its own constitution and supposedly elects its functionaries except for the post of the sar sangh chalak, which is inherited by the nominee of the previous functionary. The ban having been removed, the Sangh is again engaged in the task of organising the country into its old way of thinking.

Many questions arise regarding the fundamental objectives with which the Sangh was founded, and the methods of their fulfillment. Why were their

* Originally published in *Economic Weekly* 2, no. 4 (4 February 1950), pp. 132–38.

objectives contrary to the Congress's way of thinking and work? What was the Sangh's attitude towards foreigners in general and Muslims in particular? Was it influenced by Nazi methods of mass organisation? Was it a reaction to Muslim propaganda for power, to fascist organisations like Allama Mashriqui's Khaksar movement, or was it a purely cultural organisation, aiming to regenerate the country into one heritage, one culture, and one nation without any reference to Swaraj? The task of answering these questions has been rendered difficult because the Sangh, since it was founded, has been carrying on its organisational work silently, ever spurning publicity. Even so, an attempt has been made in this article to analyse the Sangh from the acknowledged sentiments of its founder, and his philosophy, and from the famous treatise *We*, which the present sar sangh chalak, Shri M. S. Golwalkar, M.Sc., LL.B., wrote in 1949.

The RSS was founded on Dasserah day in 1925. The founder was Dr Keshav Baliram Hedgewar of Nagpur. Victim to the operation of the Risley Circular, which prohibited students from taking part in politics, the Doctor was rusticated from the Neil High School for his *Vande Mataram* agitation. He joined the national school at Yeotmal (Berar). But the school was compelled to close, and the Doctor migrated to Poona and passed his matriculation from the national school there. In 1910, he joined the National Medical College at Calcutta. He led the batch of Maharashtrian students which occupied the Santi Niketan Lodge and, owing to his notable patriotism, came into intimate contact with highly respected leaders like Shri Shyam Sunder Chakravarty and Shri Motilal Ghosh. Shyam Sunder in particular took a liking to him, and exercised a considerable influence on his development. His life in Calcutta further cemented the feeling of affection and respect which abounded between Bengal and Maharashtra since the days of anti-partition in Bengal. In due course he secured his LMS degree and returned to Nagpur. He was, no doubt, a doctor, but he hardly ever interested himself in setting up a practice. Patriot to the core, he had dedicated his life to the cause of his country's emancipation from slavery. He preferred to remain a bachelor because of the need he felt for devoting his years to the unbroken service of the Motherland. The present writer had the good fortune to be in contact with him from late 1919 to 1923 at Nagpur. Not a day passed without our meeting. The present writer even addressed a number of public meetings at various places along with him. Dr Hedgewar was a renowned orator, he kept his audience spellbound. He was impatient of the slow progress the country was making in the direction of independence. He disliked the constitutional agitation which was being conducted by the late Lokamanya for Swaraj "within the British Empire." He wanted complete freedom without being tied to any apron strings. Mahatmaji's non-cooperation movement, having as its objective "Swaraj with one year," immediately enticed him. As the present writer recalls the proceedings of the Reception Committee of the Nagpur Congress, he remembers how the Tilak school of politics was done away with brick by brick, in which youngsters like Dr. Hedgewar took not a small part. Although the Doctor and the present writer were later accepted as Associate Members of the Rashtriya Mandal led by Dr. B. S. Moonje, which governed and ran politics in C. P. on Tilakite lines, Doctor Hedgewar in his objective of complete independence went headlong with the non-cooperation movement.

The movement having failed, the Doctor retired from it as quickly as he had entered it. He disliked the way in which the movement was conducted later on and the way the Muslim leaders were misdirecting it. The Moplah rebellion created a deep impression on him. Then came the Muslim riots in Nagpur and the weakness of Hindus became patent to all. The Doctor felt ashamed of the behaviour of the Hindu population which, though stronger in numbers, was totally disorganised and panicky. This set him furiously to the task of infusing confidence in the hearts of Hindus, and of preparing them to protect themselves. Thus was born the RSS. A fairly large number of volunteers were regularly drilled into the art of defending themselves. Timidity gave place to courage, and the next time there were riots, the Muslims had a new experience. They had to run away and leave Nagpur *en masse* for safety. They, as aggressors, had sown the wind. They had to reap the whirlwind. This success infused a feeling of courage in Hindu hearts, which was reflected in an influx of strength to the organisation.

The Doctor's pro-Hindu feeling having been awakened, it always had the upper hand. The Congress policy of appeasing the Muslims enraged him. Later, the Communal Award and the organisation of the Muslims on communal lines, not for Swaraj but for Pakistan, further spurred him into activity. Mention must be made here of the deep impression made on the Doctor's mind by Shri V. D. Savarkar's revolutionary past and his ideology which claimed Hindustan for the Hindus. The Doctor considered Veer Savarkar to be the stimulating source of all agitation for achieving the country's liberty. So when the RSS was formed, the Doctor ran to Ratnagiri where his apostle of liberty had been ordered to stay under restraint of movement. The Doctor was the present writer's guest for a morning in Bombay, when he personally explained to him the reason for his visit. He wanted to consult Veer Savarkar concerning the rules and regulations of the RSS organisation. Let it be said to the Doctor's credit, however, that although he held Veer Savarkar in great esteem, he never made his organisation subservient to the Hindu Mahasabha. The cleavage between the two became clearer as years went by until Veer Savarkar, in a speech at Panwel openly attacked RSS neutrality in respect of Hindu Mahasabha work and said, "The epitaph for the RSS volunteer will be that he was born, he joined the RSS and he died without accomplishing anything!"

So, the Doctor independently continued the activities of his organisation. His administrative methods may appear to have been shrouded in mystery. This was excusable, no doubt, because he had to work when a pro-Muslim foreign power like Britain was ruling India. His organisation kept away from party politics and worked entirely for strengthening the cultural instincts of Hindu society. There is reason to believe that Allama Mashriqui's Khaksar organisation, run positively on facist lines, copying Hitler's and Mussolini's youth movements, with its easy conquests, left a deep impression on the Doctor's mind. It seemed not altogether impossible that the attainment of shakti on RSS lines would one day mean release of forces that would not only win Swaraj for the country but would also reserve Bharat Hindus. A deep-dyed anti-Britisher as he was, freedom from the foreign yoke was one of his main aims, though having no faith in the ideology of non-violence or in the Congress way of political agitation, he entirely disbelieved that the Congress would ever be able to attain Swaraj because it lacked organisational strength. But had God granted him a longer life to see his country actually free on 15 August 1947, he would nonetheless have danced with sheer joy at seeing his dream fulfilled. Perhaps he would have even remodeled his organisation on different lines to suit new circumstances.

Instead, the country had to witness a different spectacle. All the RSS members, those at least whom the present writer knew and had met, looked as if they were in mourning on 15 August 1947. Perhaps they were overcome by a sense of frustration that Swaraj, even a sovereign republic, was coming without a violent war being waged against Britain, without any official contribution by the RSS to any of the civil disobedience movements initiated by the Congress. The ridicule they had heaped upon Congress was now flung back on them.

It was the partition of the country into Hindustan and Pakistan, however, that pained them most. Congressmen and others were soon to praise the services rendered by these RSS stalwarts who rendered yeomen service to the thousands of Punjabi and Sikh families who were uprooted from West Punjab. But the feeling of disgust for the miseries of Hindu and Sikh evacuees outweighed their joy at attaining Swaraj, a Swaraj which in expanse and greatness had no parallel in the history of Hindustan for the past 1,000 years. The dreams of Shivaji, Rana Pratap, and Baji Rao I, had at last taken physical shape; India was free, and yet the RSS continued to feel disgruntled and disappointed. The present Sar Sangh Chalak, Shri M. S. Golwalkar, in his speech at Shivaji Park, Dadar, delivered some time in November 1947 had not one good word to say about the architects who through lifelong sacrifice and labour had actually been able to attain Swaraj without bloodshed, without ill will. On the contrary, he poured contempt on Gandhiji, who according to him, had committed a series of blunders. To him, partition was the wound, and he would ignore the glorious Swaraj because it did not tally with his idea of one Nation and of an Akhand Hindustan for the Hindus. The feeling of contempt and hatred for the Congress continues even to this day amongst those of the many RSS rank and file whom the present writer happens to know. Even the assassination of Gandhiji does not appear to have touched them.

I would recommend to the reader who wishes to understand the full ideology of the RSS the treatise entitled *We, or Our Nationhood Defined,*[1] and in particular the first edition of the book, which bears a straightforward foreword by Shri M. S. Aney, now H. E. the Governor of Bihar. This foreword, for reasons best known to the author, has been omitted from the second edition. This book is regarded almost as the Geeta by the RSS rank and file, and to understand it is to understand everything worth knowing about the RSS. "The idea contained in the word Nation," says the author on page 18, "is a compound of five distinct factors fused into one indissoluble whole, the famous five 'unities':_geographical (country), racial (race), religious (religion), cultural (culture), and linguistic (language)." "Hindustan is the land of the Hindus and is the *terra firma* for the Hindu Nation alone to flourish," says the Guruji on page 45. Answering what is to be the fate of all those who, today, happen to live upon this land, though not belonging to the Hindu race, religion, and culture, the author says:

> At the outset, we must bear in mind that so far as "nation" is concerned, all those who fall outside the five-fold limits of that idea, can have no place in the national life, unless they abandon their difference, adopt the religion, culture and language of the Nation, and completely merge themselves in the National Race. So long, however, as they maintain their racial, religious and cultural differences, they cannot but be only foreigners, who may be either friendly or inimical to the Nation.

The Guruji proceeds on page 47:

> There are only two courses open to the foreign elements, either to merge themselves in the national race and adopt its culture, or to live at its mercy so long as the national race may allow them to do so and to quit the country at the sweet will of the national race. That is the only sound view on the minorities problem. That is the only logical and correct solution. That alone keeps the Nation safe from the danger of a cancer developing in its body politic of the creation of a State within the State. From this standpoint, sanctioned by the experience of shrewd old nations, the foreign races in Hindustan must either adopt the Hindu culture and language, must learn to respect and hold in reverence the Hindu religion, must entertain no ideas but those of glorification of the Hindu nation and must lose their separate existence to merge in the Hindu race, or may stay in the country, wholly subordinated to the Hindu Nation, claiming nothing, deserving no privileges, far less any preferential treatment, not even the citizens' rights. There is, at least should be, no other course for them to adopt. We are an old nation: let us deal, as old nations ought to and do deal, with the foreign races, who have chosen to live in our country.

Shri M. S. Aney, an erudite scholar and a deep thinker, who has not been able to see eye to eye with the author in respect of the above proposition, says:

> I have no doubt in my mind that a dispassionate study of the Minority Treaties of the League of Nations will not at all bear out the proposition which the author has so dogmatically laid down. There is nothing inconsistent with the sovereign position of a State in giving these culturally different minorities liberty to retain and observe their religious practices and facilities to preserve their culture, subject to conditions of public morals and public policy.
>
> No person born in the country, of parents whose ancestors enjoyed rights of citizenship for centuries together, can be treated as a foreigner in any modern State on the ground that he follows a religion different from that of the majority of the population which naturally dominates and controls it. Conversion of faith can't be a condition for nationalization of any alien in this twentieth century.

Shri M. S. Aney's wise words were probably anathema to the author of *We*. The result was that the foreword itself was omitted from the second edition of the book.

One can now well appreciate what must have been, and continues to be, the feeling of the rank and file of the RSS not accustomed to a deep, calm, and dispassionate study of a problem, *vis-à-vis* the Muslims. They do not even believe that Hindu-Muslim tension was perhaps the result of the British administrative policy of "divide and rule"; that Hindu-Muslim riots were mainly pre-arranged, or that even the last massacre in the Punjab was partly the result of some of the British military officials with passports in their pockets for a permanent route march out of the country, who refrained from exercising any restraint against the aggressor community.

Another part of the RSS Gita is the text of Shivaji's letter to Jaysingh which, as reproduced and used by the RSS chief, is not substantiated by historical evidence. It says:

> I do not know how I shall deal with thee. If I join thee, there is no manliness in it. For, brave men are not time servers. The lion pursues not the policy of the fox. Or if I lift up the sword and the axe, then, the Hindus on both sides will suffer. The greater sorrow is that my sword, which thirsts for the blood of the Mussalmans, should be drawn from the scabbard for some other purpose. If the Turks had come to fight this battle, then indeed the prey would have come to the lion in its lair. For they are Rakshasas in the guise of men, devoid of justice and religion, and are sinful.

One can well understand the makeup of the average RSS mind from the above. He would never, for instance, believe that communal killings could be got up and stimulated by a third party. If the Muslim is quiet or humbled today, the RSS man will believe that he will continue his treacherous campaign tomorrow.

Shri Golwalkar has also some unpleasant things to say regarding those great men who founded the Indian National Congress and those who fostered it into a nationwide organisation through lifelong service and sacrifice. He says: "Thanks to Sir William Wedderburn, Sir Henry Cotton, Mr. Hume and others of the type, we have almost completely lost sight of our true Hindu nationhood, in our wild-goose chase after the phantasm of founding a really democratic state in the country. Their aims are being realised. The Congress, which they founded as a safety valve to seething nationalism, as a toy which would lull the awakening giant into slumber, and instrument to destroy National consciousness, has been, as far as they are concerned, a success. Out own denationalisation under the name of nationalism is nearing its consummation. We have almost forgotten our Nationhood." A steadfast and self-sacrificing Congress worker as Shri M. S. Aney himself, in spite of his differing views regarding the communal award and other matters, could not meeky accept the views of the guruji regarding those pioneers who had founded and nursed the Congress. In his foreword, he says:

> The school of Indian patriots who have founded the Indian National Congress were the pioneers of the movement of Indian nationalism. I feel confident that their attempt to develop Indian Nationalism on lines other than those of religious grouping, were at any rate not inconsistent with the views of the Western jurists. The author has certainly done injustice to those high-souled illustrious Englishmen who helped the foundation of the Congress and its growth in its early stages by attributing to them unworthy motives. With all my difference of opinion on some of the vital problems of policy, such as communal award and others with the leading Congressmen of today, I consider it necessary to emphatically assert that much of the sentiment of nationalism that exists in India today is the result of the work done by the giants who have led and run the Congress movement, in the country during the last fifty years or more.

Whether or not the Sangh had any political objectives and whether or not it was influenced by the Hitlerian way of thinking and organising, it is clear that the Sangh was organised and developed under British rule. The Sangh had faith in *shakti* and not in parliamentary agitation or non-violence. It perhaps thought that the British would never voluntarily forsake power. It had also the firm conviction that the Congress would never be able to obtain Swaraj, much less a full-fledged sovereign republic. So a baffled sense of frustration must have overtaken the RSS when they saw independence being actually proclaimed in India. Independence, without organisation of *shakti,* without a bloody war, without the war-time ballads and display of heroics. It was unbelievable, it was frustrating!

So the RSS plan for emancipating the country from thralldom was unnecessary. What remains is its zest for the establishment of a real nation, nationality, nationalism, etc. If the RSS were just a reaction to what the Muslim League or Allama Mashriqui did, today no reason remains for its existence. It is all quiet on the communal front. With the mediaeval princely order lost for all time, and with zamindaris and landlordism fast disappearing, it is a strange new world in which the Sangh has set out to pursue its activities.

Has the RSS chief any socio-economic ideology? As is well known, everyone in the RSS, including the Guruji, is opposed to any "-isms" which are of foreign origin. As a message with dateline Lucknow, 1 September 1949 had shown, the Guruji is opposed to nationalisation of industries, and as regards abolition of landlordism, he said: "The criterion should be the betterment of the lot of the farmers, and in the case of the CP, the abolition of 'Malguzari,' which in some parts of the province had not proved in the interests of the people." The new constitution itself "was inspired by foreign ideals and was not in line with the evolution of indigenous institutions based on Hindu genius." To him democracy with an uneducated electorate was wrong. As latest reports indicate, he has aired his opposition also to the Hindu Code Bill. So here you have a picture of the whole philosophy that the Sangh, or at least the Guruji, is sponsoring.

It would be unjust for the present writer not to be cognizant of the determined spirit not only of its founder, and the present Sar Sangh Chalak, but also of the RSS rank and file. It is not an exaggeration to state that the thousands and lakhs who are pledged to the Sangh have sacrificed their career, wealth, and earthly pleasures for a cause. If only this human power were harnessed to a humane conception of society, it could yield valuable results. The signs of an evolution are not lacking. There are many in the RSS organisation itself who have begun the task of looking inward, arriving at truth and readjusting themselves to newer conditions. One devoutly prays and wishes that this organisation of determined men whose patriotism and love for the country may not be questioned will begin to discover the new-formed republic and the new thought and will to work to strengthen it.

Note

1 M. S. Golwalkar, *We, or Our Nationhood Defined* (Nagpur: Bharat Publications, 1939).

8

Sripuram: A Village in Tanjore District*

Andre Beteille

There are some who have been struck by the fact that the Indian village constitutes a kind of structural entity, and have devoted their attention to discussing the internal arrangements of this entity. This is indeed an important point of departure, and in what follows we shall have a good deal to say about the internal structure of the village under discussion. But, in addition to this, we shall have to take into account some of the major social forces which operate over a wider area, and the manner in which they exert their influence on a particular village community. The world of the village constitutes a sort of microcosm, and part of the interest of our study will be to see in what ways this microcosm is a reflection of the macrocosm which is the outside world.

2

Sripuram is an ancient village, situated about eight miles from Tanjore, to its north. A metalled road runs along the southern side of the village, which is situated about midway between Kumbakonam on the one hand and the Grand Anicut on the other. The river Kaveri flows parallel to the metalled road which separates it from the village. The main streets are on the opposite side of the metalled road, also parallel to it. The river is within a couple of hundred yards of the centre of the village site. To the east of Sripuram, and adjacent to it, is Thiruvaiyaru, of the sacred five rivers, famous throughout the Tamil country for its Shiva temple and for its association with Tyagaraja, the nineteenth century musician-saint.

* Originally published in *Economic Weekly* 14, nos 4, 5 and 6 (27 January 1962), pp. 141–46.

Sripuram does not, by itself, constitute a revenue village, but is grouped for revenue purposes along with another village which we shall refer to as Melur. Physically the two villages are quite distinct, Melur being separated from Sripuram by a distance of about one mile to its north. Each of these villages has had a distinctive history going back many centuries. Today there are many contacts between the two villages, and such contacts there have been for at least 200 years. The relationship between the two settlements is, in fact, quite complex, but we shall not enter into that here. Suffice it to say for the time being that the revenue village, which is named after Melur had, according to the 1951 Census, 457 occupied houses with 502 households numbering 2,485 individuals. In certain contexts, particularly with regard to land holding, we shall have to speak of Melur as a whole because in the revenue accounts the distinction between Sripuram and Melur is ignored.

A Brahmin Village

In the discussion that follows we shall concentrate our attention on Sripuram alone as it forms an independent unit in a number of important ways. A number of households which physically form a part of Sripuram are, for revenue purposes, associated with another unit which is located at a distance of about two miles. This association has arisen for a number of reasons which throw an interesting light on the revenue history of the area, but these problems cannot be entered into here. Because these households are physically, economically, and socially inseparable from the structure of Sripuram we shall, for the present purpose, regard them as constituting a part of it.

In the three southern districts of Tinnevelli, Kamnad and Madura, villages are regarded as belonging to either of two categories, *agrahara vadai* and *pandara vadai*. In the former the entire land, or the bulk of it, is or was until recently, held by a community of Brahmins, constituting what is usually known as the *agraharam*. In the latter category of villages, the landowners are mainly non-Brahmins. This distinction is equally an important feature of Tanjore villages, although the terms *agrahara vadai* and *pandara vadai* are not in normal use there. In this sense Sripuram constitutes an agraharam, or a Brahmin village, although this does not mean that the village is exclusively inhabited by Brahmins.

It should be made clear at the outset that in spite of the comparatively large concentration of Brahmins in Tanjore not every village in the district has an agraharam. In fact, in the majority of villages one finds only a few families of the Brahmins who act as temple priests or cater to some of the religious needs of the non-Brahmin residents. To this extent Sripuram is not a typical village in the statistical sense of the term. It is, nevertheless, of great importance as a type of village in which the interplay of some of the basic social forces in the region can be observed and analysed.

3

Physically, Sripuram constitutes a more or less compact unit. The houses are clustered together within a small area, giving the village a distinct physical entity. The total population of the village is 1,400, being distributed in 349 households. The breakdown of households and population by caste-group has been shown in the table below.

TABLE 8.1: HOUSEHOLDS AND POPULATION BY CASTE-GROUP

Caste-group	Households	Population
Brahmin	92	341
Non-Brahmin	168	688
Adi Dravida	89	371
Total	349	1,400

Source: Author's fieldwork.

Three-fold Divisions

It will be useful to begin with a consideration of the physical structure of the village as it has in some ways an important bearing on its social structure. Physically, the village divides itself into three well-defined segments, the agraharam, the *kudiana* streets, and the cheri. Of these, the first and the last are most distinctive. The agraharam runs in an almost perfect straight line from east to west, parallel to the metalled road, on its near side. It is separated from the metalled road by the backyards of the Brahmin houses and by a large coconut grove. The cheri is on the far side of the metalled road, also parallel to it. The houses of the Adi Dravidas, or Untouchables, are symmetrically arranged on either side, just as the Brahmin houses are arranged on either side of the Brahmin street. In between the agraharam and the cheri are the non-Brahmin houses, arranged in a number of streets which lack the symmetry of either the agraharam or the cheri. Some non-Brahmin houses are also to be found along the metalled road and in front of the Shiva temple which stands at the western extremity of the village.

These territorial divisions are of great importance because social values are attached to them. The agraharam is where all the Brahmin houses are located. It is the centre of their social life. A non-Brahmin does not ordinarily enter the agraharam except on some particular business. One can enter the non-Brahmin streets from the metalled road without passing through the agraharam. The social exclusiveness of the agraharam is related to its being physically sealed from the rest of the village. I am told that this exclusiveness was much more pronounced twenty-five years ago.

Brahmins Keep Away

The cheri is similarly sealed from the rest of the village. The Brahmins do not normally enter or pass through the cheri, which they consider to be filthy. Also, a Brahmin, if he has passed through the cheri, is required to take a bath prior to undertaking any ritual activity. The cheri, as we have mentioned earlier, consists of a single street with huts arranged on either side. The residents of this street are all Pallans, who constitute the largest group among the Adi Dravidas in Tanjore District. At a slight distance from the Pallan street is a cluster of huts inhabited by five households of Paraiyans. These Paraiyans also belong to the category of the Adi Dravidas or Untouchables, but unlike the Pallans, in this village they are all Christians. The physical separation between the Pallan and Paraiyan huts is clear. Their social separation is expressed through endogamy, the use of separate wells, and a number of other practices.

To me the identity of the non-Brahmin streets was most clearly brought out the day on which Sripuram was visited by C. N. Annadurai, the DMK leader. Preparations had been made in advance, and the non-Brahmin streets were decorated with paper streamers coloured red and black. An amplifier had been fitted in one of the non-Brahmin houses, and film music blared through the afternoon. All around there was bustle and activity. By contrast the agraharam seemed quiet and deserted.

The physical unity of the village, and its internal division into agraharam, kudiana streets and cheri constitute the most fundamental features of its social structure. The differentiation between the Brahmins, the non-Brahmins and the Adi Dravidas is evident not only in a ritual context but also in the economic and political spheres. And, in this regard Sripuram mirrors the basic cleavages that are present in Tamilnad today. Throughout our discussion we shall regard these cleavages as providing the framework within which relations between individuals and groups develop and are maintained.

4

Although the Brahmins, the non-Brahmins and the Adi Dravidas have each an identity of their own, this does not mean that they constitute homogeneous units. The Brahmins can be regarded as a unity only in relation to the non-Brahmins and the Adi Dravidas. Internally there are many sub-divisions among the Brahmins, just as there are among the non-Brahmins. The Adi Dravidas appear to be the most homogeneous, being characterised by a simple division into two groups as described above.

People who are united in one context may be sharply divided in another. The Brahmins of Sripuram who expressed their unity by refusing as a group to take notice of the DMK meeting are, nonetheless, divided among themselves. In fact, the Brahmins themselves are very conscious of their divisions, and point to these as the principal cause of their present decline. They often look back upon the past, to their days of power and glory, when the Brahmins of Sripuram stood united. It is difficult to ascertain whether divisions among the Brahmins have been sharpened in recent times. My own impression is that the opposite is the case. At any rate, there is evidence to show that as far back as in the 1880s they quarrelled bitterly among themselves over ritual and other matters.

As indicated earlier, the divisions among the Adi Dravidas are less conspicuous than among the Brahmins and the non-Brahmins. In the case of the two latter groups, they are based partly upon differences in wealth, occupation, and education. More apparent than these, however, and perhaps more fundamental, are the divisions based upon caste.

The categories Brahmin and non-Brahmin comprise aggregates of different castes. The term *caste* we use to refer to what are locally spoken of as *jati* or *kulam*—a small endogamous group, bound by ties of kinship, having in many cases a traditional occupation, and pursuing a more or less specific style of living. The Brahmins of Sripuram belong to a number of different castes and, in fact, represent a fair cross-section of the Brahmin castes present throughout Tamilnad. Castewise divisions among the Brahmins are not, however, represented in the distribution of their houses, which appear to succeed each other without any plan or order. Fifty to 60 years ago, I am told, the settlement pattern of the agraharam was more consistent with the cleavages between castes.

Three Language Groups

The Brahmins of Sripuram represent three language groups: Kannada, Telugu, and Tamil. The Kannada and Telugu Brahmins use somewhat corrupt forms of their respective languages when speaking at home, and Tamil for all other purposes. I emphasise the cultural diversity of the Brahmins because it highlights an important aspect of their position in the social structure. The Brahmins as a group have been far more mobile than other groups, and a Brahmin caste has generally a much wider territorial extension than a non-Brahmin caste. In the traditional system the Brahmins often moved from one region to another to settle on land granted to them by a particular king or prince. Connections were often maintained across very wide distances. Thus, some of the Tamil Brahmins of Sripuram have kinsmen in Mysore who settled there many generations ago on land given to them by the Mysore king. Some Telugu Brahmins who were granted land in Sripuram have relatives in Andhra Pradesh whom they visit to this day.

There is only one household of Kannada-speaking Madhva Brahmins in Sripuram. This household settled in Sripuram only about fifteen years ago, although the ancestors of the present head of the household had lived in Tanjore District for a number of generations. There are fourteen households of Telugu Brahmins, belonging to several castes. We shall not go into these differences here but note only one important distinction. Many of the Telugu Brahmin households have settled in Sripuram only within the last generation. Different from these are the families which have roots in the village and trace their ancestry in the male line to one of the original coparcenaries of the village. These families, which constitute the Kak-karai (one-fourth share) Shastri group, have a somewhat different position in relation to land ownership, control and management of the Vishnu temple as well as many other matters.

Jobs Draw Immigrants

Among the indigenous Tamil Brahmins there are many households which have moved into Sripuram only recently. This gives a somewhat amorphous character to the agraharam, which is rather different from other agraharams where a substantial majority of the Brahmins can be placed on a single genealogical chart. Many of the older Brahmin families have moved out of the village in course of the last fifty years. This is very much in keeping with the pattern of villages in Tamilnad as a whole. What seems, however, to be rather unusual is that many new families have moved into the agraharam during the last few decades. This is partly to be explained by local conditions, primarily the availability of teaching and clerical jobs in Thiruvaiyaru. It may be mentioned that more than a dozen families in the agraharam live in rented houses. Indeed, the rise in house rents is a minor problem for some of the Brahmin residents of the village.

The Tamil Brahmins of Sripuram themselves belong to different castes. There are two families of temple priests, one for the Shiva temple and the other for the Vishnu temple. These families do not intermarry with each other or with the other Brahmin families of the village. The rest of the Tamil Brahmins belong to the two main divisions of Smarthas (or Iyers) and Shri Vaishnavas (or Iyengars). The Smarthas are doctrinally affiliated to the eighth-century monistic philosopher, Shankaracharya, and worship both Shiva and Vishnu. The Shri Vaishnavas are doctrinally the followers of Ramanuja, the twelfth-century protagonist of "qualified" monism, and traditionally they owe allegiance to Vishnu alone.

Vaishnavas Outnumber Smarthas

In Sripuram today the Shri Vaishnavas greatly outnumber the Smarthas. This is somewhat unusual because Thiruvaiyaru and the surrounding areas are noted for the practice of Shaivism and the concentration of Smartha Brahmins. Also, Sripuram itself has an ancient and famous Shiva temple whereas the Vishnu temple is of recent origin and comparatively inconspicuous. The concentration of Shri Vaishnavas in Sripuram can to some extent be explained by historical factors which, however, cannot be discussed here.

The Smartha Brahmins of Sripuram belong mainly to the Brihacharanam group, which is one of the four primary sections among the Smarthas. There are three households of Vadamas and one of Ashtasahashrams. There are minor differences of custom between these groups and they are endogamous. The Brihacharanams again include some belonging to the Mazhanattu subsection and others to the Kandramanickya subsection. These subsections are themselves mutually endogamous, although in recent years there has been some intermarriage between them. Only a few of the Brihacharanam families in Sripuram today trace their descent from one of the original coparcenaries of the village. Until recently, the trusteeship of the Shiva temple was hereditarily vested in one of these families.

The Shri Vaishnavas or Iyengars, who constitute the bulk of the Brahmins of Sripuram, belong mainly to the Vadagalai section. Today there are only three Tengalai households, although in the nineteenth century the Tengalai group was of considerable importance. There are a number of differences between these two sections, and the men can be easily identified from the distinctive ways in which they wear their caste marks. There have been some intermarriages between Tengalai and Vadagalai, although they usually tend to be endogamous. There are subsections among the Vadagalai based upon affiliation to particular *acharyas* or preceptors, but these we shall not discuss them here. Two Vadagalai Iyengar families, namely, the Perian and the Dikshitar families, have been of importance in the history of Sripuram. Some of their descendants continue to reside in the village, although many have moved out and been replaced by new families from outside.

Clear Ranking of Castes Not Possible

The problem of assigning specific ranks to different castes has been of central importance in anthropological studies of caste until recent times. The outcome of such studies has been to show that no clear or unambiguous rank order of castes is possible except in a very broad and general way. First of all, one has to consider the question of ritual rank. Even this is not easy to determine, particularly in the case of adjacent castes. Then there are elements of economic, political, and numerical dominance, often cutting across ritual criteria, which greatly influence the attitudes of castes with regard to each other. This can be well-illustrated by making a comparison between the Kalians and the Vellalans. In terms of the general (ritual) rank order prevalent in the area, and in the view of the Brahmins of Sripuram, the Vellalans are higher than the Kalians. It is doubtful, however, to what extent this has a bearing on day-to-day behaviour, particularly in view of the present economic and political ascendancy of the Kalians.

The same problem of rank order may be raised with regard to the mutual positions of the different Brahmin castes. It may be said without much fear of contradiction that the caste of Shaivite temple priests, for instance, is lower in rank than any of the Smartha sub-castes. But what about the rank of the Smarthas in general in relation to the Iyengars? It is doubtful whether a definitive answer can be provided even after a detailed consideration of political, economic, and other "interactional" features.

Our purpose in drawing attention to the problem of rank order is to give some indication of its many ambiguities when we consider castes and sub-castes instead of caste-groups. We turn now to a consideration of the three caste-groups, namely, the Brahmins, the non-Brahmins and the Adi Dravidas, because the problem of rank order can in their case be meaningfully discussed within a short space. The differences which are so ambiguous when we compare Smarthas with Iyengars, or two sub-castes among the Vellalans, stand out sharply when we compare the Brahmins with the non-Brahmins or non-Brahmins with Adi Dravidas.

Friendships Follow Caste Divisions

It will be admitted by all, or almost all, that the Brahmins are ritually superior to the non-Brahmins, and that the non-Brahmins are likewise superior to the Adi Dravidas. There are other differences which are very important, if not equally clear. For instance, the Brahmins as a group own considerably more land than the non-Brahmins, who in turn own much more land than the Adi Dravidas. Again, many of the Brahmins are mirasdars, and not one of them engages in actual cultivation or other menial work. Almost all the Adi Dravidas engage either in actual cultivation or in other menial work and no Adi Dravida from Sripuram owns any land in the village. The non-Brahmins stand somewhere midway since they both own land and engage in actual cultivation as well as in other menial work.

The importance of the divisions between the Brahmins, the non-Brahmins and the Adi Dravidas can be illustrated finally by considering the case of personal friendship. Personal friendships often cut across caste consideration; they rarely, if ever, cut across caste groups, at least in the context of the village. There are personal friendships between Smartha, Iyengar, and Madhya young men who are school teachers. I have not come across a single instance of such personal friendship within the village between a Brahmin on the one hand, and a non-Brahmin or an Adi Dravida on the other. A Vellalan youth along with a Padayachi youth organises cultural functions among the non-Brahmins from time to time. It is doubtful whether similar relationships exist at all between any non-Brahmin and an Adi Dravida.

5

We shall now undertake a brief discussion on the economic life of the village in order to further highlight the basic cleavages in its social structure. The economy of Sripuram, as of the majority of Tanjore villages, is centred largely around the cultivation of rice through the extensive use of irrigation. The regulated supply of water enables the paddy crops to be raised with considerably less labour here than in the drier districts. It also gives the farmer a certain measure of protection against the vagaries of nature, although floods in the Kaveri may cause destruction even today. Paddy is grown both for consumption and for sale. The principal cash crop is banana, which is grown particularly on lands adjoining the river bed (*padughai* lands) and requires intensive cultivation. Betel vines, which require even more labour and attention, are grown only on a few acres, although their cultivation is extremely profitable.

Absentee Landlordism Common

Land ownership in Sripuram has acquired a somewhat complex pattern owing primarily to the migration of some of the owners, and the sale by others of their land to people who themselves do not always belong to the village. Absentee landlordism is fairly common in Sripuram. One of the four big mirasdars of the village lives in Srirangam and has his land managed by an agent. A second lives in Tanjore, but pays regular visits to the village where his widowed mother still resides. A third also lives in Tanjore, but has his land managed by his daughter's husband (also his wife's younger brother), who has taken up residence in his house in the village. The last of the four big mirasdars decided to settle in the village, having resigned from a job which he held in Madras some 15 years ago. All these four mirasdars are Brahmins and none of them owns more than 30 acres of land in this village. Some of this land again is not in their own name, but in the names of their wives, sons, daughters, sisters, etc.

The bulk of the land is owned by the Brahmins. Some land is also owned by the non-Brahmins, none of whom, however, owns more than 10 acres. It seems likely that at one time all the land was owned by the Brahmins with, however, one notable exception. A certain Maratha family, claiming descent from the princely family of Tanjore, owned about half the land in the village at one time. This family still survives, although today almost all the land has gone out of its hands. The Maratha family is even to this day quite distinct from the other non-Brahmin families, and even the ancestral house is not situated in one of the non-Brahmin streets but inside a walled garden, conspicuously separate from the houses of the Brahmins as well as the non-Brahmins.

Non-Brahmins Acquire Land

It is not possible here to give figures with regard to land holding by caste group. In any case, such figures would not give a complete picture if we take only Sripuram, or even Melur, into account. For one thing, many of the Brahmins own land in other villages, particularly in Peramur and Vishnu-puram, which, prior to the nineteenth century, appear to have constituted a single revenue unit along with Sripuram and Melur. For another, much of the land in Sripuram is owned by people from outside, and the caste affiliations of such people are not easy to ascertain, particularly if they happen to be women, as in some cases they are.

It is clear that the non-Brahmins have acquired much of their land in recent years, although even by the end of the nineteenth century they owned some land in the village. At that time most of the non-Brahmin landowners were Vellalans, none of whom, however, could be considered as a big landowner. Later, some land was acquired by a Padayachi who is today one of the bigger landowners among the non-Brahmins. More interesting is the case of the Kalians who have come up progressively in course of the last few decades. They owe their prosperity in large measure to their ownership of considerable portions of padughai lands on which bananas are grown for sale outside.

Although the Brahmins own most of the land they do not actually till the soil. There are two ways in which the Brahmins have their land cultivated, and an analysis of these will bring out their economic relationships with the two other groups, the non-Brahmins and the Adi Dravidas. One may say that these constitute the basic relations of production as far as Sripuram is concerned. It should be indicated that even in the field of agriculture these relations frequently extend beyond Sripuram or even Melur as a whole. Some of the Brahmin mirasdars of Sripuram have their land cultivated by the non-Brahmins and the Adi Dravidas from the adjoining village of Peramur. Some non-Brahmins and Adi Dravidas cultivate land in Sripuram owned by absentee landlords who in a number of cases did not ever belong to Sripuram.

Brahmins Feel Insecure

A few of the Brahmins have their land cultivated directly by engaging agricultural labourers whose work they themselves supervise, and who are paid daily wages in cash. It should be emphasised that this mode of production is exceptional rather than usual. There are two general reasons why this should be so, in spite of the fact that normally it would yield greater returns to the landowner. In the first place, many of the landowners live away from the village, and even among those who live in it there are some who engage in other occupations such as teaching or clerical work, and this makes it difficult for them to engage directly in the supervision of agriculture. Also, the Brahmins in general do not seem to have much experience of this kind of work and they try to avoid it as far as they can. Secondly, the relations between the Brahmin landowners and their non-Brahmin and Adi Dravida labourers have deteriorated rapidly over the last two decades. The constant complaint of the Brahmin landowners is that their labourers have become progressively demanding and insolent. This appears to be true, at least in part, and is indeed a reflection of the political insecurity of the Brahmins in Tamilnad as a whole. It is not easy to determine to what extent the Brahmins are justified in thinking that they cannot enforce their legitimate demands over the labourers. But the feeling of insecurity is there, and it tends to keep them away from directly supervising their farm work as this involves much closer relationships with cultivators and labourers.

The second and more usual way for the Brahmins to have their land cultivated is by annually leasing it out according to the *kutta-khai* system. Although the lease is, under the terms of the contract, for one year only, it is usually renewed automatically. In fact, quite frequently a formal contract is not even entered into. Legally the lessor can claim only 40 per cent of the yield, but usually his claims vary between 50 and 60 per cent because he forgoes the straw and certain other by-products over which he has a legal title. The lessee supplies the seeds to be sown, the plough cattle, the manure, and other prerequisites of cultivation. Usually he manages to give a little less than the actual share of the crops he has agreed to give.

The lessee himself does not necessarily till the land he has leased. If he happens to be a non-Brahmin and has some land of his own, he engages labourers who are usually Adi Dravidas and pays them daily wages in cash. Many non-Brahmin lessees, of course, till the land themselves. The non-Brahmin lessee is often able to make considerable profit by paying his Brahmin lessor a smaller share than he has agreed to pay, and by squeezing as much work out of his Adi Dravida labourers for as little money as is possible. In this he owes his success to the political decline of the Brahmin, to his own political ascendancy, and to the fact that the Adi Dravidas are as yet politically backward and unorganised.

Triangular Bitterness

The Brahmin is bitter against the non-Brahmin because he feels that the new land laws and the new political climate cheat him of his patrimony and give the rewards to the non-Brahmin, although the real work, as often as not, is done by the Adi Dravida. This, of course, is only one side of the picture. The non-Brahmin lessee feels that he earns his share of the crops by investment in seeds and manure, hard work and organisation, whereas the Brahmin sits at home and claims half the produce. The Adi Dravida is bitter against both the Brahmin and the non-Brahmin and complains that nobody will lease land to him, and he has to remain out of work half the year. I have not been able to ascertain why the Brahmins lease their land more usually to the non-Brahmins than to the Adi Dravidas. One would have thought that politically it would be of greater advantage to them to enter into relations with the Adi Dravidas who are less organised and less able to dictate terms than the non-Brahmins.

Thus, when we consider the relations of production, the cleavages between the Brahmins, the non-Brahmins, and the Adi Dravidas become clear once again. By and large, the Brahmins are the landowners, although not all landowners are Brahmins, nor are all Brahmins landowners. The Brahmin landowners lease their land to the non-Brahmins, although here again it must be mentioned that some of the lessees are Adi Dravidas. Further, some non-Brahmins themselves own land, whereas, at the other extreme, there are others who engage themselves directly as agricultural labourers. The Adi Dravidas by and large work as day labourers in one capacity or another.

The picture we have presented is a highly simplified one. We have had to level out variations in each category in order to highlight its differences with the others. A more complete presentation would require an analysis in greater detail of the many ties which cut across the cleavages between the three major caste-groups. In the sphere of economic life itself it would have to take into account the many other occupations in which the villagers engage apart from agriculture.

Today perhaps the social structure is in the process of acquiring a more complex form than it had 50 years ago. In the nineteenth century the economic differentiation between the Brahmins and the others was clearer than it is today. Land was concentrated to an even greater extent in the hands of the Brahmins. The Brahmins as a group were economically more homogeneous than they are today. A fuller understanding of these changes requires an analysis of the political transformation which Tamilnad has been undergoing in course of the last fifty years. Economic and political factors influence each other in a very intimate manner and changes in the one cannot fully be understood without considering changes in the other.

Measures for Integration

Most state governments have designated selected officers in their secretariat to deal with matters relating to linguistic minorities and national integration.

This followed a request from the Union home minister that steps taken for the safeguarding of linguistic minorities should "be coordinated, at a fairly high level."

Madras has appointed a linguistic minorities officer to prepare a note every two months, reviewing the progress of implementation of the linguistic minorities (zonal) scheme.

The arrangements made in Andhra Pradesh are similar except that the linguistic minorities officer is to prepare his review once in three months. In Mysore, the home secretary has been made responsible for coordination of all work relating to linguistic minorities. In Punjab, this responsibility has been entrusted to the secretary of the Education and Language Department, and in Rajasthan to the special secretary in charge of appointments. In UP, there is a special officer under the Directorate of Education to look after these matters.

9

Caste Orientation of Political Factions

Modasa Constituency A Case Study*

Rajni Kothari and Ghanshyam Shah

I

Modasa, an assembly constituency of Gujarat state, is situated in a relatively developed part of the otherwise backward district of Sabarkantha. Modasa town, the headquarter of the constituency and the taluka, has for long enjoyed some locational importance in the economic and social geography of Gujarat. Situated very close to the Gujarat-Rajasthan border and having easy access to important centres of business in both states, it has commanded various trade routes in the area. The taluka has also occupied an important place in the political geography of the Sabarkantha district. An island of British territory surrounded by native States and Agency areas, it acquired a number of modern features and exerted considerable influence on proximate areas. The prosperous, educated, and mobile trading Baniya community dominated the town of Modasa and extended its sway in the surrounding villages. In addition, there emerged in Modasa an outstanding political leader and a towering personality known as "Dada," who dominated the entire district for over 30 years. An architect of almost all the people's movements in the surrounding princely states as well as the anti-British

* Originally published in *Economic Weekly* 15, special number (July 1963), pp. 1169–78. The material for this chapter was collected in the course of an election study of seven legislative and one parliamentary constituencies of Sabarkantha district, Gujarat state. The authors wish to express their thanks to Surendra Shah and Bhailal Pancholi for their assistance in collecting the material.

agitation in Modasa, he continued to have a dominating role in the politics of Sabarkantha after the coming of independence.

Two points should be noted straightaway. The commercial importance of Modasa, the position of the Baniya community, and the fact that Dada himself was a Baniya gave a preponderant influence to this community in the public life of Modasa. Secondly, being part of British India and centre of the nationalist and states people's movements gave Modasa a dominant position in the politics of the district. Both these points—the predominance of Baniyas in Modasa and of Modasa in the district—provide us with a starting point to the changes that have taken place since Independence.

Major Communities

The Baniyas are split into two major castes, the Nima, a small and largely urban community, but much respected and influential, and the Khadaita, somewhat more numerous and having a much greater pull in the countryside owing to its *sahukar* (moneylending) functions. There are other minor castes among Baniyas but not so important. Between all of them, the Baniyas constitute no more than 3.5 per cent of the population. But they dominated the social and political life of Modasa for a very long period. In much larger numbers and mostly of peasant stock is the Patidar community of Modasa. A few Patidar families, the more highly placed in the social hierarchy and prosperous landowners, have migrated from outside. The large majority, however, have been relatively backward and poor. The latter are known as *anjana* Patidárs. Not much behind these in the social hierarchy are the Kshatriyas, the most numerous community group in Modasa and comprising of various castes and sub-castes. Socially very backward and

TABLE 9.1: MAJOR COMMUNITIES OF MODASA

Community	Social Status	Political Experience and Influence	Extent of Rural Penetration	Numerical Strength
1	2	3	4	5
Baniyas (Nima)	High	Longest	Hardly any	3.5 per cent
Baniyas (Khadaita)	High	Fairly long	More	
Patidars	Low (except a small minority of migrants)	Recent	Still more	16 per cent
Kshatriya	Low	Not yet	Most	40 to 50 per cent

politically dormant, the Kshatriyas account for 40 to 50 per cent of Modasa's population. There are many other castes, tribal and "backward" groupings but these are often indistinguishable from the Kshatriyas. There are also other smaller groups of artisan communities, Harijans, Brahmins, and Muslims, the latter with a substantial population in Modasa town. None of these, however, is important from the point of view of the constituency as a whole.

Two strains develop in the politics of Modasa after 1952. Firstly, the retirement from active politics and death later of Dada leads to a shift of power within the district from Modasa to Himatnagar, the district capital, from where the new line of leadership emerges. Secondly, within Modasa taluka itself, the hegemony of the Baniyas is challenged; initially, the ruling Nima group is challenged by the other group of Baniyas, the Khadaitas, and later the Baniyas as a whole by the Patidars. At the district level, too, Dada had cultivated Patidar leaders who took over after him. Thus, both the Baniya preponderance in Modasa politics and the importance of Modasa and its leadership in the district politics are affected largely as a result of the working of the electoral process. We shall consider these shifts in power in some detail below.

Congress Stronghold

Largely because of the dominant influence of Dada, Modasa remained with Congress for a long time and except for the short-lived victory of the Mahagujarat candidate in 1957 (the election was later declared void and the Congress came back in the bye-election that followed). Modasa has always voted Congress. However, a growing rift has taken place within the Congress, taking the form of clear-cut factions. What is more, this has culminated in considerable defection from the Congress, leading to an impressive performance by the Swatantra Party which lost by a very narrow margin in 1962 and finally to its victory in the Panchayati Raj elections of 1963. In what follows, we shall consider these two aspects of political change in Modasa—the intra-party factionalism in which the selection of candidates for the Congress plays the decisive role and the shift in popularity from Congress to the Opposition in which caste alignments play the decisive role.

II

In the crystalisation of factional positions within the Congress, the selection of party candidates has invariably played an important role. In Modasa, the recurrence of this event from one election to another has led, first, to competition for the party ticket between individuals and secondly, to an attempt by the unsuccessful candidate to build his strength by seeking support from various groups. An examination of the process provides a clue to the first two questions formulated in the beginning:

how factions come into being and how they get consolidated.

EMERGENCE OF FACTIONS

In both 1952 and 1957 the Congress ticket was given to a worker from Modasa town, a non-Baniya by caste but an ardent follower of Dada and a close associate of the Nima group among the Baniyas. It was denied both times to a Khadaita Baniya, wealthy and very influential in the villages. The former had the whole official organisation of the Congress with him. The latter had to build his strength on the basis of his own social and economic connections. He did this by mobilizing the support of his community throughout the constituency and by using the economic hold of this community on parts of the peasantry. Thus came into being the first substantial faction in Modasa politics. How powerful it was, was shown in two elections held in 1957, the general election and a bye-election that followed immediately. In the former, the Khadaita candidate was denied the Congress ticket and he worked against the Congress. Before the bye-election was held, however, he had been given the Congress ticket in another constituency in the district and had become an MLA. In the bye-election, therefore, this faction returned to the Congress fold and worked for it. While the Congress lost in the general election, it won by a comfortable majority in the bye-election. (In both the elections the popular appeal of the Congress was reduced because of the Mahagujarat agitation for linguistic autonomy. This accounts for the large vote polled by the Mahagujarat

TABLE 9.2: VOTING IN THE THREE ELECTIONS HELD BETWEEN 1957 AND 1962

(Percentage of total votes polled)

	1957	1957 Bye-election	1962
Congress	49	69	41
Mahagujarat/PSP	31	31	19
Swatantra Party			39
Others (including invalid votes)			9

Notes:

(1) The Mahagujarat issue was a constant factor in the first two elections. The great difference in the poll is made by the votes commanded by the Khadaita Baniyas in the constituency. These were cast against Congress in the general election and for Congress in the bye-election.

(2) The decline of the Congress vote in the 1962 general elections owes largely to the defection in 1962 of the Patidar leaders who joined the Swatantra Party. The Swatantra Party was also able to secure a sizeable section of the Kshatriya vote.

(3) The Mahagujarat was largely a PSP-sponsored alliance. In 1962 the PSP resumed its own identity. We have bracketed them together here.

candidate shown in Table 9.2. But the decisive difference was made by the bulk vote held and controlled by the Khadaita Baniyas.)

Thus before 1962 the main cleavage was between the majority group in the Congress organisation controlled by one Baniya caste and the minority group backed by another Baniya caste. The caste conflict that developed was not there from the beginning, but grew from the minority faction's attempt to consolidate its position. The other major caste groups in the Congress—the Patidars and the Kshatriyas—remained outside the main conflict and had not yet taken the form of factions. The Patidars had in 1957 argued for a "peasant candidate" but did not press their claim in deference to the Nima group. It was in 1962 that the selection was bitterly contested by them.

Political Polarisation

The Patidars had now become restive, organised themselves into a powerful faction, and put in their claim in opposition to the claims of the Nima and Khadaita Baniya candidates. An intense campaign followed and ultimately resulted in a polarisation, the traditional Nima group and the Patidars presenting a united front against the Khadaita Baniya. The Patidar faction was still prepared to withdraw in favour of a Nima Baniya but was not prepared to make room for a Khadaita Baniya who was getting to be much disliked in the countryside and particularly by the Patidars who were rapidly growing into positions of leadership in the villages.

Most of the Mandal Congress Committees, practically the whole of the Taluka Congress, and a majority of the DCC were against the candidature of the Khadaita, who was generally unpopular with the local Congress largely owing to his habit of bypassing the organisation and relying either on his castemen or on "higher authorities" at the State level. But to the surprise of everyone he managed to get the ticket by bringing pressure from the State level on the DCC where he succeeded in getting a majority.

The sequel to the selection is important. Barring the Khadaitas, most of whom were outside the fold of the official Congress organisation, Congressmen all over the Taluka were dissatisfied. The most resentful was the Patidar faction which decided to put up its candidate against the Congress. In these circumstances, it found the newly formed Swatantra Party a handy instrument to fight the Congress with. The upshot was en bloc desertion by the Patidar group from the Congress.

Here is a clear case of party factions becoming irreconcilable and leading to the desertion of a whole faction from the parent party into a new party which but for the desertion, had no base in the constituency. Party factions instead of providing a basis for accommodation and flexibility here became irreconcilable and led to an open break. It was through the Swatantra Party that the resentment could be channelled. Although in the outcome the Swatantra Party was defeated by a narrow margin, its performance was remarkable and would have been impossible without the desertion of the Patidar group from the Congress.

Attitudes to power, however, differ. Both the Nima and the Patidar groups had been deprived of the party ticket by the Khadaita candidate's strategy of "pressure from above." But while the Nima group continued within the Congress, albeit with a much reduced enthusiasm and with some of its workers withdrawing from active politics, the Patidars, known for their aggressiveness in politics and not given to taking a defeat lying down, left the Congress determined to undo it before long. Attitudes of particular groups have much to do with the precise form that political mobility takes. It is only by a combination of an extraordinary set of circumstances, as found in Modasa, that the commercial community of Baniyas has occupied such a predominant political position. With the tone of politics changing from a respectable and paternalistic activity into something acutely competitive and with the rise of new and aggressive groups, the days of the Baniyas in Gujarat politics are numbered. Modasa is a case in point. Even among the Baniyas, the more urbane and idealistic Nimas are first on their way out. The Khadaitas, moneylenders, and mortgage dealers are known to be more tough in their management of human affairs and can put their money to good effect in politics. But before the passion for politics of the Patidars and before the overwhelming numbers of the Kshatriyas even the Khadaitas will be forced to retreat. Considering the cost of politics, they will soon decide to give it up altogether. Though in the 1969 election in Modasa a Khadaita Baniya won narrowly against a Patidar, this was perhaps the last time that this could happen. The future, which was foreshadowed in the election, lay with the numerous and rising Patidars and Kshatriyas, as indeed was to be proved only a year afterwards when the Taluka Panchayat was elected.

III

The role of factions in the selection of the Congress candidate underlines the importance of caste in the politics of Modasa. We may now ask and recapitulate: how precisely have the various castes grouped themselves in Modasa politics?

Caste and Factions

Broadly speaking, the first important caste consolidation was that of the Khadaita Baniyas. This, in turn, led to another caste consolidation. The Patidars, deferential so long as Dada and the Nima group were in power, now began to feel uncomfortable. This was largely because whereas the Nimas were largely an urban caste and interfered little in rural affairs, the Khadaitas operated in areas where the Patidars made their livelihood. Moreover, in so many local events—the DLB elections, the composition of the School Board, the election of delegates to the AICC—these were the two groups that came into conflict. Finally, as we will see below, the Kshatriya community was advised in 1962 both by their regional organisation, the Gujarat Kshatriya Sabha, and the local Patidars with whom they had close social contacts, to vote for the Swatantra Party. This has since led gradually to a caste alliance between the Patidars and the Kshatriyas against the Baniyas.

Thus, starting with the activisation of intra-party groups, the gradual weakening of the ideological heirs of Dada, and the rise of new bidders for power, the political contest got organised on the basis of caste, at first within the Congress and then beyond. It is remarkable that in none of the elections did a Khadaita stand against a Khadaita, a Nima against a Nima, or a Patidar against a Patidar. What is found in some other places, men of the same caste standing against each other thus enabling politics to cut across caste groups, did not occur in Modasa where the major groups in politics are caste groups. Indeed, here it is the caste loyalties that often cut across party affiliations, such as the Congress Khadaitas working against the Congress candidate in 1957. Even the Patidar group's joining the Swatantra Party after defecting from the Congress is to be interpreted as continuation of a factional struggle within the Congress that had developed on a caste basis. The new party was no more than an instrument for carrying on the fight.

IV

Our consideration of factionalism has so far been limited to the political elite of Modasa. It should now be seen how such a form of political competition gets structured into the mass of the electorate. More particularly, it needs to be examined how far caste provides the infrastructure of political organisation and makes available to the competing groups the necessary mechanism for electoral divisions and alignments. For us, two questions are involved here: How far do the relationships between various castes of Modasa provide material for politics? In other words, what is the secular potentiality of Modasa's caste hierarchy? Secondly, how actually did these relationships provide a basis for electoral behaviour in 1962?

Change of Dominant Group

Modasa is a comparatively backward constituency. The political articulation found here is not one of horizontal differentiation (in terms of various social and political groupings) but of vertical dependence (between a dominant minority and a dependent majority). The developing cleavage is between two or more minority groups, although one may be more numerous than the other. The changes that occur are changes in the dominance pattern of politics, where one dominant community gives place to another, the large majority of people simply providing a numerical base for the contesting parties, having not yet themselves emerged as active participants in the political process. This is one point. Another point, of considerable general significance, is that such a change in the dominance pattern is initiated in the sphere of politics which then gets reflected in society. Indeed, to a marked extent the change taking place in the secular relationships between various groups in Modasa society can be understood largely in terms of the political relationships between those groups. What follows will make this clear.

Where the rival contenders for votes come from minority communities, there is no direct identification in terms of caste, occupation, interest group, or political party between the candidate and the voter that could be statistically related. The relation is indirect and can be asserted only because of supporting data collected both from a review of the last few years and other field data on the conduct of the election. But whatever statistical evidence there is goes to support the assertions we make; which increases our confidence in the analysis.

Let us first state our assertions. The Baniya community has enjoyed long political hegemony in this area, partly owing to its social and economic position and partly owing to its supply of political leadership during the Independence movement. As is usual in the politics of minority dominance, the minority itself gets split into rival factions. In Modasa these factions also took a community base, between the two sects of Nima Baniya and Khadaita Baniya. The Nimas had dominated so long as politics was largely urban-oriented. With adult franchise, this was no longer possible. On the other hand, the Khadaitas, both more numerous and exercising a greater rural penetration, began to dominate a number of local institutions. The Nimas continued to control the Taluka Congress for some time but, lacking the wherewithal by which to control the rural masses, lost in real power to the Khadaitas. But while the Nimas, found mostly in the urban areas, continued to hold certain positions because of the traditional respect in which they were held, it was the Khadaita community, both more numerous and exercising a greater rural penetration, that dominated local centres of power. With years of influence and status in the village community behind him and the wherewithal by which to control the needy and the backward, the (Khadaita) Baniya has enjoyed this position of dominance for a considerable time now.

Alliance of Rural Communities

This position, however, was not left unchallenged. The chief contestant has been the Patidar community of Modasa. Now it is true that in terms of economic power and influence, the Patidars have a long leeway to make up. But they have other qualifications. They are more numerous. They are the farmers, the sons of the soil. Many of them have made a success of farming and have prospered.

As politics became more broadbased and peasant-oriented, this increased their confidence and their sense of solidarity, especially against the Baniyas. The upshot was that the Patidars of Modasa were no longer satisfied with a dependent status in politics. Indeed, for a large majority of them, politics provided the only opening for getting out of their "low" and dependent status in society as well. Thus in the 1962 election, the first time the Patidars made a determined bid for power, it was from among the "backward" Patidars (caste Anjana) that a candidate was put up. A year later he became the President of the Taluka Panchayat of Modasa!

TABLE 9.3: SOCIAL COMPOSITION OF MODASA CONSTITUENCY

Brahmin	Baniyas	Patidar	Kshatriya*	Harijans	Muslim	Others	Total
2,010	2,099	9,121	20,193	3,122	4,644	13,184	54,373
(3.5)	(3.5)	(16)	(40)	(5.5)	(8)	(24)	(100)

Note: Figures in brackets denote the voters of a caste as a percentage of the total voters.

* We are not able to give the total figure for the Kshatriyas because of the later inclusion of a number of other communities here classified as "backward" and included in the "Others" column. The total of Kshatriya voters should be somewhere between 45 and 50 per cent of the total voters.

Far more numerous than any other caste group, economically exploited and socially handicapped, is the Kshatriya community of Modasa. An incomparable political force in terms of numbers, the Kshatriyas have all along had a dependent status, in politics as well as in society. They have conformed to whichever dominance pattern obtained in their different villages. This was so right up to the 1962 elections. But 1962 did make a difference even to the Kshatriyas. Two factors are important. The Gujarat Kshatriya Sabha, a prominent social organisation of Kshatriyas throughout the state and dominated by outstanding leaders of the community, had openly called upon the community to vote for the Swatantra Party. This was a great influence and made the community for the first time conscious of itself as a political force. Secondly, in the whole of Sabarkantha district, the numerous low caste Patidars (Anjanas) are very close to the Kshatriyas in the social hierarchy and are usually in constant social intercourse. Now that a Patidar—and that too an Anjana Patidar—had at last made bold to contest against the powerful Baniya, the sympathies of the Kshatriyas were naturally for the Patidar. The facts most emphasised by the latter was that he was a *khedul*, a farmer, and that he had joined issue with the Baniya, the traditional usurper. This provided a manifesto, a sort of ideology and one that readily carried meaning to the uneducated villager. Then there was also the fact that the Swatantra Party had given its ticket in the adjoining constituency to a Kshatriya. The latter also exerted his influence on the Kshatriya vote in Modasa.

Challenge to Congress

With all these factors, however, the Kshatriya vote was decisively split, the Congress and its Baniya candidate still retaining their dominance on the community in a number of places. This accounts for the ultimate victory of the Congress candidate over his Patidar rival from the Swatantra Party. The latter's calculation of a firm Patidar-Kshatriya alliance had to contend with the strong influence wielded by the trading class on the mass of voters that continued to be in a state of dependence, indebtedness, obligation or simply influence hallowed by tradition and usage. On the other hand, by forging such an alliance and turning it into an expanding base of political organisation, the Patidar leaders of the Swatantra Party posed a formidable challenge for the Congress, one that nearly shook her from her fort in the very first encounter and was likely to become a menace for a long time to come. To see it, however, as a Swatantra challenge to the Congress would be misleading. It was essentially the challenge of the Patidars against the dominant Baniyas, in the process also bringing in the numerous lower strata of the population and affecting time-honoured dominant–dependent relationships.

V

The foregoing analysis shows that it was the behaviour of the Kshatriya (and its contiguous "backward") vote that held the key to the 1962 elections. As said above, in spite of overwhelming social and political factors, the Congress managed to split the Kshatriyas in their voting preferences. The Kshatriyas had for long provided the backbone of the political superiority of the Congress in Modasa; they are also in most places economically dependent on the Baniyas. The Patidar leadership of the Swatantra Party succeeded in breaking this hegemony. But it did not succeed enough. Tables 9.4 and 9.5 make this abundantly clear. These tables give those polling booths where there is a high density of Kshatriya population. Potentially they provided the strongholds for the Swatantra Party, as is seen from the figures for the eleven booths given in Table 9.4. In an almost equal number of booths of Table 9.5, however, Kshatriya voters behaved in just the opposite way: they supported the Congress. The Congress in effect managed to retain the Modasa seat against the challenge of the Patidar-Kshatriya alliance by frustrating the alliance in a number of places. It too had its strongholds of economic domination and its political record and it cashed in on the same with good effect.

Congress and Rural Votes

Thus in village Ramos (booth 27) there was a "constructive worker" with a long record of work who came from the Khadaita Baniya community and was greatly

TABLE 9.4: SWATANTRA STRONGHOLDS IN KSHATRIYA AREAS

	Social Structure								Party-wise Voting			
Booth No.	Brahmin	Baniyas	Patidar	Kshatriya	Harijan	Muslim	Artisans, Menials, Tribals, Others	Total Voters	Congress	Swatantra	PSP	Total of Three Parties
8	31	10	175	289	124	9	158	796	58	308	125	491
14	–	–	228	770	2	8	–	1,008	54	438	35	527
13	19	1	231	724	43	3	70	1,091	150	434	35	619
21	14	49	157	319	–	–	353	892	183	421	35	639
22	12	–	251	416	55	4	84	822	72	477	50	599
25	4	9	87	587	–	11	326	1,024	117	467	9	593
26	–	–	30	463	–	12	177	682	84	402	6	492
48	–	4	209	338	–	14	235	800	176	376	21	573
49	–	–	163	242	38	80	97	620	50	481	4	535
56	6	17	216	584	67	19	112	1,021	163	629	3	795
60	–	12	43	286	–	3	51	395	82	206	7	295
Total	86	102	1,790	5,018	329	163	1,663	9,151	1,189	4,639	330	61,58

TABLE 9.5: CONGRESS STRONGHOLDS IN KSHATRIYA AREAS

	Social Structure								Party-wise Voting			
Booth No.	Brahmin	Baniyas	Patidar	Kshatriya	Harijan	Muslim	Artisans, Menials, Tribals, Others	Total Voters	Congress	Swatantra	PSP	Total of Three Parties
4	32	–	–	522	91	12	168	285	256	166	30	452
5	61	11	145	322	204	11	166	920	321	189	23	531
6	115	17	182	502	133	11	–	960	383	207	112	528
16	4	3	188	492	73	29	100	889	318	137	73	528
23	1	–	82	628	38	13	55	817	242	202	46	490
27	–	6	–	446	–	–	342	794	448	213	6	667
39	7	10	138	642	63	59	173	1,092	278	125	238	641
43	6	–	170	467	111	14	393	1,161	361	161	237	759
44	44	20	225	386	30	18	305	1,028	600	27	14	641
58	123	64	52	376	–	38	411	1,064	537	172	7	716
Total	393	131	1,182	4,783	743	205	2,113	9,550	3,744	1,599	784	6,127

TABLE 9.6: VOTING IN MODASA TOWN

Booths	Brahmin	Baniyas	Patidar	Kshatriya	Harijan	Muslim	Others	Total Voters	Congress	Swatantra	PSP	Total of Three Parties
30 to 38	372	681	148	362	94	3,423	2,580	7,860	1,883	393	2,361	4,737

respected. As it often happens, the wealthy and influential families to whom the dependent classes in any case turn for economic help and "advice" also throw up a noble person who can afford to devote his life to unpaid social work. This helps in further consolidating the hold of these families over village life as they are in a position to guide both the traditional and the modernist aspects of village life. The hold was further fortified in this village because of an incident that played into the hands of the Baniyas. A Patidar had beaten a Kshatriya for entering his field. The situation was cleverly exploited by the Baniyas to their own advantage. The benefit was reaped by the Congress candidate for whom the village Baniyas acted as a link. The link need not always be of the same caste. Thus village Kudol (booth 16) was dominated by a leading Muslim trading family (known as Vora) that performed the moneylending and other sahukar functions in the village. It also supplied the president of the local panchayat and general guidance in political matters. This family, because of its trade relationship with the Congress candidate, secured for him the support of the village.

Voting in Modasa Town

A still more interesting case is that of Boyal (booth 44), where the moneylending, shopkeeping, social leadership, and panchayat functions were performed by a leading Patidar family. Moreover, it was also a staunch "Congress family," the head of the family being the president of the Taluka Congress Committee. Thus, though a Patidar in caste, his outside trading contacts were with the Baniyas and political loyalties for the Congress. Moreover, he also had a caste quarrel with the Patidar candidate of the Swatantra Party over whose family stood higher in the system of hypergamy. At the same time, as he was also an Anjana Patidar, he had close ties with the local Kshatriya community. Such a combination of circumstances enabled the Congress to poll almost the entire village population in its favour in the election. The gain of the Congress was even more. In the neighbouring village of Itali (booth 43) another Patidar who was a close kinsman of the Bayal family dominated the village economically and politically. A substantial section of the latter also voted Congress. The main point in such villages is the *monopolistic* position of the family that performed the sahukar functions. Though normally Baniya, it did not matter what the caste of the family was.

These are stray illustrations but they show the ways in which the Congress was able to make inroads into the rural vote, including the votes of Kshatriyas and in some places even of the Patidars. But if the splitting of the Kshatriya vote enabled the Congress to withstand the Swatantra challenge of a rural alliance against Baniya dominance, it was the urban vote that really tilted the balance in favour of the Congress. The vote in Modasa town followed a pattern very different from the pattern in the countryside. Here it was not the persistence or decline of a dominance pattern on social or economic lines but political record and persuasion that influenced voter's decisions.

The interesting thing to note in this connection is that a recent event of explosive significance—diversion of the railway line from Modasa to another part of the district in spite of official and expert advice being in favour of Modasa, which had led to a great deal of agitation and violence—had turned the people of the town hostile to the Congress. Yet their disatisfaction could not be turned to the advantage of the Swatantra Party. There were two reasons for this. Firstly, the PSP, which had been in the forefront of the Mahagujarat movement, had also taken the lead in the railway agitation. Hence it was the PSP that derived the most benefit. Secondly, the old Nima leadership in the Congress had a good hold over the population of the town. Although thrown out of position within the party by the Khadaitas, the Nima leaders could not, like the Patidars, bring themselves to oppose the Congress or even be indifferent to it. (Some, however, subsequently retired from active politics.) They used all their influence and pressure to save the party's prestige and the name of Dada. The result was the PSP and the Congress polled between them almost the entire vote of the town, the Swatantra Party making a miserable show. The margin thus secured enabled the Congress to tilt the balance and win the election.

CONGRESS FACTIONALISM HELPS SWATANTRA

Such are the reasons for the actual outcome of the general elections, the Congress losing substantially but yet retaining the seal. A closer look at Tables 9.4 and 9.5 may be worthwhile. It is true that whereas one set of booths shows a correlation between Kshatriya concentration and Swatantra strongholds, another set of almost equal concentration of Kshatriya shows a strong preference for the Congress. The sweep of the Swatantra hold in Kshatriya areas, however, is stronger than of the Congress. Thus even in the Congress-dominated areas, the Swatantra managed to secure 27 per cent of the vote and the PSP another 10 per cent. The corresponding figures in the Swatantra strongholds are 19 per cent for Congress and 5 per cent for PSP. As a matter of fact, the shift away from Baniya dominance and towards affinity with the Patidars is clear in greater or smaller degree all over the constitutuency. This was shown in the election, with the single exception of both 44 (see Table 9.5), where the overwhelming superiority of the Congress is owing to the exceptional stand taken by the Patidars themselves to support the Congress (and advise the Kshatriyas also to do so). As a matter of fact, with the exception of booth 44, the Patidar leaders of the Swatantra Party managed to put up a three-figure performance in all booths of Kshatriya predominance. The Congress, on the other hand, failed to do so in as many as six booths. The upshot is a trend of declining Baniya dominance and rising Patidar-Kshatriya alliance against such a dominance in Modasa politics.

The trend was confirmed in the election of the Taluka Panchayat President that followed in 1963. In this election, the impressive majority of the Patidar candidate of the Swatantra Party against the Congress candidate largely owed itself to the support he got from Kshatriya and Patidar sarpanches. The caste break-up of the vote is given in Table 9.7.

TABLE 9.7: TALUKA PANCHAYAT ELECTION

Caste	Swatantra	Congress	Total
Brahmin	1	4	5
Patidar	16	2	18
Kshatriya	27	3	30
Baniya	–	5	5
Others	1	1	2
	45	15	60

Notes:

(1) The Swatantra group in this election, owing to a directive of the party, did not use the name of the party but of "Khedut Sangh," a farmers' organisation in the constituency that was created at the time of the election.

(2) Sixty members out of a total of 62 voted in this election.

The experience of the elections has opened the eyes of a section of the Congress leadership which is aware of the strong position of the Patidar leadership of the Taluka. The only way of regaining the lost position of the Congress in Modasa is to win back this group and this could be done only at one price: the present Khadaita hegemony of the Taluka Congress should go. Such a solution may indeed find favour with the DCC, which is also dominated by the Patidars. Moreover, if the DCC can enforce its line of thinking on the Taluka, Modasa too will be in their hands and the rivalry between two centres of power in the district ever since the death of Dada will come to an end. The territorial shift of power from Modasa to Himatnagar (the district capital and home of the DCC group) and the social shift from Baniyas to Patidars would be complete. The enticements for the DCC to enter into this grand design are indeed tempting but any movement on their part would depend upon (i) the success in wooing back the Patidar group of Modasa; and (ii) the ease with which the Khadaita MLA and his group can be persuaded or coerced into acquiescence. The latter would depend on the pull of the MLA with "higher level" leadership. Meanwhile, Modasa politics after a long factional process has crystallised along a pattern that seems to augur well for the opposition party.

VI

Conclusions

(1) The political orientation of this relatively backward constituency has been provided by a long period of one-man dominance followed by the political hegemony of the Congress Party since independence.

(2) This led to political competition within Congress. Opposition got internalised and the outcome was a structuring of the party into a system of factions. Starting with individual competition and frustration the process soon got crystallised along an ongoing structure of ascription, influence, and power. In the main, this derived from (a) kinship and caste alignments and (b) economic power.

(3) The process gained shape from a sequence of competitive trials provided by a series of elections over a period of twelve years (1952 to 1963) and even more by the selection of candidates for the Congress ticket for each of these elections.

(4) Such a structuring of political power along factional lines drew its sustenance from the division of the electorate on the lines of the prevailing infrastructure of Modasa society, although in the process it radically altered the power relationships of this structure by introducing new principles of organisation and affiliation.

These changes in the power relationships of Modasa can be understood in terms of the changes through which the dominance pattern in society has passed. For long this pattern was one of urban dominance in which one section of the trading community of Baniyas was all-powerful. With the growing importance of numbers and thus of the rural population, the pattern turned into one in which economic hold and a long period of rural domination gave power to another sect of Baniyas, the moneylenders and the village sahukars. Meanwhile, the more enterprising and aggressive of the farming communities, the Patidar community, was catching up and soon began challenging the dominance of the trading class. They were the new rural leaders and owing to their closeness in occupation and social hierarchy to the numerous small and landless farmers, coming from various "backward" castes but together known as the "Kshatriya", there came about a consolidation of rural power never known before. With this, the hegemony of the urban and trading communities was undermined once and for all.

Caste Orientation of Politics

(5) Such an understanding of politics in terms of an infrastructure of communities also provides a clue to the 1962 election results. The trading community with its

traditional hold on the villages on the one hand, and the conscious and articulate section of the peasantry on the other, provided the basis of the polarisation that came about in Modasa politics. When the faction representing the latter defected from the Congress Party in 1962, the factional cleavage within the party turned into a political cleavage between two parties. Underlying both, however, was the caste cleavage described here.

The decisive influence was, of course, exercised by the large and inarticulate "backward" vote of the Kshatriya communities. This vote was split. The Swatantra Party was a latecomer and had no organisational network to count upon. On the other hand, the candidate of the Congress had vast influence in the constituency, especially owing to his wealth and business links. That the balance was still in favour of the Swatantra Party is owing to the close links of its socially "backward" candidate with the bulk of the farming population of Modasa. It is significant, therefore, that it was the urban vote of Modasa town that enabled the Congress to steal a march on the Swatantra.

(6) More than the outcome, however, it is the trends revealed by the 1962 election that are important. These point to the emergence of a strong political alliance between the two farming communities of Patidars and Kshatriyas. The days of Baniya dominance in Modasa politics seem to be numbered. Whether the alliance will benefit the Swatantra Party, as it appears to have done in the local self-government election of 1963, or the Congress will stage a comeback by winning back the Patidar leadership into its fold cannot be predicted with certainty, although there are great difficulties in the way of the Congress, thanks to the powerful faction chain stretching from the taluka right to the state and national levels that could be invoked by the present Baniya MLA of Modasa. What is certain is that whichever party wins over this new rural coalition will come out successful in Modasa. The crux of political divisions in Modasa is their community and interest orientation (the latter taking an urban-rural and trader-farmer complexion), caste emerging as the relevant political category and providing the necessary structural basis for mobilisation.

(7) Such a community orientation of politics, however, should not lead to an instrumental view according to which politics is but a reflection of social cleavages that exist apart from and prior to the play of politics. Such a view of the relationship between society and politics is not borne out by the Modasa study. Indeed, the point that emerges clearly in Modasa is the *political origin of social changes*: politics is the great leveller of social distances and dominance positions found in a peasant society. The distances exist, the antagonisms are also there, but these are largely latent. It is in politics that they are crystallised and given shape. "Baniyas," "Patidars," and "Kshatriyas" were indeed the significant categories of Modasa politics, but they operated not as traditional communal groups but as

political groups, in the process passing over important social gradations or creating new gradations. What emerges from Modasa is not so much social conditioning of politics but politicization of social cleavages and the creation of new identifications and loyalties, although both were involved in the process of change. While caste provided an ongoing structure along which politics got articulated, politics provided events and opportunities by which traditional structures were found to disintegrate or reshape under the impart of new forces. Modasa is a revealing case study in the politicisation of traditional society.

10

Class and Caste*

Nirmal Kumar Bose

It is necessary to draw a distinction between the way in which Weber and Marx have used the term *class*.

Weber tried to discover by means of comparison and analysis how some societies were actually stratified into classes. One part of a community might be distinguished from another by differences in the level of consumption, or in the distribution of economic or political power, or in some other way. After having examined various ways in which classes were marked off from one another, and also how they had evolved in course of time, Weber tried to find a suitable definition of the term *class*, so that the widest range of observed phenomena might be covered under it with precision.

By contrast, the intention of Marx was something more than a scientific description of a particular kind of social phenomenon. After having examined the history of many societies, he came to the conclusion that all of them were divided into privileged and unprivileged classes; although the dividing line might be obscure in many cases. The *real* difference between classes lay in the manner in which one class laboured and produced wealth, while another, which exercised private rights of ownership over the means of production, lived more or less on the toils of the labourers.

In their own time, Proudhon, Tolstoy or Gandhi also held that, all over the world, men were divided into those who toiled, and the rest who lived on the toils of others, and were therefore thieves.[1]

It is interesting that Marx, Tolstoy and Gandhi's *ideal* distinction between producers and non-producers is never neatly defined. There may be a hundred

* Originally published in *Economic Weekly* 17, no. 35 (28 August 1965), pp. 1337–40.

ways in which the dividing line may be rendered obscure. Even labourers may be divided into subclasses, distinguishable from one another by the proportion between what they produce and what they consume, or by the power which they exercise over their fellowmen, which helps them in gathering for their own interest and use, varying fractions of the surplus value produced by the toilers. In addition, the same subclass may function as "exploiter" in relation to one below it, and "exploited" in relation to another above it.

According to Marx, it is this indistinctness which is responsible, to some extent, for the persistence of many of these stratified societies all over the world. This is true as much of the present age as of the past. Marx saw through, or he felt that he saw through, this camouflage placed over basic and real class differences. His reading of history led him to the conclusion that progress has taken place through a succession of class conflicts. Every conflict does not necessarily lead to victory of the labouring section of mankind; but it may be guided to that end. At least, that was the view strongly held by Lenin who thought that the moral responsibility of this leadership lies with the True Party which represents the interests of the proletariat.

Both Marx and Lenin, therefore, held that anything which masks *real* class-contradictions should be revealed, class consciousness accentuated, so that class conflicts may come nearer home. Indeed, even defeats are not useless. Every conflict can, at least, be utilised for augmenting class consciousness by laying bare the involved contradictions. This line of action has to be intelligently pursued, and with determination; because it leads to a shortening of the process of progressive evolution which is already taking place in human history. The revolutionist's task is to render the process of social change more economical and more efficient. He thus helps consciously and participates actively in the process of "natural" change. The polarity of interests has to be heightened by him before progress can take place with rapidity as it ought to in the present age of science.

Marx was thus not so much interested in *describing* what was happening in the world. This he did occasionally; and then he played the role of a social philosopher rather than that of a revolutionist in action. For him, the primary duty of a philosopher is not merely to *understand*, but to *change*. Marx thus used the concept of class as an operational instrument rather than as a descriptive term which would cover a wide range of camouflaged and uncamouflaged class antagonisms.

It is, therefore, not fair to say that Marx now and then contradicted himself in his use of the term *class*. To say that Weber is logically more consistent, and thus an improvement upon Marx, is also not quite correct. One was interested in classifying social phenomena, the other in fashioning an intellectual concept which would pierce through obscurities and serve as a tool of action. In the use of the same term, Marx and Weber thus stood widely apart from one another.

Caste: The Four Orders

It is possible to look upon the Indian concept of varna in the same manner as Marx's class—as an instrument of social reorganisation rather than as a description of historical facts.

The Brahminical peoples were confronted in the past by the presence of many communities with whom they came into contact either in peace or war. Such communities were frequently marked off from the Vedic people by sharp contrasts of language, beliefs, or social customs. Brahmins had already developed a system of preserving the text of the Vedas by relegating sections of it to the keeping of specific lineages. This system had worked perfectly, and it can be imagined that its success led them to transfer the pattern to the economic organisation of society as well.

The rule was established that separate communities or jatis should be in charge of separate technological processes, or of services like priestcraft, trade, defence, and so on. They were theoretically to be in enjoyment of monopoly in respect of their allotted function in each regionally distinct area; and there was to be *no competition* between such groups. Yet, a sufficient amount of resilience was introduced into the system by means of "alternative rules," or *apad-dharma*, from fairly early times. Manu has recorded this elaborately in his *Institutes of Hindu Law* (X, 74 ff).

In their time, legislators like Manu had to examine the situation arising out of the economic and social mingling of many jatis. Some of these were evidently of foreign origin, while others arose out of progressive differentiation of occupations, and as a few among them tried to rise high in social status by concealing their birth and adopting the ways of castes "superior" to them.[2] In order to bring a system into this chance conglomeration of jatis, social legislators tried to reduce them ideally into a scheme in which only four varnas were recognised.

It is interesting to note in this connection that the classification into Brahmin, Kshatriya, Vaishya, and Sudra was not confined to the world of men. Soils, temples, gems, gods, and even the stars were actually classified into the same four orders.[3]

Manu believed in the possibility of transmission of character-types from parents to children. He also held that a person or a community or jati eventually drifts into the occupation for which it is temperamentally equipped by heredity. If the origin of a jati is not known, it can be found out by reference to the ideal order in which the Brahmin is contemplative, selfless, devoted to learning; the Kshatriya is fond of fighting or ruling; the Vaishya interested in trade, and the Sudra in service. By applying this fourfold scheme, he claimed to find the origin of every jati; and then he assigned each to one or other of the four varnas by means of some other rules.

The *Manu Samhita* in its present form is considered to have been written between 200 BC and AD 100.[4] The following quotations illustrating Manu's theory of heredity are from Sir William Jones's translation.[5]

> IX, 31 Learn now that excellent law, universally salutary, which was declared, concerning issue by great and good sages formerly born.
>
> IX, 33 The woman is considered in law as the field, and the man as the grain: now vegetable bodies are formed by the united operation of the seed and the field.
>
> IX, 34 In some cases the prolific power of the male is chiefly distinguished; in others, the receptacle of the female: but when both are equal in dignity, the offspring is most highly-esteemed.
>
> IX, 37 Certainly this earth is called the primeval womb of many beings; but the seed exhibits not in its vegetation any properties of the womb.
>
> IX, 38 On earth here below, even in the same ploughed field, seeds of many different forms, having been sown by husbandmen in the proper season, vegetate according to their nature.
>
> IX, 40 That one plant should be sown, and another produced, cannot happen: whatever seed may be sown, even that produced its proper stem.
>
> X, 69 As good grain, springing from good soil, is in all respects excellent, thus a man, springing from a respectable father by a respectable mother, has claim to the whole institution of the twiceborn.
>
> X, 70 Some sages give a preference to the grain; others to the field: and others consider both field and grain; on this point the decision follows:
>
> X, 71 Grain, cast into bad ground, wholly perishes, and a good field with no grain sown in it, is a mere heap of clods:
>
> X, 12 But since, by the virtue of eminent fathers, even the sons of wild animals, as Risyasringa, and others, have been transformed into holy men revered and extolled, the paternal side, therefore, prevails.
>
> X, 59 Whether a man of debased birth assume the character of his father or of his mother, he can at no time conceal his origin:
>
> X, 60 He, whose family had been exalted, but whose parents were criminal in marrying, has a base nature, according as the offence of his mother was great or small.
>
> X, 8 From a Brahmana, on a wife of the Vaisya class is born a son called Ambastha, or Vaidya, on a Sudra wife a Nisada, named also Parasava.
>
> X, 9 From a Ksatriya, on a wife of the Sudra class springs a creature, called Ugra, with a nature partly warlike and partly servile, ferocious in his manners, cruel in his acts.
>
> X, 40 These, among various mixed classes, have been described by their several fathers and mothers; and, whether concealed or open, they may be known by their occupations.

By such rules, the people of Bengal became divided into two orders, namely Brahmin and Sudra, although there are numerous jatis or castes among them. In other parts of India, all four orders are present; and this is how many jatis became federated into an ideal system invented by Brahmin thinkers.

Class and Caste

Many authors have described caste as one variety of the class system. There is no doubt that Brahminical communities reserved for themselves a position of privilege in society, while the work by means of which people lived was relegated to the "lower" orders. Caste was thus class; and this is a fact which has been emphasised by many historians in the past, as well as by sociologists like Bhupendra Nath Datta, M. N. Srinivas and Narmadeshwar Prasad in more recent times.

We must, however, remember the fact that class antagonisms within the caste system failed to generate a sufficient amount of opposition and revolt among the subordinated communities. Narmadeshwar Prasad has tried to account for this by saying that the Brahmins successfully prevented reaction and revolt by the creation of a widespread myth about their own holiness and infallibility, by a belief in the law of karma and transmigration of the soul, and so on. M. N. Srinivas is of the opinion that the concern and value attached to ritual purity is so deep-rooted among Hindus, and the belief in karma so pervasive, that both the privileged and unprivileged remain content with the status and role into which they have been born. So much so that there is no desire to rise and revolt against gross inequality.

Srinivas also says that the "upper" classes have succeeded in retaining their positions of advantage not only by extensive indoctrination of the "lower," but also by usurping positions of authority in other ways. In the past, they did so by ownership of land and an alignment with the ruling powers. In the present age, the same upper castes have taken advantage of modern education, and progressively "westernised" themselves so as to join the ranks of the new ruling class. This they do by joining the administrative services, or by alliance with one or other of the political parties as they come into power. The upper castes have thus adapted themselves to change, and still form the upper class; while those who are below, because of poverty, lack of education, and social subordination, retain their attachment to caste's ancient values, and prefer to raise themselves in rank by Sanskritisation instead of secularisation or westernisation.

In the opinion of the present author, however, these hypotheses as explanations of the continuity of caste through the ages, in spite of political or cultural upheavals, do not appear to be wholly adequate. In any case, there are several other elements which help in creating a *positive* sense of loyalty among the subordinated classes, even when some of them know that they are suppressed. These possible causes are enumerated below:

(1) In an economy of relative scarcity, particularly when there were swift changes of rulers, the rules of caste were devised in a manner so that various communal

groups were woven together into a network of mutual interdependence.

(2) Competition was positively discouraged. An artisan or priest could seek the protection of the king, the local college of Brahmins, the village panchayat, or even of the caste if he was threatened by competition by anyone who infringed upon his preserves.

(3) Each caste was left free to pursue its specific regional or communal customs in an atmosphere of comparative freedom and equality. In other words, cultural autonomy was thus guaranteed to each of the federated communities.

(4) If class differences brought about a growing inequality of income, as they were likely to do, the evils of increasing polarisation were offset by the custom of "conspicuous expenditure." Anyone who spent lavishly in beneficent acts, or even in sheer exhibitionism, was applauded more than one who hoarded. A practice was likewise built up in connection with birth, marriage, and funerary ceremonies in which even the poorest householder had to make gifts to priests, scholars and the indigent. The more lavishly one spent, even by incurring debts, the more approbation one received.

These elements in the culture of the people mitigated, but did not obliterate, the evils and strains resulting from class differences within the caste system. And, it is the belief of the present author, that it is this fact, which might either be labelled as a camouflage or a conscious limitation of the growing ills of caste's productive system, which prevented the progressive polarisation of class differences. The latter could have led to class war in India but actually did not on account of the various safeguards thus built into the social structure.

Marxian Class and Caste

According to the Marxian way of thinking, this ingenious system helped the Brahmin-Kshatriya or upper-class leadership to preserve itself intact through centuries. This was achieved by not allowing the contradictions in the distribution of power between classes to develop as they did in the West.

The contradiction between technological progress and growth of population could not, however, be solved by this ingenuity. People remained poor, famine was followed by famine, and caste persisted because it gave a feeling of security even under the most straitened circumstances. Under the exigency of famine or natural calamity, people turned either to their joint families, or their own kinsmen or caste-men for protection or support. Ancient governments were frequently powerless to cope with such calamities, except by an extensive system of doles or gifts.

The remedy, according to the Marxian, lies in tearing aside the arrangements in the superstructure of caste, which prevent the "natural" sharpening of class antagonisms. That alone can prepare the ground for an already-belated class conflict, which will inevitably lead to the victory of the organised proletariat under the guidance of the True Party.

Comments

It is not our purpose in the present paper either to find fault with the Marxian viewpoint, or show up its differences with the Gandhian method of bringing about social change through constructive work and satyagraha, to which the author is personally committed. We have only tried to present the Marxian viewpoint with regard to caste as faithfully as possible.

But the conclusion to which we arrive is that the latter is as much an idealistic system, an instrument of social reorganisation as the Indian system of four varnas happened to be in the past. One may, of course, claim that Marx worked for human emancipation while Manu worked for preserving the rights and privileges of Brahmins. That is, however, a point which can be modified and controverted from the social historian's point of view. But we need not indulge in that exercise for the present.

The point which we have been trying to build up is that class in the Marxian sense is an intellectual instrument of action, and not a pure description of social phenomena into which Weber tried to convert it.

Notes and References

[1] For Gandhi, see Nirmal Kumar Bose, *Studies in Gandhism*, 3rd ed. (Calcutta: Merit Publishers, 1962), 1962a, pp. 1–125.

[2] See, for instance, *Mahabharata, Shantiparvan*, ch. 65.

[3] See Nirmal Kumar Bose, "Theory of Heredity in Manusamhita," "Classification of Soils," "Classification of Temples," *Bulletin of the National Institute of Sciences of India*, no. 21 (1962): 1963, 45–47; Sourindro Mohun Tagore, "Manimala, or a Treatise on Gems," Part 1 (Calcutta: self-published, 1879.), pp. 99–107, 199–201, 277.

[4] P. V. Kane, *"History of Dharmasas-tras"*, vol. 3 (Poona: Bhandarkar Oriental Research Institute, 1946), p. xvii.

[5] Manu, *The Institutes of Hindu Law: or the Ordinances of Manu, according to the Gloss of Culluca*, trans. William Jones (Calcutta: 1794).

PART IV

Analytical Frameworks

11

Keynesian Economics and Underdeveloped Countries*

A. K. Dasgupta

The relation of Keynesian economics to the problems of underdeveloped countries is a subject which has received wide attention from our economists recently. In a series of articles in the *Indian Economic Review*,[1] Dr. V. K. R. V. Rao called attention to the special features of underdeveloped economies and enquired to what extent the Keynesian propositions apply to these economies. It was a subject of discussion in the 1953 session of the Indian Economic Association, and a good many papers were devoted in the conference to a consideration of this problem. In general, the authors, despite differences in emphasis on specific points, seem to come to the conclusion that Keynesian economics, in so far as it is formulated in *The General Theory of Employment, Interest and Money*, has little validity in the context of underdeveloped economies, that Keynesian involuntary unemployment is not the kind of unemployment from which these economies suffer, and that the problem in these economies is one of long-term economic development rather than the attainment of "full employment" in the Keynesian sense. Broadly speaking, I find myself in sympathy with this general attitude. I have always felt that, whatever the generality of the *General Theory* may be in the limited sense in which the term "general" was used by Keynes, the applicability of the propositions of the volume to conditions of an underdeveloped economy, such as India, is at best limited.[2]

As early as 1942, commenting on certain aspects of an important book on India's fiscal policy in which an appeal was made to the Keynesian theory of involuntary unemployment in support of a general policy of protection for India, I said the following:

* Originally published in *Economic Weekly* 17, no. 35 (28 August 1965), pp. 1337–40.

> Has the argument any particular relevance to the case of India? Is there anything like involuntary unemployment in this country? Is it not pertinent if one asks for a demonstration of its existence before one accepts any judgement of policy which begs so delicate an assumption? Mr. Keynes, I think, had the case of his own country in view when he enunciated his theory of involuntary unemployment. A country which is in an advanced state of economic development, where population is fast coming to a stationary level, and where, further, there exists a strong trade union organisation to resist any reduction of money wages, provides a peculiarly suitable soil for the application of Keynes's theory ... Indian economy, on the other hand, is characterised by an entirely different set of conditions. It is not capital saturation, and surely not a refusal of the people to multiply that accounts for a low marginal efficiency of capital. The trade unions are just in their infancy and are not sufficiently organised, so that there is still scope for "plasticity" of wage rates. General considerations suggest that mass unemployment, in this country, is mostly seasonal, although partly also it is due to inertia and lack of mobility of capital.[3]

I developed this thesis at some length in a course of extension lectures that I delivered under the auspices of the University of Lucknow in the autumn of 1950, publication of which has been held up on account of my preoccupations outside the university for the last three years. The following notes are intended to offer a summary of the attitude that I hold on the matter, for whatever it may be worth.

(2) The propositions of the *General Theory* are by now well known. I would, however, restate them in a slightly different order, placing emphasis on certain ingredients and bringing out one or two implied assumptions which are relevant to the present enquiry.

Let me start with the definition of *full employment*, from which is derived the core of Keynesian economics: the concept of involuntary unemployment. Full employment signifies a state in which any person *willing* to work at a wage rate that corresponds to his economic contribution to social product finds a job at that wage. To put it in more precise terms, in a state of full employment, the marginal unit of labour gets a wage in real terms, the utility derived from which is equal to the disutility that the work involves. From this it follows that in a state of involuntary unemployment the utility of wage exceeds the marginal disutility of labour. Keynes does not offer an independent theory of wages. He accepts the ordinary theory that the real wage rate is equated in equilibrium to the marginal productivity of labour. But—and this is important—he emphasises that real wage is a derived concept and does not represent the actual operation of the market. The wage bargain in the market runs in money terms, and the real wage rate is derived from the money wage rate relative to the prices of wage-goods.

The period of reference is a short period over which, among other things, capital equipment and technique are given and constant, these being the result of past investment. Labour is employed upon a given capital equipment and is pushed up to the margin of profitableness. A short period equilibrium is thus envisaged for the economy as a whole. However, although Keynes's analysis runs in terms of a short period, it does not preclude longer-run inferences. For, a long period is a succession of short periods, each endowed with a different capital equipment and carrying the legacy of the past.[4]

Propositions supporting the Keynesian theory of involuntary unemployment can now be set forth.

a. Money wage rate is fixed more or less conventionally between employers and trade unions. This given money wage rate provides the measure of the magnitudes involved in the analysis. Consumption, investment, prices, etc., are measured in terms of "wage units," i.e., the money wage received by a representative unit of labour.[5]
b. Prices of wage goods, along with the general price levels, are determined by the expenditure on consumption and investment.
c. Expenditure on consumption goods is limited, with reference to a given prospective income, by the extent to which income earners are inclined to spend rather than to save (marginal propensity to consume).
d. Expenditure on investment is limited, given the market rate of interest, by the prospective marginal net yield of investment (marginal efficiency of capital).
e. A decision not to spend on consumption does not necessarily mean a decision to invest; the rate of interest which is ordinarily supposed to be the connecting link between the two is determined not just by the propensity to save but by the preference of the public to hold cash (liquidity preference).
f. The expenditure on consumption and expenditure on investment, between them, make up the aggregate demand price of output as a whole, and short period equilibrium is struck at a point where the aggregate demand price is equated to aggregate supply price.
g. Under conditions of equilibrium, therefore, the price level may be too low relatively to the given money wage rate, or, in other words, the real wage rate may be too high for full employment to be secured. More than full employment can be ruled out, for the workers have the option not to work if the real wage rate fails to compensate for the disutility of labour. But less than full employment is a probability; indeed, it tends to be a normal feature of an economy which suffers from a low marginal propensity to consume and a low marginal efficiency of capital.
h. The unemployment that emerges is "involuntary" when it is found either (i) that the labourers, being under a "money illusion," are prepared to put up with a higher price level, even though they are unwilling to accept a cut in money wage rate, or (ii) that even with a cut in money wage rate, it is not possible to effect a reduction in the real wage rate. For, in either of these cases,

while the labourers are willing to accept a lower rate of "real" wage at which the employers would also find it worthwhile offering more employment, the mechanism by which this could be effected is absent, unless special measures are taken.

i. These special measures include (i) transference of income from the relatively rich to the relatively poor, thus causing a tendency to an increase in the propensity to consume, or (ii) maintenance of a low rate of interest as an inducement for larger investment. However, the potency of these measures is limited. A tax on higher incomes, in so far as it touches profits, would prejudice investment. On the other hand, the effectiveness of interest policy is dubious, if only because the liquidity preference of the people being what it is, there is a limit below which the rate of interest cannot be brought down. Hence, what is indicated is a more direct measure, namely, public investment through deficit finance, unprofitable as it may seem at first sight. A dose of public investment, in so far as it is not at the expense of private investment, would release forces making for increased consumption, whereby the increment of aggregate output will be a multiple of the initial investment, the value of the multiplier depending upon the marginal propensity to consume.

Students of Pigou's *Economics of Welfare* will notice that, in the context of involuntary unemployment, the multiplier formula provides another conspicuous example of a discrepancy between marginal private net product and marginal social net product. Equilibrium implies that an additional dose of investment by itself is unprofitable and would not be undertaken in the private sector. But when the secondary repercussions touching the various consumption goods industries are taken into account, the investment turns out to be *socially* profitable and hence it should be undertaken by the State.

Indeed, the so-called theory of employment as a whole seems to me to be capable of being subsumed under the general theory of allocation of resources from which it is so often sharply differentiated. A deviation from full employment can be shown to be just an indication of wrong allocation, less than full employment being interpreted as a forced surrender to leisure at the expense of a more preferred object—real income. If this unemployment is caused by a low expectation of profit relative to the rate of interest, that again is amenable to treatment in terms of the time structure of production and consumption—the problem, par excellence, of allocation. And so on, one could proceed. Personally, I am inclined to believe that not only would some kind of integration between the theory of employment and the theory of allocation give formal elegance to our analytical structure, it would also provide a check to certain misdirections of public today. A theory of employment conceived outside the framework of the theory of allocation is apt to neglect long-run consequences. An employment policy, unless checked up by an allocational norm, is apt to contain seeds of ultimate disruption. Neglect of these considerations seems to me to inform much of that part of Keynes's *General Theory* which relates to capital and interest, and I doubt very much if his prescriptions regarding interest would at all be compatible with a long survival of capitalism which was so near to his heart. But that is a different story.

(3) This is Keynes's *General Theory* in its pristine form. I have tried to bring out the essentials of the theory and to put it in a form which makes it inevitable that any pushing up of employment should be accompanied by a reduction in the real rate of wages. And, of course, this is what Keynes had in mind; the hypothesis is one of diminishing returns at or near full employment.

Now, one who is acquainted with the conditions of an underdeveloped economy of the sort we have here under consideration, with the earnings of the majority of the working population practically below the minimum subsistence level, will find it hard to see how the prevailing real wage in these economies could be too high. He will surely look askance at Keynes's theory of involuntary unemployment, and perhaps on this ground alone would throw it overboard. However, let us look at the matter a little more closely.

It should be obvious from a scrutiny of the constituent elements of Keynesian economics, as enumerated above, that they pertain to an economy in which money serves as the instrument of economic operations, in which these operations include borrowing and lending, and in which, further, the ownership of the means of production is divorced from the use of these means, which is to say that labour is divorced from capital. Wherever these conditions prevail, Keynesian technique of analysis applies. And these conditions are the conditions of capitalism in that special sense in which socialists would use the term. It is under capitalism that savers are distinct from investors, that net profit is the motive force behind production and employment, and that wage rate is determined in money as a result of a bargain between two parties—the employers and the employed.

To what extent are these characteristics present in the so-called underdeveloped economies? Even in India which, in respect of the stage of economic development though not in respect of per capita income, happens to be the most advanced among the underdeveloped South Asian countries, it is only over a small field that these conditions hold good. The organised sector of our economy, with its large-scale industries and a fairly well-developed banking system, does no doubt come under the scope of Keynesian economics, for it presents features no less capitalistic than those associated with the so-called advanced economies. But the place that this sector occupies in the national economy from the point of view of its contribution to employment is surely insignificant. The waste due to "involuntary unemployment," if there is any, in this sector is surely of the second order of smalls when considered in relation to the total working population of the country.[6]

A considerable part of the economy does not fall under money economy at all, and even where it does, in so far as the organisation of the industry is such that the worker works with his own tools (e.g., cottage industries), the level of activity is determined by considerations of gross income and not of net profit. All this explains why in this country the depression of the 1930s did not affect employment so much as it did prices, and why, on the other hand, the stimulus to investment during the last war was almost immediately followed by inflation and a rise in money wages. If I am not mistaken, it is this aspect of the matter that Dr. Rao brings out in the first article in the series. Dr M. A. Khusro seems to me to have misjudged the relative significance of the constituents of Keynesian theory when, in an otherwise excellent paper,[7] he shifts the emphasis from the multiplier to interest and marginal efficiency of capital. After all, even in the context of an advanced economy, marginal efficiency is an uncertain factor and the rate of interest is of limited significance. Maybe interest policy would do some little trick here or there. Yet, in spite of Keynes,[8] concentration on this factor would lead us away from the more vital elements of the policy prescriptions which are associated with the *General Theory*. It is much more important to concentrate, as Dr. Rao does, on the marginal propensity to consume and the multiplier and to see how far, in the economic set-up in which the underdeveloped regions find themselves, a policy of deficit financing would add to the volume of employment or release forces making for inflation. It is much more important, in the context of such economics, to enquire whether saving creates wealth, as it did in nineteenth-century England, or it destroys wealth.

(4) The possibilities of involuntary unemployment is not denied, in so far as even an underdeveloped economy may contain an organised sector wherein the Keynesian propositions hold good. But its magnitude is not likely to be appreciable. Firstly, the marginal propensity to consume in a low-level economy, despite huge inequalities of income, tends to be relatively high. Secondly, although investment opportunities are limited, when account is taken of the fact that most of these economies are characterised by a rapidly growing population, they should not normally lag behind the rate at which people are inclined to save. If, in spite of growing population, the marginal efficiency of capital in these economies is found to be low, the cause is to be sought not in the Keynesian direction but rather in the direction of J. B. Say. If the curve of marginal efficiency of capital has to be raised, what is needed is, as Nurkse has so beautifully shown,[9] a simultaneous development of a number of industries, the supply of goods in one creating demand for goods produced in others. And this involves an expansion in the stock of capital resources. The limiting factor in the growth of employment in an economy such as ours is not so much a shortage of money as a shortage of real capital. With the existing capital equipment, even if we have full employment in the Keynesian sense, a large volume of unemployment will still remain in the

physical sense. When capital equipment is low and population large, marginal productivity comes down to the level of marginal disutility of labour at a stage where unemployment still persists in the physical sense, though not in the "involuntary" sense. Our economists, misappropriating a term that Mrs. Joan Robinson uses in another context,[10] often call it "disguised unemployment." In fact, however, it is a phenomenon which is not connected in any way with a fall in effective demand, nor does it go along with excess capacity in capital resources. It is there because the maximum capacity of capital equipment is inadequate to fully employ the available labour.

This suggests a notion of shifting points of full employment, a notion which I have long felt would be useful in this context and which I am happy to find elaborated in the *Indian Economic Review* articles already referred to (see note 1). With each expansion of capital equipment, the marginal productivity of labour rises and, the disutility curve of labour remaining constant, we have a higher level of full employment. The notion of an ascending level of full employment emerges readily from the hypothesis that the potential marginal productivity of labour with reference to an increasing supply of capital resources is larger than the marginal productivity as it actually is.[11] Capital saturation is marked by a stage where absence of involuntary unemployment ensures absence of unemployment in the physical sense too, barring frictions due to lack of mobility of labour.

What happens in this background about the much talked of stagnation theory? Will each expansion in the stock of capital lower the marginal efficiency of capital while it raises the marginal productivity of labour? Does expansion itself contain seeds of stagnation? The answer is again to be sought in Nurkse's hypothesis. Capital saturation is a long way off for an underdeveloped economy with a strong pressure of population and a depressed standard of living. For such an economy, an increase of capital resources, if it could be brought about, will make possible a simultaneous development of industries and will have rather the effect of raising the marginal efficiency of capital. Indeed, this points to a peculiar feature of an underdeveloped economy which distinguishes it fundamentally from a so-called mature economy.

NOTES AND REFERENCES

[1] *Indian Economic Review*, vol. 1, nos. 1, 2, and 3.

[2] Apparently, the title *General Theory* was used by Keynes to emphasise that the theory takes account of the possibility of under-employment equilibrium not envisaged by the so-called classical economists.

[3] A. K. Dasgupta, "The Indian Fiscal Policy," *Indian Journal of Economics* 22, no. 89, (October, 1942), pp. 101–14.

[4] It is important not to miss this. For it provides the basis of the famous stagnation theory. If, to anticipate our story, the "marginal efficiency of capital" depends at all upon the stock of capital

existing currently, then, in the absence of favourable exogenous factors, such as innovation and, growth of markets, etc., every act of new investment over a given period creates difficulties for the next period by enlarging capital equipment and lowering its prospective yield. However, I shall have occasion in a later section to refer to this matter, for, as I feel, so far as this longer-run aspect of Keynes's theory is concerned, the conditions of underdeveloped economics are in sharp contrast with those of mature economics.

5 Note the family resemblance between Keynes's "wage-unit" and the "labour command measure" of Malthus.

6 Assuming, for example, persons involuntarily unemployed constitute 10 per cent of the number actually employed in organised industry, and assuming further that organised industry absorbs 5 per cent of the total working population (these are hypothetical figures), we find that involuntary unemployment turns out to be just 0.5 per cent of the total working population. We do not have reliable unemployment figures for India. However, the following table showing the waste due to unemployment in certain other countries is revealing.

TABLE 11.1: AVERAGE INCOME PER HEAD OF WORKING POPULATION IN INTERNATIONAL UNITS, 1925–34

	Employed and unemployed taken together	Approximate estimate if all unemployed had been at work
USA	1,368	1,550
Canada	1,337	1,440
New Zealand	1202	1,280
Australia	980	1,090
Great Britain	1,089	1,210
Sweden	653	700
France	694	720
Germany	646	750
Norway	539	590
Austria	511	570
Czechoslovakia	455	480
Italy	343	363

The figures have been taken from Colin Clark's *Conditions of Economic Progress* (1st ed. [London: Macmillan, 1940], p. 77). They are based on the most generous assumption, namely, that the average productivity of the unemployed would have been about the same as these who were actually in work if the unemployed had been absorbed in industry. Yet, barring USA, Canada, Great Britain and Germany—countries which are definitely the more capitalistic in our sense—the waste due to unemployment during a period which includes years of one of the severest depressions known in history, is surprisingly small.

7 M. A. Khusro, "Keynesian Theory of Investment in an Underdeveloped Economy," *Indian Economic Association Papers* (December 1953).

8 The only reference to the problem of an underdeveloped economy in Keynes's *General Theory* is in the following passage, which is worth quoting: "The history of India at all times has provided an example of a country impoverished by a preference for liquidity amounting to so strong

a passion that even an enormous and chronic influx of the precious metals has been insufficient to bring down the rate of interest to a level which was compatible with the growth of real wealth." p. 337.

[9] R. Nurkse, *Problems of Capital Formation in Underdeveloped Countries*, aptly quoted by Dr Khusro in "Keynesian Theory of Investment," pp. 37–38.

[10] Joan Robinson, *Essays in the Theory of Employment* (New York: Macmillan, 1937), pp. 60–62.

[11] I am afraid Mr B. M. Bhatia misconceived the notion when; apparently referring to Dr Rao, he says, "There is a tendency on the part of some economists to argue that there are several points of equilibrium between the present employment and income conditions in underdeveloped countries and conditions of full employment in the Keynesian sense." See *Indian Economic Association Papers* (December 1953).

12

Teaching Economics*

Joan Robinson

In Cambridge, one or two of our best men, in most years, come from the subcontinent. This is not at all surprising. If talent is fairly evenly distributed in various populations, there must be eight potentially first-class men there for every one bred in Britain, and where economic problems are of great importance and the natural sciences not very well endowed, a larger proportion of talent is attracted to the subject than with us. (In the 1930s, when unemployment was an urgent problem and the discovery of remedies intellectually exciting, economics attracted more talent in England than it does now.) A small proportion come to English universities, but a small proportion of a large total comes to quite an appreciable number.

These good men who come to us to be taught (and the not-so-good ones also) go home often to teach in their turn, and their pupils, too, become teachers and influence thought through other channels. Moreover, the books and the subjects chosen for examinations bear the stamp of English teaching. We have a great responsibility on our shoulders. Are we doing more harm or good?

In a gloomy mood, I think of the harm. Most students, of course, approach their studies merely with the aim of passing an examination and acquiring a degree. (This is not a matter of natural talent, but of character and circumstance. Some who are naturally brilliant may set themselves this limited aim. Some less clever may be more serious.) The exam-passers learn the trick of saying what is expected, of not asking themselves what is meant by what they are saying (for that is disturbing and dangerous and may lead to losing marks), of repeating the particular formula which sounds as though it was relevant to each particular question. In India, especially, where the ancient belief in the power of words as

* Originally published in *Economic Weekly* 12, no. 4–6 (23 January 1960), pp. 173–75.

such is still strong, this comes quite naturally. The exam-passer who does well becomes in due course an examiner and by then he has quite lost any doubts he may once have had to stifle. He has come to believe that this kind of thing really is education. And so the system feeds on itself.

What about the few who are serious, who really want to learn something? What do we do for them? The serious student is often attracted to economics by humanitarian feeling and patriotism—he wants to learn how to choose economic policies that will increase human welfare. Orthodox teaching deflects these feelings into the dreary desert of so-called welfare economics, a system of ideas based on a mechanistic psychology of a completely individualistic pursuit of pleasure and avoidance of pain, which no one believes to be a correct account of human nature, dished up in algebraical formulae which do not even pretend to be applicable to actual data. As he goes deeper into the matter, he reads some brilliant and subtle authors who debunk the whole subject and show conclusively that its methodology was inadmissible. For most, this is too bitter a pill to swallow and they desperately cling to some scraps of what they have learned because no other way has been offered of formulating the vague benevolent feelings with which they began.

The serious student was hoping, also, to learn something that would help him to make up his mind on the great question that lies open before all the developing countries. How far can private-enterprise capitalism be made to serve national ends? Why is it that the socialist countries appear to develop faster than the democracies? Is the cost that they exact from their people necessary, or could the job be done with less pain? Must he make an all-or-none choice, or is there a middle way?

He soon begins to notice that, without any overt discussion of the question, he is being indoctrinated with notions soaked in a prejudice for laissez-faire. This is partly the result of a mere time lag. Nineteenth century economic teaching was built up round the conception of the merits of the free market and, in particular, of free trade (which at that time favoured British national interests, though it was damaging to India); the modern textbooks are still much influenced by the masters of that period. It is partly the result of the choice of curriculum. A large proportion of his time is taken up by the theory of relative prices. The question of the distribution of *given* resources amongst alternative ends, subject to the condition that there is an equitable (and not very unequal) distribution of purchasing power among the families concerned, lends itself to exhibiting a free market in a favourable light; the student is required to work out exercises devised to show how, in these conditions, interference with the free play of the forces of supply and demand causes harm to the individuals who make up the market. All this is very complicated and, when modified by modern embellishments such as the theory of oligopoly and imperfect competition, may well occupy a year of lectures and reading. The serious student is made to feel foolish if he has the hardihood to ask whether resources are given, and if income is distributed equitably: "Do you not understand that these are necessary simplifying assumptions for the analysis of prices? You cannot expect to do everything at once."

It is true that we cannot, in the time available, teach everything that we would like. But why do we pick out for treatment just that selection of topics that is least likely to raise any questions of fundamental importance?

Arid Lands

Trudging through these arid lands, the serious student still hopes to learn something about development, planning, inflation, and all that concerns the burning questions of India today. Here the mere pressure of events has forced some new questions into the curriculum, and a new theoretical apparatus of capital/output ratios and growth rates has been hastily botched up to meet the need. Systematic teaching, however, for the most part still rests at the stage of the old equilibrium theory. Take, for example, the question of choosing the capital/output ratio in framing the plans for industrialisation. The textbook theory says no more than that, if we compare two economies, each already in equilibrium, with the same total value of capital already in existence in each, the one with the lower level of real wages will have (on certain stated assumptions about competition etc.) a higher level of employment. That is where the argument is left. If the student falls into the trap of concluding that cutting wages would cause employment to increase, very likely no one will go out of their way to explain why this is a non sequitur.

The prestige of the teachers and the books bears down on the serious student with a heavy weight. He learns to distrust his native common sense and to curb his generous impulses. He submits himself to a course of miseducation and comes out, not "by the same door wherein he went" but by another door, in the wrong street.

So in my gloomy mood. But even at the gloomiest, I do not think of giving up. The subject does exist. For better or worse it has become the basis of a flourishing profession. There is no stopping it now. We must keep on pegging away and try to make the best of it.

Begin with Economic Systems

How would I like to see teaching reformed? First, do not let us bother about the exam-passers. Whatever we teach they still reduce to slogans, and new slogans cannot be more miseducating than the old ones. If the new ones are less easy to detach from reality, they might even be a shade less miseducating.

For the serious students, I would take the bull by the horns and start from the beginning to discuss various types of economic system. Every society (except Robinson Crusoe) has to have some rules of the game for organizing production and the distribution of the product. Laissez-faire capitalism is only one of the possible sets of rules, and one in fact which is unemployable in a pure form. It always has to be mixed with some measures of collective control. The Indian scene provides examples of pre-capitalist, capitalist and socialist games being played side by side. Students acquainted with the old fast-vanishing world can help in trying to puzzle out the economic analysis of its functioning and to test out the meaning of concepts such as wages and capital in non-capitalist contexts. Adam Smith, Ricardo, Marx, Marshall, and Keynes would be treated in terms of the model of an economic system that they each had in mind and of the actual problems that each sought to solve.

DISPLACE THEORY OF RELATIVE PRICES

I should displace the theory of the relative prices of commodities from the centre of the picture and make the main topic production, accumulation, and distribution looked at from the point of view of an economy taken as a whole. Keynes's *General Theory* then falls into place as the short-period section of a truly general theory. Here price theory comes in as an element in the theory of distribution, for the relation of prices to money-wage rates in the industrial sector of an economy is one of the determinants of the distribution of proceeds between workers and capitalists or the state, and the relation of agricultural to manufacturing prices is a main determinant of distribution between sectors of the economy.

Markets and the laws of supply and demand I should treat not only in terms of an ideal equilibrium already achieved but also in terms of actual dealings in commodities, with their tendency to develop cobweb cycles, and the violent shocks that are given from time to time to the communities dependent on them.

Welfare I should treat in human terms and teach the students to look not for "preference surfaces" but for objective tests of standards of nutrition and health.

In all this I should emphasise that economic theory, in itself, preaches no doctrines and cannot establish any universally valid laws. It is a method of ordering ideas and formulating questions. For this reason, I should pay a good deal of attention to method. I should insist upon the distinction between an accounting identity, a statement of equilibrium conditions, and a summary of econometric facts. Y = C + S (where Y is net value of national income of a period, C is the value of purchases of consumable goods and S, net saving,) is an identity. The word "net" covers a balancing factor (amortisation of pre-existing capital) which makes the two sides equal by definition. S = sY (where s is the proportion of national income *normally* saved) is a statement of conditions of equilibrium; its whole significance lies in the sense given to *normally*. A table of figures giving estimates of S and Y over some past period is a statement, ex post, of supposed facts; its significance depends largely on the reliability of the estimates. None of these tells us anything about causation and models built with these bricks will never stand up. To find causal relations we want to know how individuals behave and how the behaviour of various groups reacts on each other. I should try to break down the awe that students feel for formulae, not so as to induce a sceptical drift into intellectual nihilism but so as to form the habit of picking them to pieces and putting them together again, with the ambiguities cleaned off, and keeping them firmly in their place as useful adjuncts to common sense, not as substitutes for it.

All this sounds dry and formalist but, illustrated first with precise imaginary simple examples, and then with rough and inexact actual examples, leading up to questions of real importance, it can be made interesting and educational for the serious students. The exam-passers will not be any the worse for it. A generation well educated, resistent to fudging, imbued with the humility and the pride of genuine scientists, could make contribution both to knowledge and to the conduct of affairs that no one need be ashamed of.

Returning from this happy daydream, my gloom is all the deeper. To write down what I want to see emphasises how unlikely it is that I ever shall. But, courage! We must try as best we may to do a little good here and there to set in the scales against all the harm.

13

Peasant Economy as a Category in Economic History*

Daniel Thorner

Peasant economies, we suggest, have been and still are a widespread form of organisation of human society. Because of their historical persistence, peasant economies would appear to be well worthy of study in their own right and in their own terms. When we search the literature of agrarian history for discussions of peasant economies we find them scattered among such diverse categories as "subsistence," "feudal," or "oriental." In discussions of the so-called underdeveloped areas, peasant economies are frequently dealt with as conglomerations of "small-scale" units or "minifundia." Or they may be relegated to an intermediate or transition stage between "primitive" and "modern" (or "developed") economies. By contrast, we believe there is hope of rich analytical yield if we can find a way of treating peasant economies as a distinctive group.

For this purpose, it is essential to define peasant economy as a system of production and to distinguish it from other historical systems such as slavery, capitalism, and socialism. We shall accordingly set out a tentative definition of peasant economy, and then illustrate it by several examples. These will show some of the varied forms which peasant economies have assumed in different

* Published in *Economic Weekly* 15, nos 28–30 (July 1963), pp. 1243–52. (This chapter is a revised and reworked version of a paper originally submitted in Septermber 1962 to the Second International Conference in Economic History, held at Aix-en-Provence. The proceedings of the conference will be issued during the coming winter by the Ecolo Pratique des Hautes Etudes, Sixieme Section, Paris, the publishers being Mouton and Co. Paris and The Hague.) Many writers have utilised the term peasant economy to describe the functioning of individual household units. We prefer to reserve the term for entice economies having certain characteristics which we shall specify in the course of this chapter.

continents in modern times. Beneath the apparent variety we shall find in each case a common core.

Before we specify the determining characteristics of peasant economy, we should make our level of analysis absolutely plain. We are dealing here with the features of the whole economy of sizeable countries. Our units will be at the scale of kingdoms or empires (Japan, Tsarist Russia, China), nations (Mexico), and grand imperial possessions (India, Indonesia).

We exclude from our coverage little possessions, tiny states, and sub-regions of larger states. Nor do we deal with peasant sectors of economies which, taken as a whole, are not peasant economies. We do *not* exclude small nations. Quite a number of them, e.g., Ceylon, Paraguay, Syria, Sardinia, Ireland, and Scotland before the Union, have had peasant economies, and a few still do today. But in the present paper we have thought it would be clearer if we presented as our examples only countries of a substantial size.

Determining Criteria

We use five criteria for determining whether the total economy of a given country, nation, or large colonial area is to be taken as a peasant economy. All five of these must be satisfied before an entire economy of a given country can be termed peasant. Our first two criteria relate to production and working population. They are intended to help distinguish peasant economies from industrialised economies, whether capitalist or socialist. In a peasant economy, roughly half of the total production must be agricultural and more than half of the working population must be engaged in agriculture. In a word, we are saying that to be termed "peasant," an economy must be primarily agricultural. In a capitalist or a socialist state which has been industrialised, there may remain thousands or even millions of peasants, but we would no longer apply the term "peasant" to such an economy, *taken as a whole*. The question would rather become one of the peasant sector in a non-peasant economy; the setting would then be different, and a different level of analysis would be required.

Our third criterion requires the existence of a state power and a ruling hierarchy of a particular kind: one in which the "kinship" or "clan" order has weakened sufficiently to give way to a "territorial State." I am not saying that kinship or kin ties have disappeared, for that would be absurd. Rather, I require the passage, in the sense of Moret on Egypt, "from tribe to empire"[1] or, in the sense of ancient Greece, the formation of the territorial state.[2] The question of peasant economies in "feudal" regimes is delicate. So are practically all questions involving that ticklish word "feudalism"! If I were to be forced to specify now what I have in mind, I would say that I am concerned with the economies of the feudal monarchical states of western Europe in the late twelfth and thirteenth centuries, rather than with those of the disintegrated and practically non-urban regimes in the ninth and tenth centuries. Here, however, our fourth criterion also comes into play, the rural-urban separation.

We presuppose, for peasant economies, the presence of towns, and a division or break between these towns and the countryside that is simultaneously political, economic, social, and cultural. In practice, or belief, or both, the peasants are held to be a lesser or "subject" order, existing to be exploited by all concerned. In social terms, this is considered to be the "natural order." We do not consider an economy to be "peasant" unless it contains a significant number of towns with a definite pattern of urban life, quite different from that of the countryside.[3] Simply as a rough quantitative indication, we can say that the total urban population should amount to at least half a million persons; or, alternatively, that at least 5 per cent of the entire population of a given country should be resident in towns. By insisting that a peasant economy must have towns, we wish to do more than establish the mere fact that the economy is not purely agricultural. We posit a fairly marked degree of division of labour in society, and a distinct urban concentration of artisans, or other industrial and intellectual workers of various skills. By the same token we presume that agriculture is sufficiently developed to feed not only the peasants and the governing hierarchies, but also the townspeople.

Our fifth and final criterion, the most fundamental, is that of the unit of production. In our concept of peasant economy peasant family households are the typical and most representative units of production. We define a peasant family household as a socio-economic unit which grows crops primarily by the physical efforts of the members of the family. The principal activity of the peasant households is the cultivation of their lands, strips, or allotments. The households may also engage in other activities: for example, in handicrafts, processing, or even petty trade. Some members of the family may work, perhaps be forced to work, outside the household from time to time. The household may include one or more slaves, domestic servants, or hired hands. But the total contribution of these non-family members to actual crop production will be much less than that of the family members.

In a peasant economy half or more of all crops grown will be produced by such peasant households, relying mainly on their own family labour. Alongside of the peasant producers there may exist larger units: the landlord's demesne or home farm tilled by labour exacted from the peasants, the hacienda or estate on which the peasants may be employed for part of the year, the capitalist farm in which the bulk of the work is done by free hired labourers. But if any of these is the characteristic economic unit dominating the countryside and accounting for the greater share of the crop output, then we are not dealing with a peasant economy. We also exclude specifically all economies in which the most representative agricultural unit is the Roman-style slave villa or the sugar- or cotton-growing slave plantation of more modern times.

Status of Peasant

We may state categorically that in a peasant economy the peasant family members are not slaves. But we shall not try to specify whether the peasants are serfs, semi-free or free. There are, it hardly needs saying, other contexts in which the question is of the highest importance. For the *definition* of peasant economy, however, the distinction is unnecessary, and the effort to make it is likely to prove analytically sterile. We have already indicated that in peasant economies the peasantry as a group is subject and exists to be exploited by others. The peasant may very well have to work one or more days of the week for the baron or the lord of manor. He may also be obliged to make payments or presents to landlords, functionaries, aristocrats, and other important persons. At the same time, from the point of production, the peasant households constitute definite—one is almost tempted to say "independent"—entities. Because of this quality in their position, these peasantries inevitably straddle the line between free and unfree. In a sense the peasant in such economies is simultaneously subject and master.

Within a particular country at a particular time, many varieties or blends of freedom and unfreedom may coexist. It is usually difficult to say with any precision what proportion of the peasantry are serfs and what proportion are not serfs. With the passage of time, the proportions may change. In some areas, the working populations have oscillated over the centuries through most of the range, from freedom to serfdom and back again.

In a peasant economy the first concern of the productive units is to grow food crops to feed themselves. But this cannot be their sole concern. By definition, they live in a state and are linked with urban areas. They must willy-nilly sustain the State, the towns, the local lords. Hence, in one way or another, they must hand over, surrender, or sell to others part of their food crops. Although the conditions of exchange are such that the peasants usually give more than they get, they may obtain in return a bit of iron, some salt, spices, perhaps fancy cloth for a marriage.

Peasant Economy and the Market

We should be careful not to slip into the trap of imagining "pure" type of peasant household which consumes practically everything it produces and practically nothing else, as distinct from an "impure" type which produces for a market as well as for its own immediate needs. The latter is historically more common and more characteristic. In point of fact, the household units in peasant economies frequently dramatize their dual focus by growing two crops. The first is the cereal essential to their own sustenance and that of society as a whole; the second is much more likely to be a non-foodgrain (perhaps a fruit, fibre, or oilseed) produced precisely with an eye to barter, sale, or exchange of some sort. It is as habitual with peasants in many areas to grow two crops as to walk on two feet.

We are sure to go astray if we try to conceive of peasant economies as exclusively "subsistance" oriented and suspect capitalism wherever the peasants show evidence of being "market" oriented. It is much sounder to take it for granted, as a starting point, that for ages peasant economies have had a double orientation toward both. In this way, much fruitless discussion about the nature of so-called "subsistence" economies can be avoided.

We might say that in a peasant economy roughly half or more of all agricultural production is consumed by the peasant households themselves, rather than being "marketed." We do not, however, include as "marketed" produce those foodgrains handed over around harvest time by indebted or dependent peasant families to the local landlords, merchants, or moneylenders, and subsequently doled back before the next harvest, generally on unfavourable terms, to the same peasant families. Such foodgrains, in our view, have not passed through an organised market process. They have not moved on, via genuine commerce, for consumption by parties other than the original producers. Instead, they have remained in the village where they were grown and have returned to source, to the original producers. In effect, the productive unit and consumption unit is the same peasant family household. This is certainly not the indirect process, mediated by a market, which is characteristic of capitalist agriculture. Instead, in a peasant economy, the movement of foodgrains inside the village away from the producing family and back again to that same family is tied in with long-established modes of economic domination and exploitation. When such relationships are typical at the village level, we have an almost sure sign in an agricultural economy, that we are dealing with a peasant rather than capitalistic structure.

To summarize, we have defined peasant economies in terms of the predominance of agriculture, both in total product and in the working population. We have required the existence of a territorial state and a separation between town and country. We have indicated that the characteristic unit of production must be the peasant family household with a double orientation, that is, both to its own sustenance and to the greater world beyond the village. We must emphasise that no single one of these elements will suffice to determine whether or not a given economy is indeed a peasant economy. All these features must be found together and must relate to the economy of a whole country.

II

When we look for examples of peasant economy, in terms of the set of criteria just listed, we find many different kinds scattered throughout recorded history and in all continents except Australia. We shall discuss, in the present paper, only six examples, all within the 200 years since 1750. There are several reasons for limiting ourselves to the period of the Industrial Revolution and its aftermath. It is, in the first place, the period with which I am most familiar. The modern age is the one for which we have the best documentation, particularly in terms of quantitative materials. More important, under the impact of the expanding industrial system, the 200-odd years since 1750 have witnessed the most fundamental transformations in peasant economy known in history. We ourselves are living witnesses of this process of transformation, which is still continuing; in fact, it is accelerating before our eyes. We are in a position to study at first hand both the nature of peasant economies and the ways in which they resist or yield to change.

As illustrations of cases of peasant economy in this era of change, I propose to characterise in a few words the salient features of the economic structure of six different countries. Any such characterisation in so limited a space must necessarily appear incomplete and somewhat impressionistic. For this I apologise in advance. My purpose is solely to draw your attention to a few of the chief aspects of each case. My examples are Tsarist Russia, Indonesia, Mexico, India, Japan, and China.

Among the peasant economies of the nineteenth century that of Tsarist Russia had the richest and most complicated history and has left us with the largest literature. As a group, Russian scholars carried the analysis of peasant economies further than anyone else, and were perhaps the first to formulate a theory of peasant economy.[4]

In the century and a half before 1917, the imperial structure of Tsarist Russia was expanding outwardly into Siberia, while inwardly it was decaying at home. In terms of peasant economy, the most distinctive feature of the countryside in the late Tsarist era was the close interdependence of landlord estates, *mir* (village community) lands and rights, and small peasant holdings. In the centuries before the emancipation of the serfs in 1861, the bondage of the peasantry guaranteed the landlords the labour supply needed for their estates. The emancipation enabled cultivating peasant families to get more land of their own, provided they could raise oppressive redemption payments. The size and importance of the old landlord estates was much reduced. By the late nineteenth century individual peasant tenures were gradually increasing in importance.

In the decades before the First World War, a growing proportion of the peasantry devoted themselves to producing for the market with and aid of regularly hired agricultural labourers. In the same period there was a rapid expansion of railways, cities, commerce, and factory production on capitalistic lines. The significance of the growth of capitalism in city and country became a hotly debated national issue. Criteria were advanced for distinguishing peasant production from capitalistic agriculture. Many of the questions taken up in the present paper were posed at that time, in one form or another, in the works of

Chernyshevsky, Danielson (Nicolai-on), Hourwich, Plekhanov, Kossinsky, Lenin, Chayanov, and others.

In the decades after the revolution of 1917, Russia ceased to be a peasant economy, emerging instead under socialism as both urbanised and industrialised.

INDONESIA

Under the Dutch, Indonesia constituted one of the oldest and most striking examples of colonial rule in both of its major forms, "direct" and "indirect." For some decades in the middle of the nineteenth century, the peasants were compelled, under the so-called "culture system," to grow certain crops which the Dutch wanted to export. After that policy was given up in 1870, the Dutch energetically developed large plantations for the growth of export crops. For their labour supply for these plantations, the Dutch drew on the peasants from the bordering villages. There emerged, particularly in Java and Sumatra, a pattern of large plantations, village communities with group rights in land, and small peasants among whom, in the course of time, the sentiment for individual family holdings deepened.

Although the parallel must not be pressed unduly, the pattern of large estates and their labour supply, village community rights in land, and ascendant feeling for family land, bears some resemblance to late Tsarist Russia. The missing element was *indigenous* capitalism which, in a colonial setting, was practically negligible, both in city and country. As of 1949, when the Dutch relinquished control, Indonesia had very little modern industry and a quite limited urban population—barely enough in fact, to qualify under our criteria as a peasant economy.

MEXICO

Striking similarities between the peasant economies of Java and Mexico have already been observed and discussed in an important article by Eric Wolf.[5] In Mexico, during the century after the end of Spanish rule in 1823, we find a pattern of large estates (haciendas), weakening village community rights in land, and a very slow growth of individual family holdings.

A great part of Mexican history in the twentieth century turns on the savage struggle of the peasants for land and for resources with which to cultivate it. The revolutionaries, especially those led by Zapata, at first demanded and obtained in principle, the restoration of village commons which had been seized by the great landholders. In practice, however, very little land was handed back to the villages under restoration proceedings. By 1915 the revolutionary programme called for taking from the great estates land which had not previously been held by the villages, and endowing the peasantry with it. This endowment policy was implemented so vigorously under President Cárdenas in the 1930s, that eventually more than 30 per cent of the villagers in Mexico received grants of land. Tens of millions of hectares were transferred either to individual smallholders or to communities (*ejidos*).

Once set up, however, the ejidos failed to fulfil the high hopes placed in them. Much of the land turned over to the peasantry was poor in quality and in water supply. The amount of agricultural credit supplied by the government through the Ejidor Bank has been grossly inadequate. Moreover, the funds tended to be directed toward the good risks among the peasants, that is, the peasants with the most fertile land, preferably irrigated. Among the less fortunate peasantry some have leased their lands to the better-off, and gone to work for them as hired agricultural labourers. Meanwhile, there has arisen, with the aid of private credit, a new large-scale agriculture utilising modern techniques to produce profitable export crops.

During the present century industry has expanded rapidly in certain parts of the country, thanks in large part to substantial foreign investment. Hundreds of thousands of peasants have left their villages to find work in the rapidly growing cities. In recent decades well more than half of the national product has been non-agricultural; and now half of the country's population is urban. Mexico has left her phase of peasant economy (as herein defined) well behind.

India

Up to 1947, India, like Indonesia, was a colonial empire in which both "direct" and "indirect" rule prevailed. In India, as compared with Indonesia, the plantations and other large units of cultivation occupied a very minor position in the economy as a whole. There were great landlords in India, some of them holding hundreds of villages. But cultivation almost everywhere was by peasant families, most of them working very small amounts of land.

Caste and untouchability are distinctive characteristics of India. One of the principal economic functions of caste in the countryside has been to emphasise the inferiority of the lower castes who have for ages served their superiors as a cheap, dependent supply of agricultural labour. Few observers would be so rash as to say that caste has stopped serving that function in the villages of contemporary India.

During their regime, the British developed in India one of the half-dozen largest railway systems in the world. Along with this appeared many other elements of what, in economists' jargon, is called the "infrastructure" of development. Around Calcutta, Scottish houses developed a jute manufacturing industry, while in Bombay and Ahmedabad Indian entrepreneurs built up several hundred cotton textile mills. Since India attained independence in 1947, the government has thrown its weight behind the rapid development of a comprehensive range of heavy industries. In the

1950s, agriculture, principally carried on by small peasant families, still accounted for roughly half of the total national product. India is today still a peasant economy.

Japan

Less than fifty years after the Meiji Restoration of 1868 Japan had ceased to be a peasant economy. There is by now a vast literature assessing this apparently abrupt and dramatic revolution. The leading authorities today agree that the foundations for this genuine and rapid economic transformation antedate the 1868 restoration and go back, particularly in agriculture, far into the preceding period, the Tokugawa era.[6]

It was in the Tokugawa period, roughly from the seventeenth to nineteenth centuries, that the Japanese countryside took on the pattern of cultivation in small units by individual peasant families which has persisted to the present. Taxes were collected in kind from the villages for the great feudal overlords and amounted at times to as much as 60 per cent of the crop. The warrior class, for the most part, had been gathered up into the castle towns where they lived on rice stipends. In the relatively few large holdings which remained, cultivation by serfs (*nago*) and servants gradually gave way to tenancy. The 1820 reform, which permitted the mortgaging of land, was followed by the emergence of a group of moneylender-landlords (rich peasants, town merchants, petty rural capitalists, village headmen) whose tenants were often the original cultivating owners.

After the Meiji Restoration of 1868, the peasant proprietors were free from their feudal obligations and confirmed in the ownership of land they cultivated. The old rice levies were supplanted by a fixed annual tax in money payable to the state. At first a heavy burden, these taxes declined progressively in real terms with the long-run rise in the prices of agricultural products.

On the other hand, the need to raise cash to pay the taxes placed the small peasant—always at the margin of his resources—in the position of having to sell his crop at the most unfavourable moment, immediately after the harvest. The same situation worked to the advantage of the richer peasants who sometimes acted as rice brokers.

For tenants, the Meiji reforms brought no benefits. They still had to pay rents in kind and at the rate of about half of an average crop. The rise in the price of rice did not help them, since they marketed so little. In the early 1880s about one-third of all arable land was worked under tenancy; by the time of the First World War, the fraction had increased to nearly one-half.

The average area worked by Japanese peasants (i.e., the total of the several scattered strips cultivated by the household) was about one hectare (2.47 acres) around 1868, and remained roughly the same right up to 1918. In the fifty years after 1868, the total output of rice in Japan nearly doubled partly because more land was brought under cultivation, but mostly because of an increase in output per acre of the order of 50 per cent. During this period, population increased by roughly 60 per cent. Nonetheless, the level of living went up.

The story of the fostering of modern industry by the Meiji regime to too well-known to need summary here. One of its important results for the countryside was that the natural increase of rural population was siphoned off by the towns and cities. Thus the size of the agricultural population of Japan remained roughly the same (around 5.5 million households) from 1868 to 1918. We must also note that the agricultural households themselves engaged increasingly in non-agricultural side activities, such as handicrafts and other rural industries. Whereas less than a quarter of the peasant households had such activities in 1884, more than one-third were so recorded by 1919.

The decline in the relative position of agriculture in modern Japan can be indicated in three ways. First, the proportion of the population living in villages, usually defined for Japan as places with less than 10,000 inhabitants: this percentage was put at 87 per cent in 1888, then at 68 per cent in 1918, and fell to 50 per cent in 1940. Our second indicator is the proportion of the total working force returned as in agriculture. According to Professor Ohkawa, one of Japan's foremost authorities, this proportion stood at 76 around 1880, at 59 around 1915, and at 44 around 1940. Lastly, the percentage contribution of agriculture to total national income; again, following Professor Ohkawa, this stood at 64 per cent around 1880, dropped sharply to 36 per cent around 1915, and fell to only 17 per cent around 1940. In terms of our first criterion of peasant economy contribution of agriculture to total national production, Japan, by the eve of the First World War, had unmistakeably stopped being a peasant economy.[7]

China

As in India and Japan, the agriculture of China for several centuries before 1950 had been the *petite culture*. Nearly all crops were grown by families holding roughly on the average about one hectare (somewhat more in the wheat areas of the north, somewhat less in the rice areas of the south). These holdings were generally made up of tiny, uneven, scattered patches. Family members themselves did the farm labour; only a very small percentage of the cultivators, the best-off ones with the most land, used much hired labour.

Before the Revolution of 1911 there was much tenancy in China: and, as the century advanced, more peasants had to give up the ownership of part or all of their land. By the 1930s, half, or more than half, of the Chinese peasants were tenants or petty owners-cum-tenants. Rents generally were paid in kind and amounted to 50 or 60 per cent of the crop. Paying such heavy rents on their tiny holdings, the Chinese peasantry could not make do from the land alone. For most of them, unfortunately, there was insufficient alternative work.

The peasant handicrafts, which had traditionally offered supplementary employment, weakened before the competition of machine-made goods from Japan and the West. The development of modern cities was very limited and entirely inadequate to drain off (as in Japan) population from the countryside. Instead, about 70 per cent of the population continued to work in agriculture.

The difficulties of the peasantry were compounded by multiple exactions by landlords, warlords, usurers, and petty government officials. They suffered further in the course of wars, invasions, famines, civil war, and revolution.

In the years since 1950 the Peking regime has exerted tremendous efforts to transform this peasant economy. In the cities there has been an immense development of modern industry. In the countryside the vast programme of land reform began by taking away the properties of the landlords and redistributing the land in small bits to the peasants. This has been followed by a series of efforts to encourage or to impose large-scale cultivation: mutual aid in the form of work teams, village cooperatives, collective farming, and the establishment of very large rural communes.

We are not in a position to assess the extent to which these programmes have reduced the importance of peasant family cultivation in Chinese agriculture. Nor do we know whether agriculture contributes half or more of the total national product. It is hard to say with any assurance whether or not China is still a peasant economy.

* * *

Since our six examples of peasant economy have been drawn from the modern world, we have been more explicit with those criteria separating them from industrial economies than to those separating them from slave or "tribal" systems. We have, in effect, dealt only with peasant economies in their "high" or "late" phase. Nonetheless, we have seen that conditions differed in several important respects which may be worth listing:

(1) indigenous or colonial rule;
(2) small-scale cultivation only, or small-scale juxtaposed with large-scale cultivation and, if the latter, the arrangements for labour supply on the large-scale units;
(3) individual family holdings of land only, or individual family holdings in the context of larger group holdings or village community rights in land;
(4) hierarchy of peasantry at the village level: existence and social role of a class of agricultural labourers;

(5) urbanisation and industrialisation as factors in reducing the relative importance of the peasantry in the economy taken as a whole, and in leading to the transformation of peasant production.

We might say we have sketched in a preliminary way cases of countries at the exit, or seeking the exit, from peasant economy. It would of course, be possible and desirable to take up cases of entrance into peasant economy. In the largest sense, the study of peasant economies should encompass the whole process of their appearance, the change they undergo through time, and the ways in which they become—or fail to become!—transformed into modern industrial economies.

III

It may be of interest to situate peasant economy, as we have defined it, in relation to Karl Marx's well-known modes of production. Our peasant economies include societies falling under both Marx's feudal mode of production and his "Asiatic Societies." In addition, they take in those periods of history which he characterised as marked by small peasant agriculture and which he treated as transitions from one main mode of production to another.

We believe that our broader grouping, peasant economy, is justified analytically in terms of the common characteristics which we have just discussed and illustrated. It would, of course, be possible to extend the term "feudal" (with or without the prefixes "semi-," "proto-," and "pseudo-") to cover this whole range, but that would be unfortunate. The term feudalism originated in western Europe and carries with it a set of specific connotations. We cannot help but be reminded of the feudal contract, the manor, and the serf. This full complex of phenomena, however, occurs only in a small number of centuries in quite confined areas of extreme western Europe and Japan. Peasant economies, by contrast, existed long before feudalism, alongside of feudalism, and long after it. They persist in our contemporary world. No matter how the content of the term is thinned out, feudalism cannot serve to cover a historical canvas stretching eastward from the Caribbean to the China Seas.

From our perspective, European feudalism of the High Middle Ages may be seen as embodying a particular form of peasant economy. Nothing is gained by trying to view all peasant economies as variations of that one rather special form. The time has arrived to treat European experience in categories derived from world history, rather than to squeeze world history into western European categories.

Notes and References

[1] A. Moret, *From Tribe to Empire: Social Organisation among Primitives and in Ancient East* (London: Kegan Paul, 1926).

[2] The area of the ancient Greek states, however, was so small that most of them would have to be excluded from our consideration because of failure to meet our initial precondition of sufficient size.

[3] There is much literature on the separation between city and country. For the eighteenth century see Sir James Steuart, *An Inquiry into the Principles of Political Economy*, Vol. I (London, 1767). Marx considered that the entire economic history of human society could be summed up in the movement of the antithesis between town and country. See *Capital*, Vol. I, edited by Dona Torr (London, 1939), p. 345; for the German original, see the *Volksausgabe*, Vol. I (Moscow, 1932), p. 369. Robert Redfield was one the of twentieth century writers much interested in this theme, particularly in cultural terms. See his study, *Peasant Society and Culture: An Anthropological Approach to Civilization* (Chicago: University of Chicago Press, 1956). In an interesting article, Lloyd A. Fallers has carried forward Redfield's line of work: "Are African Cultivators to be Called 'Peasants'?" *Current Anthropology* 2, no. 2 (April 1961): pp. 108–10.

[4] The leading scholar appears to have been A. V. Chayanov, a number of whose studies were translated into German in the 1920s. Of these, one of the most fundamental was *Die Lehre von der bauerlichen Wirtschaft*, tr. F. Schlomer (Berlin, 1923). In the German transliterations, Chayanov's name is given as Tschajanow or Tschayanoff and is so listed in most catalogues. (Chayanov's book has just been translated into English, and is to be published in 1964).

[5] "Closed Corporate Peasant Communities in Mesoamerica and Central Java," *Southwestern Journal of Anthropology* 13, no. 1 (Spring 1957), pp. 1–18. See also Wolf's suggestive comparisons in his article "Aspects of Group Relations in a Complex Society: Mexico," *American Anthropologist* 58, no. 6 (December 1956), pp. 1065–78.

[6] See, for example, R. P. Dore, *Land Reform in Japan* (London: Oxford University Press, 1959), ch 1; and T. C. Smith, *The Agrarian Origins of Modern Japan* (Stanford: Stanford University Press, 1959).

[7] The data of Professor Kazushi Ohkawa are taken from the comprehensive summary article which he and Henry Rosovsky prepared under the title, "The Role of Agriculture in Modern Japanese Economic Development," *Economic Development and Cultural Change* 9, no. 1, Part 2: The City and Village in Japan (October, 1960), pp. 43–67. This issue of *Economic Development and Cultural Change* was a special number devoted to the topic "City and Village in Japan" and contains many other relevant contributions.

PART V

Development and Planning

14

A Case of Aborted Growth: India, 1860–1900

Some Suggestions for Research*

George Rosen

From the fragments of data available on British investment in India during the period 1860–1900 there is clear evidence of major investment activity. Much of this foreign investment was for the construction of a railroad network, but it extended to private industry and to purchase of government securities. Two sets of figures for British investment are presented below, one for total investment and the other for largely railway investment, which equalled about 50 per cent of the total. Unfortunately, there are no data for Indian investment.

TABLE 14.1: BRITISH INVESTMENT IN INDIA, 1857–1911 (IN £ MILLIONS OF POUNDS)

Year	Total British Investment	British Investment Exclusive of Private, Unguaranteed Railway, and Indian Government Rupee Debt
1857	—	14
1870–71	153.4	78
1884	260.0	150
1911	351.0	1

Sources: A. K. Cairncross, *Home and Foreign Investment, 1870–1913*, Studies in Capital Accumulation (Cambridge: Cambridge University Press, 1953), p. 185; Leland H. Jenks, *Migration of British Capital to 1870*, p. 213, p. 219.

* Originally published in *Economic Weekly* 14, no. 32 (11 August 1962), pp. 1299–1302.

The railroad network grew as follows during this same period:

TABLE 14.2: GROWTH OF RAILWAY MILEAGE IN INDIA, 1854–1913/14

Year	Railroad Mileage in India
1854	first short rise
1859	432
1865	3,000*
1869	5,015
1878	8,000*
1890	16,000*
1900	21,000*
1913/14	34,656

Sources: D. R. Gadgil, *The Industrial Evolution of India in Recent Times*; P. A. Wadia and K. T. Merchant, *Our Economic Problem*, pp. 419–20, provided bases for the starred estimates.

Simultaneously with this growth of the railway network there was a rapid development of three large industries—two processing industries and one mineral. In these industries there was a large Indian as well as English investment and ownership. Certain data with respect to the growth of these industries are presented in Table 14.3.

Apart from this industrial growth there was major investment in irrigation works and the area under irrigation rose from 29 million acres in 1880 to 44 million in 1903. This was also a period of heavy investment and rapid growth in the plantation industry—tea especially, but to a lesser extent coffee plantations also.

But No Rise in Incomes

Yet, in spite of an investment from British sources in the period of about £300 million ($1.5 billion at the then prices, and probably double that in present-day prices) and the rapid rise of several major industries, there was little change in annual per capita income. A set of very crude estimates for certain years in this period indicates an average per capita income range of Rs. 18–35 in current rupees during the same years or period. The proportion of urban population to the total remained at about 9–10 per cent; and in the 1911 Census only about 2.1 million workers were employed in factory industry; and of these over 800,000 worked on plantation. (This was probably about 2 per cent of the labour force at that time.)[1]

Although some of the rise in output was absorbed by the growth of population during this period, the rate of population increase was very low by present standards. Davis estimates that the population in 1871 was 255 million, and that by 1901 it had reached 285 million. This is a rise of 12 per cent in thirty years, or an annual rate of less than 0.5 per cent.[2] It is doubtful that the rate of increase was greater in the previous twenty years. Clearly the rise in annual output absorbed by the growing population was small at most.

The purpose of this paper is to indicate certain hypotheses from economic theory and development economics to explain this phenomenon of stagnation. These hypotheses will centre upon the arguments that in this period investment in other industries would have been unprofitable under a government not prepared to provide protection to new industries; and it would have been less profitable or far riskier than alternative investment in other non-industrial directions.

Both Schumpter and Rostow, among others, have stressed the role of "leading sectors" in European and American development: and these sectors, through the phenomenon described by Hirschman as "linkage," have stimulated growth in related industrial fields. In both England and the United States the cotton textile and railroad industries have filled the leading sector role and by their development have stimulated the growth of mineral and engineering industries. This "backward linkage" did not occur in India, except for one notable exception: the coal industry, which was directly stimulated by the growing railroad industry, to which it sold 30–40 per cent of its output during this period.

WHY COAL BUT NOT OTHER INDUSTRIES?

Why did the coal industry grow but not others, under the stimulus of the leading sectors? Coal is a bulk product whose transport cost is extremely high relative to its total price if it must be shipped from Europe to India. It would be far cheaper to mine it in India and use it nearer to the point of origin and India had the coal which could be mined and used. The same was not true for machinery products. There was no machinery industry in India, the cost of sea transport of machinery adds only a small proportionate amount to the price of the product, and the quality of English machinery was known and was high. At the same time the manufacture of machinery in India would have been most risky, with a limited market and with no protection from imports under a policy of free trade. It thus proved economic for the manufacturers (both English and Indian) of textiles and railroads to import English machinery rather than take the risk of setting up machinery plants which, at this time, would also have had to import the basic raw material—steel. When this is combined with the connections existing between English-owned firms in India and firms in England the lack of development of machine industry becomes understandable on largely economic grounds, and would help explain the absence of any backward linkage from the textile, mining, and railroad industries.

There would also be a variety of economic factors that would explain the failure of any consumer goods industries, other than the cotton textile industry, to develop. The first of these would be the very low level of initial per capita income, approximately Rs. 20, which is far below the level of per capita income in Great Britain or the United States at their early stages of industrialisation. Then the growth of the cotton textile industry was not a net investment for the economy as a whole, but was accompanied by the continued impoverishment of the textile handicraft industry—India's major rural industry. A part of any gains in worker income in the factory textile industry would be offset by declining incomes in the handicraft textile industry. At the same time it is unlikely that the real wages in factory industry were in fact far above incomes in agriculture since the pressure of population from the farms, especially in light of the occurring famines, would act to keep wages in industry low. Thus, there would be little demand for manufactured consumer goods on a mass basis, except for cotton textiles, and the demand for these would simply have replaced the demand for handicraft cotton textiles.

TABLE 14.3: GROWTH OF THREE INDIAN INDUSTRIES, 1850–1906

Year	Cotton Textile Industry [Mills (M), Spindles (S), and Workers (W)]	Jute Textile Industry [Mills (M), Spindles (S), and Workers (W)]	Coal Mining [Miners (M) and Output (O)]
1851	First mill	First mill	M: 3
1861	M: 12	—	—
1869	—	—	O: 467,000 tons M: 56
1879–80	M: 58 S: 1.4 million W: 39,537	—	—
1882	—	M: 20 W: 20,000	—
1885	—	—	M: 68 O: 1.3 million tons
1889–90	M: 114 S: 2.9 million W: 99,224	—	M: 82 O: 2.2 million tons
1895–96	—	M: 28 S: 214,679 W: 78,114	—
1900–01	M: 194 S: 4.9 million W: 156,355	M: 36 S:331,382 W: 114,795	O: 6.9 million tons
1906	—	—	O: 9.1 million tons

Source: D. R. Gadgil, *Industrial Evolution of India in Recent Times.*

EFFECT OF LOW WAGES ON DEMAND

The period from 1860 to 1900 was marked by two major periods of famine, occurring during the latter part of the decade of the 1870s and in the decade of the 1890s. Population rose in India by only 1 per cent during each of these two decades. These famines would have contributed to keeping real wages of industrial workers low, and to reducing rural demand for manufactured industrial goods. If the effects of poor crops were similar to what the present effects of poor crops are, these periods would also have been ones of high money wages and raw material prices in industry, resulting in reduced profits and industrial activities, so that much of the gain of the more prosperous years would have been reduced or wiped out. For the higher income group, the larger part of its consumption expenditure was probably on imported consumer goods in the absence of Indian production and under the influence of English consumption habits and the demonstration effect of the English rulers.[3]

Thus, on the basis of a variety of economic factors, operating within the framework of the then government's policies, it is possible to present a series of plausible hypotheses for the absence of economic development in India.

The policies of the English government during this period were essentially passive. It is unnecessary to bring in intent; the government was unwilling on philosophic grounds either to take positive steps to assist the growth of industry apart from building the railroads or to protect new industries from foreign competition. There is also the question of the extent to which the apparent volume of British investment in India was reduced by the outflow of resources to pay for past and present British services (government, pensions, etc.), interest on the Indian debt, in large part representing military expenditures.

Under all these circumstances one does not need a wide variety of sociological reasons to explain the absence of development in India. In fact a reason frequently given, that the Indians were averse to money-making, was not correct in Bombay or Gujarat, where an Indian-owned textile industry grew up (it may have some greater validity in other regions but this is doubtful); and it is unnecessary to postulate a deliberate English attempt to keep down Indian industry, if this had existed it would be difficult to explain the growth that did occur.

In summary, we have presented several largely economic hypotheses which could provide a basis for research into a period of Indian economic history that is not only of crucial interest to the economic historian of India, but is also of great interest to the development economist in general.

Notes and References

[1] See V. K. R. V. Rao, "*The National Income of British India, 1931–1932* (London: Macmillan, 1942)," p. 2; Kingsley Davis, "*The Population of India and Pakistan* (Princeton: Princeton University Press, 1951)," p. 206; D. R. Gadgil, *The Industrial Evolution of India in Recent Timesop cit*, pp. 136 and 115.

[2] K. Davis, *op. cit., Population of India and Pakistan*, pp. 26–29.

[3] See the provocative remarks by D. M Bensusan-Butt in *On Economic Growth: An Essay in Pure Theory* (Oxford: Clarendon Press, 1960), D. M. Bensusan-Butt, "On Econowmic Growth," especially pp. 40–41; 142–45; 146–50.

15

How to Industrialise an Underdeveloped Area*

Paul N. Rosenstein-Rodan

I

Economic Logistics

Economic development programmes in most underdeveloped countries, although to a much lesser extent in India, emphasise industrialisation, but they are essentially *pre-industrialisation programmes*. They aim at providing the proper framework of social overhead capital to which, in some cases, some agricultural investments (land reclamation) as well as housing are added, in the hope that once such a framework is created, spontaneous private industrial investments will follow. The implicit theory relies on removing two obstacles to industrialisation: (1) on the supply side, by creating a minimum quantum of social overhead capital without which directly productive investments could not take place, and (2) on the demand side, by creating additional employment and income through investment in the social overhead capital activities effective demand is raised in the area since the workers employed in the construction of social overhead capital will spend their wages on additional goods.

This increase in effective demand should create an additional market in an area in which formerly, due to the absence of effective demand, productive investment in industrial establishments appear doomed to failure. Some investment may now appear attractive if producers of industrial goods can sell greater amounts of their products in the region, when it formerly seemed to offer no prospects at all. It is true that the employment and additional income created

* Originally published in *Economic Weekly* 12, nos 4, 5 and 6 (23 January 1960), pp. 181–84.

by investment in social overhead capital will only last as long as the construction activities of the social overhead capital last. It will not be a permanent increase in employment; the bulk of the increase is a *revolving* employment. Both jobs and additional incomes would come to an end when the electric power stations, roads, harbours, etc., are completed. Permanent jobs created by social overhead capital activities are a mere fraction of the additional jobs created during their construction period.

While the revolving employment lasts, however, increased effective demand creates an additional market which may induce investment, if the investors anticipate that the presently increased volume of demand will also obtain in the future. The process of development relies thus, first, on the multiplier mechanism whereby additional investment in social overhead capital increases income and effective demand; and second, on the acceleration principle whereby increased effective demand (increased consumption) will feedback and induce additional spontaneous directly productive investment.

Apart from those economic logistics, both ideological and practical considerations lead many governments to confine the bulk of their direct development activities to the investment in social overhead capital activities. There is, first, the feeling that social overhead capital is the proper sphere for public investment while any direct industrial investment would be an improper encroachment on private sector activities. If "proper" activities in public investment sectors were spontaneously to induce private investment, then public investment in industries would be superfluous anyway. Besides such general economic policy or ideological considerations, there is also the practical administrative difficulty that governments are, in many cases, incapable of successfully creating and operating commercial and industrial undertakings, apart from some "pilot" operations or special cases in major heavy industrial fields in which private initiative is reluctant to take the plunge.

Catalytic Effects Indirect and Uncertain

The creation of social overhead capital cannot lead directly to a considerable increase in output. Its economic rationale consists not in the directly caused increase in income but in the hope that additional investment opportunities created will be taken up by private investment. The main emphasis is, therefore, on the indirect effects—on the catalytic action of such pre-industrialisation programmes on the directly productive development of agriculture and industry.

The catalytic effects of public investment which alone justify the public investment programmes are, however, not only "indirect" but also uncertain. Induced investment may or may not take place; it is called spontaneous but is by no means automatic. We cannot know, with any certainty or high probability, whether the hoped-for induced investment will take place, it is impossible to rely fully on the working of the macroeconomic mechanism. Some bridges between the macro- and microeconomic fields have to be crossed if we are to count on the catalytic effect of public investment in social overhead capital.

II

Not Automatic

Experience of many economic development plans, which were largely pro-industrialisation programmes (for instance, the programme for the Development of the South of Italy) shows, in fact, that induced industrialisation in a unindustrialised country or area does, by no means, take place automatically. In some cases that may be due to the insufficient size of the social overhead capital investment. In such cases, proceeding with this type of investment until it reaches the minimum quantum or threshold required is obviously sensible. In many other cases, however, it does not make sense. Induced industrialisation may not take place for reasons other than an insufficient framework of social overhead capital. The dynamo may be there but the transmission belt does not function. If one proceeded to install a second dynamo besides the first, instead of making the transmission belt function, the induced current of industrialisation would not ensue and the installation of a second dynamo would be wasteful. A whole system of different economic policy measures may be required to make the transmission belt function. While the pre-industrialisation programme with its large social overhead capital investment is a "conception" of industrialisation, the infant industry may not be born without a series of measures of postnatal control. These measures, which constitute bridges between the macro- and microeconomic fields, should be thoroughly studied with experiences sought of each of the types described under Section III, gathered in different countries.

III

Measures of Postnatal Control

Measures of postnatal control consist of both direct (A and B) and indirect (C) incentives. The need for indirect incentives is well recognised, and a varying basket of them is offered to industries in many underdeveloped countries. Whether, where and how much they will work, however, is uncertain. The effectiveness of stimulation can be fundamentally strengthened, and its costs can be incidentally lowered, if direct incentives can supplement the indirect ones. The measures of postnatal control are a system; it may not work, in spite of some flexibility in its parts, if only one part of it is used and another part (direct incentives) is left out.

Sometimes, it is true, one may hop over the micro–macroeconomic bridge on one leg; it is safer and better to cross it on both legs.

(A) The Pattern of Large- and Small-Scale Enterprise in a New Industrializing Area

The Role of Subcontracting Observations of the sequence and ease with which new industrial units are established in a formerly unindustrialised area seem to suggest that the pattern of industrialisation in the twentieth century may be markedly different from that observed in past economic history. The beginning of industrialisation in the past saw the growth first of handicrafts; then of small industries growing later to medium-scale and then large-scale industries, and at the end only giant corporations. At present many successful industrial ventures in unindustrialised areas are subsidiaries or branch establishments of a large enterprise in a developed industrial area. Such large units bring with them skilled management, including often a detailed production plan involving assembly line techniques for labour, with a few skilled workers brought in together with capital. The particular feature of a well-established management and of advanced techniques of assembly line production is that even workers who had no former industrial experience can be easily taught on the job to make the few required movements in the proper rhythm at the proper time. Many experiences suggest that workers engaged in such undertakings, despite never having held any industrial job before, acquire within a few weeks of operation labour discipline and technique to such an extent that they have ratings of productivity per man hour as high as, and rates of absenteeism as low as, those of experienced workers in old industrialised areas. In those cases the labour training problem is so much easier that the roundabout way—via producing training teachers first, then establishing vocational training schools, and only then proceeding to industrial employment of the workers—seems unnecessary.

The establishment of such big branch units with advanced labour techniques is thus the easier step and may, therefore, in marked contrast to the past, be the first step in the industrialisation of a new area. Unfortunately, this is confined to the small number of big factories (branches or new) only and does not apply in equal or even similar measure to the large network of medium-scale and small-scale enterprises which should grow around the big units. If the growth of small- and medium-scale enterprises does not supplement the establishment of the few large industrial establishments, then those will remain like islands in the sea without any economic diffusion and radiation effect in the area and may not induce additional industrial growth. In many other cases, however, such large units may place subcontracts and orders for small spare parts or intermediate products to other (small- and medium-scale) firms in the new industrialising region and thereby induce investment in small industrial enterprises dependent on and centering around the big unit.

In such cases, the diffusion effect of induced industrial investment may be considerable, and the big enterprise gives rise to the establishment of other units around it; by creating the market for their output it induces industrial investment which, without it, would not take place. It is important, therefore, that the incentives (See III C) which are often sufficient for the inflow of big industrial units whose establishment in a new area presents less problems and difficulties, should be made conditional on the degree of subcontracting which is possible under the production conditions of the particular industrial sector concerned. It is known, for instance, that shipyards in some countries (for example, the United Kingdom, Holland, and Japan) rely to a much larger extent on subcontracting to small firms of different activities like carpentering than shipyards of other countries (for instance, Italy).

Where it is appropriate (and this will be different in different industrial sectors), the types and amounts of incentives offered should be made conditional on and may be made to vary according to the degree of subcontracting envisaged and proposed in the big industrial project. In such a way, the establishment in the underdeveloped area of branch replicas of factories from developed areas will not remain an isolated industrial venture but may give rise to a complementary network of small enterprises around it. The pattern of industrialisation in an unindustrialised area might thus, in the future, be the reverse of that observed in the past: big units come first and induce the subsequent growth of small industrial units around them.

(B) Industrial Zones or Estates

The establishment of industrial zones or estates has proved to be a most effective instrument to induce the inflow of small (and medium) industrial units into a new area. It constitutes a strong inducement to invest because it can capture the otherwise volatile external economies of agglomeration. Industrial zones can save a great deal of effort, trouble, and expenses in erecting a factory: they can realise considerable economies of scale in construction of factory buildings and in the installation of public utility services. They provide for a better division of labour by securing common technical, repair, and information services which could not pay for one industrial unit alone but do pay for a series of industrial units. They can organise housing, transportation, and social amenities for workers which no single industrial project could do effectively. Applying the experience gained in the so-called special development areas in England, they could offer additional inducements by building factories and offering them for rental to prospective industrial entrepreneurs. They can thereby considerably reduce the risk of single industrial projects by transforming the stock of capital required for the building into the flow of expenses for its rental, which reduces the risk of capital loss, if the investor were to abandon the project and move out. Industrial estates can thus catalyse investments which otherwise would not take place. Many of those investments are labour-intensive; investment here means employment. Industrial zones can finally be a most effective instrument for a natural policy of industrial location—avoiding both overcrowding of certain areas which might cause increasing costs and an undue dispersion which would very soon, because of non-optimum location, reduce the volume of industrial investment in the area.

An Illustration A single concrete example might illustrate this point. A worker originating from an underdeveloped area of a country has moved to an industrially developed area of the same country and spent 30 years there as a skilled foreman in a button factory. During that time he acquired detailed knowledge of the production technique, of the sources of the raw material supply, of labour problems, and of the particular markets to which the output of the factory (buttons) has been regularly sold. We could observe that all the needs of buttons in his native underdeveloped area have been regularly supplied by factories located in the industrially developed area of the country. Having saved $20,000 during his lifetime of work, he decided to return to his native town and erect a button factory there. No technical or organisational secret was foreign to him and he was, in fact, an ideal small entrepreneur needed in an underdeveloped area. When he arrived home and talked over his plans to buy a plot for a factory, prices of land rose 100 to 150 per cent within one week since a customer was in sight. He had to spend more on the acquisition of the plot and proceeded to plan the construction, clearing of the ground, erecting of the factory, etc. Negotiations with local and municipal authorities, the need to have the plans approved, and, far worse, the time needed to have electric light, water, gas, connection with the sewerage, and telephone installed, took not only a lot of effort and trouble but also of time; eight months elapsed before all the details could be settled. These eight months represented additional costs which were unforeseen.

When the building was finally erected, he approached the biggest bank in the area for a loan of $12,000 which would serve to cover half of the machinery to be installed and overdraft for circulating capital (two to three months of raw material stocks and wage payments). The bank's reply was that the managerial qualifications and experience of the man clearly qualified him as a potential first-class entrepreneur and debtor. It is true, they said, that he put $20,000 of his own into the erection of the factory. If it were not to prosper, however, and had to be sold in a public auction, it might only fetch, at best, one half of what it originally cost, so his collateral security is worth not $20,000 but something like $8,000–10,000. He would, therefore, get a loan of only $5,000!

None of these troubles would have arisen had there been an industrial zone or estate in the vicinity of his town. The price of land would have been fixed. The cost of erecting the factory would have been lowered, and the trouble and expense of having the plans approved and installation of public utilities and services secured would have been eliminated. A more progressive credit organisation could certainly have provided him with a loan which represented one-third of the total capital invested in the undertaking. Some experience is available already and should be collected the authorities about industrial zones and estates operating in England, India, Brazil (the industrial district of Belo Horizonte), and in Italy (for instance, the industrial zone of Catania in Sicily).

(C) A System of Economic, Money, and Credit Fiscal and Tariff Incentives

A series of "indirect" incentives should supplement the direct ones (A and B) in order to induce a sufficient inflow of industrial investment. The incentives are sometimes a substitute for an infant industry protection in an unindustrialised area, and are always a more diversified and flexible supplement to it.

(1) *Economic Incentives: The Use of Long-Term Contracts* Long-term contracts may be a more effective instrument to improve the efficiency of an already existing industry in an unindustrialised area as well as for providing incentives to technical progress in the organisation of new industries. Any reorganisation which is to improve the efficiency of an existing industry requires capital. The uncertainty of whether there will be a market for the products of the industry over a period long enough to amortise and repay the new investment is very frequently an insurmountable obstacle to raising the capital required.

Where there is an operating economic development programme, the uncertainty of whether road building activities, building materials, etc., will find an outlet could be more efficiently reduced by securing long-term contracts for such firms. This will lower cost per unit of their services not for a single project or unit but for a series of them, extending over four or five years on condition that, in public tender, they will reduce their prices through time, offering, for instance, a price cut of 5 per cent, 10 per cent, and 15 per cent per unit in the second, third, and fourth year of their operation. On the basis of such contracts, firms could raise capital for reorganisation which would not otherwise take place. Long-term contracts can thus be powerful incentives to increase productivity and should be used systematically for such purposes. A hand-to-mouth operation for one house or for fifty miles of a road to be performed in six or nine months is insufficient to induce a reorganisation of the method of production.

(2) *Credit and Money Incentives* New industrial investment in an unindustrialised area may be offered a range of credit incentives. The most important incentive is to secure a sufficient *availability* of credit, up to 50 per cent of capital requirements should, for instance, be offered for approved projects. In many cases the costs of such credit could be lower than those available in a non-organised market, which is an additional though less important, incentive. In addition, there may be an interest cost, reducing contributions to certain specific parts of an investment; for instance, building irrigation canals in land reclamation projects, where a development authority does not only secure credit but also contributes part of the cost of it; for instance, contributing 3 per cent on the interest cost of a loan which costs 8 per cent, thus reducing the cost to the borrower to 5 per cent. Besides securing long-term investment credit, which may be in bond form, there is a need for a contribution to risk-bearing capital. The establishment of an institution which besides normal credit would also subscribe part of equity capital in industrial projects is undoubtedly an important task which requires careful studies.

The experience of industrial development banks in various countries can be carefully sifted; for instance, industrial development banks in India, Ethiopia, Turkey, as well as of some of the most recent experiences of Latin American fomentos (in Chile). Finally, the survey and the experience on the whole system of such credit incentives offered for the development of southern Italy by recent Italian legislation including, notably, the experience of the new industrial development banks for southern Italy (ISVIEMER) Sicily (IRFIS) and Sardegna (CIS) can throw some light on successes and failures in this field.

Over and above securing long-term investment credit there is the difficult problem of providing medium-term credit and credit to small enterprise. Even in a highly developed country like England, the "Macmillan" gap was not easily filled, and new institutions had to be created to deal with this problem. Banking institutions are diverse in different countries and can, by no means, be easily transplanted and imitated. Some lessons may be derived, however, from past experience to show how to deal with this problem in underdeveloped countries.

(3) *Fiscal Incentives* Exemption from income and other taxes for new industrial investments over a period of time, stretching from six to 12 years, is a well-established and powerful incentive to induce an inflow of industrial investment.

(4) *Tariff Incentives* Machinery and equipment to be installed in an unindustrialised area can be imported duty free. An evaluation of the advantage thus presented could be obtained by a special inquiry on experience gained with this incentive in some countries (for example, southern Italy).

16

Choice Elements in Intertemporal Planning*

S. Chakravarti and R. S. Ekaus

The utility of intertemporal or dynamic planning arises not just from its formulation of final goals but from its specification of the best means to achieve those goals. An intertemporal plan is like a guide map: it not only shows the beginning and ending but also the road to be travelled. An intertemporal plan, therefore, is necessary as a means of determining what must be done today and in each year in the future. The increasing uncertainty of longer periods, the inevitable short-run deviations from prescribed paths, the changes in the technological possibilities, for example—all such influences justify annual and short-term plans. But short plans are most effective in the context of long-term planning, and the same influences necessitate frequent replanning on a long-term basis. This means that long-term planning as well as short-term planning are not once-for-all operations but must be a continuing process with modifications in the light of new knowledge and for elaboration to greater detail.

All planning is a political as well as an economic process. Though the political constraints often remain implicit in an economic programme, they constitute the boundaries within which the economist must work. The components of economic policy are often competing, however, both as regards means as well as choice of ends, and the difficulties in political decisions arise not so much in formulating the ideals of a good life as in making the inevitable choices among

* Originally published in *Economic Weekly* 14, annual number (February 1962), pp. 189–92. We acknowledge the helpful comments of Messrs Andreatta, Harberger, and Sevaldson while retaining full responsibility for any errors.

its components. The economist has, therefore, the responsibility of defining the economic content of the political constraints given to him and demonstrating the implications of alternative policies for concrete economic magnitudes.

I

Levels of Consumption and Saving at the Beginning of a Plan

The point need not be elaborated that most of the resources required for growth in any country must be provided internally. Just as the productive resources currently available depend on past accumulation so also the endowment which the present leaves to the future depends on the manner in which current resources are allocated between consumption and investment.

The vicious circle of poverty and stagnation from which the less-developed countries are trying to escape sets limits on the proportion of output from currently available resources which can be diverted from consumption to building up productive resources for future use. The proportion can be changed, however, by individuals in some of the income brackets, at least, and by the state in pursuance of the national goals. This proportion is one of the fundamental choice elements in planning.

Most important from the viewpoint of planning is that the state can affect the initial levels of consumption and saving by the various tax and control measures at its command. The economic analyses of alternative policies should not obscure the fact that the choice is essentially political. In some countries physical coercion has been used. Where such means are abhorrent, fiscal and other indirect devices are employed and the element of state coercion becomes less obvious. These indirect measures are each likely to have a limited scope where consumption is already low, but they are not without effect.

To force down consumption by any means will be a difficult process. More often the practical issue is to what level it will be allowed to rise. The decisions have to be political but their consequences are profoundly economic. This also applies to the degree of inequality of consumption which is tolerated in the process of development. This inequality influences the level and pattern of consumption and may be as significant in the latter respect as in the former since the consumption of the upper income groups makes special demands on such particularly scarce resources as foreign exchange. Therefore, a redistribution of income, or of poverty, to put the point another way, may be required to create the initial conditions necessary to achieve the other economic goals which a nation sets for itself.

TIME HORIZON OF PLANNING

The choice of a time horizon for planning is not just a question of whether there are technical-economic reasons for a five-year plan or a 10- or 20-year plan, though these are important. Even some of the most important projects require long periods to show their full benefits. In addition, the choice of a time horizon also influences the manner in which the sacrifices and benefits of economic growth should be distributed over time. The choice of a planning horizon of fifty years, for example, at the end of which relative austerity would be relaxed, would be one aspect of a decision to deny the present generation any of the fruits of its own labour and sacrifice. A planning horizon of five years may imply the opposite.

There are technical-economic reasons for a longer plan rather than a short plan in the opportunities the former provides for foresight and continuity of effort. These reasons are not finally decisive. For example, a policy of preparation for imminent doomsday would override such arguments and dictate short-term planning in spite of its limitations.

The length of the planning horizon is more usually an implicit rather than an explicit decision in planning. Although this decision affects the path and content of economic growth in an essential, if intricate way, the alternative choices are less fully debated than, say, questions related to current consumption and savings levels which may seem to be more tangible and pressing. The time horizon issues have not been completely ignored. A common policy statement is that the present generation should participate in the benefits of the future economic growth for which it is making sacrifices. An explicit and open policy to the contrary has rarely if ever been enunciated in any country.

Yet the meaning of the policy of participation by the present generation in the returns for present sacrifices has to be spelled out. Today's patriarch cannot expect the same future benefits as the schoolboy. Still, the impossibility of promising fully equal participation does not prevent establishment of some standards of equity. One such standard would be that a representative member of the current population should have a better future. Another, somewhat different criterion would set this goal for an average person in the present labour force. For the application of such criteria the average length of life is important or, more precisely, the average life expectancy of the population or of members of the labour force. For the present population of India as a whole the average life expectancy is in the neighbourhood of thirty-two years. It is substantially less for members of the current labour force. This suggests a limit to the postponement of the enjoyment of the fruits of development on the basis of either of the above standards of equity.

Extending the planning horizon requires a lengthening look with increasing uncertainty about the goals of the future. This uncertainty is itself another limiting factor which must be taken into account in setting a planning horizon.

Rate of Growth of Consumption within the Planning Period

The rate at which consumption is allowed to grow during the plan is, like the choice of a planning horizon, another element in the decision as to how to spread the benefits of economic development over time. Moreover, it affects in a direct way the rate of growth of production and of capital accumulation for further growth. The more quickly consumption is allowed to grow, and the lower the rate of saving out of the increments of production, then the greater the current spread of the benefits of development. Development itself, however, depends on the plowback of increased output into investment. So a too-large or premature diversion to production of consumption goods of the resources which become increasingly available as the result of development could stifle that development.

The decision as to what growth in consumption will be permitted is again a political one. Ordinarily, in free societies, it will be difficult to rule out at least some increase in consumption. As unemployment, open and disguised, is reduced, there will be increasing demands for consumption goods. Another major source of pressure will be the general upgrading of the work force which takes place as part of the process of development: increasing numbers of unskilled workers acquire skills; more persons move into foreman and supervisory status, become higher civil servants, managers, entrepreneurs, and so on. As individuals participate in this process of upgrading their occupations they will also try to upgrade their consumption to the patterns of the new levels they are achieving. Thus the mere maintenance of the present relative supplies of consumption goods will mean growing scarcities of particular types as increasing numbers of persons bid for the apartments, motor scooters, automobiles, etc., of the higher income levels. Denial of these amenities is in turn certain to become a pressing political issue.

The political and economic interconnections between the choice elements in long-term planning are illustrated by the relations between the choice of initial consumption levels and of the rate of growth of consumption during the plan. Suppose the initial level of consumption from which planning starts could be reduced by reduction of the inequalities of consumption. Subsequent upgrading of consumption as occupational levels rise would then mean less overall pressure on consumption. On the other hand, the decision might be that current reduction of the inequalities of consumption is politically more difficult than delaying the upgrading process. Or there may be some planned use of both procedures.

There is, from the standpoint of economics, the fullest flexibility in the rates of consumption growth at various phases of a plan over the planning horizon: fast at first, slow later, or vice versa, or any other pattern. Each pattern of growth rates and each composition would have a different economic significance and each would pose a different political problem. High consumption growth rates in the early plan stages may be justified not only on humane grounds but on those of increasing human stamina or giving necessary encouragement for future sacrifices. On a political evaluation that it is more difficult to hold down consumption once it has begun to grow, just the reverse procedure might be dictated. The detail of alternative patterns of consumption growth must also be considered in order to have a full appreciation of their political as well as economic significance.

Terminal Conditions in Planning

Stipulation of the terminal conditions of an intertemporal plan requires the choice of one or another set of national economic goals in a general sense. These terminal conditions, therefore, may have alternative characterisations. For example, it may be specified as a political decision that at the end of the planning horizon certain minimum consumption levels should be achieved and that some particular rate of growth should be maintainable thereafter. Or it may be stipulated that a particular level of employment should be a terminal condition or that independence from external assistance be established by the end of the plan. The interrelations of the elements of these terminal conditions must be set out and it is also up to the economist to determine, if several final conditions are specified, if they are consistent as well as feasible. The particular year-by-year production targets of a plan are not terminal conditions in themselves but are the implications of such conditions taken together with the values given to the other choice elements. The annual production levels emerge as the result of the total planning process.

The content of the terminal conditions is a political decision: the overall economic goals which it is the nation's objective to achieve by the end of the planning horizon. If the goals are specified in terms of consumption levels, then the politics of consumption levels and distribution are involved in an obvious way. Statements of terminal conditions in terms of resources of productive capacity, i.e., in terms of steel capacity, or dams or power stations or machine tool production, have implications for consumption and saving as well and, therefore, are just as political. If the implications are hidden, the content of the political decisions may be obscure. It is possible that the statement of terminal conditions in terms of productive capacity raises fewer internal political issues just because the consumption, saving, and tax implications are unspecified, though not by any means undetermined.

The choice of terminal conditions for a planning period does not mean there is a lack of concern for succeeding years. Rather, it is a decision about the desired characteristics of a way station in economic growth. These characteristics may include rewards for previous effort and provide also for more future growth depending on political evaluations and satisfaction of economic feasibility requirements.

In the replanning mentioned above the terminal conditions as well as the other choice elements of the intertemporal plan may be modified in the light of new alternatives which become available or new exigencies which must be faced. If a plan is made with standards of equity in mind and if it is regarded as a national compact, the new set of choices should, to the maximum extent possible, provide for no worse standards of life for the population and exploit to the fullest any new opportunities which arise.

II

Substitution among Choice Elements

In plans as in life not every wish can be satisfied and not every element can be chosen independently. There are political constraints which we shall not attempt to explore here and economic constraints which we shall illustrate. These constraints arise out of the economic structure and the interrelationships within it. Four choice elements in intertemporal planning have been identified: the initial levels of consumption, the rate of growth of consumption during the plan period, the planning horizon, and the terminal conditions. Not all can be chosen independently. Once three are stipulated, the feasibility and in that case the magnitude of the fourth is also determined.

Suppose we think in terms of the production of a generalised output which is divided between consumption and investment. We start with the amount of resources available at the beginning of the plan. This availability in this aggregative approach is represented by the stock of capital and the productivity coefficient. As the first decision about one of the choice elements we might stipulate the initial levels of consumption and, thus, also determine the initial use of the available resources in the production of consumption goods and in capital formation. However, we provisionally leave this element to be determined by decisions about the other three choice elements. The terminal conditions will be translated into a specific level of capital stock to be reached at a particular time in the future. The choice of that time determines the planning horizon. Finally, a decision must be made about the choice of the rate of growth of consumption which will be allowed during the plan period.

Not every possible path and set of parameters are consistent, which reflects the constraints of the economic system, but we will consider only those which can be realised. The overall productivity of capital will be taken to be close to that implicit in the Third Five Year Plan. We take, as well, the 1960–61 levels of consumption of roughly 14,000 crores of rupees as the basis for comparison with the initial levels of consumption stipulated by the planning model.

The significance of alternative decisions on the choice elements in long-term planning can now be illustrated by a set of numerical examples. The *planning horizon* is set at fifteen years. The *terminal condition* is set first so that there is *no growth* in capital stock by the end of the planning period. Each row of Table 16.1 shows the necessary change in the *initial consumption* level as compared to that now prevailing as the result of a specification on the *rate of growth of consumption* allowed during the plan.[1] Thus, remembering that the rate of population growth in India is itself about 2 per cent, a small increase in consumption is permissible now, if it is intended that per capita consumption is to remain constant over the next fifteen years and if there is to be no change in the stock of productive resources by the end of the period. If the rate of growth of consumption is set at 4 per cent during the plan period, and everything else remains the same, then in order to give a 2 per cent increase in per capita consumption, current consumption levels must be cut by 4.8 per cent. A 6 per cent rate of increase in consumption implies even greater current sacrifices.

TABLE 16.1

Rate of Growth of Consumption during Plan Period	Required Change in the Initial Level of Consumption
2%	+ 0.4%
4%	– 4.8%
6%	– 10.0%

A more ambitious terminal goal has more austere implications. If the objective is to *double the stock of capital goods* by the end of the 15-year plan period, i.e., to achieve an annual average rate of growth in these resources of slightly less than 5 per cent, we have the conditions of Table 16.2. That is, the terminal goal is achievable with no sacrifice in the current or future levels of per capita consumption. But, let the current level of consumption rise by ever so little, and that goal will not be achieved. If it rises by as much as 0.1 per cent, Table 16.1 says that the capital resources will just be maintained over the plan period. If per capita consumption is allowed to rise during the plan, then there must be greater immediate sacrifice if the terminal condition is to be achieved. There must be a sacrifice of 5 per cent in current consumption for a 4 per cent of growth in the future, of 10 per cent for a 6 per cent rate of growth in consumption over the plan period.

TABLE 16.2

Required Chance in the Initial Level of Consumption	Rate of Growth of Consumption during the Plan Period
2%	+ 0.0%
4%	– 5.0%
6%	– 10.0%

These examples are not intended to be descriptive, though they are approximative with respect to the Indian economy. They are illustrative of the significance of alternative intertemporal planning decisions. They clearly demonstrate that what is done right now does make a great deal of difference for the future. Having a long-term plan, for example, does not encourage complacency or procrastination. Rather, it indicates what must be done immediately and, in the present circumstances, suggests the need for great stringency in continuing the pressures for raising consumption levels if the national goals are to be reached. This in turn implies the need for reviewing policies designed to restrict consumption at the upper income levels in order to share the burdens of sacrifice equitably.

Changing the decision about the planning horizon is not in itself so important in determining the current and future levels of consumption permissible, as is shown in Table 16.3 for a planning horizon of 20 years. Of course, this does not imply that the choice of a planning horizon may not be important on political and equity grounds as discussed above.

TABLE 16.3

Rate of Growth of Consumption during the Plan Period	Required Change in the Initial Level of Consumption	
	If Capital Stock is Not to Grow	If Capital Stock is to Double over the Plan Period
2%	+ 0.3%	+ 0.2%
4%	– 5.0%	– 5.0%
6%	– 10.3%	– 10.3%

Intertemporal, Multi-Sector Planning

The basic components of intertemporal planning have been illustrated in an aggregate model. The next stage would be to elaborate the approach in order to operate in the many-sector detail which constitutes the practical context of development programmes.

Expanding the approach to many sectors also requires more detailed specification of each of the various choice elements. The initial levels of consumption must be described in terms of the items which make up the consumer budget. The choice of a rate of growth of consumption involves decisions about the different growth rates permitted for each one of these items at various stages over the plan period. Only the planning horizon can continue to be given as a single number.

Detailed information is also required about the structural relations between the various sectors, both with respect to their current requirements and their requirements for capital expansion. Interindustry or input-output information is an essential ingredient.

The multi-sector, intertemporal planning model is essentially an extension to many sectors of the simple aggregate model already described. The result of the planning process is the determination, period-by-period, of production levels or targets which are consistent with the decisions made about the choice elements.

The possibility of replanning is always kept open. In fact, the approach is envisaged as a continuing process which permits adjustments to take into account the actual levels of achievement year by year and changes in structural relations.

This type of planning procedure does what an intertemporal plan should do and tells what must be done now in order to achieve distant goals. The approach described here is not one of general optimisation, however, and does not attempt the ambitious task of finding the best of all possible paths of development. It would be desirable to explore the implications of alternative paths by using the methods to be proposed and, in that way, provide a basis for discrimination among them.

By no means all of the problems of intertemporal planning can be handled in any such planning model. Much data collection and statistical estimation must be done outside it and fed into it. Results of the planning process must be interpreted and disaggregated. Fiscal and monetary issues have to be handled separately. Yet an intertemporal planning procedure provides the focus necessary to make all these separate activities coherent.

APPENDIX

The simple, aggregative model underlying the numerical examples is familiar to economists. The following variables and parameters are used:

- $Y(t)$ — National income or output in period t
- $C(t)$ — total consumption in period t is Ce^{rt} where C is the initial level of consumption and r the rate of growth of consumption chosen for the interplan period
- $K(t)$ — the capital stock existing in period t
- $I(t)$ — investment, or the change in capital stock, in period t, or $K(t)$

h — the output-capital ratio, or $Y(t)/K(t)$, which is set at 1/2.5 or 0.4

t — the planning period

The initial level of capital stock $K(0)$ is set at 37,000 crores of rupees. Then, substituting into the basic national income equation,

$$Y(t) = C(t) + I(t)$$

We get $hK(t) = Ce^{rt} + K\ (t)$. This is a simple differential equation which is the basis of the numerical examples.

Since this is a first order equation, it determines a one-parameter family of solutions. Further, since C is an unknown of this problem, our solution is really a member of a two-parameter family of solutions. Specification of initial and terminal capital stocks enables us to determine a specific solution in this class.

The qualitative results are independent of the value of parameters chosen.

Note

[1] These tables are based on a simple, aggregative model which is outlined in a brief Appendix.

17

Structural Linkages in the Indian Economy*

Krishna K. Bharadwaj

The intersectoral relations on the production side could be of two types. An activity (using this term interchangeably with sector industry) could depend on another whose output it utilises in its production. The linkage in this respect is of the *backward* type and is represented by the columns of the input-output table. Alternatively, the structural relations could be analysed in terms of an activity supplying its output as an input to other activities; this, represented by the rows of the input-output matrix, is designated as the *forward* linkage. A very rough measure of the extent of a sector's interconnections with the others in the economy is provided on the input side by the ratio of a sector's purchases from all other sectors to its total output:

$\sum_{j=1}^{M} X_{ij}$ where M—number of sectors, X_{ij} = deliveries from the ith sector to the jth sector and X_j = total output of the jth sector) and on the deliveries side, by the ratio of intermediate demand for the output of a given sector to its total demand or availability.

$$(\text{i.e.,} \sum_{j=1}^{M} X_{ij}$$

$$Xi \mid Xis + Xmi$$

* Originally published in *Economic Weekly* 14, no. 33 (11 August 1962), pp. 1339–42.

Xi = output of ith sector.
Where Xis = net changes in inventories of the ith sector, and
Xmi = imports in the ith sector.)

These ratios have been used to identify what have been called "key industries," to study structural change in an economy over time, and to make international structural comparisons. These, in the case of the *Indian Table* were observed to be as in Table 17.1.

TABLE 17.1: STRUCTURAL LINKAGES IN THE INDIAN ECONOMY

Description Sector and Code (in brackets)		Backward linkage	Forward linkage
High (above 50 per cent) backward with high (above 50 per cent) *Forward Linkage*		$\dfrac{\sum_{i=1}^{M} X_{ij}}{Xj} \times 100$	$\dfrac{\sum_{i=1}^{M} X_{ij}}{Xi + Xis + Xmi} \times 100$
Other Metals	(7)*	70	86
Cement	(10)	55	98
Chemicals	(9)	53	71
Iron and Steel	(6)	57	85
Leather	(17)	57	52
Small-Scale Metal Products	(20)	53	61
Food, Drink, and Tobacco	(12)	66	23
Cotton Textiles	(13)	60	27
Other Textiles	(14)	59	36
Jute and other Fibers	(15)	57	20
Small-Scale, Food, Drink, Tobacco	(23)	62	5
Small-Scale others (nec)	(26)	58	41
Other Transport	(28)	64	14
Constructions	(32)	54	**
Defence Materials	(35)	±	6
Low Backward with High Forward Linkage			
Plantations	(2)	19	95
Animal Husbandry	(3)	43	56
Coke and Coal	(4)	18	78
All Other Minings	(5)	9	74
Building Materials	(11)	36	58
Glass and Glassware	(16)	45	61
Electricity	(19)	33	68

Small Scale: Building Materials	(21)	21	70
Banks, Insurance, etc.	(30)	17	67
Large Scale, unclassified	(36)	15	67
Communications	(27B)	11	(52)
Engineering	(8)	43	53
Low Backward and Low Forward Linkage			
Agriculture	(1)	23	32
Paper and Paperboard		41	31
Small Scale, Textiles	22)	41	3
-do- Glassware	(24)	22	–
-do- Leather Products	(25)	40	–
Railways	(27A)	25	33
Trade and Distribution	(29)	14	23
Personal and Institutional Services	(31)	14	17
Residential Property	(33)	3	–
Public Administration	(34)	n.a.	1

* Numbers in brackets indicate sector codes as in the input-output table.
** All deliveries to final demand.
± No information was available regarding value added in the sector; consequently, output was equated to material inputs.

Although the numerical results as presented in the table speak for themselves, a few observations are in order. It will be noticed that the intermediate activities like metals, cement, chemicals, etc., have higher values for both backward and forward linkages. The consumption-oriented activities, like textiles, food, drink, and tobacco, possess a high backward linkage but a low forward linkage. This is natural since a greater proportion of their output goes to final demand. The primary activities, like animal husbandry and plantations, show a weaker backward but stronger forward linkage.

However, the linkage effects calculated as above, are extremely aggregative. Also, being an average measure, they do not give the distribution of the inputs for deliveries amongst various sectors. They assume thus implicitly that the indirect or secondary linkage effects that might arise due to the simultaneous character of production relations are proportional to the direct or primary linkages in whatever manner the inputs (or deliveries) might be distributed. Thus, for example, they cannot differentiate between a sector with a very skewed input or deliveries distribution (meaning dependence entirely or highly on only a few inputs or deliveries entirely or in the most part to a few sectors) and another whose structural relations might be more evenly characterised. The use of these ratios to estimate structural characteristics intertemporally or internationally, or to draw generalisations regarding the relative importance of the sectors is rather limited since these aggregative rough comparisons do not allow for the variety of production structures which are to be estimated or compared.

Limited Operational Use

The operational meaningfulness of these ratios is extremely circumscribed. It would be erroneous, for example, to claim, in absence of other supporting evidence, that a high backward linkage necessarily implies that by increasing the particular sector's output we set into operation more powerful stimuli to expand the output of input-providing industries other than in the case of a sector with a lower backward linkage effect. A high backward linkage ratio could come about either because of heavier reliance on purchased inputs measured in absolute amounts or as a consequence of low productivity of inputs used, which makes the input-output ratio high. The economic implications of the two situations are extremely different. It could then be observed that a manufacturing activity operating with an advanced technique and on a large scale might have an equivalent ratio to that of a small-scale household enterprise. This would occur for the simple reason that whereas high market-reliance for the inputs in the case of the former tends to increase the numerator in the ratio as compared to the latter, its higher productivity vis-à-vis the latter might also tend to increase the denominator relatively to that in the case of the small-scale enterprise. The two tendencies might balance to give equivalent ratios in the two cases, or might even in some cases give a lower backward linkage effect for the more productive technology enterprise. The same objection could be raised against international structural comparisons based on these ratios between countries of unequal development. Moreover, even when two activities producing the same output and operating on different scales have the same backward linkage, the effectiveness of the stimulus provided by them to the input-providing activities might be different since the scale of their operation would determine the absolute magnitudes of inputs required. This would be so especially when initiation and not merely expansion of input-providing activities is concerned.

A more refined way of estimating structural interconnections is suggested by Rasmussen.[1] He defines an index of power of dispersion as

$$U_j = \frac{\overset{i}{M}}{\frac{1}{M^2}\sum_{j=1}^{M} Z_j} \qquad (j - 1, 2 \ldots m)$$

where m = no. of sectors,

$$Zj = \sum_{1 = i}^{M} Zij$$

where Zij is an element in ith row and jth column of the inverse matrix $(I - A)^{-1}$, A being the matrix of input coefficients. The economic significance of the index Uj is akin to the backward linkage effect; as this index is based on the inverse matrix of input coefficients, it takes into account both direct and indirect intersectoral dependence and "describes the relative extent to which an increase in final demand for the products of industry no. j is dispersed throughout the system of industries" or "the extent of the expansion caused in the system of industries in general by an expansion in industry no. j."[2] The magnitude of the index exceeding unity would imply that any industry taken at random will need a comparatively large production increase to make feasible the unit increase in the final demand for the output of industry no j. Analogous to the forward linkage effect is defined another index, namely that of sensitivity of dispersion. Represented symbolically it is:

$$Uj = \frac{\frac{1}{M} Zj}{\frac{1}{M^2} \sum_{j = 1}^{M} Zij} \qquad (i - 1, 2 \ldots m^5)$$

$$\text{where} = Zi = \sum_{j = 1}^{M} Zij$$

(other symbols as in previous representation). It expresses "the extent to which the system of industries draws upon industry no. i," or, in other words, the extent to which industry no. i is affected by an expansion in the system of industries.[3] For reasons mentioned, these average measures need to be supplemented by a measure of variability or characteristic parameters describing the distribution of Z_{ij} for given j and i = 1, 2 … n and vice versa. These are defined as two indices V_j and V_i, the former indicating the extent to which industry no. j draws on the system of industries evenly or otherwise and the latter, in its turn, indicating the extent to which the system of industries draw evenly or otherwise on the output of sector i. Symbolically,

$$Vij = \frac{\sqrt{\frac{1}{M - 1} \sum_{j = 1}^{M} \left(Zij\, 1 - \frac{1}{M} \bullet Zij\right)^2}}{Zij}$$

$$\text{and } Vi = \frac{\sqrt{\frac{1}{M-1}\sum_{1=1}^{M}\left(Zij - \frac{1 \bullet Zi}{M}\right)^2}}{Zi}$$

Thus, whereas a high value for V_j implies that industry no. j depends for its inputs heavily on a few sectors, that for V_i implies that the output of sector i is absorbed relatively highly by only a few sectors of the economy. These four indices were computed for the Indian economy and have been shown in Table 17.2.

TABLE 17.2: INDICES OF POWER OF DISPERSION, SENSITIVITY OF DISPERSION AND MEASURES OF VARIABILITY COMPUTED FOR THE INDIAN ECONOMY

Description and Code (in brackets)		Power of Dispersion U	Variability V_j	Sensitivity of Dispersion U_i	Variability V_i
High (exceeding unity) value of V_j and V_i					
Other Metals	(7)	1.2735	3.8336	1.2222	3.9431
Chemicals	(9)	1.1427	4.0356	1.4835	3.1474
Cotton Textiles	(13)	1.2138	3.9830	1.1951	4.0420
Iron and Steel	(8)	1.0623	3.7118	1.1481	3.4459
High Value for U_j and Low (Less than Unity) for U_i					
Defence Materials	(35)	1.5222	2.7269	0.6709	5.8098
Other Textiles	(14)	1.2203	3.7416	0.8424	5.3834
Small Scale: Food, Drink, Tobacco	(23)	1.2173	3.4322	0.6601	5.7288
Small Scale: Other (N E C)	(26)	1.2168	3.4225	0.8547	4.6285
Other Transport (Excluding Railways)	(28)	1.2151	3.1763	0.8383	4.4409
Large Scale: Food, Drink, Tobacco	(12)	1.1998	3.5897	0.8989	4.44386
Small Scale: Metal and Metal Wares	(20)	1.1793	3.2848	0.6522	5.7252
Leather Manufactures	(17)	1.1740	3.3112	0.7571	5.0979
Jute Manufactures	(15)	1.1209	3.6198	0.8006	4.8461
Cement	(10)	1.1092	2.8197	0.6729	5.8371
Trade and Distribution	(29)	0.7468	5.1230	2.7226	1.4217
Glass and Glassware	(16)	1.0113	3.7625	0.6470	5.8371

Agriculture	(1)	0.8443	5.0311	2.6492	2.1569
Animal Husbandry	(3)	0.9972	4.2885	2.0122	2.0696
Nonferrous Metals	(5)	0.7072	5.4956	1.7467	2.3034
Coal and Coke	(4)	0.7858	4.9946	1.1190	3.5092
Railways and communication	(27)	0.8384	4.4963	1.0724	3.4776
Low value for both U_j and U_i					
Plantations	(2)	0.7838	4.7811	0.8092	4.6175
Building Materials	(11)	0.9924	3.2006	0.6912	5.4348
Paper and Paperboard	(18)	0.9924	4.1975	0.8273	5.0096
Electricity	(19)	0.9138	4.3460	0.8284	4.7537
Small Scale: Building Materials	(21)	0.8293	4.4951	0.7055	5.2924
Banks, Insurance, etc.	(30)	0.7574	4.9689	0.7136	5.2547
Personal & Institutional Services	(31)	0.7490	4.9674	0.8409	4.4346
Large Scale N E S	(36)	0.7874	4.7821	0.7733	4.8550

Comparing Tables 17.1 and 17.2, we observe that the rankings of the sectors would be somewhat different depending upon which method is adopted. To illustrate, whereas sector 8 (engineering) has a low backward linkage and a high forward linkage according to Table 17.1, it has both high power and sensitivity of dispersion as in Table 17.2. However, the variability of the distribution of inputs and deliveries does not seem to create any great problem in this case, since those sectors which generally have lower values for either power or sensitivity of dispersion or for both have generally a higher corresponding variability index. Interestingly enough, we notice that the small-scale sectors— generally known for their low productivity in India — compare well with their highly organised counterparts in the manufacturing sector, strengthening our earlier contention that lower productivity might counteract lower intersectoral purchases to give a high backward linkage effect.

II

The backward linkages, especially, have received considerable attention as a basis for fixing investment priorities, particularly in the "productive" sectors (meaning sectors producing physical commodity outputs), a sector with a higher linkage effect being favoured.[4] A number of objections could be raised against such an approach. The inclusion of this tool in the criteria-box is based upon the fact of technological interdependence, namely, "that every non-primary economic activity will induce attempts to supply through domestic production the inputs needed in that activity [backward linkage effect] and every activity that does not by its nature cater exclusively to final demand will induce attempts to utilise its outputs as inputs in some new activities" (forward linkage effect).[5]

The backward linkage effects are considered to be stronger than the forward linkage effects in inducing development through compulsive sequences. It is, of course, recognised that the strength of these effects, interpreted as the probability that the derived demand for the input-providing industries would succeed in establishing those industries or in expanding their output, is different from the potential importance of linkage effects. A realistic assessment of the total effective linkage effect will have to be based on the summation of the products of potentially inducible net outputs in other industries and the probabilities that they might so be induced.[6] Even with this modification these ratios might not be of much help in fixing up sectoral priorities. The very simultaneous character of economic relations on the production side which forms the theoretical justification of an input-output system would favour a choice between alternative programmes rather than between individual sectors. The combined backward linkage effect of two sectors might add greatly to the induced occurrence of an industry which, considered individually, might have had very little effectiveness. This might be particularly so in cases where the economically profitable size of the induced industries requires higher demand than set by either of the sectors individually.[7] The probability that one would attach to the potentially induced outputs, therefore, would depend upon the complete investment programme.

The structural relationships as depicted in the input-output scheme are instantaneous; still pictures abstracted from time patterns of inputs and outputs and investment priorities based upon the comparison of two activities as such will be very crude indeed. Moreover, the three most significant constraints, namely those of capital, labour, and foreign exchange are kept out of the picture.[8] Treating inputs on a separate basis from domestic production would be ignoring the possibility of domestic production as a substitute for imports. Treating them, on the other hand, as not different from domestically available inputs would assume away the special difficulties in paying for imports. The labour constraint (specified either in terms of minimum employment desirable or maximum skilled labour available) or the capital constraint (the maximum available capital) cannot be explicitly treated, implying that both capital and labour of the specific type would flow into the industry as and when required and in appropriate amounts.

No Guarantee of Growth Potential

However, technological interdependence alone is no guarantee of the growth potential of a sector. The linear homogeneity and additivity assumptions underlying the input-output analysis neither allow for the existence of external economies or diseconomies nor for a divergence between marginal and average input requirements which are at the heart of the problem of growth and consequently crucial for investment decisions. The divergence between marginal and average input requirements might be predominant, especially in land and natural-resource-oriented activities. Considerations of returns to scale are even more significant to the underdeveloped countries. Hirschman, among others, suggests that the input-output relationships as depicted in an advanced country's technology matrix could be utilised fruitfully to determine sectoral priorities since the technical relations are more or less evolved completely in their case. With many reservations,[9] such a technology matrix could be, at best, viewed as a terminal picture to be attained. It would not, however, offer the strategy to attain it. Such a procedure would assume away the real problem of growth, namely the maximisation of productivity through reaping the maximum benefits of external economies and increasing returns to scale whose sector-wise magnitude and location are bound to be different in an underdeveloped country from that of a developed one.

Another equally important aspect of economic interdependence—namely, that on the demand side—is totally left out, at least in the open input-output system, where consumption is exogenously determined. Thus, income effects are completely ignored. Whereas the input-output scheme would be useful to approximate the production requirements of a given final demand vector or to adjudge the compatibility of a set of production targets, it would, in absence of complementary information, dictate very little as to the significance of different activities in the final goods sector.

Productivity of the activities will have to be separately considered. If the same output is produced by two activities and depicted as columns in the input-output scheme, one requiring twice the amount of inputs as the other per unit of output, the former would not be a desirable activity despite its higher linkages. What is required is not the maximisation of a certain statistical ratio for whatever it stands. The targeted programmes will have their varying welfare contents depending upon their composition, and the problem as to which sector, in what magnitudes and at what "cost" are the linkage effects propagated is an extremely important consideration.

As is clear from Tables 17.1 and 17.2, the backward linkage effects (or the power of dispersion) and the forward linkage effects (or the sensitivity of dispersion) differ markedly in many sectors, for instance, in agriculture. The fact that a primary activity does not draw heavily on material inputs does not reduce its importance in the economic structure. It might be a very important "input-provider," in which case the index of sensitivity of dispersion might be as important a consideration for growth as the index of power of dispersion. Whereas, it is true to a certain extent, that by setting high stimulus to provide inputs, growth could be more quickly generated, this process of creating compulsive sequences has its own limitations.

Inputs whose production is more-or-less demand inelastic, in particular, whose economic scale of operation is much beyond the extent of the stimulus or whose marginal requirements differ significantly from average, might have to be provided for to begin with, irrespective of their low backward linkages.

Thus, whereas the input-output system could be used profitably for determining the compatibility of a targeted programme or to analyse static situations or even, within limits, for purposes of short-run projections, its use for setting investment priorities is questionable.

Notes and References

[1] P. N. Rasmussen, *Studies in Inter-sectoral Relations* (Amsterdam: North Holland Publishing Company, 1956).

[2] Ibid., p. 135.

[3] Ibid., p. 136.

[4] Even the proponents of this criterion accept that it cannot be applied to sectors like transportation (where capital inputs are more significant than flow coefficients) and other social overheads like communications.

[5] A. O. Hirschman, *Op Cit, The Strategy of Economic Development* (New Haven: Yale University Press, 1958), p. 100.

[6] Ibid., p. 101.

[7] Hirschman recognises this fact explicitly (Ibid., pp. 103–04) and points out the possibility of cumulative development through such occurrences. However, he does not carry the logic of his statements further, which invalidates any probabilistic estimates attached to the derived demand effects independent of the entire investment programme chosen.

[8] A closed input-output model could bring the labour and foreign exchange inputs within its framework only at the cost of realism by assuming strict technical relations to hold in the foreign trade and the household sectors also.

[9] The optimal pattern of technical relations to be attained by an economy would be entirely based on its own resource base and ophelimity patterns.

18

Relative Rates of Growth

Agriculture and Industry*

Ashok Rudra

One, of course, knows qualitatively the effects to be anticipated. Shortage of agricultural raw materials for domestic industries would tend to slow down the growth of industries dependent on such raw materials. Shortage of agricultural products for export would reduce foreign exchange earnings. Shortage of foodgrains, other food products, and consumer goods based on agriculture would exert pressure on their respective prices; the pressure would be transmitted to wages which in turn would tend to raise the general level of prices. If the shortages are to be met by imports, it would be necessary to curtail the import of capital goods and raw materials for industries and this in turn would tend to reduce the growth of the industries sectors unless, of course, one is capable of as well as prepared to draw upon external assistance to an indefinite extent.

What we propose to do in the present paper is to obtain certain quantitative measures of these effects. It may be emphasised that the numerical results presented here are of more than illustrative value. They are as much relevant to policy making purposes as any numerical results based on Indian economic statistics may ever be. We can make this assertion as the model from which the results are derived is not a demonstration model but a planning model the parameters of which have been estimated on the basis of extensive empirical research.

* Originally published in *Economic Weekly* 16, no. 45 (7 November 1964), pp. 1773–88. (Most of the mathematical and computational results presented in this chapter have been borrowed by the writer from the research works of Smt. Pushpam and Shri A. V. Ramsunder. The writer alone is, however, personally responsible for the interpretation made of them. The official organisations with which he is associated also have no responsibility for the results and views presented.)

We shall examine the dependence of industry on agriculture in three of its aspects, namely, (1) industry's dependence on agriculture as a supplier of raw materials and as a consumer of industrial raw materials and capital goods; (2) industrial wage earners' dependence on agriculture for the supply of wage goods and raw materials for industrial wage goods; and (3) industry's dependence on foreign exchange earned by agriculture.

As to inter-industrial interdependence, it does not require any model to observe that the interdependence is not of such a nature as to impose a limit on the growth rate of the industry sector as a whole, given the growth rate of agriculture as a whole. That is because, while it is easy to think of industries that are directly and totally dependent on agricultural raw materials (e.g., rice and wheat milling, sugar, vegetable oil, and vanaspati, jute, textile, cotton textile, leather products etc.), it is equally easy to identify industries that are not even remotely dependent on agriculture for any of their important raw materials. Moreover, it is to this latter group that the so-called heavy industries that have been picked out in our planning for top priority treatment belong. Steel, aluminium, cement, fertilisers, machinery, petroleum refining, and such industries can develop at rates quite independent of the rate of growth of agriculture. The industrial products consumed by agriculture are also not of such a proportion to the total supply of industrial products as to make much difference to the growth of industries taken as a whole. It can, therefore, be stated that one can go ahead with a programme of industrial development at the annual rate of 12 per cent or any other rate without any physical bottlenecks arising from a low rate of growth of agriculture, provided that one remembers that a relatively slow rate of growth of industries directly dependent on agriculture would have to be counterbalanced by a relatively high rate of growth of other industries dependent primarily on minerals.

While one may presume this feature of the relationship between agriculture and industry from one's general knowledge about different economies, the extent to which it is true of a particular economy can only be known as a result of empirical research. The degree of inter-industrial dissociation between agriculture and industries directly based on agriculture on the one hand and the rest of the economy on the other is sharply brought out by the following inter-industry table for Indian economy for 1960–61 (Table 18.1). The corresponding inter-industrial coefficient matrix is presented in Table 18.2. If one chooses to substitute a coefficient by zero every time the corresponding flow in 1960–61 constitutes less than 5 per cent of the total flow (note that this condition has no relation with that of the coefficient being smaller than .05), we obtain the coefficient matrix given in Table 18.2a. It would follow that the inter-industrial feasibility conditions may be approximately written as:

TABLE 18.1: INTER-INDUSTRIAL TRANSACTIONS FOR INDIA 1960–61

(In Rs. crores at 1959–60 producers' prices)

Output of Sector	Input into Sector			Other Industries	Total Inter-mediate Consum-ption	House-hold Consum-ption	Govt. Consum-ption	Gross Capital Formu-lation	Export	Import	Stocks	Total Final Demand	Gross Output
	1	2	3										
1. Agriculture and Industries Based on Agriculture	2,059.7	187.8	21.0	206.6	2,475.1	7,220.7	104.9	–	401.1	322.0	197.7	7,611.4	1,00,805
2. Mining and Industries Based on Mining	106.7	1,126.4	159.8	147.0	1,600.8	500.2	225.1	2,002.0	57.9	790.9	33.2	2,036.5	3,637.3
3. Coal, electricity Railways and Motor Transport	199.3	232.3	137.9	276.7	846.2	219.2	4.7	–	1.8	0.1	0.2	225.8	1,072.0

Note: See Note 1 for explanations.

$$x_{1t} \geq 0.204\, x_{1t} \quad (1)$$
$$x_{2t} \geq 0.310\, x_{2t} \quad (2)$$
$$x_{3t} \geq 0.030\, x_{3t} + 0.064\, x_{2t} + 0.129\, x_{3t} \quad (3)$$

Where x_{it} is the output level of sector i in year t, measured in the producer's prices of 1959–60. The first two conditions being tautologically true, it follows that the growth rate of the first does not exert any influence at all on the growth rate of the second and vice versa.

TABLE 18.2: INPUT COEFFICIENTS 1960–61

Output	Input sectors		
	1	2	3
1	0.204	0.052	0.020
2	0.017	0.310	0.149
3	0.020	0.064	0.129

TABLE 18.2A: INPUT COEFFICIENTS 1960–61

Output	Input Sectors		
	1	2	3
1	0.204	0	0
2	0	0.310	0
3	0.020	0.064	0.120

In order to study the dependence of industry on agriculture as the supplier of wage goods and the earner of foreign exchange, we replace the inequalities written above by equalities by stipulating conditions to be satisfied by final demand; we also allow for a non-zero coefficient for the input of industrial raw materials into agriculture, to take care of likely technological changes in the latter. To start with we write:

$$x_{1t} - a_{11}\, x_{1t} = h_{1t} + g_{1t} + s_{1t} + o_{1t} + e_{1t} - m_{1t} \quad (4)$$
$$x_{2t} - a_{21}\, x_{1t} - a_{22}\, x_{2t} = h_{2t} + g_{2t} + s_{2t} + o_{2t} + c_{2t} - m_{2t} + k_t \quad (5)$$
$$x_{3t} - a_{31}\, x_{1t} - a_{32}\, x_{2t} - a_{33} + x_{3t} = h_{3t} + g_{3t} + s_{3t}\, o_{3t} \quad (6)$$

where a_{ij} is the usual inter-industrial coefficient, h_{it} household consumption of commodity i in year t, g_{it} government consumption, e_{it} its export, m_{it} the import, and s_{it} the addition to stocks. o_{it} is intermediate consumption in sectors not covered by the left-hand side of the equation. k_t stands for capital formation, and the sectors have been defined in such a way that the commodities that go into capital formation—machinery and construction—are all products of sector 2. Also, the third sector is so defined that it has neither exports nor imports. The unit of measurement all through is the constant price of 1959–60.

In order to study the mutual relation between the rates of growth of output x_{it}, available supply for household consumption h_{it}, and available supply for net exports $(e_{it} - m_{it})$, we eliminate from the above equations the other expressions—namely, g_{it}, s_{it}, o_{it}, and k_t—by making suitable assumptions about them. Government consumption, g_{it}, we treat as an exogenous variable taking the value g_{it}^0. Stock formation and consumption by the residual sectors, s_{it} and o_{it}, we treat as proportional to the level of output:

$$s_{it} + o_{it} = x_{it}\, b_{it}$$

As to capital formation, k_t, we assume that it is made up of two parts, a part k_{dt} financed by domestic savings and a part k_{ft} financed by external assistance. We treat k_{dt} as bearing a certain proportion to the household consumption of the products of the sectors considered:

$$k_{dt} = \theta_t\,(h_{1t} + h_{2t} + h_{3t}) \tag{7}$$

As to k_{ft} we treat it as equal to the surplus of imports over export earnings:

$$k_{ft} = (m_{1t} + m_{2t}) - (e_{1t} + e_{2t}) - e_0 \tag{8}$$

Where e_0 is the invisible earnings plus domestic trade and transport margin on exports (see note 2).

Basing ourselves on the inter-industry table for 1960–61 and making allowances for structural changes to be expected between this base period and 1970–71, one may make the following numerical assumptions for t = 1970 (see note 3):

$\theta = 0.35$	e_0 = Rs. 220 crores
$b = 0.050$	g_1^0 = Rs. 250 crores
$b^1 = 0.030$	g_2^0 = Rs. 560 crores
$b_3^2 = 0.300$	g_a^0 = Rs. 10 crores

$$0.746\, x_1 = h_1 + (e_1 - m_1) + 250 \tag{9}$$

$$0.640\, x_2 - 0.040\, x_1 = h_2 - (e_1 - m_1) + (h_1 + h_2 + h_3) \tag{10}$$

$$0.35 + 340$$

$$0.571\, x_3 - 0.020\, x_1 - 0.064\, x_2 = h_3 + 10 \tag{11}$$

An interesting feature of the set of equations written above is that only the export surplus of sector 1 enters the picture: *no assumptions are required and no results derivable about export and import of the second sector. Further, the rate of growth of industries (sector 2) is directly dependent on the rate of domestic savings but has no relation with the rate of investment.*

We shall now try to answer the following questions:

(1) What are the "balanced" relative rates of growth of the sectors valid for the period 1960–61 to 1970–71 that would ensure that the relative prices would remain steady all through at the 1959–60 levels?
(2) What would be the pressure on prices of consumer goods if the relative rates of growth be different from the balanced rates?
(3) If the pressure on prices is to be averted by drawing upon the rest of the world, what would be the pressure of foreign exchange shortage?

In order to answer the first question, we shall assume for e_1 a given projection representing the maximum extent of agricultural exports possible by 1970–71, namely, Rs. 570 crores. We shall also assume for m_1 the relation:

$$m_1 = m_1^* = 0.010\, x_1 \tag{12}$$

Where m_1^* represents the minimum content of non-competitive imports in the supply of agricultural goods visualised for 1970–71 (See Note 5).

We may therefore write the following relations between the output levels and available supply for household consumption:

$$0.756x_1 = h_1 + 820 \tag{13}$$
$$0.640x_2 - 0.050x_1 = (h_1 + h_2 + h_3)\, 0.35 + h_2 - 230 \tag{14}$$
$$0.571x_3 - 0.064\, x_2 - 0.020\, x_1 = h_3 + 10 \tag{15}$$

We now make use of the following conditions to be satisfied by h_1, h_2, and h_3 if the relative prices are to remain unchanged at the 1959–60 levels—a result derived by a modified application of the linear expenditure system developed by Professor Richard Stone and his associates to National Sample Survey household consumption data (see note 4 for more details about the econometric basis of the results):

$$h_2 = 0.07485\, h_1 - 24.96 \tag{16}$$
$$h_3 = 0.03226\, h_1 - 10.76 \tag{17}$$

The striking simplicity of these two linear relations need not give rise to any scepticism about their accuracy or validity: the demand function on the basis of which they have been arrived at provide very much better fit to NSS demand patterns over the different rounds than any other tool of demand analysis that has been tried upon them so far.

Substitution of the relations (16) and (17) in (13), (14), and (15) yield the following linear relations in the output levels:

$$x_2 = 0.623x_1 - 1011.20 \quad (18)$$
$$x_3 = 0.147x_1 - 167.06 \quad (19)$$

These relations permit us to calculate alternative sets of "balanced" relative rates of growth. The results are presented in Table 3 . We notice that the *assumption being very widely made currently that a 5 per cent rate of growth of agriculture is in balance with a 12 per cent rate of growth of industry is very much off the mark.* A 12 per cent rate of growth of industry calls for a 6.9 per cent rate of growth of agriculture.

TABLE 18.3: BALANCED RELATIVE RATES OF GROWTH

Sector 1 Agriculture	Sector 2 Industries	Sector 3 Coal, Electricity, and Transport
1	2	3
.02	6.21	4.30
.03	7.41	5.50
.04	8.57	6.59
.05	9.75	7.71
.069	12.00	9.80

Note: See Note 4 for explanation.

We now take up the third question. We consider four alternative rates of growth for agriculture, namely, 2 per cent, 8 per cent, 4 per cent, and 5 per cent per annum, and a constant rate of growth of 10 per cent per annum for industries. We also consider the combination 12 per cent rate of growth for industries and 5 per cent rate of growth for agriculture. For each combination we calculate for 1970–71 on the basis of the conditions of (i) the relative prices of consumer goods remaining stable and (ii) export targets of Rs. 570 crores for agriculture, Rs. 200 (in producer's prices) crores for industries and Rs. 220 for invisibles (including trade and transport margin on commodity exports) the following:

(1) the volume of import of foodgrains and other food products necessary to keep prices stable;
(2) deficit in foreign exchange earnings if import is to be strictly restricted to non-competitive items only; and

(3) the competitive import of industrial products and the corresponding gap in foreign exchange earnings and requirements if a desired level of gross fixed capital formation is to be reached, irrespective of the available supply of domestic savings for the purpose. The results are presented in Table 18.4.

The algebraic basis of the computations are as follows. By substituting in (9) and (10) for fe_a and h_3 from (16) and (17) and eliminating h_1, we get the following expression for the export surplus of sector 1.

$$e_1 - m_1 = 0.268\, x_1 - 0.488\, x_2 + 127.842 \tag{20}$$

This permits us to calculate h_1 from equation (9) and h_2, h_3, and k_d from relations (16), (17) and (7). In order to calculate the minimum volume of imports, in addition to (12), we make the following assumption for the non-competitive imports content of the supply of sector 2 products:

$$m_2 \text{ (in producer's prices)} = 0.085\, x_1 \tag{21}$$

As to competitive imports, the results for agriculture $m_1 - m_1$ (in producer's prices) are arrived at by using (20) for export surplus together with the given projection for e_1 and the definition (12) for non-competitive imports. In order to calculate the noncompetitive imports $m_2 - m_2$ (in producer's prices) of industrial goods, we assume that the target for gross fixed capital formation to be achieved irrespective of the growth rates of agriculture and industry is Rs. 6,176 crores, the value at market price corresponding to the "balanced" rates of growth of 6–9 per cent and 12 per cent for which case competitive imports are assumed to be zero. (For further details see Note 5).

It may be noted that for the combination 5 per cent rate for agriculture and 12 per cent for industry, capital formation under assumption A (Rs. 6,454.6 crores) is more than the figure corresponding to the "balanced" combination (Rs. 6,176.6 crores). This may be interpreted as meaning that the imbalance of the combination (5 per cent, 12 per cent) is such that the non-competitive import requirements alone would generate an import surplus and result in a capital formation higher than would follow from the balanced combination (6.0 per cent, 12 per cent). While the balanced combination would result in a fixed capital formation of Rs. 6,176.6 crores with only Rs. 160.5 crores of deficit in foreign exchange, the unbalanced combination would result in a fixed capital formation of Rs. 6,454.6 crores but at the cost of a deficit of Rs. 1,035.6 crores in foreign exchange!

We now take up the second question, namely, what the pressure on prices would be if foreign exchange deficit is not to be allowed to increase beyond the requirements of non-competitive imports. In order to treat of prices we have to

TABLE 18.4: FOREIGN EXCHANGE DEFICITS RESULTING FROM UNBALANCED GROWTH

Rates of Growth		Competitive Import of Agricultural Products	Competitive import Industries Products		Deficit of Foreign Exchange		Gross Fixed Capital Formulation	
Agriculture	Industry		Assumption A	Assumption B	Assumption A	Assumption B	Assumption A	Assumption B
1	2	3	4	5	6	7	8	9
2%	10%	1,215.1	–	722.5	1,150.1	1,872.6	5,381.9	6,176.6
3%	10%	870.8	–	818.3	818.4	1,636.7	5,276.5	6,176.6
4%	10%	501.7	–	921.0	462.8	1,383.8	5,163.5	6,176.6
5%	10%	85.8	–	1,036.7	62.1	1,098.8	5,036.2	6,176.6
5%	12%	001.0	–	–	1,035.6	1,035.6	6,454.6	6,454.6
6.9%	12%	–	–	–	160.5	160.5	6,176.6	6,176.6

Assumption A: No competitive industrial imports deficit determined by minimum import requirements over and above a fixed projection for export earnings of Rs. 990 crores.

Assumption B: Foreign exchange deficit determined by shortfall of domestic savings below desired level of gross capital formation.

Note: See Note 5 for explanation.

introduce a commodity classification scheme different from the sector classification scheme used so far. Once again we consider only three groups, but this time the groups are: foodgrains, other food, and non-food products. On the basis of the eighty sectors inter-industry table for 1960–61 and making allowance for higher rate of consumption of industrial products in agriculture as before and also making similar or identical assumptions regarding government consumption, intermediate consumption in other sectors, stock formation, and fixed capital formation, we find that we can write the following set of equations where X_i stands for the output of commodity i and H_i, G_i, E_i, M_i, etc., different modes of final consumption of the products:

$$H_1 = 0.874\, x_1 - 0.026\, x_2 \quad (22)$$
$$H_2 = 0.712\, x_2 - 500 \quad (23)$$
$$1.35\, H_3 = 0.502\, x_3 - 0.040\, x_2 - 0.040\, x_1 - 0.35\, H_1 - 0.35\, H_2 \quad (24)$$

We can now write for H_1, H_2, and H_3 the following equations in terms of their prices (expressed as index numbers with base at 1950–60):

$$p_1 (H_1\, 12.07 \text{ X } 10^{-4} - 8.7206) - p_2 (H_2\, 4.98 \text{ X } 10^{-4} - 1.5897) - p_3 (H_3\, 11.51 \text{ X } 10^{-4} - 1.7690) = 0 \quad (25)$$
$$-p_1 (H_1\, 5.64 \text{ X } 10^{-4} - 1.7375) + p_2 (H_2\, 9.62 \text{ X } 10^{-4} - 2.9737) - p_3 (H_3\, 9.39 \text{ X } 10^{-4} - 1.4434) = 0 \quad (26)$$
$$-p_1 (H_1\, 6.43 \text{ X } 10^{-4} - 1.9832) - p_2 (H_2\, 4.64 \text{ X } 10^{-4} - 1.4340) - p_3 (H_3\, 20.90 \text{ X } 10^{-4} - 3.2125) = 0 \quad (27)$$

These relations are once again the results of a modified application of the Linear Expenditure System to N.S.S. consumption data (for details see Note 4). Assuming the same varying rates of growth for agriculture and industry, the equation system (22) to (26) is used to calculate the changes in the relative prices to be expected in 1970–71. The results are presented in Table 18.5. As one would not expect any reduction in the industrial prices, the ratios in columns (3) and (4) represent the minimum rise in prices of foodgrains and other food products to be expected—minimum, as our calculations *do not* take into account price rises in industrial products as a result of price rises in foodgrains and food products and further price rises in the latter as a result of the rise in general price level. As can be seen, if the targets of 5 per cent rate of growth of agricultural production and 12 per cent rate of growth of industrial production are achieved, a minimal price rise of 109 per cent is to be expected in foodgrains prices by 1970–71. However, if, as is more likely, agriculture is to grow at a much lower rate, the rise in prices to be expected is much larger.

TABLE 18.5: PRICE REPURCUSSIONS OF IMBALANCED GROWTH

Rates of Growth		Relative Prices in 1970–71	
Agriculture	Industry	Foodgrains to Non-Food Products	Other Food Products to Non-Food Products
1	2	3	4
2%	10%	4.10	20.71
3%	10%	2.59	6.76
4%	10%	1.72	3.53
5%	10%	1.14	2.64
5%	12%	2.09	3.74

Note: See Note 4 for explanation.

IN LIEU OF CONCLUSIONS

No conclusions have been attempted to be drawn in this paper. The results presented in Tables 18.4 and 18.5 only indicate the price that might have to be paid for pushing ahead with a high rate of industrial growth in the teeth of a slow-growing agriculture. If one is prepared to face an *initial* and *minimal* price rise of 159 per cent in foodgrains and 576 per cent in other food products, one may well say that a 3 per cent rate of growth in agriculture need not deter one from trying to achieve a 10 per cent rate of industrial growth. I may not also be accused of pessimism or fatalism. It is not being suggested that the industrial growth rate should be reduced to bring about compatibility with the slow agricultural growth. The results may equally well be used to recommend that the rate of growth of agriculture has to be raised in order to be compatible with the high rate of growth of industries desired.

NOTES AND REFERENCES

[1] This inter-industry flow table has been condensed from a thirty-sector inter-industry table constructed by the writer and some of his younger colleagues of the Indian Statistical Institute. This particular condensation was worked out by Shri A. V. Uamasunder. The coverage of the first two sectors is as follows:

- Agricultural production proper (main products only), plantations, animal husbandry, and fishery, forestry, food industry, textile industry, leather and leather products, rubber and rubber products.
- Mining, metallurgical industries, cement, chemicals, crude oil and petroleum refining, glass and non-metallic mineral products, engineering industries, and construction.
- It is to be noted that all other sectors (e.g., trade and commerce, transport other than railway and motor transport, professions, services, and housing) are ignored as output sectors, though input into these sectors is shown under the column headed "others."

[2] The sector "Others," by definition, is a residual sector and its treatment in terms of technological input coefficients may not be expected to give very satisfactory results. Similarly, the treatment of stocks in terms of the capital-output ratio is much less satisfactory than the similar treatment of fixed capital formation. The simplicity achieved by treating these two flows in terms of fixed percentages of the total flow is not counterbalanced by the loss in realism. It is to be remembered here that the "Others" for this purpose would include not only the industries left out in our model but also those industries included in the model for which the input coefficients have been treated as zero for achieving simplicity. The parameter is an innovation introduced for convenience. It is obviously related to the rate of gross savings. It is, however, to be noted that k_d does not equal gross savings. That is because k_d and k_f are both measured in the producers' prices of capital goods. Investment, however, equals the value of capital goods at their market prices. k_f is assumed to be equal to the import surplus over exports (inclusive of invisibles). e_0 includes not only the net invisible earnings but also the domestic trade and transport margin on e_1 and e_2. It is to be remembered that m_1 and m_2 are measured at their c.i.f. prices, and in order to be comparable, the exports have to be measured at their f.o.b. prices.

[3] The numerical values for the coefficients b_1, b_2, and b_3 are based on the inter-industry table for 1960–61 for which the values are 0.04, 0.05, and 0.27. The high figure for b_3 is largely accounted for by the large consumption of electricity by commercial enterprises. The value of 0.35 for θ for 1970 corresponds to a rate of gross savings of about 19 per cent. The value of θ for 1960–61 is 0.20 corresponding to a rate of gross savings of about 13 per cent. The increase of 18 per cent to 19 per cent no doubt represents an ambitious target but no more so than currently made assumptions. It is to be remembered here that higher the rate of gross savings, higher would be the rate of growth of industries that would be in balance with a given rate of growth of agriculture. Hence, by choosing a high figure for θ for 1970 we are actually prejudicing our work in favour of a high rate of growth for industries. As to government consumption, it is assumed that its overall magnitude goes up by 150 per cent between 1960–61 and 1970–71 due to expansion of the public services. The composition in terms of the sector and commodity classification is assumed to remain more or less constant. The values for exports according to the sector and commodity classifications are of the nature of projections. The input coefficient for industry into agriculture for 1960–61 is .017. This is raised to .040 to take into account technological changes to be expected in agriculture between 1960–61 and 1970–71 (more of chemical fertilisers, electricity, oil for diesel pumps, etc.). The corresponding coefficients of non-food products into foodgrains and other food products in the equation system (22), (28), and (24) are .022 and .027 for 1960–01. They are also each raised to .040.

[4] The Linear Expenditure System developed by Professor Stone and others (See *Economic Journal* 64 [1954]) satisfies three of the four desirable conditions of a demand function, namely, the conditions of additivity homogeneity and symmetry. The basic relation is:

$$q_i p_i = q_i p_i \mid b_i \left[\sum_{i=1}^{n} p_i (q_i \bar{q}_i) \right]$$

$$\text{for } i = 1, 2, \ldots \ldots n$$

$$b_i \geq 0 \qquad q_i \geq 0 \qquad \sum_{i=1}^{n} b_i = 1$$

Where q_i is consumer demand for commodity i in quantity, p_i its price. b_i and q_i are the parameters. $i = 1, 2 \ldots n$ constitute an exhaustive classification of all consumer commodities. An extensive application of this function to N.S.S. data had been carried out by Smt. Pushpam and her results show that the function gives excellent account of the variations in the N.S.S. consumption pattern from round to round in relation to the variations in the prices. In the present paper I have made use of two of the interesting fits carried out by her. They are both based on the N.S.S. rounds 8th to 15th and consider three commodity groups, namely, foodgrains, other food products, and non-food products. In each case the prices are expressed as index numbers with base at 1952–53. In one case the quantities are treated as given and the prices treated as dependent variables; the results of this fit are used for calculating the price equations (25), (20), and (27). In the other case the quantities are treated as dependent variables and the prices treated as given: the results of this fit are used for calculating the relations (10) and (17) between the demands for the products of the three sectors compatible with stable relative prices. The values of the parameters q_i and b_i for these two fits are presented in Table 18.6 along with indications regarding the goodness of the fits.

It is seen that the goodness of fit, as measured by the product moment correlation coefficient between observed and fitted values of quantities demanded and prices respectively, are in each case extremely high. It may also be mentioned in passing that none of the tools of demand prediction currently in use in India (mostly constant elasticities based on single rounds of the N.S.S.) give anywhere near comparable fits to observations ranging over a period. In order to obtain relations (25), (26), and (27) we have made use of the following relations between H_1, H_2 and H_3 (which are total annual consumption at 1960–61 producers prices) and q_1, q_2, and q_3 (which are monthly per capita consumption figures at 1952–53 market prices):

$$H_1 = \frac{q_1 \times 10^6}{1898}$$

$$H_2 = \frac{q_2 \times 10^6}{1363}$$

$$H_3 = \frac{q_3 \times 10^6}{2108} \times \cdot 7617$$

It is to be noted that q_3 represents all non-food consumer goods according to N.S.S. definitions whereas H_3 represents only non-food products covered by the 30 sector inter-industry classification scheme. In order to obtain the relations (16) and (17) between h_1, h_2, and h_3, which are the household consumption of the products of sectors 1, 2, and 3, we first write out a set of relations akin to (25), (26), and (27), but not identical to them as we now use the quantity fit for the demand functions. Then we eliminate from these expressions p_1, p_2, and p_3 by substituting for them their values at t = 1959–60 (the values are 1.074, 1.229 and 1.168) and then substitute for H_1, H_2, and H_3 by h_1, h_2, and h_3 in terms of the following relations:

$$h_1 = H_1 + 0.535H_3$$
$$h_2 = 0.325H_3$$
$$h_3 = 0.140H_3$$

Household consumption of food products, H_3, is split up into three parts in the proportions 0.535, 0.325, and 0.140. The latter two parts are composed of the products of sectors 2 and 3. The first part is a product of the first sector which also accounts for H_1 and H_2.

[5] It is an interesting feature of the two models represented by the equation systems (9), (10), and (11) and (22), (23), and (24) that the exports and imports of industrial products do not enter

TABLE 18.6: MODIFIED LINEAR EXPENDITURE SYSTEM FITTED TO NSS DATA

Commodity Group	Quantity Fit			Price Fit		
	Parameter			Parameters		
	a_i	b_i	Correlation Coefficient between Observed and Expected r_i	a_i	a_i	Correlation Coefficient between Observed and Expected r_i
1	2	3	4	5	6	7
Foodgrains	6.00*	0.355	90.5%	5.85*	0.364	99.0%
Other Food Products	4.34	0.302	92.1%	4.23	0.297	98.0%
Non-Food Products	4.98	0.343	96.1%	4.80	0.330	98.2%

* In rupees at 1952–53 prices.

Note: See note 4 for explanation.

in any way the relations between output, household consumption, and the prices of consumer goods. That is because in either case fixed capital formation takes place entirely out of the products of a single sector: sector 2 in the model represented by equations (9) to (11) and sector 3 in the model represented by equations (22) to (24). The import surplus of that sector gets cancelled against the same quantity occuring as a part of the excess of capital formation over domestic savings. The indeterminacy of the import surplus of industrial products is matched by the indeterminacy of the size and rate of investment. It is, however, necessary to make certain assumptions for c_2 and m_2 if one wants to calculate the difference between foreign exchange earnings and requirements. As to exports we take the approach of making simple projections, for non-competitive imports we link them to corresponding domestic production by fixed coefficients. The coefficients 0.010 and 0.085 for agriculture and industry represent the maximum limits of import substitution that may be expected to be reached by 1970–71. Competitive import of agricultural products would be called for to satisfy the condition of maintaining stable relative prices as well as fulfil the export targets. Competitive import of industrial products would, however, be called for only if one desires to have (this constitutes assumption B) a level of capital formation higher than what would result from domestic savings plus only such import surplus that would result if the imports consist exclusively of the non-competitive import requirements (this constitutes assumption A). Capital formation thus resulting corresponding to various relative rates of growth is shown in column (8) of Table 18.4. Competitive import of industrial products is shown in column (5), and the foreign exchange deficits under the two assumptions in columns (6) and (7). If the entries in column (5) do not equal the difference between columns (9) and (8) that is because the entries in these two columns are at market prices whereas those of column (5) and all other figures are in producer's prices. The formula for capital formation at market price is:

$$(k_{dt}+k_{ft}) \qquad 1.10$$

Where k_{dt} and k_{ft} are as in (7) and (8) and the factor 1.10 is brought in to transform the measure from producer price units to market price units. The fact that competitive import of industrial products increases while that of agricultural products decreases is explained by the fact that the former is called for only to meet the shortfall in domestic resources in relation to a desired level of capital formation. Hence greater the import surplus in agricultural products less the need for import surplus in industrial products.

PART VI

Policy Debates: Agriculture

19

The Shifting Fortunes of Agriculture

The General Setting*

W. Arthur Lewis

The fortunes of agriculturists depend not only upon the prices they receive, but also upon their productivity. If real prices halve but productivity doubles, they are no worse off than before. In practice, farmers are interested not only in their own absolute standard of living, but also in how their earnings compare with earnings in other occupations. So, in comparing members of the same community, the terms of trade which matter are not the commodity terms of trade but the factoral terms of trade. The behaviour of the factoral terms of trade depends on three movements:

(1) the comparative rates of growth of demand for agricultural and for non-agricultural products,
(2) the comparative rates of growth of productivity in agricultural and in non-agricultural industries, and
(3) the mobility of the population into and out of agriculture.

The balance between these various rates of growth is so different in different phases of economic development that it is not feasible to speak in the same breath about the newly developing and the advanced countries. Broadly speaking, the advanced countries produce too much food, while the newly developing countries produce too little. I propose therefore to speak separately about these

* Originally published in *Economic Weekly* 10, no. 35 (30 August 1958), pp. 1135–38. Text of the chapter submitted to the Tenth Conference of International Agricultural Economists, held at Mysore, 24 August–3 September 1958. Published courtesy of the CIAE.

two groups. It is not possible in 1958 to say anything about these matters which is both startling and true; I shall make only some random introductory remarks.

The Role of Agriculture in Economic Development

The economic development of most countries is unbalanced, in the sense that not all sectors come alive and show vigorous growth simultaneously. From the point of view of the role of agriculture in economic development we may distinguish three cases:

(1) Where development begins outside agriculture,
(2) Where development begins with agricultural exports, and
(3) Where development begins with greater productivity in food for the home market.

We can dismiss the third of these cases, because it is seldom if ever self-sustaining. Since the elasticity of demand for food is less than unity, an increase in home food production when other sectors of the economy are stationary is almost certain to drive the farmers bankrupt. It is true that at low levels the farmers may eat nearly the whole of their extra production, so that they may be better off in terms of food, even though the increase in their marketings causes them to have less of other commodities. It is also true that the rest of the economy benefits from the reduction of food prices, but since this means selling less to the farmers, the effect may be to increase urban unemployment rather than to stimulate non-agricultural production. One can conceive of a case where economic development begins with increased productivity in food and is sustained because farmers move rapidly out of food into other occupations as their productivity rises; but I cannot think of any case in history where the initiative in development (as distinct from the response to development) has been taken by the food farmers, and has been sustained. I suspect that Malthus was right in thinking that the only long-term effect would be that more of the farmers' children would live, and that equilibrium would be re-established with a larger population.

The farmers' position is quite different if development begins outside agriculture. This is quite common: minerals are discovered; or new technologies are applied to manufacturing industry; or a tourist trade develops; or shifts in trade favour a particular port; or some other stroke of fortune stimulates the non-agricultural sector. This in turn generates an increase in demand for agricultural products, and so development spreads from sector to sector. Ricardo believed that this could not sustain itself because the failure of food output to grow adequately would turn the factoral terms of trade against the non-agricultural sector, and so stop its expansion. Indeed, I believe that we have here the main reason for the very slow growth of manufacturing industry in India and China during the past century, as compared with Japan, where increases in agricultural productivity have been spectacular. Similarly, agricultural stagnation helps to explain why French manufacturing industry made so little progress before 1944, when compared with the rest of Western Europe.

FOOD AND BALANCE OF PAYMENTS

However, Ricardo did not tell the whole story, since he was writing of the closed economy. The open economy can import agricultural products to match an expansion of industrial output and employment. This, however, may lead to a balance of payments crisis, as in contemporary England and contemporary India, and then force the nation to adopt one or more of three policies: to cut investment, which is the English and the Indian solution, and leads back to Ricardian stagnation; or to make a big drive to export more manufactures, which is the German and Japanese solution; or to raise agricultural productivity as rapidly as possible.

The obstacle to the third of these solutions is mainly psychological; we know how to increase agricultural productivity in newly developing areas by spending on water, on the distribution of high-yielding strains, on agricultural extension and so on at a cost which is a fraction of what governments spend on their other programmes. Governments are beginning to realise that food production is as important as anything else, but there is still hardly any country in Asia or in Africa where the Ministry of Agriculture is occupied by a senior cabinet minister.

If development begins with an increased demand or supply of agricultural exports, the country does not run into these awful balance of payments difficulties, partly because the supply of output from other home sectors is fairly elastic in response to farmers' demands; and even more importantly, because the exports provide the foreign currency with which to pay for imports. Countries which begin this way will have balance of payments deficits if they live beyond their incomes, and especially if they borrow abroad more than their incomes can support; but they have no balance of payments problem if they live within their incomes. On the contrary, since the marginal propensity to import is less than unity, and since there is a time lag in the multiplier, such a country, if living within its means, would always tend to have a balance of payments surplus. This is the main reason why virtually nothing was heard about balance of payments crises during the seventy-five years before the First World War, although this was a time of rapid development all over the world; whereas these words are on everybody's tongue today. In the former period development was concentrated in export sectors; whereas nowadays nearly every country plans for home demand, for public utilities, and for public services but forgets about exports. Since development always increases imports, one of the most important chapters in any development plan is that which tells what is to be done to increase exports, whether of manufactures or of agricultural products.

Terms of Trade

Though development through agricultural exports works wonders, it has also its disadvantages. A well-known disadvantage is the fact that it discourages manufacturing industry. It certainly provides demand, but this demand is easily met by imports. At the same time, it creates the wrong atmosphere for industrialisation. Everything is geared to agricultural exports research, training facilities, public utilities, representation of vested interests in the legislature, etc. To get money spent in ways that are favourable to manufacturing industry requires a great effort in these circumstances. All this is well known, and generally accepted. It is merely an extension of the old infant industry argument.

An even more serious disadvantage in the tropical countries, is the difficulty of getting favourable terms of trade for agricultural exports. Tropical agricultural exports are small in relation to agricultural production as a whole; the main output is of foodstuffs for home consumption. Hence the supply is very elastic. The incomes of farmers producing for export cannot rise significantly above the incomes of farmers producing for the home demand. Naturally there are lags, frictions, and some inelasticities, which modify the argument, and create temporary or permanent gaps between home and export incomes, but the two are chained together. The incomes of farmers producing for export are determined not by their own productivity, but by the productivity of the food farmers, which is very low in comparison with the productivity of food farmers in the temperate zones—whose incomes are in turn linked to those of industrial producers in the temperate zones. We have then the following relationship. Suppose that temperate farmers earn 60 per cent as much as industrial workers and produce eight times as much food per head as tropical farmers. It will then follow that the income of tropical exporters of agricultural products cannot be much more than 7.5 per cent of the incomes of industrial workers in the temperate zones. However much productivity may rise in tropical agricultural export crops, the terms of trade will always adjust themselves to keep down the farmer's standard of living.

Balanced Development

It follows that tropical countries cannot rely for major development solely on incomes derived from agricultural exports. Neither can they become prosperous simply by producing more food for home consumption, since in the absence of expansion in other sectors of the economy, this would merely bankrupt the farmers. They must look instead to balanced development. If productivity and investment are raised in all sectors, the growing manufacturing and service sectors will absorb both an increasing output of food, and also agricultural labour rendered surplus; and at the same time the real incomes of agricultural exporters will rise as the gap between food productivities in the temperate and the tropical zones closes.

I do not rule out the possibility that the people of one small country may grow prosperous by raising their productivity and exporting more agricultural products at constant prices; but the tropics as a whole cannot do this, and improvements in the export sector spread fairly rapidly from one tropical country to another. Neither do I neglect the fact that time lags in supply may bring temporary windfalls, as to the cocoa producers today. But it remains true that a general improvement in tropical terms of trade will occur only when there is an all-round increase in tropical productivity in all sectors for home consumption.

MOBILITY IN AGRICULTURAL ADJUSTMENT

This brings me to the problems of the advanced economy since, from the point of view of this discussion, the distinction between the undeveloped and the advanced country is that in the latter one can normally expect a substantial increase in agricultural productivity per man from one decade to the next. The starting point of farmers' troubles in these countries is the fact that the demand for food tends to grow less rapidly than the supply; whereas the starting point of the planners' troubles in newly developing countries is that the demand for food grows more rapidly than the supply.

It is a well-established proposition that consumers' expenditure on food rises less rapidly than income. There is a little doubt about this in poor countries, but no doubt in wealthier countries where the average daily intake per person exceeds, say, 2,500 calories. Farm receipts rise even less rapidly than consumers' expenditure on food. As incomes rise, consumers want their food prepared and served more elaborately; it must be processed, or preserved and served out of season, or brought from the far corners of the earth or served in restaurants with music. Hence the "value added" after it leaves the farm becomes an increasing proportion of the whole to the increasing disgust of the farmer. The farmer's only consolation is that as incomes grow the wastage of food by the average household seems to grow even more.

The reverse happens to the agricultural raw materials: they are more and more carefully economised. The income elasticity of demand for manufactures exceeds unity in the poorer countries, though it is probably not greater than unity in the richer countries, where increases in income go much more to services than to purchasing further knick-knacks. This high income elasticity is favourable to agricultural raw materials, but it is not decisively favourable. In the first place, since raw materials for industry are only a small part of agricultural production, the elasticity of supply is high, and prices are determined more by what is happening to food prices than they are by the demand for raw materials. Secondly, there is continuous economy in the use of raw materials, and especially in the utilisation of by-products. And thirdly, raw materials are menaced all the time by synthetics, which are a means of substituting cheaper and more abundant raw materials for more expensive ones. The only thing the farmer can say in praise of synthetics is that they tend to stabilise his market. For these synthetics are often made by monopolistic industries, which hold prices more or less constant through boom and recession. Thus the price of rubber is now pretty stable after two decades of wild confusion; and the emergence of detergents seems similarly to have reduced the fluctuations in the prices of vegetable oils.

The Remedy: Fewer Farmers

If the demand for food grows slowly, while productivity grows rapidly, the terms of trade must move against the farmer unless the proportion of the population engaged in agriculture contracts. Poets and other romantics have always deplored this change, but it is inevitable in the arithmetic. As far as the agricultural economist is concerned, the main remedy for the farmer's ills must always be to have fewer farmers.

The speed with which the proportion must contract depends entirely upon the rate of growth of consumption per head of population, and the rate of growth of productivity per person in agriculture. The required contraction is greater in rich than in poor countries. Thus, if consumption per head grows by 0.5 per cent per annum and productivity by 3.0 per cent, over twenty years the proportion must contract by 37 per cent—i.e., the proportion of the population in agriculture must fall from, say, 20 per cent to 13 per cent. On the other hand, in a poor country, where consumption can grow by 1.0 per cent per annum, and productivity by 2.0 per cent per annum, the proportion contracts over twenty years only by 18 per cent or, say, from 60 per cent to 49 per cent of the population.

Moreover, the difficulty of making this contraction depends upon how rapidly population is growing (though this does not affect the required proportions). If population is growing only by 1.0 per cent in the wealthier country, to reduce the proportion in agriculture from 20 to 13 per cent in twenty years means that the absolute number in agriculture must be reduced by 24 per cent. Whereas, in the poorer country, if population is increasing by 2.0 per cent per annum, a fall in the proportion in agriculture from 60 to 49 per cent is consistent with an increase in the absolute number by 22 per cent.

These calculations illustrate the point that in a closed economy the farmers would have a harder time in a rich country than in a poor one because of slower population growth, smaller increases in food consumption per head, and faster increases in farm productivity. However, there is no closed economy. In practice most of the world's farmers, with the notable exception of North American farmers, would stay reasonably prosperous if imports of food were prohibited. What troubles them is neither the slow growth of demand in their countries, nor the speed with which their own productivity is rising, but the rising tide of supplies in a very few other countries.

FOOD IS TOO CHEAP

The international division of labour requires that countries which are short of arable land should import food and export manufactures. Thus Britain, Germany, Japan, India, China, Java, and one or two other countries should export manufactures, while North America, South-East Asia (excluding Java) and others should import manufactures and export food. Alas, the international division of labour does not have its way.

The main reason why the international division of labour does not have its way is that food is too cheap: at current prices farmers' real incomes are substantially lower than the real incomes of other occupations. This causes food exporting countries to be anxious to industrialise rather than continue exporting food, and causes food importing countries to try to keep imports down for the sake of their own farmers.

Now food is too cheap because farmers are not sufficiently mobile; agriculture contracts too slowly. In the poorer countries of the world this is primarily due to lack of opportunities outside agriculture. Not enough investment is occurring in manufacturing industry or in other sectors to draw off the rural surplus. However, neither Asia nor Africa suffers from a surplus of food. In the over-populated parts of Asia the rural surplus should be drawn out of agriculture—but not in order to reduce the food supply, which would, by definition, not be affected. The problem of these countries is simultaneously to increase food supplies while finding other work for the rural surplus. Africa has no rural surplus except in a few small areas; but neither has Africa, at present, a surplus of food. The African problem is to start an upward movement of productivity, so that other sectors of the economy can be expanded, without running short of food.

It is in the other continents, especially in North America and in Europe, that the immobility of farmers is keeping down farm prices, and here the cause is not failure of other sectors to expand, but the unwillingness of farmers to move. Investment proceeds so rapidly in these parts of the world that even the largest conceivable exodus from farms to towns would be snapped up in a very short time, just as Western Germany has absorbed millions of refugees. It is true that demand does not grow steadily; there are Kitchin, Juglar, Kuznets, and even possibly Kondratieff cycles. Farmers are used to having a decade of prosperity succeeded by a decade of poverty. Nevertheless, in times of prosperity the non-agricultural sector can absorb all who want to leave farming. If there are still too many farmers, it is because too many people want to be farmers.

I doubt whether this problem is capable of solution. There will always be occupations which attract too many people—farming, teaching, shopkeeping, music, acting, and many others—and the economy will always retaliate by paying people in these occupations less than they could earn in others. They, in their turn, resenting this, will do whatever they can to get higher rewards, by restricting entry to their trades, by tariffs and quotas, by parity price formulas or by any other regulative device for which they can win acceptance. Their philosophers—in our case the agricultural economists—will wrangle among themselves over these devices, some supporting, others denouncing, and yet others confining themselves to measuring. That is what we have assembled here to do, and I hope that you will find enough material in this chapter to make a start.

20

Retrospect

The Shifting Fortunes of Agriculture

The Experience of Less Fully Developed Countries*

D. R. Gadgil

Programmes of research and education are, in the long run, of fundamental importance. In the context of the actual fortunes of the agriculturist they assume importance when they come to affect his costs or his income. This is also true of any programme of rationalising layout or other rearrangements of the holding. There is, however, one aspect of land reform which may immediately affect the fortunes of agriculturists. This is where, through the abolition of a superior holder or the reduction of levels of legal rent, etc., the outgoings of the agriculturists are reduced. It appears that the largest changes in the fortunes of agriculturists in this manner have been brought about in the centrally planned economies. China is the most important recent example. However, to a lesser extent the abolition of intermediaries and reductions of rent have taken place in countries like Burma, India, Pakistan, Philippines, Egypt, Turkey, Guatemala, Bolivia, and Puerto Rico. The difficulty of assessing the actual change brought about by these programmes lies in judging of the effectiveness of actual implementation of legislation. Careful surveys have revealed large failures in this regard in particular areas.

Programmes relating to credit and marketing could improve, within a short time, the economic position of the agriculturist. They have the aspects of reduction of costs borne currently by the agriculturist, such as interest, commission, etc.,

* Originally published in *Economic Weekly* 10, nos. 36–37 (13 September 1958), pp. 1187–91. Text of chapter submitted to the Tenth International Conference of Agricultural Economists, held at Mysore, 24 August–3 September 1958. Published courtesy of ICAE.

and of increasing receipts through greater and more effective outlay made possible by more ample and timely credit or through a better price obtained because of more orderly marketing. The results of credit programmes are comparatively readily recorded. These programmes have been elaborated in only a small number of the less developed countries and in 1955 the FAO judgment regarding them was no more than that "they have slightly augmented the flow of institutional credit to agriculture."[1] The latest data indicate no great advance. Among the underdeveloped countries the amounts of institutional agricultural credit advanced in recent years appear significant chiefly in Turkey and Egypt in the Near East; Puerto Rico, Columbia, and Argentina in Latin America; and the Philippines, Ceylon, India, and Indonesia in the ECAFE region.[2]

Price Support and Stabilisation

The most considerable effect on the fortunes of the agriculturist is likely to be produced by measures of direct subsidies or by price support and stabilisation measures. Subsidies may be granted as part of a long-term development programme for purposes such as the improvement of land or of irrigation source. In terms of current operations, they are used chiefly for encouraging adoption of improved products or methods such as through subsidising prices of fertilisers, improved planting material, or tractor ploughing. Though useful in the implementation of certain plans, these subsidies do not represent amounts significant in the context of the total operations of a farmer.

Price policy could affect materially the agriculturist's entire economic situation. The simplest objective of such policies could be the elimination of seasonal fluctuations. For example, reserve stocks of grain could serve not only as insurance against crop failure but could bring down very substantially the annual seasonal variation in prices.[3] Usually, however, the objective has a longer period in view and aims at obtaining a fair average price, over the years, for the produce. Where the commodity whose price is controlled is also an important export commodity the operation may amount to an insulation of the domestic market, with internal prices being in some years above and in others below the international price level. Price stabilisation or support policies are fairly widespread in the less developed countries. Generally, the prices of only a small number of agricultural products, particularly those entering into international trade, are thus controlled.

The governments of all the major Latin American countries, like Argentina, Chile, Uruguay, Brazil, and Columbia, control prices. In tropical Africa, the outstanding feature is the operation of the marketing boards. For many years these boards kept the domestic price of cocoa, for example, at a lower level than the international price, but also in years of depressed prices after 1954 were able to maintain them, in some cases at levels higher than the international. Among the Middle East countries, Egypt and Turkey have adopted price support policies. The Egyptian government controlled both acreages and prices of wheat and cotton and used these for stabilising both farmers' incomes and export earnings. In Turkey, government provides price support for a much larger number of agricultural commodities than in Egypt. Government sets prices at which it is prepared to buy any quantity of these agricultural products, particularly grains. This, together with government organisation for storing and issuing grains, has brought about a great increase in the production of grains in Turkey since 1950. In the underdeveloped countries of the ECAFE region, many of which are rice economies, price stabilisation or support policies for rice had been followed, notably in Philippines, Ceylon, Thailand, and Burma. In Burma, in particular, the elaborate price and marketing policy has been directed not only towards stabilising farmers' incomes but also towards obtaining resources for development of the economy. Where state marketing monopolies have operated long enough to build up their own reserves the stabilisation operations have been fairly successful and have been maintained even in the face of falling international price.

The operations of these price policies must be considered as an extremely important new factor in the economy of the agriculturists. In the underdeveloped countries these policies cannot increase the share of the agriculturist in the total national product as the agriculturist is here the majority not the minority group. But, through any incentive effects that they have, they might increase total production and might increase the average real level of incomes through elimination of uncertainty and fluctuations. However, in view of the large variety of types of support policies and the variations in their administrative efficiency, it is not possible to make any general statement as to their effects.

COMMODITY AGREEMENTS

It has been generally recognised that action by individual countries could not, by itself, prove adequate for stabilising the level of agricultural prices, and efforts at international action towards this end have been marked since the depression of the thirties. The considerable increase of government-to-government transactions during years of war and after, and fears of a depression in the immediate post-war period led to attempts at international commodity agreements on a much wider scale than before. The chief new feature of these was the attempt to associate both producers and consumers in one agreement. International organisations like the FAO have actively backed the formation of international commodity agreements. It remains true, however, that the International Wheat Agreement and the International Sugar Agreement are the only two which today affect agricultural producers in large areas in the less developed countries.

In the absence of international agreements primary exporting countries have attempted to secure their position by entering into bilateral agreements with the chief importing countries of their products. Burma has been one of the most active in seeking these. In regional terms the Latin American countries have tended to look to guaranteed purchases by the USA. The vital importance to economies of less developed countries of secured export markets was recently emphasised by the agreements regarding sales of cotton by Egypt and Syria to the USSR. The possibility of mutual help among the less developed countries has been indicated by the Rubber-Rice Agreement between Ceylon and China.

Evaluation of State Policy

It is difficult to judge the effects of state policy, especially in the short run. Policy which brings about better distribution such as that relating to land reform and to cooperative organisation of marketing and credit may prove the starting point, may indeed be a condition precedent, of greater and more diversified production. The immediate betterment of the fortunes of the agriculturists through such policies is not, however, easily discerned. The effects of price support and stabilisation policies are even more difficult to assess. For example, Burma has followed through many years a policy of a low stabilised rice price for the farmers and of canalising the gains of rice exports into development. India, on the other hand, has had no well-defined policy in this regard and has almost let things drift. Only a detailed, many-sided study of the situation in the two countries could lead to a firm judgement regarding the relative merits and propriety of the two different approaches.

In the post-war period social welfare policies have been responsible for improving the conditions of the people in a number of countries. However, significant programmes of social security, etc., have not been undertaken in most of the less developed countries, and in countries like India and Pakistan expenditure even on education for the rural population gets surprisingly low allocations.

Agriculture and National Income

In recent years, use has been made of the national income data for obtaining some idea of the relative condition of agriculturists. Comparison of per capita incomes in agriculture, forestry, and fisheries with per capita incomes in all other occupations, taken together, shows that in all the less developed countries the agriculturist is relatively inadequately rewarded. As a rule, in these countries, the per capita income in agriculture, etc., is less than 50 per cent of the per capita income in all other occupations and the percentage may be as low as 30. This percentage depends on a variety of economic considerations and it is not possible to generalise on its basis. In the present context, interest attaches to whether this percentage is increasing or not. In absolute terms, the income of the agriculturist, ordinarily, increases with an increase in total national income. In view of existing inadequacy of the earnings of agriculturists, it is important that the agriculturist's income should increase faster than the national income. The data for judging of this are scanty but those available indicate large variations in the situation. For example, it appears that in Turkey the per capita income in all other occupations was 30 in 1938, 51 in 1948, and 60 in 1952; in the Philippines, it varied between 29 per cent and 34 per cent between 1948 and 1952 without showing a definite trend.[4] It is obviously dangerous to generalise on the basis of the data for a few years, especially in the case of income in agriculture. It would appear that in the years between 1946 and 1952 the trend in regions like Latin America, the Middle East, and Africa was for incomes in agriculture to rise at a rate faster than the national income. The data after 1952 do not present a consistent picture. Fully reliable information regarding the occupational distribution of the population is not available for all countries and, where available, it pertains only to particular years. It is necessary, therefore, to confine attention to movements of total income in agriculture instead of attempting to estimate per capita figures for studying trends after 1950.

Examination was made of the data for the six years 1950 to 1955 for some of the larger among the less developed countries in different regions in which the share of agriculture is larger than 25 per cent of the total domestic product. These were Brazil, Burma, Colombia, Egypt, India, Pakistan, Philippines, Thailand, and Turkey. The examination revealed that in Brazil and Philippines, the share of agriculture (valued at current factor cost) rose continuously from 1950 to 1955 at a rate faster than the total domestic product and that consequently the share of agriculture in the total was larger after 1952 than in earlier years. These data also indicated very large fluctuations in the value of the product of agriculture from year to year in some countries. In Burma and Colombia, in addition to Brazil and Philippines, there was a steady movement upwards in the value of both agricultural and total products between 1950 and 1955. In Turkey also, the movement was continuously upward except for a drop in the value of agricultural product in 1954. On the other hand, in Egypt, India, Pakistan, and Thailand, there were variations in both directions from year to year and some of these variations were large. In interpreting these data, it is necessary to remember that differences in the pattern of production and in price support policies, etc., would lead to differences in the situation of the agriculturists from country to country.

Vicious Circle

In this context, there are also other limitations of the data of total product of agriculture. For example, because of stratification within the agricultural community, the benefits and disadvantages might be very unevenly distributed among its members. For example, it has been reported that both in north and tropical Africa agricultural activity, which has proved specially profitable during the last decade, has been concentrated in the hands of small groups of European settlers; overall indicators may mislead in relation to the fortunes of the bulk of farmers in such instances. Further, in a large number of underdeveloped economies the share of landlords, moneylenders, and traders in the total product of agriculture may be substantial and this might become even larger in proportion in periods of instability. Surveys in such countries have revealed that primary producers fail to profit from temporary favourable changes and that the effects of an occasional very bad year may be felt by them for a number of years afterwards. This makes it necessary to exercise caution in estimating effects of favourable changes, which have not been stabilised or trends which are not persistent.

Recent studies have shown that the main factors responsible for low relative incomes in agriculture are economic instability of agriculture and immobility outwards associated with mobility inwards. Economic instability stems from both instability of yields and of agricultural producers' prices. Increase in the inelasticity of the demand for food products, enhanced possibilities of displacement of agricultural raw materials by synthetic products, etc., and emergence of surpluses have intensified demand instability in the post-war period. And all national and international attempts to make markets and prices for the agriculturists more stable have achieved little real success. Rapid growth in population continually adds large numbers to the largest existent occupational group, namely agriculture, and the limited number of openings in other occupations reinforces the other reasons for outward immobility. In the older, the poorer, and the more populous of the less developed countries all the factors operate in a cumulative manner. Unless, in some way or another, the vicious circle is broken there is little prospect of the beginning of an upward trend, relative or absolute, in the fortunes of the agriculturist.

Notes and References

1 Food and Agriculture Organisation, *The State of Food and Agriculture: Review of a Decade and Outlook* (Rome: FAO, 1955), p. 40.

2 Food and Agriculture Organisation, *The The State of Food and Agriculture 1957* (Rome: FAO, Annex Table 16, 1957).

3 For recent experience in South Korea supporting this view, see *Economic Development and Planning in Asia and the Far East: Economic Bulletin for Asia and Far East* (November 1957), p. 6.

4 Food and Agriculture Organisation, *Agriculture in the World Economy* (1955), p. 54.

21

A Note on Cooperative Farming*

Amlan Datta

This article has no claim to originality. It seeks merely to bring together certain fairly well-known facts, which in their totality do not seem to have sufficiently entered into the consciousness of policy makers in this country.

First, a word about large-scale and small-scale farming. Farming on a relatively large scale is essential for mechanised cultivation: tractors, for example, cannot be used on plots of land of the average size of holdings in India. But, generally speaking, mechanisation does not lead to increased productivity per acre of land.

Increased productivity of land is due principally to such factors as more careful selection of seeds, better manuring, improved water supply, etc. These are quite compatible with small-scale farming. Whether the use of tractors contributes to raising or actually lowering the productivity of land depends on the quality of the soil. There is a respectable volume of expert opinion that, in a country like India, it is likely in general to impair the fertility of the soil in the long run, as has been the case in a number of other countries.

There are also other reasons, in a sense more fundamental, why large-scale farming tends to be inefficient. These reasons are rooted partly in peasant psychology and partly in organisational problems in the field of agriculture, noted by competent observers since a long time back. Thus, Adam Smith wrote:

> A small proprietor who knows every part of his little territory, who views it with all the affection that property, especially small property, naturally inspires, and who upon that account takes pleasure not only in cultivating but in adorning it, is generally of all improvers the most industrious, the most intelligent, and the most successful.[1]

* Originally published in *Economic Weekly* 9, nos. 3–5 (19 January 1957), pp. 119–20.

The Japanese, treating their small farms with almost the same care as gardening receives in other parts of the world, have by their results lent striking support to this view.

Managerial Optimum

In the field of agriculture, the managerial or supervisory optimum is reached much earlier than in the field of industry. This is the basic fact which economists, well versed in theory but lacking acquaintance with the special problems of agriculture, tend to ignore. Yet this is one of those elementary facts that a student of agriculture comes to recognise at a quite early stage. Thus, Shri A. N. Sharma, in his careful and factual study on "Some Economic Aspects of Large-Scale Farming," concludes: "Supervision becomes less effective as the size (of the farm) increases."[2] At a much higher level of mechanisation, the trend is perhaps reversed over a certain segment of the curve; but this happens under circumstances which hold for us no practical interest.

While mechanisation does not, generally speaking, lead to increased productivity of land, it does result in increased productivity per unit of labour, by making it possible to cultivate the same land with a smaller labour force. This does constitute a case for the introduction of mechanisation in a country like the USA or the USSR, but not in a country like India, or in any other country where there exists on land more excess population than can be absorbed in industries in the near future. In such countries, mechanisation should only be adopted in marginal cases such as for purposes of land reclamation, where the soil is, say, too heavy to be worked by hand and simple implements.

If, in a country like India, mechanised cultivation can only be adopted as an exception rather than as a rule, the same remark holds good for large-scale farming. Small-scale cultivation, preferably individual peasant farming, ought to be the rule. This does not, of course, exclude the consolidation of individual holdings, which seems to be desirable in most cases.

Cooperative Servicing

Small farms, be it noted, have one considerable disadvantage compared to large farms. This disadvantage shows itself not so much in field work as in work outside the field.

In sale and purchase, supply of credit, research and the like, there are definite advantages in favour of organisation on a large scale. Even where actual cultivation is carried on in individually owned farms, these farms to show maximum result must be surrounded by a host of cooperatives or public agencies, taking charge of bulk sale and purchase, supply of credit, and other essential services which cannot be organised with any degree of efficiency except on a large scale. Indeed, if such common servicing is provided for in all necessary directions, the organisation of giant farms becomes unnecessary even where mechanisation is adopted. "Mechanical cultivation," writes Prof. W. A. Lewis, "can be combined with small farming (by Western standards) if the machinery is owned by a central agency which cultivates the land for the farmers in return for a fee, while leaving each farmer to plant, weed and reap on his own account."[3] A word may be added on research. In the field of agriculture, government-sponsored research is playing today a significant role in a number of countries. Cooperatives can serve here as convenient channels. For instance, the government may finance agricultural research, while the agricultural extension workers may meet the farmers through their cooperatives. Through these cooperatives the farmers may also, as in some countries like Denmark, hire the services of agricultural specialists.

A firm distinction must be made between cooperative servicing and cooperative farming. While the one is a condition of efficient agriculture, the other is not. This notwithstanding the fact that intellectuals in this country, including our prime minister, feel a righteous but, if the following argument is correct, misconceived enthusiasm for cooperative farming as a golden mean between capitalist and collectivist farming, an enthusiasm which this writer shared till rather recently.

Basic Dilemma

The basic dilemma that besets cooperative farming can be simply stated: either a cooperative farm accepts the egalitarian principle of distribution according to needs, etc., in which case incentives tend to weaken and efficiency suffers, or it adopts the principle of distribution according to work performed, in which case supervisory costs rise sharply, assessment of work being particularly difficult in the field of agriculture. One may feel tempted to challenge this statement by referring to Israel. But Israel is a special case and, even as such, her position is not perhaps entirely stable.

This does not mean that a country, like China, which adopts cooperative farming, cannot raise its agricultural productivity. It can secure an increased agricultural output by bringing new land under cultivation. It can even raise productivity per acre of land through improved irrigation, more effective use of fertilisers, seed control, precaution against infectious diseases of plants, and a hundred other ways. Merely because these measures are adopted at the same time as cooperative farming is introduced, it should not be concluded that the resulting rise in productivity is due to cooperative farming and not to these other measures.

The crucial test lies, of course, in comparing productivity of land under cooperative and other forms of farming, where these different forms exist side by side and where "other things are equal." In communist countries, other things are not generally equal: cooperative farms are specially encouraged and individual peasant farms are discriminated against systematically. Under the circumstances, if productivity in individual farms is higher than in cooperative farms, this is almost a decisive evidence against the relative efficiency of cooperative farming, whereas higher productivity in cooperative farms is not an equally decisive evidence against individual farming.

There is at least one communist country for which the relevant facts have recently been made available. Gomulka, speaking at the eighth plenum of the Polish Communist Party Central Committee on 20 October 1956, presented the following facts: "When estimating the value of overall production per hectare of arable land, we arrive at the following picture: individual farms 621.1 zlotys, cooperative farms 517.3 zlotys, and state farms 393.7 zlotys, at constant prices." Gomulka concludes, "This is in brief an outline of the economic picture of cooperative farms. It is a sad picture. In spite of great outlays they had smaller results and greater costs of production."

To Extract Surplus

From the economic point of view, there is one and perhaps only one solid argument in favour of the establishment of cooperative farms as a rule rather than as an exception. That argument runs in terms of capital accumulation. It is easier for a political centre to control a small number of large farms than a large number of small farms, and such control may be necessary to extract surplus from the peasantry in amounts beyond what would be possible otherwise. But such extraction of surplus is also possible through an agricultural tax. In Japan, in the early stage of industrialisation, no tax was so productive of revenue as the land tax. It is only if a government decides to extract surplus in excess of what it hopes to be able to obtain through such a tax, only if a government thinks it necessary to break the power of resistance of the peasantry that it may discover a basic justification for organising cooperatives of the so-called more advanced type, that is, the type under which the peasant ceases to have any land which he can call his own and on which he can fall back to resist what he considers an unjust imposition from above. This may be essential to totalitarian planning, but in India we profess to follow the democratic way.

The golden mean between capitalist and collectivist or State farming, if such a mean exists, lies in individual peasant farming based chiefly on family labour, and supported by cooperative servicing. Strictly speaking, this is no mean at all, but a third way; but it is, perhaps, the only democratic way. In a democratic country like India, there is every justification for the government to display increased initiative in organising agricultural training, extension work, and research, and in other ways helping the peasant to improve the productivity of the land that he loves, while, at the same time, taxing away a part of the fruits of such improvement; and for strengthening the texture of communal life in the rural areas so that, through improved communication of ideas and social cooperation, innovations or better techniques of production, first adopted by a few, are quickly passed on and shared by the whole community. But this can be called the cooperative way only in the very broadest sense of that term.

Notes and References

[1] Adam Smith, *The Wealth of Nations*, book 3, ch. 4.

[2] A. N. Sharma, "Some Economic Aspects of Large-Scale Farming," *Economic Weekly* 8, no. 50 (15 December 1956), p. 1433.

[3] W. A. Lewis, *The Theory of Economic Growth*, pp. 130–31.

22

Context for Cooperatives in Rural India*

Daniel Thorner

In order to find out how agricultural cooperatives were functioning and were likely to function in the future I decided to go and see things for myself. Accordingly, between December 1958 and May 1959 I visited some 117 cooperatives scattered throughout most of the states of India.

The particular societies which I visited were not selected by me. Rather, they were selected by the local authorities, but not at random. Since I was interested in the prospects for successful cooperation, I asked the local people (from the cooperative departments, in most cases) to take me to their best societies. Since they would want to show me their best, there would be no harm in asking them to do what they were, in any event, almost certain to do. Further, the places in which I halted while on tour were, wherever possible, well-known for their achievements in the field of cooperation. Hence it was not by chance that my itinerary included Baroda, Salem, Kolhapur, Nilgiris, Mandya, and Anakapalla. In this way I saw not merely good cooperative societies, but the best of the best. These societies, however, did not constitute a properly drawn sample, whether of all cooperatives or of good cooperatives. They are merely cases or illustrations which happened to be brought to my attention when I asked for the best.

As it happened, my field tour followed close upon an important shift in governmental policy with regard to cooperatives. A decision had just been taken at the highest level to go no further with the integrated credit scheme which had been taken up at the recommendation of the Reserve Bank. As against the Reserve Bank's larger-sized societies, the new policy emphasised single village, multi-purpose service cooperatives. These, it was stated, ought to serve as a

* Originally published in *Economic Weekly* 14, annual number (February 1962), pp. 251–66.

transition to cooperative joint farming. Since the implementation of the Reserve Bank programme had begun only three years earlier, the reversal had an upsetting effect on many cooperators. On the other hand, the government's unprecedented stress on cooperation as an instrument of development made the subject a live one wherever I went.

The Leading Cooperators

When I arrived at the office of a village cooperative society, the first persons who came to meet me, or indeed were already waiting, were usually the members of the managing committee. In discussion I tried to ascertain the social make-up of the village and to find out which groups were represented in the cooperative and which in the managing committee. In quite a few places the people whom I met were anxious to impress upon me the importance of the heads of their cooperatives. They took pride in telling me that these cooperators were big men in trade, in government contracts, in rice-milling, in land-holding, and in local politics. In general, I found that the heads of cooperatives were the big people of the villages and that they had their fingers in many other pies as well as cooperation.

For example, the leading figures of the multipurpose cooperative at Saadhi in Baroda District of Gujarat are all landholders from the dominant local community, the Patels. They own enough land so that they do not have to work with their own hands. They have managed to get around the land reform, and some of them were giving out land on a 50-50 cropshare basis to the lesser folk of the village. Some of the leading figures in the cooperative appeared to be lending money informally on a private basis. The previous head of the cooperative had gone on to become the chairman (sarpanch) of the village panchayat (the council of the village).

Power Concentration in Single Family

One of the outstanding cooperative joint farms in Gujarat is located at Rasulabad, ten miles north of Baroda. It seemed to be well run, and the benefits of the members included purchase of schoolbooks for their children. But it was functioning as a one-family show, operated mostly on family land by one of the landlord families of the village. Three brothers from this single family were serving respectively as the chairman of the managing committee, the managing director, and the farm manager. More of the work of the farm appeared to be done by hired labourers than by the members themselves.

Sadoli in Kolhapur District affords a different kind of illustration of concentrated power of a single family. Seven brothers here constituted the village's leading family and wielded the greatest influence in the multipurpose cooperative. One brother was village sarpanch, another was director of a lift irrigation cooperative, while a third was director of a nearby cooperative sugar cane factory. In addition to owning more land than any other family, the seven brothers also owned five mechanical vehicles (tractors, bulldozer, car, lorry). During the busy season they employed more than fifty labourers. In the Sadoli multipurpose cooperative, half of the outstanding short-term loans (Rs. 95,000 out of a grand total of Rs. 191,000) had been made to only eleven members.

In Salem District of Madras, perhaps as celebrated as any in the state for work in cooperation, one family has dominated the movement for a generation. In 1959 one member of that family was simultaneously the president of no less than six cooperatives and the director of several others. The cooperative movement of the district seemed to be little more than an extension of his personality.

Work Done by Hired Labour

At a joint cultivation cooperative in Coimbatore District of Madras only three out of 28 members actually went out and helped till the society's fields. In another joint cultivation society in North Arcot, three-quarters of the members were absentees, and none of the full members living in the village actually did physical work in the fields. In both cases the cooperatives served as a form of organisation whereby the full members could receive aid from the state and yet get their work done for them by the employment of hired labourers.

Nauranga in Kanpur District of UP is perhaps the best-known in North India of the large-sized societies of the type recommended by the Reserve Bank. The society appears, however, to be under the wing of the local landlord, the ex-zamindar, who used to hold not only Nauranga but several other villages as well. He has been serving as a director of the Kanpur District Cooperative Federation. Peasant members of the new society assert that the big people, the ex-zamindars, get first preferential treatment from the cooperative, while application from the lesser folk are handled in dilatory fashion.

Chairman, Patel, and Sarpanch—All Three in One

The chairman of a new, large-sized society in the Sehore area of Madhya Pradesh was simultaneously the village patel (headman of the village), the sarpanch, and director of at least two other cooperative societies. He lived in a splendid house and was one of the three largest cultivators in the village, with four farm servants working for him full-time all year round.

In the Hyderabad District of Andhra the president of a new large-sized society founded in 1956 was a military contractor owning a mansion and a new car, while the secretary-treasurer was one of the largest landowners. Similarly, at a nearby and highly reputed single-village primary society, the president, in addition to being the largest holder in the village, was also a PWD (public works) contractor.

Mysore furnishes the example par excellence of leading families who completely control village affairs, including the cooperatives. These are the *mukhyestaru*, the local "all-in-alls." To an extent perhaps unequalled anywhere else in India, they are at one and the same time the principal landowners, chief traders, main moneylenders, shopkeepers, and village officials. The mukhyestaru have generally opposed the formation of cooperatives. Once these are established, however, they join the societies to take them over for their own purposes.

Masters and Servants

Let us now take a closer look at the range of activities of the bigger people who are so often found at the helm of the cooperatives. Their holdings, as we have noted, are likely to be the largest, or among the largest, in their villages. These they can either cultivate directly through hired labourers, or they can give them out for others to cultivate on payment of rent in cash or in kind. In actual practice the bigger people often do both. They keep some of their land directly in their own hands, and they give out the rest to others. To the extent that land is given out, they are likely to be giving out the most. As such, they wield great power. The little people, desperate to get land, cannot sit as equals with the important people who have significant amounts of land to give out. It is doubtful that they can work together on a cooperative basis.

Insofar as the large landlords are also big cultivators, they are the principal employers of agricultural labour. When the labourers are utterly landless, they are, with rare exceptions, not enrolled as members of the local cooperative. By contrast, there are numerous cases in which the labourers own tiny patches or take in bits of land on lease or cropshare. Some of these labourers may well have joined the cooperative. If so, there is almost certain to be a wide gap between them and the top people by whom they are hired. The employer is the master, and his hired labourer is the servant; in the languages of India there are no terms for distinguishing an employer-employee relationship from that of master-and-servant.

The relations of master and servant are typically complex. The labourer or his father may have borrowed money from the master, either in time of distress or for a major ceremony like marriage. Or the labourer may simultaneously be taking some pieces of land from the master on cropshare (*batai*). The masters may come from one caste and the labourers from another that ranks lower. The implications of caste differences and caste rivalries have been so widely commented on that we will not attempt to add anything to that subject here.

We cannot overlook, however, the question of attitude toward physical work in the fields. There is very little belief in India in the dignity of labour. For the most part, whoever can escape it considers manual labour an indignity. The surest way by which a family whose fortunes have been improving can stake a claim to higher standing in the village is for the members to abstain from manual labour. It is safe to say that in most of India the distinction between those who work with their own hands and those who do not cuts deep. It is idle to expect those who do not soil their hands, and their hired labourers who do, to work together in the spirit appropriate to a cooperative. Not only may the masters not be prepared to "work together," they may simply not be prepared to work at all!

Moneylenders in the Societies

One cannot help but be impressed by the position occupied in the cooperatives by one or another type of person who lends money. The cultivator who also does some moneylending figures prominently in cooperatives in Baroda, Saurashtra, Hyderabad, and Rajasthan. The trader-cum-moneylender is found in societies in Saurashtra, Mysore, the Nilgiris, Nellore, and Kashmir. The formidable combination of the cultivating moneylender-cum-trader dominates the scene in Mysore and coastal Andhra. If the aim of the cooperative credit societies has been to free the cultivators from the grip of the moneylenders, then the moneylenders do not belong in the societies, let alone in the leadership. How, then, have persons who lend money come to occupy so prominent a place in the cooperative movement?

Here we have to bear in mind that the need of the villagers to take loans is crucial and chronic. The bullock may die in the middle of the ploughing season; a son may be seriously ill; in the period between one harvest and the next, the foodgrains in the family jars may run out, etc. At such times the peasant must borrow and he cannot be choosy about rates of interest. He will have to pay whatever is asked. Hence, the lending of money is a very paying proposition. Bigger peasants whose crops have done well may find themselves with funds to spare. In such situations they may very well do a bit of moneylending. Among the well-off peasants, including those who are members of cooperatives, the growth of moneylending may almost be termed a natural process.

Persons well supplied with funds to lend are *ipso facto* important in the villages. If, as we have seen above, they are also active in cultivation or trade, they may be doubly important. As regards cooperatives, such persons may initially resist their formation. Once the societies are established, however, persons who lend may join the cooperatives, perhaps in order to get direct access to the society's funds. When an important person in the village wants to join the cooperative, it is usually hard to keep him out.

We must also note that it may be government policy to bring the moneylenders into the cooperatives. Perhaps in no area of India in the 1950s did cooperatives expand so rapidly and achieve such complete coverage as in

Saurashtra. In case after case among the best cooperatives, the leadership turns out to be the trader-moneylender.

SAHAKARI OR SARKARI?

In many parts of the country the role of government in the cooperatives is so great that the members consider the societies not as their own but as an instrument of the state. To them the cooperatives appear as a source from which they borrow government funds. In Sehore District of Madhya Pradesh the chairman and secretary stated that they fostered this impression because it helped to facilitate recoveries of loans. Similarly, in a well-reputed society near Trivandrum, the members were stated to believe that the loans they got from the society were sums from government. Their term for a loan from the society is, in Malayalam, *sarkar vaipa*, which means government loan.

The state in which these attitudes and feelings are most pronounced is Madras. There the hand of the Cooperative Department bureaucracy seems to be everywhere, in the person of officials on deputation to run the affairs of local societies. The members of one of the best cooperative agricultural banks in Coimbatore District, for example, consider that the sums they borrow from the society are government loans. The borrower feels ("has that fear") that since the loan is from government he must repay in time. The term in Tamil for a loan from the cooperative society is *sarkar kadan* (government loan).

The societies in Madras appear to be bound down very closely by the Cooperative Department's book of rules and regulations. The consequence not only in Madras but in other states as well, is an inelasticity that has been the curse of the movement. In the Nilgiris, members of small and large societies feel that government control is very rigid. In bad seasons they cannot count on the government-controlled societies to see them through. Instead, they must turn to the trader-moneylender, no matter how oppressive he may be; when they most need help, they get a kind of "cooperation" from him. But in their hour of need what they get from the cooperative society is a form of "non-cooperation."

POLITICAL FORCES IN THE COOPERATIVES

The impact of politics upon the cooperatives seems to be getting heavier and more direct. In several states the leadership of the cooperatives is heavily sprinkled with active politicians. In Kashmir, Mysore, and coastal Andhra, for example, there are many MLAs (members of the legislative assemblies) in the top cooperative posts.

Persons who succeed in becoming elected to the legislative assemblies are usually, if they are villagers, from the important and best-off families. They tend to use the cooperatives as levers or weapons in jostling for position with their rivals. Or they show their importance by the number of societies which they keep under their wings. In this connection it has to be borne in mind that the people in power in the capitals of the various states are pretty much the same people in the seats of power in the villages, only occupying larger chairs. When the government decides upon a policy of vigorous support to cooperatives, then the people in power bring in their friends and loyal political supporters to implement the policy. Thus, under the Congress regime in Saurashtra in the early 1950s, Congress workers were encouraged to start cooperatives. During the Communist regime in Kerala, Communist workers were active in promoting cooperatives.

There is a danger that in this process the cooperatives may become political footballs. No matter how well a society may be run, if it is the other party's or the other faction's society, then a change in state regime may take the ground from under its feet. A dramatic illustration of this is afforded by the Anthikad Toddy Tappers' Cooperative Society in Trichur (Cochin), Kerala State. Early in 1959 the local officers of the Kerala Cooperative Department were proud of the success of the society; visitors were struck by the fact that 11 out of 12 of the directors of the society were themselves tappers who still climbed trees to bring down the toddy.

When the new anti-communist regime in Kerala assumed power after the elections early in 1960, one of its first main decisions was to end the system whereby toddy shops were given on negotiated contracts to the toddy tappers' societies.[1] So intimate a relationship between politics and cooperatives does not augur well for the prospects of the movement.

Reserve Bank's "Integrated Scheme of Rural Credit"

The most elaborate plan ever devised for the development of cooperatives in India was put forward at the end of 1954 under the auspices of the Reserve Bank. The basic features of this programme were spelled out in the *General Report* which constitutes Volume II of the Reserve Bank's All-India Rural Credit Survey. Essentially, the Reserve Bank called for a more business-like approach to peasant farming. This was to be achieved by concentrating credit on the productive needs of farm business. The cooperatives were to make advances to the cultivators as producers of crops (not as owners of land). The loans were to be given on the basis that a crop was anticipated, and the amounts of the loans were to be related to the estimated outlay for raising the crop. The recoveries were to be made, as and when the crop was sold, from the proceeds of the sale.[2]

The "integrated" aspect of the Reserve Bank's Integrated Scheme of Rural Credit is the effort to link credit and marketing. The credit cooperative was to finance its members on condition that the produce of the member is sold through the nearest marketing cooperative. One of these marketing societies was to serve a number of credit societies. The credit cooperatives were to arrange for collection and transport of the members' produce to the marketing centre. The sums due to the members for their produce were to be paid through the credit society, which would first deduct for outstanding loans. In this way the integrated scheme was intended to ensure recoveries of loans to members.[3]

The scheme, of course, rests on the assumption that the members of the cooperatives produce crops primarily for sale. As it happens, the main crops of India are foodgrains, most of which the peasant families do not sell but retain for their own consumption. A system such as the Reserve Bank proposed would work best with growers of perishable cash crops like sugarcane or potatoes, which require heavy investment and must be sold quickly after each harvest. But the areas under such special items are limited and they can never displace foodgrains as the dominant crop of the country.

We may also note that the Reserve Bank's scheme did not face up squarely to the credit needs of the peasantry to carry on their existence as social beings. From time to time the peasantry must spend on marriages, education, illnesses, funerals, journeys, pilgrimages, etc. Ceremonies and festivals are either the most solemn occasions of life, or occasions for the greatest rejoicing. The peasantry can and will do without neither. One of the main points made in the Rural Credit Survey was that the borrowings of the peasants must be understood as an overall "balancing factor." Peasant families, the Survey Report observed, get accustomed to a certain level of living. They go on trying to live at that level whether or not in any given year their total resources are sufficient. When they fall short, they borrow. Their loans are a "balancing factor," making up the difference between their total current needs and their total current resources.[4]

It is the strength of the moneylender that he is prepared, at heavy cost to the peasant, to play the role of overall "balancing factor." On this crucial ground, the Reserve Bank's integrated scheme, by contrast, offered him no competition. The bank's scheme made rather vague and grudging allowance for "subsistence" needs in its system of crop loans: "Such needs will be automatically covered if the quantum of crop loans at so much per acre of the particular crop cultivated is properly fixed for each area after taking into account all relevant considerations."[5] One can roughly allocate manure on a crop acreage basis, but it is not so easy to do so with marriages! To be fair, the Reserve Bank did not really attempt to do so; but instead of trying to deal with such problems, the bank fobbed them off with the suggestion that each credit cooperative should also sponsor a "mutual help" fund ("chit fund").

In India, "chit funds" are known well only in the extreme South. There they are loosely organised, take many forms, and have a spotty record.[6] The particular version that the Reserve Bank has suggested is exceedingly complicated and no indication is given that it has ever been tried anywhere. This seems surprising in view of the importance which the Rural Credit Survey has attached to credit requirements for family living. Borrowings for "family expenditure" of all types, the Survey Report stated, many times overshadowed those for investment or for current production purposes.[7] To have put forward an intricate and untested scheme for dealing with these prime needs was neither business-like nor responsible.

The Issue of Size

When it was put forward in 1954–55, the Reserve Bank's "integrated scheme" was well received. The Government of India accepted the main features of the programme and its implementation figured prominently in the Second Five Year Plan (1956–61). In the second half of 1958 the scheme fell into official disfavour, and the government policy shifted to "service cooperatives." The discussion of this change in policy has centred on the question of size, the Reserve Bank's "larger-sized" societies (covering many villages) being contrasted unfavourably with societies limited to a single village (or, at most, say, three villages).

As we shall see, the question of size was not really the basic issue. But it is convenient to take it up first. The Reserve Bank called for "larger-sized" societies so that each could afford to have a trained, full-time paid secretary. For this purpose it has been estimated that each society would have to make a minimum of at least Rs. 50,000 in loans per year. Judged by this criterion the traditional single-village primary societies were, in most cases, too small. Unless each of the societies had a properly trained secretary, the Reserve Bank argued, they would not be viable. Following the Reserve Bank's recommendations, the various states formed thousands of larger-sized societies by mergers of a dozen or so of the older-type, single village societies.

From the time the Reserve Bank's proposals appeared, however, there were those who viewed with regret the way the scheme gave up the single village as the basic unit of rural credit. In their eyes a peasant cooperative did not have much meaning unless the members knew each other well and kept in personal touch. This could not be expected in a cooperative which covered a dozen or more villages. Rather, such societies would tend to be not cooperatives but rural banks.

The prime minister, who had initially welcomed the Reserve Bank proposals, announced in 1958 that he had been mistaken. Mr. Nehru stated that he no longer agreed with the idea of substituting bigger cooperatives for smaller ones. The bigger societies, controlled by an official, might do some good, but they would also do infinite harm in the sense that they would not teach people self-reliance. Rather, they would encourage the habit of looking to government for everything. The Reserve Bank recommendations, Mr. Nehru lamented, had encouraged the tendency of government officials to boss over the people. "We should try to get out of it as quickly as we can and aim at small cooperatives without official interference."[8]

COOPERATIVES AND LAND REFORMS

When the All-India Congress Committee met at Hyderabad in October 1958, they adopted a resolution calling for doubling of India's agricultural production in the next ten years.[9] As might be expected, there were differences of opinion as to what would be required to reach so ambitious a target. An Agricultural Production Sub-Committee was set up to make specific recommendations. Meeting in New Delhi, 6–7 November 1958, the committee drew up two parallel and linked three-year programmes, one involving land reforms, the other involving cooperatives.

Regarding land reform, the committee recommended that comprehensive, thoroughgoing legislation should be enacted in all of the states by the end of March 1959. These measures should include ceilings (limits on the larger holdings), which would result in surpluses being taken away from the bigger owners. Implementation of these laws should take no longer than three years, and should be completed by the end of 1961 (i.e., before the next general election). The surpluses taken away from the larger holders, however, were not to be redistributed in tiny bits. Instead, in the interests of developing a more progressive and better-yielding agriculture, these were to be handed over for cooperative working.

During the same three years that the land reforms were to be implemented, the committee recommended that multipurpose service cooperatives should be formed to cover all the villages of India. These cooperatives should be small enough (covering only one or two villages) to allow for personal touch and intimate knowledge among the members. Such cooperatives, however, were not to be considered ends in themselves. If India's infinite number of small holdings were to be able to take advantage of modern farming methods, they would have to be brought together into larger units. Cooperative farming was inevitable, but it would have to come in stages.[10]

The "service cooperatives" were to be the first stage. The next stage would be joint cultivation, in which small holdings would be thrown together to permit farming on a larger scale, while the property rights of the individual holders would remain separate. In his press conference on 7 November 1958, the prime minister emphasised the linkage among production ceilings and cooperative farming: "We think that in every village there should be joint cultivation. Broadly, that is the approach, and the question of ceiling is more tied up with cooperative farming. Otherwise there is the danger of production going down."[11]

Tasks of the Service Cooperatives

In addition to providing credit, the service cooperatives are expected to collect, to store, and to arrange for the marketing of the produce of their members. Except for special crops in particular areas, cooperatives have had very little success in this field. Progress in the development of cooperative marketing may be expected to lag several steps behind the growth of cooperative credit. A large number of the private parties who lend money are also traders. It has been their custom to take their debtors' crops at prices below the going market rates. So long as substantial numbers of peasants depend for loans upon such traders, the scope for cooperative marketing will remain limited.

One way in which the government may try to strengthen the cooperatives is by making the societies the chief agents for the distribution of fertilisers and improved seeds. Such a favoured position, however, may not turn out to be an unmixed blessing. In practice the handling of seeds is a tricky matter. If the reputation of the cooperative is not to suffer, the right seeds must be ready at the right times, in the right places, in the required quantities.

To a considerable extent the problem is the same with fertilisers. It is also the case that for some years to come fertilisers are expected to be in short supply. The officers of the cooperatives may find the gratifications offered to them for special favours in the distribution of fertilisers almost irresistible. In this connection the diversion to cash crops of fertilisers provided for the Grow More Food Campaign is worth recalling.[12]

The service cooperatives have also been called up to promote such assorted activities as animal husbandry, contour bunding, consolidation of holdings, and more effective use of irrigation water. It is by no means clear how the efforts of the cooperatives along these lines will be integrated with the work already taken up by the community projects and the state agricultural departments. Half a century or more of experience in these fields shows that where achievements have been registered, they have followed upon sustained hard work on a full-time basis by qualified persons. It would seem unsound to expect much by way of accomplishment in these fields from the service cooperatives.

Cent Per Cent Enrolment

The goal of enrolling 100 per cent of the village families in the service cooperatives is relatively easy to attain. Saurashtra has shown how it can be done. There is no reason why similar successes cannot be scored in other parts of the country. In the abstract, the idea of having all the village families in the same cooperative might appear attractive. It would seem to represent a social advance by ensuring the inclusion of the bottom half of the population. Because of their weak economic position, the labourers, artisans, cropsharers, and village servants have generally been kept out of the societies and have failed to benefit from the cooperative movement. These are the elements in village society which have the greatest difficulty in making ends meet and consequently have the most trouble in repaying loans. It might seem heartless to leave them to the mercy of the moneylender while providing cooperative credit and other services to their better-off neighbours. The fact remains, however, that simply bringing the weaker families into the cooperatives does not automatically improve their basic economic position. To gather all these insolvent people up into the cooperatives is doubtless a dramatic gesture. But it means that they carry all their unsolved problems with them into the cooperative. To enroll such families wholesale into the cooperatives before putting their affairs on a better footing is to invite the danger that they will drag the societies down with them.

It must also be realised that cent per cent village membership guarantees equally the enrolment of all the village traders, moneylenders, and landlords. Why should they stay out of the cooperatives when government will be going to such trouble to funnel funds, supplies, equipment, and assistance through the new societies?

THE WEAK AND THE STRONG

People like to think that a comprehensive, well-supported, well-thought-out governmental programme of setting up cooperatives will change the pattern of village power. The evidence suggests that the structure of village power has imposed, and will continue to impose, its own pattern on the cooperatives.

This is not to say that in recent years there have been no important changes in village life. A great deal has happened, but not enough to enable the mass of ordinary villagers to shake off the grip of a few dominant families. The great zamindars of the north and once-haughty mirasdars of the south have lost much of their grandeur. A good deal of land has changed hands. Universal suffrage has come. Compulsory labour (*begar*) has mostly gone. Nonetheless, in areas where the former men of power have declined, others have risen up in their place. Newly arrived men may show their strength by acting more arrogantly than effete aristocrats. In western Uttar Pradesh where the old zamindars have been brought down, the local Jats have talked of buying tractors and driving the Harijan labourers (Chamars) bodily out of their villages. In the south, landowning Thevars have been accused of burning down the quarters (*cheris*) of the labourers.

The fate of land reforms since 1947 furnishes ample testimony to the power of the little oligarchs who run village life. In the past dozen years the states of India have put on the statute books perhaps the largest body of land reform legislation passed in so brief a span of years in any country known to history. The village oligarchs have made a mockery of this legislation, devising 1001 ways of blocking or getting around the law. Their relations and friends in the state legislatures have eased their task by putting numerous loopholes in the laws or adding crippling amendments.

Bombay in recent years was generally considered to have been the best administered of the states. The Bombay Tenancy Act of 1948 has been cited as a model land reform law. A detailed study made for the Planning Commission found the implementation from 1948 to 1953 to have been a dismal failure. The overriding social and economic power of the landlords against their tenants was so great that they did not even bother to take cognisance of the reforms. "For all practical purposes," the authors concluded, the Bombay Tenancy Act "did not exist."[13] The top families in the Bombay villages were, in other words, able to disregard with impunity land reforms carrying the full sanction of the law.

In the eyes of the dominant families the ordinary people are inferiors, dependants, or servants. The little people lack land, education, influence, connections, staying power, resources. Often they even lack work. The top village families are not great lords, but they are strong enough to get the small folk to do their bidding. The dominant families try to abstain from the actual work of cultivation; they get others to turn their sod and lift the water for their fields. Nevertheless, the dominant families consider themselves the principal "cultivators." They are precisely the top groups who, according to report after report of the Planning Commission's Programme Evaluation Organisation, have been securing for themselves the main benefits of the community projects. Similarly, with the water from many of the vast new irrigation projects: they see to it that their fields get the water first and foremost, and leave the rest for the ordinary, weaker folk. Where the panchayats function, these *bare admi* are in the chairs. If labour is demanded in the name of village, the ordinary people must go out in the hot sun. The men from dominant families do not; they send money or lend the use of a tractor.[14]

Firmly lodged in the chief positions of village power today, the dominant families stand ready to seize the lion's share of the vast programme of cooperative development. As the UP peasants say: "*Jiske pas jitna hai, utana use milta hai.*" (To him that hath much, much shall be given.)[15]

Cooperative Joint Farming

It is hard to believe that the service cooperatives will provide a transition to joint farming. Here we have to note that the pressure for such group farming does not spring from India's villages. It is rather a policy laid down in New Delhi. The village strong have not asked for joint farms; they do not intend to surrender control of part or all of their land in favour of their tenants, cropsharers, labourers, or poorer neighbours. Nor, indeed, have these small folk demanded to be allowed to farm jointly with the bigger people. To the extent that the small people of the villages have asked for anything, it is to have in their own right some or all of the land now in the hands of the dominant families.

In the Indian framework today, if cooperative farming is to come, it would have to be imposed. The Government of India have made it clear to all those willing to listen that they do not intend to impose cooperative farming. Even if they were to try, there is no reason to believe that they could succeed. After all, to date the Government of India have not been able to get the panchayats, land reforms, or community projects to work along the lines laid down in New Delhi.

At the centre, in the states, and in the districts, the administration is manned by men who do not believe in cooperative farming. If anything, they have less faith in this latest governmental policy than in panchayats and community projects, to say nothing of their hostility to land redistribution.

There are, however, two kinds of cooperative farms which are likely to increase in number. First is the type so useful in evading land reform, the so-called cooperative which is really a single-family enterprise. Once a group of relatives convert themselves into an agricultural cooperative, they are eligible for such benefits as loans, subsidies or outright grants from government; priorities in securing good seeds and scarce fertilisers; and the free services for several years of a trained secretary. The official review of the cooperative movement in Punjab for 1958–59 reported that "a very large number of cooperative societies are, in effect, owned exclusively by influential families with a bogus membership of some outsiders to give them the appearance of cooperative bodies."[16]

A second type of which we may see more specimens is the kind of state-sponsored cooperative farms I found at Belligetti in Dharwar District (formerly in Bombay, now in Mysore), Kumbhapura in Mysore, Ashokpuri in the Etawah pilot project area (UP), and Jehangirpura near Bhopal (MP). Here poor or previously uncultivated lands were made available by government to special groups of Harijans, labourers, evicted peasants, or displaced persons. Situation, quality of soil, and availability of water were usually unpromising. The initiative in forming these joint farms had come from outside. The motive power to keep them going was furnished primarily by the state governments, which provided money, officers, supplies, and equipment. Joint farms of this description are expensive and unrewarding.

CONCLUSION

Experience in many countries has shown that cooperatives can serve as a means by which peasant cultivators can help each other to improve their position. But the success of rural cooperatives presupposes a modicum of social equality, political democracy, and economic viability among the villagers. These preconditions have not been present in village India and are still not present today. If the cooperative movement in India is to get anywhere, two things must happen first: (1) the power of the village oligarchs—the leading people, the mukhyestaru, to use the Kannada expression—must be curtailed; and (2) the government must become an instrument of the ordinary people and must be considered as such by the ordinary people.

What is happening in India today is that the cooperatives are being asked to create their own pre-conditions, to reconstruct village society so that the ordinary peasants can make effective use of the cooperative method. This is too much to expect. To rush ahead prematurely with cooperatives is to invite failure and give to cooperation a bad name.

Notes and References

[1] *The Hindu*, 3 March 1960; see also *The Times of India*, 14 May 1960.

[2] *General Report*, pp. 386, 433 and 452–53. For a comprehensive assessment of the Rural Credit Survey, see Daniel Thorner, "The All-India Rural Credit Survey Viewed as a Scientific Enquiry," *Economic Weekly* 12, Special Number (4 June 1960), pp. 949–96; the article has been reprinted in *Land and Labour in India*, eds Alice Thorner and Daniel (Bombay: Asia Publishing House, 1962).

[3] *General Report*, p. 454.

[4] *Survey Report*, p. 262.

[5] *General Report*, p. 433.

[6] V. Krishnan, *Indigenous Banking in South India* (Bombay: Bombay State Cooperative Union, August 1959), pp. 130–43.

[7] *Survey Report*, p. 402.

[8] *The Times of India*, 13 April 1958.

[9] *The Times of India*, 13 April 1958. *The Hindu*, 20 October 1958.

[10] *The Times of India*, 8, 10 and 19 November 1958; *The Hindu*, 29 November 1958.

[11] *The Hindu*, 8 November 1958.

[12] "Government of India, Ministry of of Food and Agriculture," *Report of the Grow More Food Enquiry Committee* (Delhi, 1952), pp. 45–46.

[13] V. M. Dandekar and G. J. Khudanpur, *11 Working of Bombay Tenancy Act, 1948: Report of Investigation* by V. M. Dandekar and G. J. Khudanpur, Gokhale Institute, (Publication No. 35, Poona: Gokhale Institute,, 1957), p. 187. The general pattern of land reform in India is discussed in my book, *The Agrarian Prospect in India: Five Lectures on Land Reform*, (Delhi: Delhi School of Economics, University Press, Delhi, 1956).

[14] Cf., "Charter for a Rural Plutocracy," *Economic Weekly* 12 (12 March 1960), pp. 438–39.

[15] For this free but apt. translation, I must thank Mr Thomas B. Keehn.

[16] Cited in *The Hindu*, 14 March 1960.

23

Agrarian Structure in Twelve Districts*

M. L. Dantwala

Distribution of Owned and Operated Area

The feature of our agrarian structure which has attracted most attention is the concentration in the ownership and operation of land. In the twelve districts which were covered by the Second Follow-up Survey, it was found that "big" cultivators, who formed 10 per cent of the total number of cultivating families, held 40–42 per cent of the total cultivated area in seven out of 12 districts. In 10 out of 12 districts, about 60 per cent or more of the total area of cultivated holdings was held by large cultivators who comprised only 30 per cent of the cultivating families. At the other end, the share of "small" cultivators (30 per cent of the total number) was less than 10 per cent in all but two out of twelve districts.

Concentration: A Statistical Phenomenon

Thus, while the fact regarding concentration is undeniable, for any meaningful policy decisions and administrative arrangements it is necessary to have some idea about the size of holdings of the substantial cultivators. The relevant point for enquiry is whether and to what extent the size of the owned and cultivated holdings of such persons is excessive both from the social as well as the agronomic point of view, particularly the latter. It may be noted that the average cultivated area per family of the big cultivators (top 10 per cent) exceeds 25 acres in five out of 12 districts and exceeds 50 acres in the case of only one district (Akola, where the average size of holding of all cultivators is 23.3 acres). Whether a size of holding

* Originally published in *Economic Weekly* 13, nos. 27–29 (8 July 1961), pp. 1159–60.

of less than 25 or 50 acres should be considered as excessive—say, for the purpose of the ceiling legislation—will perhaps be answered differently by different people depending upon their social and economic philosophy, but it would be possible to maintain that the concentration is more of a statistical phenomenon reflecting overall scarcity rather than predatory acquisition by the top few.

Incidentally, it may also be noted that the quality of the land of the big cultivators is generally inferior to that of the small cultivators. If the value per acre of land cultivated by the big and the small cultivators is an indication of the quality of the land, in seven out of 12 districts it was larger for the lands of the small cultivators. In three other districts, though it was smaller, the difference was insignificant.

Another indicator of the "bigness" of the farms of the big cultivators is the value of the gross produce of their farms. The value of gross produce per family of big cultivators exceeded Rs. 4,000 in only two districts (Jullundur—Rs. 4,052, and Akola—Rs. 6,450) out of 12. It was below Rs. 2,000 in seven out of 12 districts. These are our big (top 10 per cent) farmers!

Land Tenure Pattern

The Report of the Follow-up Survey contains information regarding the land leased in and leased out by different classes of cultivators. Before we analyse the data on this question, it may be noted that the definition of ownership—and consequently of tenancy—adopted in this survey differs from the one adopted both by the Population Census and the National Sample Survey. Ownership of land was taken to mean proprietory rights, including the right to sell, lease, mortgage, bequeath or otherwise transfer ownership of land. The NSS, on the other hand, considers a person as an owner if he has the right of permanent heritable possession of the land with or without right to transfer the title which is vested in him. The consequence of this difference in definitions would be that less land would be shown under ownership and more under tenancy by the Follow-up Survey than by the NSS.

The most important feature to note in this connection is that all classes of cultivators—big, medium and small—lease-in and lease- out land. Contrary to the popular belief, the big (top 10 per cent) cultivators lease in anywhere between 3 to 35 per cent of their total cultivated area. In view of the fact that their holdings are relatively larger, even a smaller percentage would constitute a large proportion of the total leased-in land. It is true that as we go from the big to the small cultivators, the proportion of leased-in land to the total cultivated area goes on increasing; and in the case of the small cultivators, it varies from 9 to 47 per cent. Similarly, in regard to owned land given on lease, contrary to the general belief, the small cultivators lease out larger proportions of their owned land compared with the big cultivators. This was so in nine out of twelve districts investigated by the Follow-up Survey. The tenancy legislation in many states which does not discriminate between the small cultivator who leases out land and the big one—for example, in the matter of the right of resumption—and seeks to protect the tenant, may be ironically protecting the big cultivator-tenant against the small cultivator-landlord.

PRODUCTIVITY OF LAND

Another significant feature of the agrarian economy in these districts—which is corroborated also by other enquiries—is that the value of the gross produce per acre is generally lower on farms of the big cultivators compared with that of the small cultivators. Table 23.1 reveals that it was so in nine out of the twelve districts investigated by the Follow-up Survey. In two other districts where it was larger, it was so by an insignificant margin. An interdistrict comparison will also reveal that in Sorath and Akola, the two districts with comparatively larger holdings, the per acre gross produce was distinctly low. This confirms the widely held view that as far as the return to land is concerned, the small farm is not at a disadvantage.

TABLE 23.1: INTER-DISTRICT COMPARISON OF GROSS PRODUCE PER ACRE

District	Value of Gross Produce per Acre for Cultivators (in Rs.)	
	Big	Small
Burdwan	234	214
Monghyr	76	119
Deoria	85	187
Jullundur	147	174
Jaipur	44	47
Sagar	37	46
Sorath	78	108
Akola	70	68
Nizamabad	109	207
Bangalore	91	110
Chingleput	130	178
Quilon	167	162

Source: Report of the Second Rural Credit Follow-up Survey, 1957–58.

Value of Assets

Another interesting feature of the agrarian economy which is of some interest to the credit policy is the composition of the assets of the different classes of cultivators. By the very definition, the value of the assets of the small cultivators would be markedly lower than that of the big cultivators. It is the composition of these assets which has some distinct characteristics. It is observed that the value of livestock and houses—particularly the latter—as a percentage of the total value of the assets is much higher in the case of medium and small cultivators as compared with big cultivators. Correspondingly, the value of land as a percentage of total assets is lower. The value of houses of the families of small cultivators as a percentage of the value of total assets is 25 or more in the case of eight out of twelve districts; but this is so only in two districts in the case of big cultivators. Similar disparity is noticed in regard to the percentage value of livestock in the total assets position of the small and big cultivators. On the whole, it may therefore be said that the composition of assets, from the lender's point of view, is less favourable in the case of the small cultivators.

24

Major and Minor Irrigation Works

A Preliminary Comparison of Costs and Returns*

Ranjit Gupta

For the purposes of this analysis, data about major works of irrigation have been obtained from the study of the Bhakra-Nangal by Dr. K. N. Raj.[1] For minor works, comparable data have been collected through a survey of an experimental project being operated jointly by the Indian Co-operative Union and the Union Ministry of Food and Agriculture.

The project, located in an arid zone of Delhi—in a village called Sultanpore—has been in operation since 1960. It is a large *kutcha* well, about 60 feet deep with a diameter of 200 feet at the top and 40 feet at the bottom, and is fitted with a diesel-driven pump for lifting the water to the embankment and releasing it into the field. Normally, the rate of water discharge is about 16,000 gallons per hour with a capacity to maintain the flow for about ten hours a day. Through a network of *pucca* channels, the well now provides irrigation to about 100 acres of land per crop season or 200 crop-acres a year.

The well has been dug entirely by unskilled labour. With 100 adult men working, the task can be performed in about 4–5 months. Fresh employment opportunities resulting from such works in the villages thus range between 12,000–15,000 man-days. Judging from the experimental well, the total expenditure involved, including the cost of capital equipment and pucca channels, can be fixed at Rs. 60,000 and the cost of operation—salary of the engine driver, cost

* Originally published in *Economic Weekly* 13, no. 50 (16 December 1961), pp. 1857–59.

of fuel, and depreciation and maintenance—at about Rs. 5,000 a year or Rs. 25 per crop-acre.

A comparative study of the Bhakra-Nangal project and the pilot well may be attempted in terms of the criteria suggested by Dr. Raj for selecting between different types of investment. Since projects like the Bhakra-Nangal would besides providing irrigation water, generate electricity while minor projects, like the pilot well, would not, we compare the two projects only as irrigation works.

Investment in irrigation works will be examined in terms of (i) the difference between the private and social costs of the labour employed on an investment scheme, (ii) the difference between the private and social costs of the materials used in the construction of the project, (iii) the difference between the private and social costs of depreciation, (iv) the increase in the social product attributable to the investment, whether through additional input of labour or through greater productivity of labour, and (v) the social coat involved in the time factor.[2] The term "social cost," as used here refers to "the opportunity cost from the social point of view incurred by the use of a scarce resource."[3]

Breakdown of Costs

For the purpose of our study, knowledge of the shares of major elements of costs in the total cost of different types of irrigation works is essential (see Table 24.1). The difference in the absolute cost of the two types of units also needs to be noted. The investment in Bhakra-Nangal (for irrigation only) is enough to meet the cost of construction of nearly 2.5 lakhs experimental wells.

It will be seen from the table that expenditure on unskilled labour is about two-thirds of the total expenditure for the pilot well, and only about one-seventh for the Bhakra-Nangal. Since the machinery and equipment needed for the pilot well are of an elementary type and are produced in the country, the part of expenditure which requires foreign exchange is practically nil for such wells. For the Bhakra-Nangal, expenditure involving foreign exchange constitutes nearly "40 to 45 per cent of the total, since apart from the machinery and equipment and the foreign technical personnel required, almost all the spare parts, and also the bulk of the fuel and the lubricants necessary for the machinery, have to be imported."[4]

Again, while expenditure on internally produced materials is 17.5 per cent for the pilot well—mainly on construction of pucca channels—in the case of Bhakra-Nangal, it is much greater, about 26 per cent. A large part of this expenditure is on cement which has alternative uses and is relatively scarce. In fact, so much cement was needed for Bhakra-Nangal that it necessitated the opening of a cement factory, employing about 2,000 workers, near the site of the project. The construction of the Bhakra Dam thus calls for "resources which

TABLE 24.1: MAIN ELEMENTS OF COST IN MAJOR AND MINOR IRRIGATION WORKS

(As percentage of total cost)

	Pilot	Well	Bhakra-Nangal*	
1. Manpower				
(a) Unskilled	66.6	67.6	14	32.0
(b) Semi-skilled and skilled	1.0		18	
2. Machinery and equipment		8.3		30.0
3. Materials				
(a) Relatively scarce (fuel, oil, bricks, cement, etc.)	3.0	17.5	16	26.0**
(b) Others	14.5		11	
4. Miscellaneous		6.6		12.0
		100.0		100.0

Note: The discrepancy in the totalling, as Dr Raj explains, is due to rounding off.
Source: K. N. Raj, *Economic Aspects of Bhakra Nangal Project*: p. 46, Table 6.

are relatively scarce in the economy, involving by implication a higher social cost, and offers relatively limited scope for the use of man-power which the economy has in greater abundance."[5]

It is usually assumed that when there are large reserves of unemployed labour, their utilisation in investment projects does not result in reduction in output elsewhere. Such employment, therefore, does not involve any social cost. In other words, "projects whose construction requires more labour are not more costly from the social point of view than those which require less; indeed, if the use of more labour helps to save other scarce resources in construction, the former would be preferable to the latter."[6]

GREATER USE OF LABOUR

From this point of view, projects like the pilot well offer much greater scope for the utilisation of idle man-power than projects like the Bhakra-Nangal. More than 66 per cent of the investment on the well, as compared to 14 per cent of that on the Bhakra-Nangal, is on unskilled labourers. Significantly, the period during which such employment opportunities were created coincided almost exactly with that during which the Second Agricultural Labour Enquiry Committee found agricultural labour to be unemployed.

Further, since the additional income generated by the investment in small projects goes to the lesser-privileged class in the rural society, the increase in consumption expenditure is on articles like food and clothing, which do not involve any draft on foreign exchange. The social cost of investment which leads to consumption involving draft on foreign exchange "must be reckoned as higher the greater the premium that needs to be placed on foreign exchange."[7]

Major works, on the other hand, require recruitment of highly paid managerial and technical personnel. This results in an increase in the demand for articles like watches, radios, cars, refrigerators, etc., which involves heavy draft on foreign exchange.

Further, since the investment on pilot well projects seeks to increase production of foodgrains in the shortest time possible, the additional demand created, in so far as it is for food articles, can be assumed to be met from the increase in supply. The same would hold true for major irrigation projects also if the execution of such projects did not involve long gestation periods, often extending to over a decade. During this time the increase in the output of foodgrains as a result of the investment is almost negligible.

Cost of Materials and Equipment

What has been said about the social cost of employing labour holds true for the social cost of materials, machinery, and equipment used for the construction of the project. The use of certain types of materials, like sand, earth, gravel, etc., which are available in abundance in the country, do not require their diversion from other uses. The only social cost involved, if any, in the use of such materials is the employment of labour for digging them up and processing them into usable forms. Since such works would have already been accounted for in computing the social cost of employment of labour, no further adjustment is necessary.

But the social cost of materials which are scarce and have alternative uses, like cement, steel, etc., has to be regarded as "at least equal to the cost to the agency undertaking the investment, but it may be more to the extent that their use involves a draft on foreign exchange."[8] The greater the premium placed on foreign exchange, the higher would be the social cost.

The pilot well does not involve costs since the materials needed mostly consist of bricks, clay, and sand. Machinery and equipment required are also available from domestic supplies. Consequently, even though expenditure on machinery and equipment amounts to 8.3 per cent of the total expenditure, the element of social cost involved is negligible. For major irrigation works, however, such expenditure is as much as 40 to 45 per cent of the total investment and practically all of it involves foreign exchange resources. Further, these projects, relying heavily on capital equipment, usually take much time—in planning for equipment and awaiting deliveries, and as a result of breakdowns of machinery on account of which utilisation of the plant is often reduced to only 52 per cent.[9] If such delays are also taken into account the time factor goes against the use of heavy machinery.

THE TIME FACTOR

The time factor involved in the execution of irrigation works calls for the greatest consideration, for the longer the time taken in the completion of the work, the greater the delay in the increase in production. From the standpoint of the durability of the project also, the time factor is important, since the longer the expected life of the project, the lower the rate of physical depreciation.

Evaluated on the basis of these considerations, minor irrigation works possess definite advantages over major works. Take the pilot well, for instance. Under normal conditions it can be completed in about four months. Its expected life-period, as estimated by the engineers, is about a 100 years. The rate of physical depreciation per annum would thus be 1 per cent only. Excluding the cost of the pump engine, which is Rs. 5,000, from the total cost of Rs. 60,000, this would mean that the rate of depreciation would be Rs. 550 per annum. Add to this the depreciation on the pump engine at 20 per cent per annum since its life is expected to be five years—and the total depreciation on the well would be Rs. 1,550 per annum only, or about 2.6 per cent.

In assessing the economic consequences of the gestation period the stream of output from the project has also to be taken into consideration. Minor works, like the pilot well, are definitely superior in this respect to major works. This is substantiated by the working of the pilot well. The increase in yields per acre as a result of completion of the project and intensive agricultural development programmes was over 65 per cent. The increase in gross farm income of the farmers who participated in the project was about Rs. 600 per acre. Increase in farm expenses on account of the operation of the well and the use of seeds, fertilisers, and chemicals for improved cultivation, on the other hand, was about Rs. 100 per acre. The net increase in farm income was, therefore, Rs. 500 per acre.

This phenomenal increase in yield and income was no doubt chiefly due to the extremely low levels of yield and income prevailing in the area prior to availability of irrigation facilities. Thus, before irrigation became available, the per acre gross and net farm incomes were only Rs. 138 and Rs. 111 respectively. This also pinpoints the importance of irrigation and the miracles that can be brought about through effective planning of minor works. The increase in farmers' incomes would, in fact, within a few years result in a surplus large enough to meet the initial cost of the project. Since, however, the rate of increase in farm income from year to year would vary and cannot be precisely ascertained, the period in which total investment would be realised can only be projected on the basis of assumed rates.

An annual rate of increase as low as 7 per cent would generate during the expected life period of the project an additional income equivalent to the investment on it. On the other hand, if the average rate of increase is placed at 25 per cent, the total investment becomes realisable within a period as short as 10 years.

Gestation Period

For major irrigation works such information is not available. But the gestation period is too long even on a conservative estimate. These projects take from five to 10 years to complete. Their long lifetime even if assumed to be over a 100 years, that is longer than that of the pilot well—hardly reduces the rate of depreciation. In fact, because of intensive use of machinery and capital equipment, the rate of depreciation tends to become much higher than in the case of minor works. This can be seen from the estimate worked out by Dr Raj for Bhakra-Nangal. It shows that

> for the machinery employed on the project taken as a whole, the cost of depreciation is on the average about 25 per cent of the total cost of operating the machinery, that the share of fuel, oil grease and waste is another 25 per cent, of labour about 15 per cent, of repairs and spare-parts another 15 per cent and of other miscellaneous items about 20 per cent … *that the depreciation of the machinery will in all amount to 75 per cent of the capital cost of the machinery.*[10]

Imputation of cost to time thus makes significant changes in total social cost. Longer the gestation period, higher are the social costs. Investment schemes which involve shorter gestation period, even if less durable, and yield larger gross output are therefore, preferable. "An even more important consideration, weighing the scales in favour of projects with less durability," as Dr Raj aptly concludes,

> is that though a project which is less durable may have a higher rate of physical depreciation, the amortisation quotas of the early years may not actually be required for replacement. These quotas, therefore, represent further investible surplus during the period, and the increase in output accruing from the investment of this surplus may more than cover the resources required for the replacement of the depreciated capital stock at a later stage. This means that, even if the net output of the two schemes is the same after allowing for the different rates of depreciation, there might be a case for preferring the scheme with the larger gross output, i.e. the one with the shorter life.[11]

It is not our purpose to reject major works of irrigation completely. Certainly, they have a role to play in areas where, due to paucity of subsoil water reserves, irrigation facilities cannot be made available by any means except through a network of canals. But where subsoil water reserves are available, planners must recognise the fact that major works are not only a waste of resources and energy but definitely detrimental to the country's progress. Essentially it is a question of striking a balance—of appreciating the merits of the two types of irrigation works and letting each play its role. The official approach lacks this touch of realism. It is blurred by its eagerness to do things in a big way.

Notes and References

[1] K. N. Raj, *"Some Economic Aspects of the Bhakra-Nangal Project: A Preliminary Analysis in Terms of Selected Investment Criteria,"* (Bombay: Asia Publishing House, 1960).

[2] Ibid., pp. 7–8.

[3] Ibid., p. 17.

[4] Ibid., p. 46.

[5] Ibid., p. 46.

[6] Ibid., p. 17.

[7] Ibid., p. 20.

[8] Ibid., p. 21.

[9] Ministry of Irrigation and Power, *"Report of the Construction Plant and Machinery Committee,"* (Ministry of Irrigation and Power, Government of India, 1954), ch. XV15.

[10] Raj, *Some Economic Aspects*, p. 43.

[11] Ibid., p. 20.

25

Size of Holdings and Productivity*

Amartya Kumar Sen

Before we proceed further, a point relating to the background of all this controversy should be stressed. The inverse relationship between the size of holdings and productivity per acre that has been derived on the basis of size-class data, is not yet something that can be taken as a well-established fact. I hasten to add this because I have not yet seen any attempt to use individual holding data to establish this conclusion, and when one deals with averages, it is possible to be misled. My own guess is that I have not been widely misled, but it is still worth bearing in mind that the statistical basis of the observations around which all this controversy is centred, is not really something that has been proved beyond the legitimate doubts of exacting statisticians. With that reservation, I proceed to explain the observation, assuming it to be true.

Three alternative lines of explanation should be distinguished. We can call them, respectively,

(i) technique-based,
(ii) labour-based, and
(iii) fertility-based explanations.

In principle we can suggest a fourth, viz., a capital-based explanation, if we wish to suggest that the smaller farms may be more productive because they can have more capital investment per acre. But the causation of such a process is not immediately obvious, particularly because a bigger farmer usually (a) has more capital to invest per acre, and (b) can borrow money at a lower rate of interest because of his greater "creditworthiness." There is, however, a sense in which

* Originally published in *Economic Weekly* 16, Annual Number (February 1964), pp. 323–26.

capital investment is cheaper for the small farmer, and this can be discussed in the context of the labour-based explanation.

LABOUR-BASED EXPLANATION

I find the technique-based explanation the weakest of the three, though I would not like to rule it out altogether. In its simplest form this can take the shape of assuming "diseconomies of large scale." In this form the argument is open to the obvious objection that diseconomies of scale can be avoided by the big farmer by splitting his big piece of land into small bits and cultivating them in these smaller units. In fact, there is very little evidence of any such diseconomy proper associated with scale. There is, however, a more sophisticated form of this argument. Because of personal participation and supervision that a small business allows, a small holding may permit the use of some techniques—efficient ones—that cannot be used in larger holdings. Some techniques require not only inputs in the usual sense but also loving care, and Adam Smith had directed our attention to the "affection" that small property inspires. It may be difficult to make a paid labourer do what the owner himself would. For a well-reasoned development of this line of argument I have only to refer the reader to Amlan Datta's essay on the subject (*Essays on Economic Development*, Essay 7).

The second line of argument is the one I adhered to in my earlier note referred to above. In a situation of widespread unemployment, the opportunity cost of labour to a family-based farm is very low, but for various reasons (mainly perhaps sociological), the wage rate does not go down below a certain level, considerably higher than the opportunity cost. As a consequence, the family-based farmer applies labour more liberally with less restraint than the wage-based farmer, and this naturally leads to a higher productivity per acre of the small farms because these are mostly family-based farms rather than wage-based ones. Before this argument is further developed, a few preliminary questions can be sorted out, including the ones that Dipak Mazumdar has raised.

First of all, it should be noted that an extreme case of this difference is given by the possibility of marginal opportunity cost of labour being zero in a family-based economy. This will be the case when unemployment is really rampant. In a more general case the relevant opportunity cost may be given by the wage rate suitably weighted by a certain probability of finding a job, the probability being less than 1. If p is the probability of getting a wage-job, and w the wage rate, the opportunity cost of labour can be taken to be equal to (p.w). Since $p < 1$, (p.w) will be below w. In the extreme cases of full employment we have $p = 1$, and the two values coincide; in the other extreme case of hopeless unemployment, $p = 0$, and the value of the opportunity cost becomes nil. But as long as $p < 1$, we shall expect, given other things, a lower output per acre for wage-based farms, because labour will be applied there with greater restraint, and will not be carried beyond the point where marginal productivity of labour is equal to the wage rate. On the family-based farm, however, labour will be applied more freely up to the point where marginal productivity of labour equals (p.w). The extreme case only heightens this contrast.

Secondly, if there is full employment in a "busy" season and unemployment in a "slack" season, the argument still holds. Since there is complementarity between labour applied in different seasons, the lower opportunity cost of labour in the "slack" season (compared with the corresponding wage rate) makes the cost of a composite unit of labour less than the average wage. Thus, greater utilisation of labour takes place even in this case for smaller farms. This, as I understand it, is the core of Mazumdar's argument, shorn of its somewhat more complex background. It is really an extension of the cheap-family-labour line of explanation rather than a new kind of explanation. But I think it is an important extension.

Thirdly, Mazumdar's argument for preferring the above explanation to the one I had put forward does not seem to me to follow from the data he quotes. He says, in criticising my explanation, "the explanation breaks down when we note the fact that in the data presented by the Farm Surveys, both small and large farms make use of some hired labour. So long as any hired labour is used, the marginal supply-price of labour to the farm will be given by the ruling wage rate, and consequently input of labour would be carried to the same point in farms of various sizes, so long as the production function is the same."[1] This argument overlooks the fact that the data presented by the Farm Management Surveys are size-class averages and do not state the position of any individual holding. Just because in the average data it is found that in each class a certain amount of hired labour is used, it does not follow that all or even the bulk of the farms in the smaller size-groups use hired labour at the margin. Mazumdar takes the given amount of hired labour in each size-group, and assumes that it is spread evenly on all pieces of land of that size-group (somewhat like butter on a toast). In fact, in the other extreme we might find a case when hired labour is used in a very small number of farms, and even then the class-average will show some hired labour for this size-group. I am not claiming that this last is in fact the case, which it probably is not, but only that the data that Mazumdar quotes is insufficient for his argument. We require not only the average figure for his argument but also some information on the proportion of farms where any hired labour is used. In fact, more complete individual holding data are what are needed to substantiate (or invalidate) Mazumdar's line of explanation.

Fertility-based Explanation

Now, irrespective of whether we take the simpler version of the labour-based explanation or the extension proposed by Mazumdar, we have a picture of a more free application of labour in smaller holdings and a consequent larger output per acre. We can now look at the third approach. The fertility-based explanation is quite different from all this. What we could suggest here is that the smaller farms have higher output per acre because they are more fertile. The only work I know of in this line is that of A. M. Khusro in his unpublished note, "Some Basic Generalisations in Indian Agriculture." The Farm Management Surveys deal with crude figures of acreage without any correction for fertility. Khusro finds that when a correction for fertility is made, "farm business-income per corrected acre is now seen in almost all States to increase slightly by the size of farm," which is the reverse of the relation with uncorrected acres.

Khusro does not go into any explanation of his important observation, but if I had to justify the fertility-based explanation, I should proceed this way. Even if we start from a situation of no relation between fertility of land and the size of holdings, a positive relation between the two will be soon established through a more rapid expansion of population on the more fertile land than on less fertile ones. If two pieces of land are of the same size but holding A is more fertile than holding B, the former will provide a greater opportunity of earning income, so that family size may expand faster in the former case. This will lead to quicker subdivision of A than of B, and soon a correlation may be established between smallness of the size of the holdings and fertility of soil. This argument is easy to see in the context of interregional variation, because it has been often observed that in fertile areas population expands faster both because of natural increase as well as migration. But the picture can be expected even within a given region, particularly because the ability of a family to withstand famines and other catastrophes is greater if the land it owns is fertile than if it is not. Thus, the correlation between size and fertility is not an odd result, but one that can be expected on good economic grounds.

Having put forward this explanation, I should, however, like to express a reservation about empirically testing the validity of the hypothesis of fertility variation. Fertility data are notoriously difficult to come by, and in some publications what is taken to be fertility is often nothing more than a figure based on past productivity per acre, which tends to make the fertility-based explanation of productivity differences quite circular. Khusro does not take data of this kind, but takes land revenue data as indicators of fertility. I personally have some reservations also on this because very often land revenues are based on other considerations such as ability to pay which may be more related to productivity than to fertility. But Professor Khusro's attempt to bring fertility into the discussion seems to be on the right line.

Now in this note I have done no more than state some hypotheses and have tried to clarify their economic bases. On the economic grounds put forward here I would expect some truth in the fertility-based explanation. Professor Khusro's data seem to support this, and it will be interesting to have other empirical studies taking some basis for evaluating fertility other than land revenue. But again, on economic grounds I would expect some truth in the labour-based explanation also. And we should further note the fact that the amount of labour applied per acre does seem to be greater for smaller farms, a fact that was quoted in my earlier note.[2] This lends support to the labour-based explanation, and its theoretical basis is indeed quite sound. We can also bring in capital in this context, because a substantial part of capital investment in small farms takes the form of direct labour input in capital projects, so that the cheap cost of labour is reflected in the cheap cost of capital of this type. The technique-based hypothesis is also not to be dismissed, at least not in its more sophisticated form, even though my guess will be that this is a much less important factor in the context of present Indian farming. The real question is, it seems to me, not which of these hypotheses is right, but what are their relative importance. And that can be determined only by an empirical study, and the main object of putting forward these hypotheses in this note is to stimulate precisely this kind of empirical work.

Notes and References

1 D. Mazumdar, "Relative Efficiency of Small Farmers," p. 1259.

2 A. Sen, "An Aspect of Indian Agriculture."

26

Problem of Numbers in Cattle Development*

V. M. Dandekar

The problem of numbers in cattle development is getting worse, judging from the Livestock Census in 1961. The problem is both of the old and useless stock as also of the surplus young stock.

The present solution, which apparently does not offend anybody's susceptibilities, is to keep the numbers under control through a process of neglect and starvation. This has not altogether prevented the numbers from growing, and as numbers grow, even greater starvation will have to be resorted to in order to achieve the required results.

For now, with epidemics such as rinderpest brought under control and veterinary services improving, the rate of mortality from disease will decline and that from starvation will have to be stepped up. Those who survive starvation are not necessarily those who should survive. As a process of weeding out, starvation is thus indiscriminate. It is also uneconomical and wasteful.

True, slaughter of cattle is not in consonance with our cultural tradition and values. But which is more humane and more in harmony with our cultural tradition and values: slaughter or killing through starvation?

Whatever the choice we make, let it be firmly understood that there is no escaping from the elementary principles of livestock husbandry, namely, that without adequate weeding out through appropriate selection between sex and age and between one animal and another, there can be no efficient management of stock.

If we neglect these elementary principles, we shall only be postponing and making more difficult the development of cattle in this country. The elementary

* Originally published in *Economic Weekly* 16, Annual Number (February 1964), pp. 351–55.

truth shall prevail: without some measures to control their numbers, cows will not grow—only their numbers will grow.

The All-India Livestock Census taken in 1961 shows that the cattle population of the country has increased by about 10 per cent over the five-year period 1956–61. This would be considered as quite satisfactory if all the cattle population could be regarded as wealth. Unfortunately, this is not so. As is well known, the quality of our cattle is generally very poor. All our cattle is not wealth and much of it probably a net burden on the resources of the country. One of the principal reasons for the poor quality of the cattle is its large number in relation to the available fodder and feed resources, and it is evident that in order to improve the quality of the stock, something will have to be done to reduce and to regulate the numbers.

The problem of numbers in relation to resources is now generally well-recognised with regard to the human population and the need for a population policy is accepted. In regard to cattle, however, because of the sentiment surrounding the cow, the problem of numbers has not so far been discussed dispassionately. As is well known, cattle and buffaloes are bred and reared as draught and milch animals rather than for meat. There is practically no breeding and rearing of cattle for beef, as a majority of the population does not eat beef. Not that cattle are not slaughtered at all. But generally it is the useless animals that find the way to the slaughterhouse and that too, through devious ways. It is this fundamental aversion to slaughter of cattle, as distinct from killing of smaller animals like sheep and goat, that has stood in the way of an economic approach to the problem of cattle development in this country. The problem is both a delicate and a difficult one. But it is for that very reason that a dispassionate discussion is all the more necessary.

Birth Control Ruled Out

Whether it is the human population or the cattle population, a population grows every year by the balance of births over deaths. Until recently, death took a fairly heavy toll of life of both men and cattle and did not leave much balance of births to add to the total number. But recently, the situation has changed radically. For both, epidemics and diseases have been brought under fairly effective control and improved health or veterinary services have greatly reduced mortality. As a result, an increasingly larger balance of births over deaths is being added annually to the total number. It is thus that the recent censuses have shown very large increases in numbers both of the human and the cattle population.

In the case of the human population, the consequences of a fall in the death rate are now well-recognised. A fall in death rate is of course to be desired. Indeed, it should be one of the primary objectives of economic and social policy. With improved standards of living, no one should die prematurely; everyone should live up to a ripe old age. However, this is impossible to achieve without a limitation of numbers. The corollary is therefore accepted that fewer must be born. Thanks to science, this has now become possible. Family planning figures prominently today as an important state policy.

The consequences of a fall in the death rate in the cattle population are similar but the solution has to be different. Here the control of births is not possible. A cow is maintained because she drops a calf and gives milk. Even if the calf were not needed, a cow must drop a calf every year if she is to remain in milk. Therefore, if births of calves are controlled, a cow would cease to be in milk for long periods. At present, because of their emaciated condition, only one-third of the adult cows are found to be in milk. If birth control is adopted as a means of checking growth of numbers, not even one-tenth of the cows could be kept in milk and it would be impossible economically to maintain such a herd of cows.

The Alternatives

This is a major point of difference between human and cattle population. There is reluctance to admit that there is this difference and much sentiment is brought to bear on this issue. In particular, a great deal of argument is spun out of the symbolisation of the cow as the mother. This merely clouds the issue. There is no point in denying that there can be no analogy between the cow and the mother. There are several practices which have now come to be accepted in respect of the cow, such as cross-breeding, artificial insemination, and economic recovery of the carcass, which do not quite fit the analogy of the mother. It should therefore be explicitly understood that whatever be our sentiment, the reason why a cow is maintained is that she drops a calf and gives milk, and gives it in sufficient measure to justify her feeding. If she failed to do that, she would not be fed.

Thus, the control of cattle population through control of births is not possible. The only choice left is therefore that of controlling the population through the operation of a higher rate of mortality. There are three alternative methods of doing this. One is to allow more deaths by disease and epidemics. This is obviously not desirable. Diseases not only kill, they also disable the living and reduce their work efficiency; and epidemics might endanger entire herds. Increased mortality through disease and epidemics cannot therefore be allowed. The second alternative is to slaughter, which we are unwilling to contemplate. The only choice then left is to let the animals that it is uneconomic to maintain die of neglect and starvation. It is thus that we are at present trying to keep the numbers down in the cattle population. The consequences are to be seen in the census figures.

Less Cows than Bullocks

As an illustration, let us examine the census figures for Maharashtra. According to the 1961 livestock census, there were in Maharashtra 85.5 lakhs of bullocks and 67.8 lakhs of cows. The number of cows is thus about 20 per cent less than that of bullocks. How did this difference in numbers come about? Not by sending more cows to the slaughterhouse but by the higher mortality of cows. Between a bullock and a cow, the bullock is the more valued and needed animal. Cows are needed primarily to breed bullocks and secondarily for the milk they give. In order that they may be able to do draught work, bullocks have to be fed adequately. Cows do not have to be fed as much in order to be able to breed. Therefore, bullocks are the first charge on the available fodder and feed supplies, and cows get only the residue. It is this differential feeding and care that leads to differential rates of mortality among bullocks and cows and ultimately results in 20 per cent fewer cows than bullocks.

Let us look at the figures a little more closely. The distribution of bullocks and cows in different age-groups was as follows:

TABLE 26.1: DISTRIBUTION OF BULLOCKS AND COWS IN DIFFERENT AGE GROUPS

Number in Lakhs

Age Group (Years)	Bullocks	Cows	Total
0–1	9.7	9.6	19.3
1–3	10.9	11.8	22.7
3–	64.9	46.4	111.3
Total	85.5	67.8	153.3

Source: All-India Livestock Census 1961.

It will be seen that the number of bullocks and cows in the two young age-groups, 0–1 and 1–3, are about equal, which means that no selection takes place as between male and female youngstock. However, in the adult stock above three years of age, the number of cows is almost 30 per cent less than that of bullocks, thus indicating that a definite process of selection operates against the cows. The process of selection does not operate through slaughter of female stock for beef or even slaughter of useless female stock. In fact, there is evidence to suggest that more bullocks are sent to the slaughterhouse than cows. For instance, the Annual Administration Report of the Department of Animal Husbandry, Bombay State, for the year 1958–59 records that in that year, as many as 1,22,000 bullocks and only 10,000 cows were slaughtered in the recognised slaughterhouses in Maharashtra. It is clear, therefore, that the process of selection operates against the cows through higher rates of "natural" mortality among the adult stock of cows. In other words, because the cows cannot be fed, nor can they be killed, they are neglected, starved, and left to die a "natural" death.

YOUNG STOCK STARVED

It is not only the old and unproductive animals that are left to starve. In fact, the problem of numbers is not merely the problem of old and unproductive cattle. That is only one aspect of the problem. The problem is more fundamental. It is simply this: a cow is not productive and economic unless she is in milk. To be in milk, she has to drop a calf every year or every other year. On an average a cow thus drops, say, eight calves during her productive life; but so many young animals are not needed to replace and maintain a given stock. Probably only two or three calves per cow would suffice to maintain the stock at a given level. The remaining are surplus and must be culled.

The Indian farmer is denied the facility of culling his young stock. He must therefore take recourse to "natural" mortality through neglect and starvation. This is what he does.

Let us again refer to the census data for Maharashtra. As we have seen, the total young stock, male and female together, in the two young age-groups, 0–1 and 1–3, was 19.3 and 22.7 lakhs, respectively. Now, if there were no mortality in the young stock, the number in the age-group 1–3 would be about twice as large as the number in the age-group 0–1. In point of fact, the number in the age-group 1–3 is only about 20 per cent more than the number in the age-group 0–1. This is on account of the losses due to mortality. Taking these losses to be more or less uniform over the age groups under consideration, the number in the single age years were probably as follows:

TABLE 26.2: NUMBER OF YOUNG STOCK IN SINGLE AGE YEARS

Age in Years	Youngstock Male and Female (in Lakhs)
0–1	19.3
1–2	13.3
2–3	9.4

Source: All-India Livestock Census 1961.

The average ages in the three groups are 0.5, 1.5, and 2.5 years respectively. The above figures then mean that a little over 30 per cent of the youngstock is lost in the year between the ages 0.5 and 1.5 and that a little under 30 per cent of the stock is lost in the next year from the age 1.5 to 2.5. To assess the total mortality in the first three years of life, we must add to this the mortality in the first six months of life, namely, between age 0.0 and 0.5 and also the mortality in the six months prior to completing the third year of life, namely between age 2.5 and 3.0. Taking the incidence of mortality in the first six months to be 20 per cent and in the last six months to be 10 per cent, the following may be inferred.

Substitute for Culling

The recorded stock of 19.3 lakh in the age-group 0–1 implies that there are about 24 lakh of births annually, and the recorded stock of 22.7 lakh in the age-group 1–3 suggests that only about 8.5 lakh animals complete their third year of life every year. In other words, out of 24 lakh annual births, only 8.5 lakh, which is about 35 per cent, survive the first three years of life. Thus clearly, because the number of youngstock is large and so much adult stock is not wanted or cannot be supported, the youngstock is allowed to die. The fact that the mortality among the male and the female youngstock is about the same suggests that no more bullocks than their present number are needed or can be afforded. Consequently, no special care is taken even of the male youngstock. The youngstock, male and female alike, is left more or less to shift for itself. Under these conditions about 35 per cent of the young survive and become adult. Unfortunately, as it turns out, even this rate of mortality is not adequate to arrest the growth in total stock.

Thus the problem of numbers in cattle development is not merely the problem of the old and unproductive animals. The problem is more fundamental, namely, that an adult stock of given size gives birth to youngstock much larger than is needed to replace and maintain the stock of given size. It is for this reason that stock control through appropriate selection and weeding has been accepted as one of the cardinal principles of scientific stock management. Rather than facing these facts squarely and accepting selection and weeding of youngstock as the method of stock control, solutions are sought in other directions.

Dual-Purpose Breed No Solution

It is sometimes argued that the problem of surplus youngstock arises because the present Indian cow is by and large not a dual-purpose animal. The breed which gives good draught animals does not give good milch cows. And because premium is placed on the male stock for draught purposes, the female youngstock is regarded a surplus. It is therefore hopefully suggested that if we had a really good dual-purpose breed, there would be no problem of the surplus youngstock because the male as well as the female calves would be equally useful However, without questioning the usefulness of a dual-purpose animal, it should be clearly understood that dual-purpose cattle do not solve the problem of numbers, neither of the old and useless cattle nor of the surplus youngstock. To see this, one should appreciate that even with dual-purpose cattle, the difference between a cow and a bull remains. It is not as if one and the same animal gives milk and provides draught power. Therefore, one must still decide as to how many bulls one needs for draught work, how many cows to supply the needed male stock and milk, and how much youngstock is milk, and how much youngstock is needed of either sex to replace and maintain the requisite numbers. All the rest is surplus and has to be weeded out.

Let us, as an illustration, consider again the census data for Maharashtra. Let us suppose for a moment that all the cattle in Maharashtra are a good dual-purpose breed and examine the requisite size of the youngstock needed to replace and maintain a given size of adult stock. At present, the adult stock consists of 64.9 lakh bullocks and 46.4 lakh cows. Let us suppose that the present number of bullocks is required and is adequate. From the fact that the stock has been increasing by 2 per cent per annum, it is obvious that the present stock of cows is more than adequate to replace the present stock of bullocks.

DELIBERATE WEEDING-OUT NEEDED

We have seen that the present stock of cows gives birth to 24 lakh calves annually. With a stock of cows better fed and better in health, it can be shown that about 40 lakh cows are enough to produce a crop of 24 lakh of calves annually. Further, we have seen that in the present conditions of feeding and care of the youngstock, of the 24 lakh calves being born annually, only about 8.5 lakh survive the first three years of life. This is because of the high mortality among the youngstock arising out of neglect and starvation. If this mortality is reduced to even half its present level, which needs no more than a little better care and feeding of the youngstock, it can be shown that only 18 lakh of new births are needed annually to produce the same adult stock of 8.5 lakh every year. This means that a stock of no more than 28 lakh adult cows would be needed to replace and maintain an adult stock of 65 lakh bullocks. Thus, in the adult stock, the female stock need be no more than 40 per cent of the male stock. But the proportion of male and female in the youngstock would be more or less equal and hence it is evident that at least 60 per cent of the young female stock will have to be weeded out every year.

Such deliberate weeding out at an early stage will help reduce the size of the youngstock and will enable it to be fed and looked after much better and hence will lead to higher survival rates in the same. Also, if the stock of adult cows is reduced in due course from its present level of 46.4 lakh to no more than 28 lakh, that will itself enable the stock to be fed better and thus improve the milk yields. This reduced stock of cows can then give all the milk and much more than what the present large stock gives. However, if someone argues that there is no need to weed out the young female stock and that we could let the entire female stock grow and have more milk, he must understand that it means that we shall then have more than 28 lakh adult cows that we need in order to breed the requisite male stock, that, consequently there will be more than 18 lakh annual births and that ultimately we shall have to weed out not only the female stock, but also the male stock.

Overburdening the Resources

Let it be firmly understood that under no circumstances can we let the entire youngstock to grow into adult stock without allowing the total stock to grow without limit, thus overburdening the resources and in consequence deteriorating the stock and the resources. Therefore, with or without dual-purpose cattle, the need for selection and weeding out remains paramount.

Thus the problem of numbers in cattle development is the problem of both the old and the useless stock as also of the surplus youngstock. The present solution, which apparently does not offend anybody's susceptibilities, is trying to keep the numbers under control through a process of neglect and starvation. As experience has shown this has not altogether prevented the numbers from growing. It is evident that as numbers grow even starker starvation will have to be resorted to in order to achieve the required results. Moreover, until recently, epidemics and diseases helped in the process. A neglected and famished animal easily fell prey to epidemics and diseases and did not have to suffer the agony too long. But now with the epidemics such as the rinderpest brought under effective control and with veterinary services improving it will not be so easy to die of a disease and the animal will have to suffer the pains of hunger over longer periods. Therefore, to be effective, the process of starvation will have to be not only starker but also longer.

Quite apart from the agony to which the animals are subjected in the process, elimination by starvation is indiscriminate whereas weeding through slaughter can be selective. The maxim of the survival of the fittest is only a tautology; those who survive are certainly those who are fit to survive, but not necessarily fit for anything else. In particular, those who survive long periods of starvation are not necessarily those who should survive. As a process of weeding out, starvation is thus indiscriminate. It is also uneconomic and wasteful. The carcass of a healthy and well-fed animal has many uses and is thus of much economic value. The same animal put through a long process of starvation eats up most of its economic value and finally leaves behind a carcass with nothing but bones and much inferior hide. But the process is uneconomic for other reasons as well. Slaughter, while it kills some, enables the rest to be fed better. The process of starvation on the other hand requires a much larger number to be underfed and starved than need be eliminated.

NOT FAIR TO THE FARMER

Thus, compared to slaughter, elimination through a process of starvation is indiscriminate, uneconomic, and wasteful. True, slaughter of cattle is not in consonance with our cultural tradition and values. But it must be a matter of opinion and taste as to whether slaughter or killing through starvation is more in harmony with our cultural tradition and values.

Faced with these alternatives, it must indeed be a difficult choice to make. A farmer with more animals on his hand than he can adequately feed, has to face these alternatives every day but the choice is not left to him. Today, if he resorts to starvation, it is not because of a free choice but because he is denied the other choice. In continuing to deny him such choice, let us check if we are not imposing on the farmer certain values which without any justification we are claiming to be somehow more humane and more in line with Indian tradition and culture.

Whichever the choice we make, let it be firmly understood that there is no escaping from the elementary principles of livestock husbandry, namely, that without adequate weeding through appropriate selection between sex and age and between one animal and another, there can be no efficient management of stock. If we neglect these elementary principles, we shall only be postponing and making more difficult the development of cattle in this country. The elementary truth shall prevail, namely, that without some measures to control their numbers, cows will not grow—only their numbers will grow.

27

The Marketable Surplus Function for a Subsistence Crop

An Analysis with Indian Data*

Raj Krishna

In the experiments reported here only data collected already by different agencies have been used. "Marketable surplus" and "marketed surplus" (or "market surplus" or "sales") have not been distinguished in this paper.[1] All disposals other than family consumption are treated as the marketable surplus. Disposals other than consumption and actual sale, e.g., retentions for seeds, gifts, and payments in kind, are important. But they cannot be analysed separately, for, in the first place, they have not been consistently recorded in the data available, and, secondly, it is reasonable to suppose that the quantity not retained for consumption but disposed of in kind is "marketable" and is being increasingly "marketed" as the economy gets progressively monetised.

The data required for time series analyses of marketable surplus relations are not yet available. While in time series analysis interest is focused on the response of the marketed supply to price movements, the object of cross-section analysis is to identify, and measure the effect of, the other factors which determine how much of the output of a subsistence crop will be taken to the market by different peasant families in a poor, partially monetised economy.

The Empirical Functions

A number of experiments with data relating to villages in different regions of India and the main subsistence crop (wheat or rice), revealed that in most cases there

* Originally published in *Economic Weekly* 17, annual number (February 1965), pp. 309–20. The author is grateful to A. C. Harberger and T. N. Srinivasan, who made very helpful comments on an earlier draft of this chapter.

exists a strong linear, and in some cases a strong non-linear, relation between the quantity produced and the quantity sold by different peasant families.

The linear relation may be written simply as:

$$(1)\ M = a + bQ$$

where Q denotes the total quantity produced and M the marketable surplus. We may describe this relation (or its non-linear counterparts)[2] as *the marketable surplus function.*

Table 27.1 shows the coefficients of this equation estimated from data relating to twenty-three samples from villages in eight Indian states. Twelve of the samples cover *all* the families growing the subsistence crop in a village. Two are random samples of farmers drawn from randomly chosen villages in development blocks. Four are samples drawn purposively so as to include "big" as well as "medium" and "small" farmers coming to sell in grain markets. The remaining five (PB) are also purposive samples consisting of a cross-section of peasant families in the Punjab State whose production, sales, and consumption are recorded annually in the *Farm Accounts* and *Family Budgets* published by the Board of Economic Inquiry, Punjab. The Punjab board samples include one to three farm families selected from every district of the state. The farms are selected by the board so as to represent the varying conditions in different regions of the Punjab in respect of farm size, irrigation, and cropping pattern.

The Madras, Andhra, and Orissa equations and one of the Maharashtra equations relate to rice and the rest to wheat as they are the main staple food crops of these regions.

The results presented in Table 1 show that there is a high correlation between sales and output. The regression coefficients are highly significant in all cases. All the (linear) equations have negative intercepts. Column 9 of the table shows the minimum subsistence output where market sales begin. Below this output the peasants apparently do not have enough to feed their families and might even be purchasing grain for consumption.

IMPLICATIONS OF THE FUNCTION

The Linear Cases

The marketable surplus function turns out to be linear[3] in the case of a majority of the samples analysed. The linearity of this relation has important implications. It implies that in the areas covered by these samples the *marginal propensity to sell* out of the output of a subsistence crop is constant over a wide range of output above the *minimum subsistence* output.

TABLE 27.1: MARKETABLE SURPLUS FUNCTIONS FOR WHEAT AND RICE—SOME INDIAN VILLAGES

Equation Symbol	State, Region or Village	Year	a Crop	Nature of b Sample	N	Estimated Equation	r^2	Minimum Subsistence Output where M = O C (*Mds*)
(1)	(2)	(3)	(4)	(5)	(6)	(7)	(8)	(9)
PB-51	Punjab	1950–51	W	P	12	M = – 16.50 + 0.85 Q (5.75) 0.02)	.96	19.41
PB-58	Punjab	1952–53	W	P	16	M = – 20.10 + 0.091 Q (5.14) 0.07)	.93	22.09
PB-55	Punjab	1954–55	W	P	14	M = – 14.69 + 0.88 Q (8.79) 0.23)	.89	16.72
PB-57	Punjab	1956–57	W	P	19	M = – 23.80 + 0.96 Q (3.93) 0.04)	.98	24.79
PB-59	Punjab	1958–59	W	P	25	M = – 17.25 + 0.87 Q (3.11) 0.05)	.93	19.77
P-Mo	Punjab: Moga	1957–58	W	P	63	M = – 45.06 + 0.80 Q (7.45) 0.03)	.92	56.32
P-K	Koloyee	1958–59	W	C	31	M = – 2.35 + 0.52 Q (1.47) 0.06)	.74	4.52
P-S	Sochania	1958–59	W	C	23	M = – 12.87 + 0.92 Q (1.51) 0.02)	.99	13.99
P-Mi	Mirka	1959–60	W	C	62	M = – 3.96 + 0.48 Q (2.05) 0.09)	.72	6.83

MD-C	Madras: Coimbatore	1957–58	R	P	30	M = – 36.14 + 0.99 Q (12.22) 0.02)	.99	36.24
MD-T	Tanjore	1957–58	R	P	30	M = – 39.60 + 0.92 Q (8.34) 0.09)	.99	43.04
UP-H	Uttar Pradesh: Hapur	1957–58	W	P	50	M = – 12.53 + 0.51 Q (5.90) 0.07)	.55	24.57
UP-B	Bhanwapur	1959–60	W	C	51	M = – 6.70 + 0.73 Q (0.76) 0.01)	.99	9.18
UP-W	Walidpur	1959–60	W	C	47	M = – 8.94 + 0.55 Q (2.80) 0.05)	.72	16.25
MP-Be	Madhya Pradesh: Betul	1959–60	W	S	48	M = – 1.28 + 0.86 Q (6.86) 0.02)	.97	1.48
MP-Ba	Bawariakalan	1958–59	W	C	49	M = – 4.17 + 0.56 Q (1.20) 0.04)	.82	8.85
MP-M	Misrod	1958–59	W	C	61	M = – 4.25 + 0.48 Q (1.45) 0.03)	.77	7.45
D	Delhi: Alipur	1959–60	W	S	48	M = – 12.86 + 0.56 Q (7.45) 0.04)	.80	22.96
O	Orissa: Biribati	1959–60	R	C	40	M = – 2.96 + 0.36 Q (3.26) 0.03)	.75	8.22
MH-K(W)	Maharashtra: Kasbe Sukene	1960–61	W	C	27	M = – 1.51 + 0.33 Q (0.61) 0.07)	.78	4.56
MH-K(R)	Kasbe Sukene	1960–61	R	C	26	M = – 4.57 + 0.48 Q (0.89) 0.04)	.86	9.52
AP-J	Andhra Pradesh: Jalipudi	1956–57	R	C	206	M = – 19.58 + 0.91 Q (0.68) 0.01)	.97	21.52

(contd.)

(Table 27.1 contd.)

Equation Symbol	State, Region or Village	Year	Crop[a]	Nature of Sample[b]	N	Estimated Equation	r^2	Minimum Subsistence Output where M = O (Mds)[c]
(1)	(2)	(3)	(4)	(5)	(6)	(7)	(8)	(9)
AP-K	Kumudavalli	1956–57	R	C	118	M = – 49.42 + 0.96 Q (4.71) 0.01)	.99	51.48

a W-Wheat; R-Rice (cleaned rice in the Orissa sample and paddy in other samples).
b P-Purposive Samples; O-Census; and S-Random Sample.
c Maund is an Indian measure of weight equivalent to 82 2/7 lbs.

Sources: See Appendix at the end.

The *average propensity to sell* or the sale ratio (M/Q), on the other hand, increases as output increases, above the minimum subsistence output, but at a decreasing rate. And the *elasticity of sales* with respect to output is positive and high; it ranges in most cases between 1 and 5 at low output levels, e.g., 10.25 or 60 Mds. (above the minimum output); and *decreases* as output increases, remaining greater than unity at high output levels e.g., 200, 500 or 1000 Mds (See Table 2) .

In a *linearity zone* the *aggregate marketable surplus* of the zone represented by a sample can be easily predicted from knowledge of the coefficients of the linear equation, a and b, the number of farm families growing and selling the subsistence crop, and the aggregate output of the zone. For

$$(2)\ \sum_{i=1}^{N} \hat{M}i = Na + b\sum_{i=1}^{N} Qi$$

where N is the number of farm families.

The *elasticity (E) of the aggregate surplus* ($S = \Sigma M_i$) with respect to aggregate output ($W = \Sigma Q_i$) equals the marginal propensity to sell divided by the *aggregate average propensity to sell* or the sale ratio:

$$(3)\ E = \hat{b}\frac{W}{S}.$$

This is evidently independent of the number of farm families. For the samples analysed the estimated elasticities of the aggregate surplus are tabulated in Table 27.3. They range from 1.04 to 1.60 in most cases.

These findings should weaken the widely held belief that output increases on relatively small farms are always likely to be swallowed up in consumption whereas those on large farms are likely to flow into the market. The truth seems to be that in many areas the small as well as the large producers producing more than a minimum output[4] sell (consume) the same additional quantity out of every additional unit of output. Thus, in an important sense, the market supply behaviour of small and large farmers is similar in these areas.

Wherever the marginal propensity to sell (or consume) is indifferent to output size, it follows that the usual discussions about changes in the farm size structure having a favourable or unfavourable effect on the marketable surplus of a subsistence crop have a lean empirical basis. There may be important reasons for altering the farm size structure. But in areas of constant sale propensity the necessity of increasing the marketable surplus need not be one of them.

Another policy implication of a linear marketable surplus function is that if governments concentrate on, and succeed in, stabilising and increasing output, peasants who sell any output at all would naturally and voluntarily increase their sales in at least the same proportion as output, for the output elasticity of sales exceeds unity. Unless, therefore, a government wishes to extract from the additional output a proportion far greater than the proportion by which output itself increases, there is no need for administrative measures to induce or force peasants to sell grain. It is sufficient, in linearity zones, to increase output; the marketable surplus will automatically increase correspondingly.

The Non-Linear Cases

All the 23 samples were tested for deviation from linearity. In the case of 10 samples the deviation from linearity turned out to be significant and quadratic equations were estimated.

$$(4)\ M = g + h\,Q + k\,Q^2$$

These are shown in Table 27.4.

In four of these ten equations, the Q^2 term is not significant. (PB-51, MD-C, MP-M, and MH-K(W)), but in the other six cases (P-S, UP-H, MP-Ba, MH-K(R), and AP-K) Q^2 is significant, and there is a noticeable increase in the explained variance due to the addition of the Q-term.

It is evidently important to inquire whether any special features characterise these six villages (samples). The Hapur Sample (UP-H) is not a village sample, and neither income nor acreage data are available for it. But it turns out that four of the other nonlinear village samples are characterised by very low mean income or mean holding or mean output of the subsistence crop. Thus, Bawariakalan village (MP-Ba) has the lowest mean income of all samples and the third lowest mean output (see Table 27.5). The Orissa village (O) has the second lowest mean holding size. The Kasbesukene rice (MH-K(R)) sample has the lowest output mean. The Sochania (P-S) sample has the fifth lowest mean holding size. In the case of 3 of these samples (MP-Ba, O, and MH-K(R)) the variance of acreage or output is also very low. Kumudavalli village (AP-K) is peculiar in having the lowest mean holding but the highest mean income.

These facts seem to suggest that very poor villages with very low dispersion of income (or output or holding size) are more likely to be characterised by a non-linear marketable surplus function than other villages. In a general atmosphere of *extreme* poverty, the marginal sale propensity of those few who produce more than the rest is likely to be greater than that of the rest.

On the other hand, the sample AP-K and to some extent the sample MH-K(R) suggest that relatively "rich" villages are also likely to have a nonlinear marketable surplus function. After a certain level of income has been reached the cultivation of the subsistence crop becomes highly commercial and the marginal propensity to sell rises with output.

In other words, we ought to hypothesise that the general marketable surplus function is likely to have the form shown in Figure 27.1.

FIGURE 27.1: HYPOTHETICAL FORM OF THE GENERAL MARKETABLE SURPLUS FUNCTION

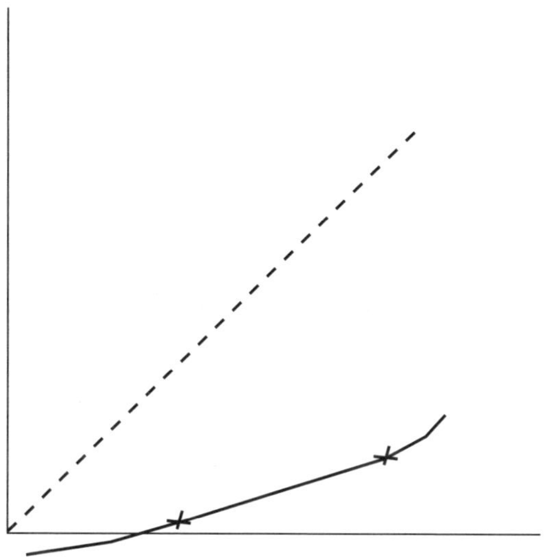

In the *non-linear zones*, of course, the prediction of the aggregate marketable surplus of a subsistence crop would require the knowledge of the output-size distribution of farm families as well as the total output and the marginal propensity to sell at different levels of output. And in such zones the increase in the marketable surplus brought about by a given increase in output would depend critically on the distribution of the output increase between farms in different output size classes. A given (absolute) output increase would be accompanied by a greater surplus-increase if the former is mainly concentrated in larger farms (see Table 27.6).

The policy implication is that in non-linear zones, in order to maximise the increase in the marketable surplus, output growth should be fostered most in relatively large farms. Where the non-linear zones are extremely poor, this is a very unpleasant implication.

Also, in such zones, an alteration of the farm size structure can, by itself, increase the marketable surplus out of a given output. This possibility, however, rests on the assumption that the density of consumer units in different size groups does not alter with an alteration of the farm size structure.

The number of consumer units dependent on the given total output must *fall* for the surplus out of that output to increase following a change in the farm size structure. But this is a big assumption to make in dense areas.[5]

Other Hypotheses

So far, we have specified the output of the subsistence crop (0) as the only variable explaining the cross-section variations of marketable surplus. But other alternative explanatory variables can be and have been proposed. The two important ones are income and acreage. Therefore, experiments were made to see how they compare with output as explanatory variables.

As for income (Y), the simple specification

(5) Log M = 1 + mLog Y + nLog F

TABLE 27.2: OUTPUT ELASTICITY OF MARKETABLE SURPLUS

Equation Symbol	Low Output *(Mds)*	Elasticity*	High Level *(Mds)*	Elasticity*
(1)	(2)	(3)	(4)	(5)
PB – 51	25	4.47	200	1.11
PB – 53	25	8.58	200	1.12
PB – 55	25	3.01	200	1.09
PB – 57	60	1.70	200	1.14
PB – 59	25	4.84	200	1.11
P – Mo	60	16.33	1,000	1.06
P – K	10	1.82	200	1.02
P – S	25	2.27	500	1.03
P – Mi	10	3.15	200	1.04
MD – C	60	2.55	1,000	1.04
MD – T	60	3.54	500	1.09
UP – C	60	1.92	200	1.17
UP – B	25	1.58	1,000	1.01
UP – W	25	2.86	200	1.09
MP – Bc	10	1.17	200	1.01
MP – Ba	10	3.92	200	1.04
MP – M	10	8.73	500	1.02
D	60	1.62	200	1.13
O	10	5.62	200	1.04
MH – K(W)	10	1.84	200	1.02
MH – K(R)	25	1.62	200	1.05
AP – J	25	7.18	1,000	1.02
AP – K	60	7.00	1,000	1.05

* From linear equations.

Source: Based on Table 27.1.

TABLE 27.3: OUTPUT ELASTICITY OF AGGREGATE MARKETABLE SURPLUS

Equation Symbol	Elasticity*
1	2
PB – 51	1.26
PB – 53	1.50
PB – 55	1.25
PB – 57	1.37
PB – 59	1.35
P – Mo	1.49
P – K	1.32
P – S	1.35
P – Mi	1.24
MD – C	1.04
MD – T	1.14
UP – M	1.47
UP – B	1.51
UP – W	1.61
MP –Be	1.04
MP – Ba	1.56
MP – M	1.13
D	1.56
O	1.36
MH – K(W)	1.17
MH – K(R)	2.55
AP – J	1.20
Ap – K	1.18

* From linear equations.
Source: Based on Table 27.1.

where F is family size, explained a much smaller part of the variance of M than the relation M = f(Q). (See columns 2 and 3 of Table 7). But if the marketable surplus is estimated from income *indirectly*, we get much better results. We may hypothesise that the critical magnitude that is first determined by the peasant is the quantity to be retained for home consumption. This quantity (C) may be specified, as is usual in demand analysis, as a function of income and the family size.

(6) Log C = p -f q Log Y H- r Log F

The consumption so estimated may be deducted from the total output of each family to arrive at the estimated marketable surplus. Thus:

(7) $M = Q - C$
$= Q - (p + q \text{ Log } Y + r \text{ Log } F)$

The accuracy of the prediction of the surplus by this method can be measured by the coefficient of determination between the predicted and actual sales. This coefficient is given in column 4 of Table 27.7.

If we compare r^2 in columns 2 and 4 of Table 27.7 we find that in the case of 5 Punjab samples income turns out to be a better predictor of sales than output. But in all other samples r^2 A is MM equal to or slightly less than r^2 MQ.

TABLE 27.4: MARKETABLE SURPLUS (QUADRATIC) FUNCTIONS

Equation Symbol	Estimated Equation				$\bar{R}^2$ **
(1)	(2)				(3)
PB – 51′	M =	1.18 +	.64 Q +	.00015 Q^2 *	0.956
^	^		(.19)	(.00077)	
P – S′	^ ^ M = –	1.51 +	.54 Q +	.00095 Q^2	0.990
			(.08)	(.00030)	
MD – C′	M = –	14.77 +	.99 Q +	.000001 Q^2 *	0.990
			(.04)	(.000007)	
UP – H′	M =	12.12 +	.33 Q +	.00409 Q^2	0.775
			(.18)	(.00080)	
MP – Ba′	M =	0.36 +	.17 Q +	.0038 Q^2	0.857
			(.10)	(.0010)	
MP – M′	M = –	4.46 +	.49 Q +	.00002 Q^2 *	0.766
			(.12)	(.00030)	
O′	M = –	0.74 +	.13 Q +	.0015 Q^2	0.774
			(.99)	(.0008)	
MH – K(W)′	M =	3.63 +	.16 Q +	.0013 Q^2	0.792
			(.10)	(0.008)	
MH – K(R)′	M = –	0.75 +	.06 Q +	.0053 Q^2 *	0.990
			(.12)	(.0014)	
AP – K[1]	M =	15.96 +	.88 Q +	.000074 Q^2	0.990
			(.02)	(.000013)	

* Q^2 not significant.

** R^{-2} is R^2 adjusted degrees of freedom.

Source: Based on Table 27.1.

We may, therefore, conclude that income and output are almost equally good predictors of sales. Output, however, may still be regarded as a somewhat superior predictor, not only because it explains a larger part of the variance of sales in a

TABLE 27.5: RANKS OF THE MEANS AND VARIANCES OF INCOME, OUTPUT AND HOLDING SIZE IN NON-LINEAR SAMPLES (WITH SIGNIFICANT Q^{2-})

	Y^a		Q^b		A_T^c	
Equation Symbol	$\bar{Y}$	$\tilde{Y}^2$	$\bar{Q}$	$\tilde{Q}^2$	$\bar{T}$ A	$\tilde{T}^1$ A
1	2	3	4	5	6	7
UP-H	–	–	14	11	–	–
MP-Ba	16	821	21	13	15	
I	–	–	18	17	17	18
MH–K(R)	6	11	23	23	4	5
P–S	10	7	13	7	14	7
AP–K	1	5	13	1	18	12

Y is income
Q is the output of the subsistence crop
AT is the total acreage cultivated
a – Total number of samples – 16
b – Total number of samples – 23
c – Total number of samples – 18
Source: Based on Table 27.1.

majority of cases, but also because we cannot predict sales from income without knowing output, whereas we can predict sales from output without having to estimate total income.

As regards the use of acreage as a predictor of sales, there are two choices. The acreage devoted to the subsistence crop itself can be considered as a proxy for the output of the crop. It is evidently a bad proxy for the yield per acre varies widely as between farms. That is why r^2 MA. where A is the acreage in wheat or rice, shown in column 5 of Table 27.7, is in all cases much less than r^2 MQ.

The *total* area cultivated by a farmer or the size of the holding can similarly be treated as a proxy for total income. But it is obvious, again, that it is a bad proxy. Though income and the size of the holding should be positively correlated, the relationship depends also on the quantity and quality of all the inputs other than land. Still, since attempts to correlate the marketable surplus with the size of the holding are very popular in the literature on marketable surplus, the coefficients of determination between the two (r^2 MA^T, where A^T is total acreage) were also estimated (see column 6 of Table 27.7). It will be seen that the size of the holding turns out to be the predictor of the marketable surplus.

TABLE 27.6: MARGINAL PROPENSITY TO SELL AT DIFFERENT OUTPUT LEVELS IN NON-LINEAR CASES

Equation Symbol		Low Output Level (*Mds*)	$\frac{dM}{dQ}$	High Output Level (*Mds*)	$\frac{dM}{dQ}$
PB – 51′	*	25	.65	200	0.70
P – S′	*	25	.59	200	0.90
MD – C′	*	60	.99	500	0.99
UP – H′		60	.16	150	0.90
MP – Ba′		10	.24	100	0.93
MP – M′	*	10	.48	500	0.48
O		10	.16	200	0.68
MH – K(W)′	*	.17	200	0.68	
MH – K(R)′	10	.17	75	0.86	
AP – K′		60	.89	500	0.95

*It may be recalled that the Q-term is not significant in these equations. Hence the increase in $\frac{dM}{dQ}$ at high output levels is not as large in the dQ case of three of these equations as in the case of others.

Source: Based on Table 27.1.

TABLE 27.7: COEFFICIENTS OF DETERMINATION BETWEEN ACTUAL MARKETABLE SURPLUS AND MARKETABLE SURPLUS PREDICTED FROM OUTPUT, INCOME AND ACREAGE

Equation Symbol	r^2 MQ	$\bar{R}^2$ M = f *** (Log Y, Log F)	r^2 $M\hat{M}$ (C = F (Y, F))	r^2 MA	r^2 MAτ
(1)	(2)	(3)	(4)	(5)	(6)
PB – 51	.96	.42	.99	.63	.09
PB – 53	.93	.29	.95	.02	.05
PB – 55	.89	–	.92	.51	.06
PB – 57	.98	.56	.96	.26	.24
PB – 59	.93	.19	.95	.27	.16
P – Mo	.092				
P – K	.74	.63*	.74	.55	.39
P – S	.99	.88*	.99	.88	.90
P – Mi	.72	.57*	.73	.53	.54
MD – C	.99	–	–	–	–
MD – T	.99	–	–	–	–
UP – H	.65	–	–	–	–
UP – B	.99	.31*	.99	.98	.87
UP – W	.72	.65*	.68	.59	.42
MP – Bc	.97	–	–	.92**	.25**
MP – Ba	.82	.08	.78	–	.03**

MP – M	.77	.25	.74	–	.29**
D	.80	–	–	.49**	.47**
O	.75	–	–	–	.60**
MH – K(W)	.78	.64	.62	.66	.51
MH – K(R)	.86	.43	.83	.79	.08
AP – J	.97	.85	.99	.92	.92
AP – K	.99	.99	.99	.94	.94

* In these cases, gross income was used instead of net income for want of data.
** In these cases, the area has not been standardised for want of information. In all other samples, the area is in standard unirrigated acres. 2
*** R^2 is R^2 adjusted for degrees of freedom.
Source: Based on Table 27.1.

SUMMARY AND CONCLUSIONS

On the whole, then, it is clear that by far the best predictor of the marketable surplus is the output of the subsistence crop itself. Income is a good second-best predictor, provided output is also known. Acreage, especially the size of the total holding, is the most unsatisfactory predictor of marketable surplus.

In most areas the sales-output relation (which we designate as the *marketable* surplus function) is linear. In very poor and very rich areas it is likely to be non-linear.

Where it is linear, the aggregate surplus can be predicted from the aggregate output, if the number of families is known and the marginal propensity to sales is estimated from a representative sample. A change in the farm structure will not increase the marketable surplus. And since the elasticity of sales with respect to output, above the minimum subsistence output, is greater than unity, any increase in output is likely to be accompanied by a more than proportionate increase in the marketable surplus.[6]

Where the marketable surplus function is non-linear, the aggregate surplus can be predicted only if the total output, the output size-distribution of families, and the parameters of the non-linear relation are known. A change in the farm size structure in favour of larger farms can increase the marketable surplus provided that it is accompanied by a corresponding reduction in the number of consumer units dependent on the total output. An increase in output will lead to larger proportionate increases in the marketable surplus, the more the increase in output is concentrated on large farms. But since most of the non-linear areas are likely to be very poor, such a policy would be highly regressive.

The overall policy implication of the analysis is that it is best for governments to concentrate on inducing increases in farm output without any special discrimination in favour of small or large farms. The nature of the marketable surplus function is such, in most areas, that the usual arguments for discrimination in favour of large farms do not hold. Even with the farm size structure remaining what it is, output increases will lead to more than proportionate increases in marketable surplus without a discriminatory or coercive policy.

Appendix: Sources of Data

Punjab and Uttar Pradesh:
Agro-Economic Research Centre, University of Delhi, Delhi.

Madras:
Economic and Statistical Adviser, Ministry of Food and Agriculture, Government of India, *Report on an Enquiry into the Pace and Pattern of Market Arrivals of Foodgrains, 1958–59*, (New Delhi, 1959).

Madhya Pradesh (Betul) and Delhi:
Directorate of Marketing and Inspection, Nagpur.

Madhya Pradesh:
Agro-Economic Research Centre, Gwalior.

Orissa:
Department of Rural Economics and Sociology, Utkal University, Bhubaneshwar.

Maharashtra:
Gokhale Institute of Politics and Economics, Poona.

Andhra Pradesh:
Agro-Economic Research Centre, University of Madras, Madras.

Notes and References

[1] For a discussion of this, see Raj Krishna, "A Note on the Elasticity of the Marketable Surplus of a Subsistence Crop," *Indian Journal of Agricultural Economics* 17, no. 3 (July–September 1962), pp. 79–84.

[2] See Section IV.

[3] In the sense that the deviation from linearity was found to be non-significant. See section IV.

[4] The proportion of farmers producing less than the minimum subsistence output varied widely from 5 to 46 per cent in the various samples. The implicit minimum per capita consumption also varies widely as between different regions due to differences in grain yields, food habits and family size.

[5] We may note here that family size has not been specified as an explanatory variable in the marketable surplus functions because experiments revealed that if it is specified as a variable in addition to output it turns out to be nonsignificant in most cases. The reason for this seems to be that in the economics of subsistence farming, the peasants determine the size of the output (or, rather, the acreage, assuming normally expected yields) of the subsistence crop itself keeping their family needs in view. The output variable itself reflects family size.

[6] It is also implied, of course, that a decrease in output is likely to be accompanied by a more than proportionate decrease in the marketable surplus.

PART VII

Policy Debates: Industry

28

Small-scale Industries

Problem of Technological Change*

K. N. Raj

I

The controversy regarding the policy to be adopted towards household and small-scale enterprises in the Second Plan has now gone on for over a year. In this controversy, there has been a tendency on the part of economists to take the view that the case for fostering such industries through protection depends primarily on humanitarian and political considerations. They seem to argue that on "strict economic considerations" there is no case for such protection, and that where this policy involves preventing or regulating the introduction of improved technology (as in the standard issue of handlooms versus automatic looms), it is positively injurious to economic progress.

This approach needs to be scrutinised a little more closely, particularly because it is a line which satisfies, almost instinctively, the intellectual and emotional needs of most of those who are called upon to deal with the problem. Economic progress has been historically associated with improved technology, and so it seems logical to them that any policy which retards or slows down the pace of technological change is necessarily detrimental to development. At the same time, it is obvious that the displacement of labour from existing techniques carries with it a certain amount of dislocation and human misery which, in all conscience, cannot be ignored. It does not, therefore, seem to them as inconsistent or opportunist to hunt with the hounds, advocating the need for technological change, and simultaneously run with the hares, openly declaring support for "the man behind the loom." The

* Originally published in two parts in *Economic Weekly* 8, no. 14 (7 April 1956), pp. 420–21; and *Economic Weekly* 8, no. 15 (14 April 1956), pp. 435–38.

whole approach leaves so much elbow room and flexibility as to permit one to take positions on a purely ad hoc basis, which is its advantage and also its danger.

It is not necessary, in an analysis of this problem, to disavow the importance of humanitarian and political considerations. Indeed, the distinction that is sought to be drawn between them and what are referred to as "strict economic considerations" does not make much sense in terms of pure logic. But it is important to be clear about the assumptions and the criteria that are applied, and perhaps the best way of making them clear would be by defining precisely what one means by "economic" considerations and by being explicit about the assumptions regarding wage levels, minimum subsistence requirements, and the agencies which would maintain those displaced from employment.

There are two criteria which are often mixed up when people speak of economic considerations. One is the maximisation of output and the other is the maximisation of the rate of growth of output. These have different implications, as we shall presently see.

It is not clear from the 'Draft of the Draft Plan-frame' which of the two criteria was the one in terms of which small-scale enterprises were favoured initially. The first impression one gets from a general reading of this draft is that maximisation of output was the criterion. For it speaks of the need "to increase the production of consumer goods as much as possible through the household or hand industries," and explains how this increased supply will meet the additional demand generated by investments in heavy industries and thus prevent undesirable inflationary pressures.

But elsewhere in the same draft there is evidence of an uneasy recognition that perhaps maximisation of the output of consumer goods will not by itself be sufficient to curb the inflationary pressures generated by increases in investment in the heavy industries. For it goes on to say that "the greater the *marketed surplus* of consumer goods in the household or hand industries the greater will be the possibilities of investments in heavy industries without any fear of inflation" (emphasis mine). To what extent such marketed surplus is likely to emerge, and whether it would be adequate for sustaining the rate of investment visualised, are not however pursued any further. Indeed, the whole problem raised here is forgotten in the very next sentence, which claims with satisfaction that "by expanding the household and hand industries and construction work, the aggregate national consumption would increase continually."

The lack of clarity in this matter is perhaps explained by an unconscious effort on the part of the framers to be loyal to both Keynesian and Marxist tools of analysis. In terms of the Keynesian system, savings from current income are merely "leakages," and the problem is primarily to match the increases in demand generated by the initial dose of additional investment with increases in supply. If, therefore, the required elasticity of supply is assured, there is little more to worry about. But in the Marxist model, it is the surplus in one department (i.e., in consumption goods industries) which maintains consumption in the other (i.e., in producer goods industries); accordingly, the size of the surplus, rather than the volume of the output which yields this surplus, is what matters; and if this surplus is small no increase in the rate of investment activity is possible.

Since the different modes of reasoning represented by these two theoretical systems entered, apparently unnoticed, into the exposition of the logic of the Plan-frame, it is no wonder that a sharp difference of opinion regarding the role of small-scale enterprises has been quick to develop even among those who are otherwise agreed in their support of the Plan-frame. Those with a Keynesian bias have, on the whole, tended to support the emphasis on small-scale enterprises (in company with the Gandhians), partly because of their larger employment potential, but more so on the ground that the low capital-output ratios in these enterprises will help to meet more adequately, with a minimum of investment, the demand generated by investment expenditures. On the other hand, those who have been applying the Marxist model (not all of whom are, by any means, Marxists!) have been, by and large, inclined to deflate the importance of small-scale enterprises and the advantage of low capital-output ratios. They see an inconsistency in the logic of the Draft Plan-frame and argue that expansion of marketed surpluses implies more and not less capital-using techniques of production, since these surpluses can emerge only through rapid increases in the productivity of labour.

The reasoning on Keynesian lines is all right as far as it goes: if increases in demand generated by additional investment can be matched by increases in supply, the rate of investment and the volume of employment can both be raised without adding to inflationary pressures. In fact, if there are fairly long lags between successive rounds of expenditure and income generation in an economy, the rate of investment and the volume of employment can be raised in this way even when the marginal propensity to save of the income recipients is nil. But there are two points which are often overlooked in using this line of reasoning for supporting the role allotted to small-scale enterprises in the Draft Plan-frame.

The first is that even if there are time lags to prevent explosive increases in demand, it will be necessary to have a constantly rising volume of output to sustain the same rate of investment year after year, as long as the marginal propensity to save is itself small. The plan-frame visualises not merely a rise in the rate of investment but a steadily rising rate of investment, and so one may enquire whether the increases in the output of consumer goods planned for would be adequate to meet the cumulative growth of demand. Secondly, even if the increases in output planned for are adequate, it does not follow that the minimum investment with which these increases can be realised is necessarily through relying on small-scale enterprises. For there is no reason to believe that the capital-output ratio is, or should be, always higher for the more advanced techniques involving larger units of equipment and organisation.

It follows from these two considerations that even though an adequate elasticity of output can, up to a point, be depended on for initiating higher rates of investment, we cannot either ignore the importance of creating surpluses in order to sustain steady increases in the rate of investment or even take for granted that small-scale enterprises have, in all cases, the merit of economy in capital. This much must be conceded to those who argue against relying on small-scale enterprises for promoting a process of growth.

But the line of reasoning developed with reference to the problem of surpluses, and in terms of which unfettered technological change is advocated, needs also to be scrutinised more closely. For it has not been uncommon for those who have put this forward to ignore all the really significant issues involved by making two assumptions: (i) that the income of those engaged in small-scale enterprises is likely to be very small, that this is likely to be spent away entirely in consumption, and that, therefore, these enterprises cannot yield any surpluses at all, and (ii) that, when new techniques yielding larger output per unit of labour employed are introduced, the wage rates in these establishments will not rise, and also that the minimum subsistence requirements of those who are displaced from productive employment will not be a drain on the surplus yielded.

II

Given these two assumptions, the case for unfettered technological change is of course unchallengeable, because not only will those displaced by the change be inevitably reabsorbed but their reabsorption will go alongside the higher rates of investment sustained by the larger surpluses. It is then only if the capital-output ratio is higher in the more advanced techniques that one need even make a choice between maximisation of output and maximisation of the rate of growth of output, and since differences in capital-output ratios are not usually brought into the model, the economic considerations are in perfect harmony with the "humanitarian" and "political" considerations.

But when we are concerned with applying a theoretical model in a specific situation, particularly in the context of a five-year plan, we need to be more careful about our assumptions.

In the first place, there is very little basis for the assumption that the incomes of those engaged in small-scale enterprises will necessarily leave no margin for saving. Indeed, as a matter of historical experience, the instinct for accumulation has been found to be as strong among small craftsmen and traders as among the larger capitalists. It is the institutional setting, and the incentives which it provides, that is of importance from this point of view rather than the size of the productive units or even the levels of income of those engaged in them.

Secondly, it is a fact which cannot be ignored that there are considerable differences in wage rates as between different types of organisation. Wage rates in factory enterprises are invariably higher than wage rates in small workshops, and wage rates in small workshops are higher than can be imputed to family labour in productive households. A changeover in techniques and in the type of organisation cannot, therefore, be assumed to leave wage rates constant.

It is also a fact that there is no clear tendency on the part of capital to move towards areas and types of organisation in which wage rates are low. This may have something to do with railways and other "overhead" facilities being available only in certain concentrated urban areas, but obviously there are also various kinds of imperfections in the capital markets, attributable to a variety of social phenomena and motivations, which work in the same direction.

It is clear from these two considerations that the consequences of immobility of labour and capital cannot be ignored, particularly in underdeveloped economies, in any analysis of the means for maximising rates of growth. Technological progress in limited sectors, we must remember, means also usually higher wage rates in these sectors, and this reduces the surplus available for investment. The fact that, despite this, the capitalists want to introduce new techniques does not, by any means, prove that the surplus yielded by investment in these techniques is larger than could have been tapped with less advanced techniques in the low-wage types of organisation. It is a tenable thesis that in pressing forward with technological change, the capitalists are more concerned with reducing the labour force in their establishments for fear of possible conflicts with labour in the future and ensuring for themselves a reasonable rate of profit than with maximisation of profits, as is often taken for granted.

We must also take into account the likely leakages from the surpluses for maintaining, at the minimum subsistence standards, those displaced from employment through introduction of new techniques. When the problem is looked at from the point of view of only one industry or firm, it may be legitimate to assume that the surplus will not be affected as a result of the change in techniques. But if the labour displaced by technological change in one industry has to be maintained in one way or another by those engaged in another, the consequent reduction in the surplus of the latter will at least offset to some extent the increase in the surplus of the former.

It is very often implicitly assumed in this context that when technological change displaces labour in underdeveloped economies, the amounts available for consumption in the productive households will somehow be redistributed among a larger number, and that the surpluses created will not therefore be drawn upon to any significant extent. This implies two things:

(1) that the productive households which are compelled to carry a larger number of dependants do not have, and are not expected to have, any surplus which they might be otherwise inclined to draw upon; and
(2) the minimum subsistence requirements of all those involved are lower than the standards they enjoyed prior to the displacement of labour from productive employment.

Taking the two together, it will be clear that what is really assumed is that there is a surplus available for being extracted from existing levels of output, but that the only practical way of getting at this surplus is by pushing out some of those at near-subsistence levels to be maintained for a time by others who are also at near-subsistence levels. This is, by no means, an "economic" consideration; it is essentially a political and administrative judgement.

It will be, on the whole, more realistic and appropriate to allow for some leakage on this account. For if labour is displaced on any significant scale through technological change, it will either become necessary for the state to provide relief of some kind for the unemployed or the households still in productive activity, which could otherwise have some surplus (i.e., in agriculture), will be compelled to divert part of it for maintaining the additional dependants.

When considering the case for technological change from the point of view of maximising the rate of growth of output, we must, therefore, take into account all these factors, because they are relevant to the size of the surplus that will be available for investment under alternative techniques. To begin with, we must remember that we are concerned with improvements in technology which, even if they do not involve more capital per unit of output, imply certainly more capital per unit of labour employed (for, otherwise, the problem of technological unemployment does not arise). This means that though a larger surplus may be generated per unit of labour employed through improved technology, the number that can be provided employment with a given initial investment ceiling will be smaller. The aggregate surplus thus thrown up will also be smaller the larger the leakage we have considered, namely those on account of (a) higher wage rates under the improved techniques, and (b) diversion of resources, directly or indirectly, made necessary for the maintenance of those displaced from employment. If, in addition, the capital-output ratio is also higher in the more advanced techniques (as may well be the case, though not necessarily), the aggregate surplus will be reduced still further. It follows that, even if the surplus per unit of labour employed in the less efficient variants is only a fraction of that possible on the basis of the more efficient ones, the total surplus available for capital accumulation in the former case could still be larger.

The simplest way of bringing all these considerations together, and of stating the conditions in which introduction of improved technology can be justified on grounds of maximising the rate of growth of the economy, might be as follows: Given two alternative technical variants, A and B, the former involving higher capital cost per unit of labour and also a somewhat higher wage rate for the labour employed than the latter, Variant A would be preferable to Variant B only if the proportion of the surplus per worker in the former (after making an allowance for the leakage for maintaining the labour displaced by its introduction)[1] to the surplus per worker in the latter is larger than the proportion of the capital cost for employing a worker in Variant A to the capital cost for employing a worker in Variant B.

If this formula is applied to the possible variants in each industry, and it is observed that there are tendencies towards introduction of techniques which do not satisfy the condition laid down, there is indisputably a case for arresting such tendencies through state intervention, even on the "economic" criterion of maximisation of the rate of growth of the economy.

Thus, to give an illustrative example, let us take three alternative techniques in weaving in the textile industry, and see how it would work out on the basis of certain assumed values for the relevant variables in each case (see Table 28.1).

TABLE 28.1

	Technique I	Technique II	Technique III
Capital cost per loom	Rs. 50	Rs. 200	Rs. 10,000
Capital cost per worker	Rs. 50	Rs. 200	Rs. 1,60,000
Output per loom per day	4 yds	20 yds	80 yds
Net value added per loom per year (on the assumption of four annas per yard and 300 working days per year)	Rs. 300	Rs. 1,500	Rs. 6,000
Net value added per worker per year	Rs. 300	Rs. 1,500	Rs. 96,000
Wage per worker per year	Rs. 300	Rs. 900	Rs. 1,500
Surplus per worker per year	Nil	Rs. *600	Rs. *94,500

(*No allowance is made here for "leakages" on account of the need to maintain the labour displaced from employment.)

This is probably not an altogether unrealistic representation of the relative magnitudes involved today in the choice between different types of technology in the textile industry (though no specific claim of that kind is implied here). Technique I conforms broadly to the more primitive type of fly-shuttle handloom which is now surviving on a very precarious and unsatisfactory basis; Technique II to the improved "Banaras" semi-automatic loom referred to in the *Report of the Textile Enquiry Committee* (1954); and Technique III to the advanced automatic loom, several of which can be operated simultaneously by one worker (assumed here to be 16 per worker).

It will be seen that it is advantageous to move from Technique I to Technique II because there is no surplus whatever in the former, while a relatively small investment per worker yields a substantial surplus in the latter. But it is not worthwhile to shift from Technique II to Technique III (except to the extent necessary for earning foreign exchange).[2] For, though the surplus per worker in Technique III is considerably larger, the increase in the capital cost per worker, involved in the shift, is even larger. Or, to put it in another way, if the amount available initially for investment is Rs. 1,60,000, not only is the employment provided by Technique III limited to one worker but the surplus thrown up with this investment will be only Rs. 94,500, while, if Technique II is adopted, employment will be available for 800 workers and, at the same time, the surplus will add up to Rs. 4,80,000. If, nevertheless, there is not evident a strong tendency to move into Technique II, it can be only because of imperfectness of competition and insufficient private enterprise, which it is the business of a plan to remedy.

On this line of reasoning, there is of course no case for "freezing" technological change, but regulation of such change, and active measures to prevent the introduction of certain types of advanced techniques, appear entirely justified. For it shows that there is such a thing as an optimum technique from the larger social point of view in any given set of conditions, and the techniques actually adopted by private entrepreneurs may not conform to it. It is, therefore, the function of the planning authority to take such positive and negative measures as may be necessary to bring about movement towards the optimum.

That it is not their inherent technical inferiority so much as organisational deficiencies which stand in the way of certain techniques close to the optimum, appearing to be "inefficient," is again illustrated by the references in the *Report of the Textile Enquiry Committee* to certain experiments with improved handlooms organised on the basis of co-operative societies. For instance, Annexure E to the report gives the history and the details of the working of the Vemmiganur Weavers' Co-operative Society. This society was started in 1938, with a paid-up capital of Rs. 170, when most of the looms in the area were throw-shuttle looms. In the course of the last two decades, the only important technical change introduced has been their replacement with fly-shuttle looms. But the society has, in the process, accumulated a paid-up capital of over Rs. 1 lakh (almost wholly out of a thrift fund into which one anna in every rupee of the wage earned by members is paid), developed another common good fund which meets the expenses of a comprehensive system of health insurance among the members, established its own dye factory, printing section, and a factory for the manufacture of furnishing fabrics, and also initiated a scheme by which houses are built by the society and the members purchase them over a period on an instalment basis—all of which, obviously, is attributable to the surpluses created by its 1,800 members.

On the line of reasoning advanced here, it will be also obvious that while positive steps are being taken for a planned transition from one technique to another, it is not inconsistent with the objectives implicit in such a policy to give a measure of protection to those who are to be assisted to move into the better techniques but who may, in the absence of protection, be displaced in the meanwhile. The case for such protection, whether it involves direct subsidisation or not, is no less strong than the infant-industries argument which has been accepted for some time as respective economics.

Notes and References

[1] This deduction from the surplus per worker will be greater the larger the number displaced by the introduction of the technique, but it will also depend on the institutional set-up.

[2] The concession to be made in regard to production for foreign markets depends on the premium which it is necessary to place on foreign exchange in the context of the investment programme. The greater this premium, the greater is, in effect, the imputed value of the products earmarked for exports.

29

Mill versus Cottage Industries

A Method of Appraisal*

Jan Tinbergen

(1) In matters of economic policy it is not always worthwhile to use very refined methods of appraisal. When, however, very substantial interests are involved, the trouble and cost inherent to complicated research may pay themselves off. This seems to be true for the controversy concerning the Indian cotton industry. In order to judge the merits of the alternative views with regard to the future development to be aimed at for this industry, the application of the most sophisticated methods would seem justified. As the readers of this journal will be aware, quite some thought has recently been given to the methods by which to decide whether, say, mill production or household industry should be preferred.

(2) The method by which the individual private firm would make its choice is relatively simple: preference should be given to the production process yielding the largest profit rate. It is well known, however, that this method does not necessarily lead to the best choice for the nation at large. The advantages to the country to be expected from either process of production are a more complicated set of phenomena several of which are, as a rule, disregarded by the private investor. In principle these advantages—or disadvantages, as the case may be— may be found in a variety of consequences of each process, all of them of some relevance to the community as a whole. It is the purpose of this article briefly to discuss some of these consequences in their mutual relationships. In this discussion I shall even neglect some aspects outside the purely economic sphere which it will be difficult to measure but which may as well have to exert their influence on the policy-maker's decision: the purely psychological and social aspects.

* Originally published in *Economic Weekly* 9, nos. 3–5 (19 January 1957), pp. 81–84.

SETTING OUT THE PROBLEM

(3) In order to discuss the problem as precisely as possible we have, first of all, to set it out. Even this setting out of the problem can be done in different ways. I propose to ask: if we are going to invest an additional crore of rupees in textile industry, shall we invest it in mill capacity or in household industry capacity? Essentially, our problem now consists of comparing what happens in the two alternative cases mentioned: call them M (mill) and H (household). In principle, all consequences for the future net product of the nation in case M and case H will have to be estimated and appraised. Two alternative developments have to be compared, quantitatively and qualitatively.

The task before us is complicated because of the large number of dimensions or aspects characterising economic development whatever its nature. The following aspects call for a separate consideration:

(A) complementary factors of production needed;
(B) products to be obtained;
(C) industries or activities involved;
(D) time periods involved;
(E) qualitative aspects; and
(F) prices to be used in appraisal.

Let us discuss these aspects in succession.

NUMBER OF DIMENSIONS

(4) Complementary factors of production needed will be, before all, the various quantities of labour. These will have to be specified, subdivided according to the aspects (C) and (D). They depend on the specification to be given of the capital goods represented by the initial crore invested. Much less labour will be needed in case M than in case H to operate the same quantity of capital.

Products to be obtained will be different, too, in cases M and H, and will have to be estimated on the basis of technical data available.

Industries or activities involved: Here the complications become evident not only for the production process under consideration, say weaving. We will have to collect the figures just briefly indicated, but in principle for the economy as a whole. Different quantities of labour will not only be used, and different quantities of product obtained, in the weaving process, but also in many other industries and activities. Their number is so large that drastic simplification is called for. Most important are:

(i) the activities technically connected with the process considered: spinning, cotton growing, and trading on the one side, finishing and further operations on the other side;
(ii) the activities connected in a more general way through the economic process: these may be the consequences in competing industries or the consequences of income changes.

An example of considerable interest is the influence that may be exerted on the volume of savings and hence on the general development process by the fact that under M, much higher incomes will be earned by a few people—as against under H where a larger number of people will earn low incomes. The example illustrates that, in principle, we have to have a picture, however rough it may be, of general economic development in the two alternative cases studied. It is here that some techniques of general programming will be of value.

Time Preference

(5) Time periods involved: As will be clear from what precedes, the estimates will have to extend over a certain period of time. In principle this period will even have to be infinite. In practice gross simplification will also be necessary here, but still some rough subdivision in periods is indispensable. Maybe a general description of the process of development by one coefficient of annual growth will be sufficient; but the point is that that coefficient may be different for cases M and H, both for the textile industry and for general development. Some help may be had from a time discount factor to be applied for later periods (see section 6), which automatically reduces the relevance of figures for remote periods.

Qualitative aspects: The two alternative processes also differ in quality of product obtained as well as in labour and capital goods needed. Such qualitative differences have to be specified and the prices to be applied chosen accordingly. The problem is interesting from a more general point of view; not always will a mechanised process yield a better product: sometimes it is the other way round.

Complex of Factors

(6) Prices to be used in appraisal: Perhaps the most difficult operation involved in the appraisal consists of the choice of the prices to be applied. It is natural only that the private investor applies the prices he expects actually to pay. But it is equally natural that for the nation as a whole this is not the best course to follow. Market prices do not always reflect the "true" value of a good or a service to the national economy. With certain types of labour overabundant, the value of such labour to the nation is near to zero: the "product foregone" by the use of an

unemployed man is nothing and only the cost of moving him to his new location represents a real national sacrifice. On the other hand, the value of capital may well be, in the near future, considerably higher than market interest rates indicate. Once India's development would gain momentum the demand for capital will in all probability outrun its supply.

The interest rate will enter into the calculations as a discount applied to values obtained in later years. As such it represents the well-known complex of factors enumerated in capital theory. It is sometimes maintained that the nation as a whole should not have a time preference proper, as the well-being of future generations should count just as much as that of the present generation. Although this may be true, there are counterarguments in that with a well-devised development plan future generations will live under better conditions than the present population and that capital will then be less scarce. All these considerations illustrate the difficulties involved in arriving at a correct numerical estimate (of section 7).

Unjustified Partition

It is sometimes maintained that the value of previously unemployed labour is not as near to zero as just suggested. The increased consumption of this man, it is said, represents a drain on the country's resources and should be considered a cost element. In the set-up chosen here this phenomenon is not denied but accounted for elsewhere, under the item (C) "industries or activities involved" sub (ii) (see section 4). The reason for doing so is that the phenomenon is part of the general development of the economy and worthwhile being studied explicitly even in this context. One may add the remark that this increased consumption is the very aim of all economic activity and that hence it is somewhat queer to consider it as a cost. It is based on an unjustified partition of the economy into those inside the producing group and those outside and implies a non-acceptable contrast between the interests of the economy as a whole and those of the unemployed.

As a third example of prices that may not reflect the "true" value to the economy, we may mention foreign exchange rates. For a country in balance of payments difficulties the true value of, say, a dollar, is higher than indicated by the official rate.

"Accounting" or "Shadow" Prices

(7) A practical question of some weight is what numerical values should be taken for the prices just mentioned, to be called "accounting" or "shadow" prices. As already discussed, the value of certain types of labour can sometimes safely be put at almost zero. But for other types of labour, for capital, and for foreign exchange the

question is less simple. It is also less simple if we want to apply different prices for different time periods. It depends very much on the nature of the price considered whether something can be done in the nature of a more precise estimate.

In the case of capital, some clue may be derived from the profit rates currently earned on new investments—with some correction for risk. In the case of foreign exchange some estimate may sometimes be possible as to which rate would equilibrate the balance of payments. But very often, it has to be admitted, all such figures are not much more than intelligent—let us hope—guesses. Still it is important that at least some of these guesses be applied in order to find out whether the result of the calculations is much influenced by them. If not, all the better. If it is, caution is in place anyway.

Role of Prices and Planning

(8) The role of the accounting or shadow prices just mentioned is, as is the role of all prices, to help the economy to find the optimum allocation of its resources. The reason why especially in an underdeveloped country considerable divergence may exist between market and shadow prices is that there is a disproportion between its factor endowment; that is, too little capital and land in comparison with the labour supply. It is in the best interests of such a country if the use made of its scarce factors is as good as possible and, in particular, that labour be used instead of them wherever possible. Thus the shadow price of labour should be lowest in regions and in periods where its abundancy is most pronounced, in order so to "deform" the country's production programme as to fill the gaps between supply of and demand for labour wherever possible.

This role of prices can to some extent be played also by the direct method of national economic planning. In fact, the two procedures could and should supplement each other. From the plans for the nation as a whole now available the probable abundance of certain types of labour may be derived, leading to an insight into the shadow prices to be applied for future years. But at the same time the plans will themselves already be the best method of so to allocate resources in future years as to avoid too big gaps between supply and demand.

30

Size, Technology and Economics

A Study of the Indian Cotton Textiles Industry*

J. C. Sandesara

This paper is divided into four parts: part I sets out the hypotheses and the scope of the paper; part II presents the broad outline of the approach; part III consists of the analyses; and part IV comprises of the conclusions, their limitations, and implications. The basic tables are presented in the Appendix.

I The Hypotheses

It is commonly held that small industrial units are labour-intensive and large industrial units capital-intensive. That is, the former use less capital per worker than the latter. It is furthermore held that small units have lower productivity per worker, lower wage per worker and also lower surplus per worker; and that they have higher output but lower surplus per unit of capital than the large ones.

Since, as noted above, labour intensity is held to be immanent in small units, it is also held, almost as a corollary, that the labour-intensive technology has lower productivity per worker, lower wage per worker, and also lower surplus per worker; and that it has higher output but lower surplus per unit of capital than the capital-intensive technology.

This writer is currently engaged in an empirical examination of these hypotheses with reference to Indian manufacturing industries. This larger study, under preparation now, may take about a year in publication. Meanwhile, an

* Originally published in *Economic Weekly* 17, no. 30 (24 July 1965), pp. 1171–76. The writer acknowledges his gratitude to M. M. Dadi, I. S. Gulati, V. N. Koihari, D. T. Lakdawala, B. V. Mehta, and C. H. Shah for their comments on the draft of this chapter.

opportunity is being taken here to present the results of the enquiry into the cotton textiles industry not only because of its topicality but also with a view to provoking comments and discussion since some of the results obtained challenge the notions commonly held.

II The Approach

The enquiry is based on the Census of Indian Manufactures for the years 1953–58.

The census is conducted with the factory as the unit of enumeration. It is confined to the units registered under the Factories Act, 1948, employing 20 or more workers on any day, and using power. The censuses for the years 1953–58 give data on the coverage of factories, capital, and labour employed, output produced, wages, etc., and value added by size of factories as denoted by the number of persons employed—the size groups being below 20, 20–49, 50–99, 100–249, 250–499, 500–999, 1,000–1,999, 2,000–4,999, and 5,000 and above workers.

On the basis of relevant data given for these size groups, we have worked out capital-labour, output-labour, wages-labour, surplus-labour, output-capital, and surplus-capital ratios. While for the detailed connotation of the terms used reference should be made to the census, the following may be permitted even in this short paper.

The term capital is used for total productive capital employed—working and fixed together; the term labour for the average number of persons employed; the term output for value added; the term wages for salaries, wages, and other benefits or privileges, all as defined in the census. The term surplus is defined to cover the residual of value added after wages are deducted.

The data are presented in three tables. Table 30.1 gives the rank correlation coefficient between size and (a) technology (i.e., capital intensity). Table 30.2 gives the rank correlation coefficient between size and (b) output-labour, (c) wages-labour, (d) surplus-labour, (e) output-capital, and (f) surplus-capital ratios. The data to the left in Table 30.3 give the rank and those to the right the product-moment coefficient, correlations between technology and each of these five characteristics. The basic tables are presented in the Appendix.

III The Analyses

(A) Size and Technology

The hypothesis tested here is that size and capital intensity are positively associated—that small units are labour-intensive and large units capital-intensive.

The data for the years 1953–58 do not lend any support to the hypothesis of positive association. In fact, they may be taken as an indication that size and technology are negatively associated; that is, small units are capital-intensive and large units labour-intensive.

It would be seen from Table 30.1 that the correlation was negative for all the six years. The value was less than the critical value, having a minus sign, at the 2.5 per cent level of significance, for three (1953, 1954, and 1957) out of six years. Here the hypothesis of independence is rejected at the 2.5 per cent level of significance against the alternative that there is negative association.[1]

TABLE 30.1: VALUE OF THE RANK CORRELATION COEFFICIENT BETWEEN SIZE AND TECHNOLOGY, 1953–58

Year	Value
(1)	(2)
1953	– .83
1954	– .73
1955	– .57
1956	– .61
1957	– .82
1958	– .52

(B) Size and Economic Characteristics

The hypotheses tested below are that (i) size and (b) productivity per worker, (c) wage per worker, and (d) surplus per worker are all positively associated; (ii) size and (e) output-capital ratio are negatively associated; and (iii) size and surplus-capital ratio are positively associated.

The rank correlation coefficients were consistently positive for all the six years in all the five cases. It would be furthermore observed from Table 30.2 that the value was greater than the critical value, having a plus sign, at the 2.5 per cent level of significance, for all the six years for output-labour and output-capital ratios; for three years (1953, 1954, and 1955) for the wages-labour ratio; and for two years each (1954 and 1955) for surplus-labour and surplus-capital ratios. Here the hypotheses of independence are rejected at the 2.5 per cent level of significance against the alternative that there are positive associations in these cases.

TABLE 30.2: VALUE OF THE RANK CORRELATION COEFFICIENT BETWEEN SIZE AND ECONOMIC CHARACTERISTICS, 1953–58

Year	Output-Labour Ratio	Wages-Labour Ratio	Surplus-Labour Ratio	Output-Capital Ratio	Surplus-Capital Ratio
(1)	(2)	(3)	(4)	(5)	(6)
1953	.98	1.00	.58	.98	.63
1954	.98	.92	.73	.98	.30
1955	1.00	1.00	.70	1.00	.98
1956	.92	.53	.35	.85	.47
1957	.93	.57	.18	.73	.35

The data above seem to support the hypotheses of positive association between size and (b) productivity per worker, (c) wages per worker, and (d) surplus per worker; and (f) surplus per unit of capital. But the evidence above does not support the hypothesis of negative association between size and (e) output-capital ratio. In point of fact it may be taken as suggesting positive association between size and output per unit of capital. Thus, small units can be said to have lower productivity, lower wage, and lower surplus per worker; and lower output and lower surplus per unit of capital than large ones.

(C) Technology and Economic Characteristics

The hypotheses now tested are that (i) technology and (b) productivity per worker, (c) wages per worker, and (d) surplus per worker are all positively associated; (ii) technology and (e) output-capital ratio are negatively associated; and (iii) technology and (f) surplus-capital ratio are positively associated.

The rank correlation was consistently negative for all the six years in all the five cases. The value of the coefficient was less than or equal to the critical value, having a minus sign, at the 2.5 per cent level of significance for five years (i.e., excepting 1955) for the output-capital ratio; for three (1953, 1956, and 1957) for the output-labour ratio; for two years (1956 and 1958) for the surplus-capital ratio; and for one year (1953) for the wages-labour ratio. Thus, here too, the hypotheses of independence are rejected at the 2.5 per cent level of significance against the hypotheses of negative association in all these cases.

Except in the case of wages-labour ratio, which was positive for two years (1956 and 1958) though negative for the other four years, the product-moment correlation was consistently negative for all the six years in the other characteristics.

The value of this coefficient was less than the critical value, having a minus sign, at the 2.5 per cent level of significance for five years (i.e., excepting 1958) for the output-labour ratio; for four years (1953, 1954, 1955, and 1958) for the

TABLE 30.3: VALUE OF THE COEFFICIENTS BETWEEN TECHNOLOGY AND ECONOMIC CHARACTERISTICS, 1953–58

Year	Rank Correlation Coefficient					Product-Moment Correlation Coefficient				
	Output-Labour Ratio	Wages-Labour Ratio	Surplus-Labour Ratio	Output-Capital Ratio	Surplus-Labour Ratio	Output-Labour Ratio	Wages-Labour Ratio	Surplus-Labour Ratio	Output-Capital Ratio	Surplus-Capital Ratio
(1)	(2)	(3)	(4)	(5)	(6)	(7)	(8)	(9)	(10)	(11)
1953	–.87	–.83	–.60	–.87	–.66	–.69	–.58	–.95	–.48	–.76
1954	–.43	–.59	–.40	–.82	–.53	–.91	–.33	–.96	–.36	–.82
1955	–.60	–.57	–.35	–.57	–.58	–.74	–.57	–.80	–.76	–.86
1956	–.70	–.16	–.48	–.93	–.68	–.69	+.22	–.28	–.80	–.45
1957	–.78	–.42	–.33	–.95	–.44	–.87	+.19	–.51	–.40	–.62
1958	–.63	–.38	–.27	–.95	–.77	–.42	–.45	–.78	–.81	–.51

surplus-labour ratio; and for three years each for the output-capital (1955, 1956, and 1958) and surplus-capital (1953, 1954, and 1955) ratios. Thus, here again the hypotheses of independence are rejected at the 2.5 per cent level of significance against the alternatives of negative association.

Thus, the data above do not support the hypotheses of positive association between technology and (b) productivity per worker, (c) wages per worker, and (d) surplus per worker; and (f) surplus per unit of capital. On the other hand, they may be taken as suggesting the hypotheses of negative association in all these cases. The evidence on the relationship between technology and (e) output-capital ratio seems also to support the hypothesis of negative association. Thus, in an overall view, the evidence may be taken to suggest that the labour-intensive technology has higher productivity, higher wage, and higher surplus per worker; and also that it has higher output and higher surplus per unit of capital than capital-intensive technology.

IV Conclusions, Their Limitations, and Implications

(A) Conclusions

The above analyses may be taken as tending towards the following conclusions:

(1) Small units are capital-intensive and large units labour-intensive.
(2) Small units have lower productivity, lower wage, and lower surplus per worker; and also lower output and lower surplus per unit of capital than the large ones.
(3) Labour-intensive technology has higher productivity, higher wage, and higher surplus per worker; and also, higher output and higher surplus per unit of capital than capital-intensive technology.

The trouble with the small units, it would seem, arises not because they have paucity of capital, but possibly because they suffer from a plethora of it! For the small units are found to be capital-intensive.

(B) Limitations

These conclusions are to be considered with reference to their context. In the first place, they are for the cotton textiles industry. Secondly, they are based on the analyses of data for six years, 1953–58. And thirdly, they are confined to factories employing 20 or more workers on any day and using power. It is only fair to emphasise here again that the smaller units, or the units which one would like to label as really small (such as the completely manual units—the handspinning or the handweaving type—and the small power-based workshops employing not more than 19 workers on any day—the power loom type) are not covered by our source.

Since these conclusions are based on the analyses of the census data, the limitations of the latter would naturally plague the results. Some of these are: use of the actual output data; valuation of capital as per books of the units; relating capital stock as at the end of the year instead of at the mid-year date with the output or its divisions; arbitrary method in arriving at surplus; limited reference period of six years only; and exclusion of the really smaller units from the coverage of the source. It is not possible to discuss in detail the influence of all these on our conclusions. It may, however, be noted that our conclusions portray only a relative picture; and the relative position will remain undisturbed if the factors concerned influence the size-groups in a uniform manner and/or in an equal measure. The influence of these limitations is being examined in the larger work referred to above. By way of an interim note, it may be added that the tone and the tendency of these conclusions are not likely to be much disturbed.

(C) Implications

How can we explain our results? And what is their significance for economic policy?

The large-sized units reveal a use of resources superior to or more economical than that in the small-sized units. Possibly, the organisational economies or the economics of scale as such, arising out of bulk buying and selling, easier availability of finance and on more favourable terms, better supervision and management, and superior entrepreneurial ability are more important than the technological economies or the economies arising out of employment of capital-intensive technology. In a word, the technological economies are perhaps not so sensational, or perhaps do not accrue in as great a measure in practice, in this industry at least, as may be commonly thought. The large units are possibly headed by entrepreneurs who very effectively combine factors of production, as is revealed by our results. The crucial factor which could possibly explain our results may well be the factor of enterprise.

Secondly, the underlying assumption of the public policy of promoting small industrial units in a country like ours seems to be that such units use capital, the scarce resource, sparingly, and labour, the plentiful resource, abundantly, in the sense that they embody a technology which produces more output and employs more labour per unit of capital than the large units. This assumption is not borne out by our data. Perhaps the case appears to be quite the contrary. Such virtues as are claimed or tacitly assumed for the small units are to be found precisely in large units! To the extent that our conclusions are valid, such a policy would be tantamount to promoting those which should be penalised and penalising those which should be promoted. Surely the large units do seem to deserve a new and better deal.

APPENDIX: BASIC TABLES

TABLE A-1: CAPITAL-LABOUR RATIO BY SIZE, COTTON TEXTILES INDUSTRY, 1953–58

Size (As Denoted by the Number of Persons Employed	Capital-Labour Ratio					
	1953	1954	1955	1956	1957	1958
(1)	(2)	(3)	(4)	(5)	(6)	(7)
Less than 20	29,108	42.201	8,585	9,921	40,367	25,129
20–49	6,236	4,663	4,091	4,222	4,282	3,045
50–99	3,881	3,357	3,210	3,541	7,085	6,497
100–249	4,767	4,941	4,052	5,812	6,714	8,674
250–449	3,920	4,567	4,525	4,152	5,277	6,334
500–999	3,987	4,009	4,416	5,151	5,354	5,286
1,000–1,999	2,160	3,135	3,243	3,647	4,229	4,494
2,000–4,999	3,350	3,418	3,353	3,623	4,027	4,278
5,000 and above	3,199	3,317	3,034	3,248	3,815	3,875
All	3,440	3,420	3,351	3,648	4,174	4,473

TABLE A-2: OUTPUT-LABOUR RATIO BY SIZE, COTTON TEXTILES INDUSTRY, 1953–58

Size	Output-Labour Ratio					
	1953	1954	1955	1956	1957	1958
(1)	(2)	(3)	(4)	(5)	(6)	(7)
Less than 20	1,127	1,240	298	889	–95	–394
20–49	529	781	1,013	1,013	1,167	1,507
50–99	1,275	1,072	1,032	1,756	1,419	1,532
100–249	605	1,305	1,305	1,338	1,559	1,467
250–449	1,299	1,738	1,524	1,722	1,433	1,687
500–999	1,469	1,864	1,864	2,047	1,605	1,592
1,000–1,999	1,701	1,848	2,002	2,003	1,728	1,857
2,000–4,999	2,146	2,092	2,265	2,324	1,901	2,177
5,000 and above	1,942	2,105	2,404	2,227	2,384	2,290
All	1,926	2,003	2,194	2,207	1,954	2,060

TABLE A-3: WAGES-LABOUR RATIO BY SIZE, COTTON TEXTILES INDUSTRY, 1953–58

Size	Wages-Labour Ratio					
	1953	1954	1955	1956	1957	1958
(1)	(2)	(3)	(4)	(5)	(6)	(7)
Less than 20	679	762	603	1,599	1,466	722
20–49	706	733	694	757	839	829
50–99	735	678	706	674	1,181	2,028
100–249	787	793	815	803	778	715
250–449	915	912	902	909	976	993
500–999	984	1,041	966	1,076	1,132	1,165
1,000–1,999	1,335	1,288	1,238	1,290	1,386	1,499
2,000–4,999	1,511	1,524	1,496	1,585	1,651	1,698
5,000 and above	1,518	1,498	1,575	1,669	1,754	1,737
All	1,425	1,411	1,413	1,497	1,566	1,588

TABLE A-4: SURPLUS-LABOUR RATIO BY SIZE, COTTON TEXTILES INDUSTRY, 1953–58

Size	Surplus-Labour Ratio					
	1953	1954	1955	1956	1957	1958
(1)	(2)	(3)	(4)	(5)	(6)	(7)
Less than 20	–1,806	–2,001	–305	–719	–1,561	–1,116
20–49	–177	48	320	256	329	679
50–99	540	393	326	1,082	238	491
100–249	–182	512	491	534	780	747
250–449	384	826	621	812	457	694
500–999	485	822	898	970	473	427
1,000–1,999	346	560	764	714	342	358
2,000–4,999	636	568	769	739	250	479
5,000 and above	424	607	829	608	629	553
All	501	592	782	711	388	472

TABLE A-5: OUTPUT-CAPITAL RATIO BY SIZE, COTTON TEXTILES INDUSTRY, 1953–58

Size	Output-Capital Ratio					
	1953	1954	1955	1956	1957	1958
(1)	(2)	(3)	(4)	(5)	(6)	(7)
Less than 20	–.04	–.03	.03	.09	–.002	–0.1
20–49	.08	.17	.25	.24	.272	.49

(contd.)

(Table A-5 contd.)

Size	Output-Capital Ratio					
	1953	1954	1955	1956	1957	1958
(1)	(2)	(3)	(4)	(5)	(6)	(7)
50–99	.328	.30	.231	.50	.20	.24
100–249	.13	.26	.322	.23	.23	.17
250–449	.331	.38	.34	.41	.271	.27
500–999	.37	.46	.42	.40	.30	.30
1,000–1,999	.48	.59	.62	.55	.41	.41
2,000–4,999	1.30	.61	.68	.64	.47	.51
5,000 and above	.61	.63	.79	.70	.62	.59
All	.56	.58	.65	.60	.47	.46

TABLE A-6: SURPLUS-CAPITAL RATIO BY SIZE, COTTON TEXTILES INDUSTRY, 1953–58

Size	Surplus-Capital Ratio					
	1953	1954	1955	1956	1957	1958
(1)	(2)	(3)	(4)	(5)	(6)	(7)
Less than 20	–.06	–.05	–.04	–.07	–.04	–.04
20–49	–.03	.01	.08	.060	.076	.22
50–99	.139	.1010	.10	.31	.03	–.07
100–249	–.04	.1036	.12.	.09	.12	.09
250–449	.098	.1807	.14	.1956	.086	.109
500–999	.12	.21	.20	.188	.088	.080
1,000–1,999	.097	.1785	.24	.1957	.080	.079
2,000–4,999	.19	.17	.23	.204	.06	.11
5,000 and above	.13	.1829	.27	.187	.16	.14
All	.15	.17	.23	.19	.09	.11

Note: More than two decimal points occurring in Tables A-5 and A-6 in some columns are for a clearer ranking.

NOTE

[1] Readers not conversant with statistical reasoning may find the following note helpful.

The critical value of the rank correlation coefficient to be used in testing the hypothesis of independence, at the 5 per cent level of significance, against the alternative hypothesis that there is association (either positive or negative) when n = 9 (as in the present case) is .68. The hypothesis is tested in the following manner:

Pr either ($r < -.68$) or

($r < +.68$) = .05

$$\Pr(r < -68) = .025$$
$$\Pr(r < +.68) = .025$$

To elaborate: If r is less than or equal to –.68 or greater than or equal to +.68, the hypothesis of independence is rejected at the 5 per cent level of significance against the alternative hypothesis that there is association (either negative or positive). If *r* is less than or equal to –.68, the hypothesis of independence is rejected at the 2.5 per cent level of significance against the alternative that there is negative association. If *r* is greater than or equal to +.68, the hypothesis of independence is rejected at the 2.5 per cent level of significance against the alternative that there is positive association.

PART VIII

Public Finance and Distribution

31

Federal Finance Perspectives*

Bhabatosh Datta

The appointment of the Finance Commission has raised the prospect of reopening the entire question of financial allocation, and has provided scope for re-examining the basis of the present system. The main difficulty about the present system is that it is largely a patchwork. One can find in it traces of the 1870 Mayo system and every subsequent revision. And of course the whole scheme is overwhelmed by the provisions of the Niemeyer Award. The post-1947 modifications were all attempts at making adjustments within a given system, and none of these did, or could, take a whole view based on the changed situation and changed perspective. The Finance Commission has no doubt to make its recommendations within the overall limits placed by the Constitution of India, but it can certainly open many issues considered closed by the Central Finance Ministry or the Sarkar Committee or C. D. Deshmukh in his capacity as an allocation arbitrator.

The change in the situation has been brought about by many factors. Some of the older provinces have disappeared from the Indian map. Some provinces have been changed thoroughly, and in one case almost out of recognition. Many new units—the Part "B" states—have entered the main picture. The Central Government's functions have increased, are increasing, and ought perhaps to be increased still further. The need for a strong unitary control over the financial machinery, with a view to serving an overall expansion of employment and output, fostering capital formation, and at the same time countervailing inflationary forces, has come to be generally recognised. And at the same time the political choice in favour of a federation has been definitely made.

The result has been unfortunate. The operation of the financial allocation plan has left the states dissatisfied, and the Centre finds it difficult to perform

* Originally published in *Economic Weekly* 4, no. 16 (19 April 1952), pp. 400–03.

the dual task of securing a satisfactory devolution of financial responsibilities and of acting as the responsible guardian of a big, wayward family. The demand on the Centre has been insistent—for a higher income-tax divisible pool, for larger state-shares in the pool, for reimbursement against specific revenues lost because of recent changes, and for grants-in-aid under Article 275 of the Constitution. It has become tempting for the states to adopt a policy of deficit budgeting, simply to press home the claim for special consideration.

There are probably three main ways in which the Finance Commission can approach the problem. The first is the Deshmukh method of hearing petitions for claims and then giving an award. This is obviously inadequate and unfair when a long view is taken; the Deshmukh method could be justified only on the ground that a definitely short-period formula was aimed at, and that no major change would be desirable before the Finance Commission has gone into the whole question. The second method is that of negotiations; the Union and states representatives can meet together and examine their claims and counterclaims. Given goodwill and a real desire and ability to see the viewpoint of the other side, there is no reason why negotiations should fail to bring about an agreed formula. But, in the present context, the necessary presumptions are perhaps rather bold, and it may be difficult actually to reconcile the conflicting viewpoints that would be presented.

The third alternative would be to begin by a clarification of the basic conditions and principles. And it is here that the economist should perhaps have something to say.

An essential preliminary step would be to eliminate the unnecessary confusion in our financial system between reimbursements and grants. A case for reimbursement arises when a particular tax source is taken away from the states by the Centre—generally for administrative reasons—and the Centre reimburses the affected states for the loss of revenue. The revenue lost actually belongs to the states and the states therefore get back their own legitimate dues. Article 270 of the Indian Constitution seems to imply the acceptance of this principle. The Union is responsible for the "levy and collection" of income taxes and has a statutory liability to distribute a part of the collection among the states in which the taxes are levied. Though there is no constitutional bar against under- or over-reimbursement, it would appear that the main idea was that there would be an administrative centralisation with a sharing of revenue. The sharing takes, superficially, the form of Central allocation to the states, but is really based on the idea that the states contribute a part of their territorial revenues to the Centre.

Perhaps the most contested problem that the Finance Commission would have to decide on would be that of the size of the income-tax divisible pool and its allocation. It would, however, be easy to settle the problem of the size of the pool. No state wants that the income tax receipts other than those specifically reserved for the Centre should come wholly to the states, and the Centre is not likely to claim anything more than 50 per cent (the Centre can always increase its effective share by putting a special surcharge). A 50-50 rule would not mean great dissatisfaction on any side and a 40-60 division would go a long way in meeting the demand of the states. Considering the fact that the Centre can put a surcharge for its own benefit, and that it can determine the basic income-tax rates (i.e., considering the fact that the Centre can reduce the income tax rates and convert the concession into a surcharge), it can afford to adopt a 40-60 rule. It may, therefore, be expected that there would not be any serious wrangling about the primary division formula.

In respect of inter-state allocation of the distributable amount, the major difficulty has arisen because of the feeling in some states that they have been unfairly treated. Here perhaps the more important step would be to demarcate very clearly reimbursements from grants, so that what appears as reimbursement based on the derivation principle is nothing but reimbursement, and all grants appear undisguisedly as grants. The Constitution seems to have this end in view, and even if it did not specifically lay down any rule of guidance, it would be logical to interpret Articles 270 and 275 in a manner that would conform to the logic of sound economics. There is in the present system (the Niemeyer-Deshmukh rules) an unnecessary and confusing mixing up of the principle of refunding according to derivation, and that of grants on the basis of financial needs. There are, as a consequence, some states which are getting disguised grants in the form of income-tax reimbursement. If, for example, a state contributes Rs. 10 crores to the divisible pool (and is thus entitled to a Rs. 5 crore reimbursement under a 50-50 rule) and actually gets Rs. 7 crores as its share in the pool, it is really getting a disguised grant of Rs. 2 crores—a grant which could have more openly been given under Article 275.

There may exist excellent reasons for making a grant of this amount to this state. But the fact remains that this extra Rs. 2 crores is not reimbursement, but a needs-subsidy, and it is desirable for many reasons that it should be openly shown as a subsidy. Besides, it is fair neither to the recipient state, nor to the others that bear the ultimate incidence, to consider the problem of grants in such a piecemeal manner. The best course would be to decide on the reimbursement issue according to straight accounting rules of derivation. When this has been done a clear picture of the grant needs will be available, and the deciding authority can proceed to the next step of considering the right principle for estimating the needs.

It is quite possible that the final arithmetical result of such an approach would be exactly the same as that of a set of piecemeal subsidies, some given openly under Article 275, and some masked as income-tax refund. But even then, a separation of the logical issues will have its advantages. If the state which is entitled to a straight Rs. 5-crore reimbursement is actually getting Rs. 7 crores, and is also getting an open needs-grant of Rs. 1 crore, and if it is agreed that the state cannot do without this Rs. 8 crore total, it would be better to show that it is getting a Rs. 5 crore reimbursement and a Rs. 3 crore grant. Such a separation would have many advantages. Firstly, it would point out precisely what part of a state's receipts is a grant from outside; secondly, it would prevent the recipient state from feeling complacent about its financial position (a small open grant and a large disguised one may easily lead it to believe that things are better than they actually are); thirdly, it would tell other states exactly what this one is getting as grant; and lastly, it would provide a sound basis for comparing from time to time the "needs" position of the different states.

Once the reimbursement side of the problem has been satisfactorily solved, the Finance Commission can take the question of grants as one single problem. This single problem will of course have many facets, and, besides, one can define "needs" in a number of different ways. It is, however, necessary at the outset to distinguish between the needs of a *state* and the needs of a *state government*. These two have often been confused, so that a relatively developed state, with a general standard of life above that of its neighbours, has been able to speak about the "needs of the state" on the ground that its government budget has been persistently unbalanced. We shall show later that there is a strong case for eliminating deficit in the state budgets—if necessary, with Central assistance—but one should keep clear the distinction between a *backward state* and a *deficit state*. A backward state requiring special grants for raising the standard of life of the people may have a strong budgetary position, and it is quite usual for a relatively prosperous state to have a consistently weak position in the matter of government finances.

The estimation of the needs of a state requires the consideration of many points, including its population and area, the occupational distribution and average income, resources, the potential "speed of reaction" of development expenditure, etc. In the present situation, the first essential would be to equalise as far as possible the standard of life of the average person in all states, and though it is difficult to suggest an all-correct formula, it should not be difficult to decide which states require the largest amounts of developmental expenditure.

It is, however, important to remember that the existence of backwardness-needs does not necessarily justify a Central grant-in-aid to the state government concerned. A grant to a state can easily be made without making a grant to the state government. The central government has a large capital programme of its own and the choice of the *situs* of the programme or of any part of it is an important factor. Thus, if Alpha is a backward state and requires development expenditure, the end can be achieved not simply by making development grants to the Alpha government, but also by undertaking centrally controlled development expenditure in Alpha. So long as there is a large and expanding central capital budget, it is not essential that state "needs" should be covered by grants-in-aid to the state government. Grants-in-aid to one state have generally some incidence on other states; they at least produce perverse psychological reactions. And it may be easier for every state to accept the principle of needs-based expenditure in particular areas, if this expenditure is directly Central.

The problem of deficit in the state government budgets of course remains. Here it appears that important factors have often been ignored. There has recently been too much talk about Central surpluses or deficit vis-à-vis capital formation or inflation, without considering the fact that it is the "net budgetary effect" of all government expenditure that counts. It is common to speak, for example, about the disinflationary effect of the Rs. 93-crore revenue surplus of 1951–52 or of the reduced overall revenue-cum-capital deficit; it is overlooked that the net effects of the state budgets may neutralise a large part of the net effects of the Central budget. One can speak about the capital-forming effect or the disinflationary effect of a revenue-surplus only when one takes into consideration the Central and the state budgets together, and preferably, the budgetary results of the operation of municipalities and other local superiorities as well. Full details for 1951–52 are not available, but it is noteworthy that the Central revenue surplus of Rs. 8 crores in 1950–51 was secured alongside a combined revenue deficit of Rs. 5 crores in the Part 'A' states. And it seems that the 1952–53 budget estimate of a Central revenue surplus of Rs. 33 crores (Rs. 18 crores, if the anticipations regarding food-department expenditure do not materialize) would be considerably weakened by a combined total of deficit in the Part 'A' and Part 'B' states.

A full computation of the final figures for the net budgetary effects would require a consideration of the revenue surplus or deficit of the Centre, of all categories of states, and of other public authorities (avoiding some items of double counting), a careful examination of the capital budget surplus or deficit (bringing the accounts in different areas up to the same pattern of presentation), and an aggregation of the overall surplus or deficit for each relevant account. The combined revenue surplus or deficit would show the contribution which the government financial system can make towards capital formation, while the combined overall result (plus/minus the relevant balance-of-payments figure) would indicate the net inflationary or deflationary pressure of all categories of financial operations undertaken by public authorities.

If the Central Government is to remain responsible for counteracting by its own financial operations the inflationary or deflationary pressure generated by other factors, there would be a strong case for centralising the net budgetary effects—for centralising all deficits and surpluses in public expenditure. A theoretically perfect system would be one under which the states and the local authorities have balanced budgets in all circumstances, their deficit being made up by the Centre, and their surpluses appropriated by the Centre, and the central budget explicitly showing the net total of the deficit, or surplus, of all governmental financial operations.

The Central Government then can proceed confidently to the task of choosing suitable correctives or stimulants. This of course is unpractical at the present stage, and with the present form of government; it means in effect a return to a completely centralised and unitary administration of the finances in which the state treasuries become really administrative departments working within dictated financial plans, no longer responsible for the results of their own actions. When a political choice in favour of a federal form of government has definitely been made, this becomes an unattainable and undesirable financial ideal.

It is possible, however, to evolve a compromise formula which constitutes such an allocation of expenditure heads and revenue resources to the states as to make the state finances more or less cycle-insensitive. But even this is not now practicable—the states are not, for example, likely to give up their right to impose sales taxes, which are naturally highly cycle-sensitive. It may, however, be possible to arrange things in such a way that the states would not be allowed to run into overall deficit (except within a narrow range, which administrative factors might make necessary), and that all actually accrued revenue surpluses could be carefully ploughed back into the states' own capital operations.

In other words, if a deliberately adopted Union policy of surplus-budget or deficit-finance is to succeed, the Union must have full control over the net surplus or deficit of the expenditure of all public authorities. To secure this, the state budgets must either be fully coordinated with the Centre, or they must be maintained with Central help, if necessary, on a near-balanced level. The former alternative means the rejection of our political choice in favour of a federation. If the political choice is taken for granted, one has still to remember that there can be no effective financial policy in the country, with the states running into deficit, while the Union Government is trying disinflation or capital formation through revenue surplus, or with the states collecting comfortable surpluses when the Union Government is deliberately aiming at the multiplier effects of deficit finance.

To prevent this contradictory state of affairs, it may be advisable to plan development expenditure and grant-in-aid for terms longer than the budget year—say, for five years at a time. The term "quinquennial settlement" has an unhappy association for the student of Indian financial history. But some long-term or at least medium-term arrangement would be unavoidable if there has to be a common overall financial policy with income and employment targets. The grants-in-aid, once fixed for five years, should not be allowed to vary appreciably from year to year, any necessary change being met by variations of the Central development expenditure undertaken within the relevant area. Within the planning period, the state governments should be required to apply all revenue surplus to capital formation (unless of course the inflationary pressure is so great as to require a cutting down of the capital programme and sterilising the surplus). The states should also be encouraged to eliminate deficit by reduction of expenditure and new taxation and not to look up to the Centre for filling up accrued gaps.

For the success of this type of arrangement, the first essential is the elimination of the scramble for revenue and shares in revenue, and of the feeling of injustice which is common under the present system. This can be done by arranging the reimbursement schemes as straight refund of collections, and making them completely independent of any consideration of needs. It is only then that a fair picture of the needs of the states can be obtained; the requirements of the backward states can then be broadly estimated. A large part of these requirements can be met effectively—and in a manner satisfactory to all units—by the allocation of Central capital expenditure. If this is not adequate, or if the development expenditure required in a state is of a type that can be better undertaken by a state government, there would be a clear case for specific grants-in-aid to the state finances. All this should work under the overall constraint that the state budgets as a whole should always be at a near balanced level, all net surpluses or deficit being made to appear in the Central budget. The Centre then would be in a position to adopt a financial policy that would be appropriate in view of its income-output targets, and the particular phase of the inflation-deflation cycle through which the country may be passing. It is difficult to secure in a federal state the full advantages of the lessons of the new economics—one notices easily the discomfort of the American economists writing on deficit finance and fiscal policy—but it may not be impossible to find a practicable compromise if everyone tries to get at the basic issues with an objective and detached mind.

The conclusions to which one comes after a consideration of these basic issues can now be summarised.

Firstly, there should not be any unnecessary mixing up of reimbursements and grants—and grants should not be disguised in any way.

Secondly, the needs of a state and the need of a state government are not the same thing, i.e., a deficit state is not necessarily a backward state.

Thirdly, a backward state requires development expenditure, but this does not necessarily justify a grant to the state government; there is the alternative of locating centrally controlled capital expenditure within the territorial area of the needy state.

And lastly, the financial position of the state government has to be considered from an entirely different viewpoint—namely, that of the undesirability of a dispersal of public authorities' surplus or deficit: the grants actually made to the state governments, and the tax allocation and reimbursement schemes should take into consideration the need for keeping the state budget continuously at a balanced or near balanced level, and for centralising the net budgetary effects.

32

Tax Reform in India*

Nicholas Kaldor

An effective system of progressive direct taxation is vital to the survival of democratic institutions in India. The need for this arises not merely on financial grounds to raise adequate resources for purposes of accelerated economic development but in order to bring about the degree of social cohesion and cooperation that is essential for the successful functioning of a democratic system. In a community where there is such a wide gap between the position of a privileged minority of well-to-do and the vast majority who live in dire poverty, social cohesion can only be achieved if economic inequality is effectively lessened and the tendency towards increasing concentration of wealth is effectively counteracted. This can only be done through the instrument of taxation. It is in any case inevitable that heavy burdens should be laid on the broad masses of the population if India is to attain a satisfactory rate of development in the coming decades. It will not be possible to carry through this programme successfully with the consent and cooperation of the people if the privileged minority of the well-to-do are not made to bear a fair share of this burden. Moreover, in matters of taxation, like in the administration of the law, it is not enough that justice should be done. It must also be seen to be done. If, owing to defects in the tax law, or in their administration, highly progressive taxes on wealth or income have no visible effect on the prevailing economic inequality or in the standards of living of the rich, the mere enactment of advanced tax legislation will prove fruitless.

* Originally published in *Economic Weekly* 11, nos. 4–6 (24 January 1959), pp. 195–98. Substance of an address given to the informal consultative committee of the Parliament in New Delhi on 16 December 1958.

A FAIR START

In the last few years India has made a fair start towards creating an effective system of progressive taxation with the introduction of the new taxes on capital gains, on wealth, on personal expenditure, and on gifts. It has thus laid the basis for a system which may serve as a model to other democracies, both developed and underdeveloped. But it is no use blinking the fact that the reforms so far introduced are, at best, a beginning; that the legislation of some of the new taxes is seriously defective whilst the measures for their effective administration have not yet been provided; and that other and equally important reforms in the field of business and company taxation have not been tackled at all. Unless some of the recent legislation is amended in important respects, and unless it is supplemented by legislation in other fields and by far-reaching reforms in the administrative field, there is a serious risk that this noble attempt at creating an egalitarian democracy will end in failure.

Whether the political or social urges which led to the recent reforms continue to prevail or not, I am convinced that the Indian tax system could not be frozen still at the point which it has now reached. If an effective tax structure is to be created, reform will have to be carried a great deal further; on the other hand, if political forces were to become dominant which would effectively bar this development, there would be little point in preserving such a complicated system of taxation.

Among the new taxes the expenditure tax and the gift tax are so heavily riddled with loopholes and exemptions that they bear only a superficial resemblance to the taxes whose introduction I originally recommended. Though the new capital gains tax represents a considerable advance on the form in which it was originally enacted in India, it still suffers from serious shortcomings which undermine the basic purpose of personal income taxation of securing equality of treatment between different tax payers. The wealth tax alone was enacted in a form that is comparatively free from loopholes, though this too contains features that could justifiably be criticised.

DEFECTS OF EXPENDITURE TAX

The most serious defect of the Expenditure Tax Act is that it ties the liability to this tax to a minimum income limit. This opens the door to endless manipulations and is bound to make the tax largely ineffective in practice. Expenditure represents an alternative base to income for measuring spending power or ability to pay. The difference is only that the latter taxes savings and exempts dissavings, whereas the former exempts savings and brings dissavings into charge. There is much to be said (for administrative and other reasons) for making use of both principles of taxation by levying some of the taxation on an income base and some on an expenditure base. But it is essential, in this case, that the liability to the one should not be made dependent on the extent of the liability to the other. By making the liability to the expenditure tax dependent on the size of income, a concession is made to savings without making a corresponding charge on dissaving.

This is far more serious than it may appear at first sight since it is always open to any tax payer to make his income smaller than it could be (even though he may not always be in the position to make it larger). This provision thus makes it possible to a taxpayer to telescope his income into particular years in which his spendings are kept low, and to telescope his spending into those years in which his income is kept low enough to entitle him to exemption from the expenditure tax. It is therefore bound to have a highly destructive effect—one is almost tempted to say that this particular provision alone makes the tax little more than a showpiece.

In addition, the Expenditure Tax Act contains a long series of exemptions of various kinds—such as expenditure on marriages, on medical expenses, election expenses, the purchase of cottage industry products, etc.—which have no counterpart in the income tax laws and which will make administration very difficult. I do not wish to argue the moral or economic justification for exempting any particular form of personal expenditure from taxation—any one of these exemptions may have something to be said for it, either on grounds of fairness or expediency. But it is surely inequitable to exempt particular categories of personal outlay from expenditure taxation if these are not also exempted from income taxation.

For the great majority of people income provides the sole source of expenditure; their ability to spend is confined by income taxation just as effectively as by expenditure taxation. If it is not justified to reduce a man's liability to income tax on account of his having exceptional expenses to bear on illness or on a wedding for example, why is it justified to reduce his liability to expenditure tax? Why should people whose source of spending is capital as well as income be more leniently treated than people whose only source of spending is the income which they earn? And (bearing in mind the high exemption limit to expenditure tax and the low exemption limit to income tax) why should the necessitous expenditures of large spenders be so carefully looked after when the necessitous expenditures of small and moderate spenders are not? From the point of view of equality of treatment whatever concessions are made on grounds of necessitous expenditure for the one tax ought to have their counterpart in the other tax.

Gift Tax Equally Defective

Analogous criticisms can be made against the Gift Tax Act, which in its final legislative form is only a pale shadow of what it was originally intended to be.

The purpose of a gift tax, like that of the estate duty, is to restrict the freedom of individuals to pass on their property rights to others. As the American economist Henry Simons once said, the whole of private property, and the income derived from it, is a gift from the community. It is only by the will of the community that particular individuals can enjoy the privileges of ownership protected by law and administration; and the constantly evolving property laws define the actual nature of the rights which these privileges confer. Inheritance taxes are, in effect, a form of limitation on the privileges conferred by ownership: they allow an individual (subject to various limits circumscribed by law) the unfettered enjoyment of his own property, but they do not allow him to pass on his property unhindered to the next generation. But if this limitation is held to be justified, on what basis can one differentiate between inter vivos gifts and gifts by deed of will?

There is a long list of exemptions in the present Gift Tax Act which has no counterpart in the Estate Duty Act. Further, the provisions of that Act are so framed as to make it possible for an owner through the mere process of spreading the gifts over time to reduce the incidence of the gift tax to a small fraction of that of the estate duty, or even to avoid the tax altogether. As is well known, it was the introduction of the estate duty which led to the wholesale passing on of property by means of inter vivos gifts so as to avoid that duty—hence the need for a gift tax. But the present tax, by failing to integrate gifts over successive years for tax purposes, and by giving a series of exemptions to gifts of particular kinds (including a large annual exemption) entirely fails in this purpose.

These loopholes in the expenditure and the gift tax legislation are bound to reduce the yield of these taxes to a small fraction of what they should have been. This in turn is bound to create agitation for their complete removal. Opponents of these taxes are certain to ask, if such complicated taxes yield so little, what is the point of having them at all? Of course, they would be ignoring the fact that the low yield will be the consequence of the very loopholes and exemptions on which they insisted. In the absence of loopholes, the gift tax and the estate duty taken together at the current rate schedule, could be expected to yield some 20–30 crores of rupees annually. As it is, the combined yield will amount to less than one-fifth of this sum. The expenditure tax, properly administered, and in the absence of the present loopholes, should yield at least 15–20 crores of rupees at the current schedule of rates. In its present form it will hardly yield one-tenth of this sum.

INCENTIVE TO CONVERT INCOME INTO CAPITAL GAINS

With regard to capital gains the new legislation has the great advantage over the old one in that capital gains are now integrated with other forms of income for income tax purposes. But they are not liable to super tax, which means that they are only liable to a maximum rate of tax of 27.5 per cent, whilst other kinds of unearned income are liable to a maximum rate of 84 per cent.[1] There is therefore still a very considerable incentive for converting income into capital gains, thereby reducing the effective taxation of those who are in a position to benefit from it to well below the rates applicable to other tax payers. Moreover, while the new law disallows certain of the exemptions provided in the original Act, the important loophole of exempting transfers of property through inter vivos gifts and through inheritance remains open, which means (if American experience is any guide) that only about one-third of the capital gains made by each generation come effectively within the tax net.

The effective rate of taxation of capital gains, even in the absence of any evasion, will thus not be 27.5 per cent, but something more like 10 per cent.

There is undoubtedly some force in the contention that a high rate of tax on capital gains (such as the combined maximum rate of income tax and super tax at present) might have highly undesirable economic effects. But this provides an argument not in favour of a discriminatory treatment of capital gains, but in favour of reducing the rates of taxation on ordinary income. There is no real justification for continuing the discrimination between income which takes the form of capital gains and other income; they both generate the same spending power, and both represent the same taxable capacity. The maintenance of the high marginal rates of income tax thus serves neither the interests of equity nor of revenue if it provides the justification for the continuance of the differential treatment of capital gains or for the maintenance of other equally serious loopholes in income-tax legislation.

Elastic Definition of Expenses

Of these loopholes, the wide and elastic definition of deductible expenses in the case of business profits is undoubtedly the most important. So long as the owners, directors, and managers of businesses are able to pass off so much of their living expenses as business expenditure the incidence of taxation is bound to remain highly arbitrary, and the effective rate of taxation on the business community will remain much below the apparent rate. In my report I suggested that the range of deductible expenses should be confined to "expenses wholly, exclusively and unavoidably incurred in earning the profits of the year" (as against the present rule which permits the deduction of all such expenses which are "wholly and exclusively laid out or expended for the purpose of trade"). This would undoubtedly strengthen the hands of the Revenue in disallowing expenses of various kinds, though the extent to which it will succeed in bringing the treatment of business incomes fully into line with that of contractual incomes will depend on the interpretation given to it by the courts. It is a matter for consideration therefore whether, in addition to a stricter general rule for deductive expenses, the deduction of particular types of expenses (such as the so-called "expense accounts," entertainment outlays, private cars, etc.) should not be explicitly prohibited.

A further source of loopholes arises from the non-integration, or incomplete integration, of total family wealth and income. To close this it would be necessary to aggregate minors' income and property with that of the parents, and to include agricultural income and property within the scope of the Union income tax, wealth tax, and capital gains tax. This latter reform may require a constitutional amendment which, however, might well be carried with the support of the states, if the revenue resulting from the extension of these taxes to agriculture is earmarked to the states.

Tax Evasion

Even if these loopholes were plugged, the administration of the system will not become effective until far-reaching reforms are introduced for checking tax evasion. The compulsory disclosure of *benami* holdings, the abolition of the system of blank transfers of shares and of bearer shares are essential ingredients of this. The introduction of a comprehensive reporting system on capital transactions and of a single comprehensive return for direct taxation are other necessary ingredients. These are matters within the purview of the Direct Taxes Administration Enquiry Committee recently set up and it is very much to be hoped that their recommendations will pay due regard to these basic requirements of the efficient administration of an integrated tax structure.

In closing, I should like to refer to two particular matters on which the Government of India has frequently been criticised for its failure to follow my original recommendations. One relates to the failure to reduce income tax to the maximum rate of 45 per cent and the other to the extension of the wealth tax to companies.

45 Per Cent Income-tax

I fully maintain the view that with a system of direct taxation of the kind I suggested, the maximum of rate of income tax should not exceed 45 per cent. It should be evident, however, that this system has by no means been fully adopted; nothing has been done to tighten up business taxation, while the new taxes, owing to the truncated form in which they have been adopted, will only produce a fraction of yield which they would have produced otherwise. In their present form, and with the present administrative techniques, the new taxes will hardly yield Rs. 20 crores.

In the absence of these gaps in legislation and with an efficient system of administration, they should produce at least Rs. 50 crores more—quite apart from the gain in income tax revenue resulting from lower tax evasion, and the disallowance of certain classes of business expenses. As against that, the loss of revenue resulting from the reduction of income tax to the celling rate of 45 per cent would only amount to Rs. 18 crores. I doubt whether the interests which agitate for the latter would willingly exchange the present high rates of surtax for these further legislative and administrative changes which would involve them in additional taxation amounting to several times this sum.

Wealth Tax on Companies

As regards the wealth tax on companies, I would agree that this does not serve the same purpose of securing equity in the distribution of the burden of taxation as the wealth tax on individuals. On the other hand, it is no more inequitable than the taxation of the profits of companies. As such, they both involve the taxation of legal entities over and above the taxation of individuals who own them, and on principles which are unrelated to the taxable capacity of the owners. But considered as an alternative to a higher rate of profits taxation on companies, its economic effects are distinctly more favourable than that of the profits tax. For it penalises firms who earn a low rate of profit on the capital which they employ and favours those firms whose earning power is high. It thus rewards efficiency and penalises inefficiency, and in the present stage of India's development, it is well worthwhile to offer special inducements to companies who use the resources at their command efficiently. For this reason I should favour putting more of the burden of taxation on companies in the form of a wealth tax, and less in the form of a profits tax—in other words, raising the wealth tax rate (which at 0.5 per cent is very low) if the combined income-and-profits tax rate on companies were correspondingly reduced. Many other features of the present company tax legislation, such as the excess dividend tax, run completely contrary to this, and these ought to be abolished and the whole system of company taxation rationalised and simplified without delay.

Note

[1] I cannot, incidentally, see the advantage of maintaining the distinction between earned and unearned income once the wealth tax is introduced—it means using two separate instruments for the same purpose. It is true that the present wealth tax rates are very moderate. The effective rates are only one-third of the Swedish rates and yield only about two-thirds of the schedule of the rates which I recommended. But it is better in that case to increase the rates of the wealth tax than to maintain the surcharge on unearned incomes.

33

Economic Growth and Rural-Urban Income Distribution

1950–51 to 1960–61*

V. K. R. V. Rao

It is not easy to allocate India's national income between the urban and rural sectors nor the change in their respective magnitudes over the 10-year period. Fortunately, the two terminal points of our period coincide with the decennial census, and it is possible to make a somewhat rough estimate of the relevant magnitudes. There are, however, differences in definition of the urban area between the two censuses of 1951 and 1961 that prevent a straight comparison of the urban population in the two years. The 1951 census had included in the urban sector all places with a population of 5,000 and over as well as some places with a smaller population but possessing definite urban characteristics. In the 1961 Census, while all places like municipalities, cantonments and other areas possessing recognised local administrations continued to be treated as urban, for other places the criteria for inclusion were made stricter. Thus, in order to count as urban, they had to have a population of not less than 5,000, have a density of not less than 1,000 per square mile, and have at least 75 per cent of their working populations engaged in pursuits other than agriculture. On this definition, urban population in 1961 was only 17.8 per cent as compared with 17.0 per cent in 1951. On a reclassification of the data for 1951 in terms of

* Originally published in *Economic Weekly* 17, no. 8 (20 February 1965), pp. 373–78. This chapter is based on the author's forthcoming book, *Distributional Aspects of Economic Growth in India: 1950–51 to 1960–61*.

the definition of 1961, however, it is found that the increase during the decennium is higher, being 17.8 per cent in 1961 as against only 15.6 per cent in 1951. It was therefore possible to identify the increase in urban population on a uniform basis.

Proportion of Workers

When it came to the number of workers, it was more difficult to bring about comparability. The 1951 Census had classified the population under three categories, namely, "self-supporting," "earning dependent," and "non-earning dependent." A self-supporting person was defined as one who earned enough at least to maintain himself, the earning dependent as one who had some income, while the non-earning dependent had none. The 1961 Census abandoned this classification and instead introduced only two categories, namely, "working" and "non-working." The principal means of livelihood was no longer linked with the proportion of the income earned but to the activity to which the respondent devoted the major part of his working time. This resulted in a large increase in the number of workers in the 1961 Census, mainly under female workers in agriculture, the index number of female cultivators which stood at 109.9 in 1951 with 100 as base in 1900 now jumping to 1,947 in 1961. It must be added that, as the bulk of the abnormal increase was accounted thus under agriculture, the definitional difference is not likely to have affected to any significant extent either the comparability of workers in other sectors or their distribution between urban and rural areas.

In any case, for calculating urban and rural incomes, we have used the proportion of workers and their income differentials in each individual industrial sector and not the actual number of workers in the urban and rural areas. The proportion of workers has been based on the paper (mimeographed) by B. R. Kalra on "1961 Census and Its Implications in Terms of Labour Force, Growth and Employment" along with the official 1961 Census paper no. 1, and the official country statement for India presented before the Asian Population Conference in 1963.

Net Output in Sectors

For determining the distribution of net output in individual sectors, our figures are based on the estimated income per worker. In the more organised sectors like mining, factories, railways, communication, and government administration, where income does not depend upon location, no wage differentials are assumed to exist. For agriculture and allied activities, the net value of output has been taken, while for the remaining sectors like small industries, construction, trade, unorganised transport, professions, and liberal arts, data on income differentials have been gleaned from a number of miscellaneous and scattered sources for 1951 and from individual reports of the National Sample Survey for 1961. These data are admittedly rough, are not strictly comparable, and do not always pertain to the specific years 1951 and 1961. Nevertheless, we have been compelled to use them for want of more reliable data and also because, in our judgement, they do broadly represent the relevant orders of magnitude.

For such sectors where no income differentials are used, incomes originating in urban and rural areas have been obtained on the basis of the ratio of workers in the two areas as given by the Population Census results. For those sectors where income differential is assumed to exist, the method adopted is to work out the ratio of rural sample earnings to the corresponding urban figure in each such sector, and the ratio of rural workers to total workers in each sector, and combining the two ratios determine the share rural income in each sector.

The urban income in each sector is then derived as a residual. Table 33.1 gives the result of our calculations for urban and rural income in 1950–51 and 1960–61.

DISPARITY WIDENED

It will be seen that while urban income has increased from Rs. 2,790 crores to Rs. 4,803 crores or by 72.15 per cent, the increase in rural income is only 39.0 per cent, being Rs. 9.396 crores in 1960–61 as against Rs. 6,760 crores in 1950–51. The share of urban income in the national product has increased from 30.3 per cent to 33.8 per cent over this period. In per capita terms, the urbanites have fared even better, the increase being 43.2 per cent as compared to only 12.6 per cent in the case of rural residents. In spite of a slight fall in the proportion of rural to total population and an increase of nearly 19 per cent in the national per capita income, rural per capita income, which was 0.843 of the all-India per capita income in 1950–51, declined to 0.805 by 1960–61. During the same period, the ratio of urban per capita income to the rural counterpart increased from 1.83 to 2.33.

These figures are of course qualified by the extent to which the size of the net transfer of income from urban to rural areas increased over the 1950–51 level, but this does not appear to have been of a significant magnitude. It is also true that the comparison is between two terminal points, but as 1960–61 was not a bad agricultural year—indeed it was particularly good year for foodgrains—this should not lead to any underestimation of the comparative position of rural income. The conclusion emerges therefore that in spite of ten years of economic planning, the disparity between the urban and rural sectors has widened significantly, with urban per capita domestic product standing at Rs. 607 in 1960–61 as against Rs. 261 of its rural counterpart or more than 2.3 times the rural per capita domestic product as against 1.8 in 1950–51.

In order to get clearer understanding of how this has come about, it is necessary to examine the changes in the net domestic product of the two sectors by their industrial origin. Relevant data are presented in Tables 33.2 and 33.3.

TABLE 33.1: SHARE OF URBAN AND RURAL INCOMES IN NET DOMESTIC PRODUCTS

	Income (Rs. Millions)				Percentage to Total Net Output by Each Sector			
	Urban		Rural		Urban		Rural	
	1950–51	1960–61	1950–51	1960–61	1950–51	1960–61	1950–51	1960–61
(1)	(2)	(3)	(4)	(5)	(6)	(7)	(8)	(9)
Agriculture and allied activities	1,700	1,580	47,200	67,320	3.5	2.3	96.5	97.7
Mining, manufacturing, and small enterprises	6,700	15,940	8,600	10,030	42.5	61.4	56.5	38.6
Commerce, transport, and communication	10,500	16,430	6,400	7,040	61.8	70.00	38.2	30.0
Other services	9,000	14,080	5,400	9,570	63.0	59.5	37.0	40.5
Net domestic product at factor cost	27,900	48,030	67,600	93,960	30.3	33.8	69.7	66.2
Index of per capita income with all India – 100	424.2*	607.5*	231.6*	260.9*	175.3	187.5	84.3	80.5

* Per capita income in rupees.

TABLE 33.2: NET DOMESTIC PRODUCT OF RURAL AREAS BY INDUSTRIAL ORIGIN

(In millions of Rs.)

	1950–51	1960–61	Percentage of Rise
(1)	(2)	(3)	(4)
Agriculture and allied activities	47,200	67,320	42.6
Mining & factory establishments	3,200	5,130	60.3
Small enterprises incl. construction	5,400	4,900	9.3
Railways and communication	700	1,180	68.6
Organised banking and insurance	200	460	130.0
Other commerce and transport	5,500	5,400	1.8
Professions and liberal arts	2,100	2,920	39.0
Government service	900	3,510	290.0
Domestic service	400	940	135.0
House property	2,000	2,200	10.0
Net domestic product	67,600	93,960	39.0

FALL IN RURAL INDUSTRIES

It is seen from these tables that as far as the rural sector is concerned, its highest increase has been in its income from government services, being as much as 290 per cent, indicating clearly the extent to which the bureaucracy has been enlarged and expanded in the rural areas for promotion or development. Increase in the income from agriculture has been substantial but not in per capita terms in view of the big increase in population during the period and the insignificant fall in the ratio of rural to total population. It is significant that there has been an actual fall in the income arising from small industries, construction, and commerce and transport, while the negligible rise in the income from house property indicates the want of progress in rural housing. The increase in the income from domestic service is substantial, being as much as 135 per cent, but this is probably due to the fall in employment in commerce, rural industries, and even rural transport of the traditional variety, as also to the opportunities opened out by the emergence of a comparatively well-off, though not numerically very large rural middle-class.

In striking contrast, the urban sector shows a significant rise in the income originating from organised industry. It seems clear that faster progress in the modern sectors of the economy and their larger presence in the urban areas has contributed significantly to the comparatively higher rate of economic growth in the urban sector.

TABLE 33.3: NET DOMESTIC PRODUCT OF URBAN AREAS BY INDUSTRIAL ORIGIN

(in millions of Rs.)

	1950–51	1960–61	Percentage of Rise
(1)	(2)	(3)	(4)
Agriculture and allied activities	1,700	1,580	−7.1
Mining & Factory establishments	3,000	9,670	222.3
Small enterprises incl. construction	3,700	6,270	69.5
Railways and communication	1,500	3,030	100.2
Organised banking and insurance	500	1,150	130.0
Other commerce and transport	8,500	12,250	44.1
Professions and liberal arts	2,600	4,490	72.7
Government service	3,400	5,490	61.5
Domestic service	900	1,000	1.1
House property	2,100	3,100	47.6
Net domestic product	27,900	48,030	72.2

Urban Share of Gain

The larger share that the urban areas have obtained of the gains from development during the first ten years of planning is seen even more clearly from Table 33.4 that sets out the share of the urban and rural areas in the overall national increase in the net domestic product during the period.

It will be seen that except for agriculture, domestic service, and government service, the rural areas have had roughly only about a fourth of the national aggregate of the increased income in the different sectors of economic activity. There has been a significant fall in its share in the income from small industries and construction, the increase in the urban share being 124 per cent of the difference between the two years in the national aggregates of the income from this sector. The rural sector does not also appear to have had any share of the aggregate increase in the income accruing from commerce and transport other than railways. It is also remarkable that if we leave out the increase in the income from agriculture, as much as 41.8 per cent of the increase in its income from all the other sectors comes from government service. Evidently, planning has led to a large increase in the number of government employees and their income in the rural areas, but this does not seem to have a sufficiently stimulating effect on the growth of income in other sectors in the rural economy.

The case for more effective attention being paid to rural development, both in the agricultural and non-agricultural sectors, seems clear from this analysis.

TABLE 33.4: DISTRIBUTION BETWEEN URBAN AND RURAL AREAS OF INCREASE IN NET DOMESTIC PRODUCT BETWEEN 1950–51 AND 1960–61 BY INDUSTRIAL ORIGINS

(in millions of Rs.)

	Urban	Rural	Total of Urban and Rural Income	Percentage to Total of Each Head	
				Urban	Rural
(1)	(2)	(3)	(4)	(5)	(6)
Agriculture and allied activities	– 120	20,120	20,000	– 0.6	100.6
Mining & Factory establishments	6,670	1,930	8,600	77.6	22.4
Small enterprises incl. construction	2,570	– 500	2,070	124.2	24.2
Railways and communication	1,530	480	2,010	76.1	23.9
Organised banking and insurance	650	260	910	71.4	28.6
Other commerce and transport	3,750	– 100	3,650	102.7	– 2.7
Professions and liberal arts	1,890	820	2,710	69.7	30.3
Government service	2,090	2,610	4,700	44.5	55.5
Domestic service	100	540	640	15.6	84.4
House property	1,000	200	1,200	83.3	16.7
Net domestic product	20,130	26,360	46,490	43.3	65.7

The analysis also shows that urbanisation is attended with a faster rate of growth of per capita income for the urbanites, but this alone cannot be a remedy for the Indian situation, as it will take many five year plans to increase the proportion of urban to total population in India to the level reached even in the latest among the developed countries. Meanwhile, disparities will widen between the urban and rural areas and threaten the whole process of economic development with political and social instability.

Our study of the incidence of economic planning on rural and urban areas makes it abundantly clear that India from placing prime emphasis on rural development in order to have there is no escape for a country like economic growth with stability.

34

Distribution of Public Health and Education Services*

N. Bhattacharya and B. Dey

The village with 468 households was subjected to complete enumeration. For each household in the village, a schedule was filled in by the interview method. The following items of information were collected in this schedule:

(a) household size and composition;
(b) average monthly consumer expenditure on all items during the last year;
(c) educational particulars of different members with details of receipt of public education services during the last year in the form of fees exempted, scholarships/stipends, and in other forms; and
(d) receipt of free public health services during the last quarter by different members of the household.

By last year and last month will be meant last 365 days and last 30 days, respectively, preceding the date of survey.

Two investigators carried out the field work and the households were divided between them at random. This gave two interpenetrating subsamples of the sample households. We do not present the subsample estimates but they were used at the stage of drawing conclusions.

A preliminary analysis of the data has been reported here. The objective is to show how the benefits of (free) public health and educational services are being shared by different sections of the population in this particular village. It is

* Originally published in *Economic Weekly* 17, no. 23 (5 June 1965), pp. 929–32. The authors are indebted to M. Mukherjee, Head of the Planning Division, for suggesting the problem, and to S. Nandi, S. Dhar, P. Mazumdar, and A. Mondal for conputational assistance.

obviously unsafe to generalise from one village which has more than one hospital within its boundary and a number of primary and secondary schools.

Attempts were made in this pilot enquiry to collect cost data from medical and educational institutions. It may be possible to present in a subsequent note the estimated money values of benefits received by different groups of people. But this line of work is extremely laborious and the results may not be worth the trouble. In any case, collection of cost data for a large-scale enquiry would be practically impossible.

Material and Analysis

As already stated, the investigators collected figures for the average monthly value of domestic consumption of all items (usually called total holdhold expenditure) by each household, averaged over the last year, i.e., 365 days preceding the date of survey. Only a rough figure was obtained through a few minutes' enquiry.[1] The households were then ranked in an ascending order of levels of living as measured by per capita total consumer expenditure per month; ten decile groups were then formed by grouping households contiguous in the ranking. The bottom decile comprised households having the lowest values of per capita consumer expenditure; the second decile from bottom, the households having the next lowest values of per capita expenditure; and so on. The limits of per capita expenditure were so determined that each group contained nearly 10 per cent of the total population in the 468 households surveyed.[2]

Table 34.1 shows the formation of the decile groups. The average household size is 6.66 for the entire population and shows very little trend over the decile groups. The lowest observed value of per capita monthly consumer expenditure was Rs. 8.57, and the overall average is Rs. 28.44. These figures show that Madhyamgram is not a typical village. Column (7) of the table shows the inequality in the distribution of domestic consumer expenditure. Whereas the bottom decile gets a share of only 4.21 per cent, the top decile has 19.22 per cent of the aggregate consumer expenditure of the entire Madhyamgram population. This column is repeated in the subsequent tables.

Table 34.2 shows the distribution of all students by decile groups. The different columns are self-explanatory. "Students" include all boys and girls continuing their studies in public educational institutions like schools and colleges, universities, and other institutions which impart training to the students and are financed and/or governed partially or wholly by public bodies. This excludes those institutions which are run with a motive of making and appropriating profit by individuals or groups of individuals. For example, tutorial schools and colleges, some of the commercial colleges, kindergarten schools etc., run under proprietorship are

TABLE 34.1: TOTAL CONSUMER EXPENDITURE AND SHARE OF TOTAL CONSUMER EXPENDITURE BY DECILE GROUPS—AVERAGE MONTH OF LAST YEAR

Decile Group (Per cent)	Number of Households	Persons	Average Households Size	Consumer Expenditure (Rs) Per Person Per Month		Per Cent Share of Consumer Expenditure
				Upper Limit	Average	
(1)	(2)	(3)	(4)	(5)	(6)	(7)
0–10	45	310	6.89	14.28*	12.04	4.21
10–20	47	313	6.66	18.18	16.42	5.80
20–30	50	310	6.20	20.00	19.50	6.82
30–40	39	308	7.90	22.72	22.45	7.80
40–50	46	313	6.80	25.00	24.73	8.73
50–60	43	314	7.30	29.16	28.42	10.07
60–70	56	313	5.59	33.33	31.80	11.23
70–80	40	306	7.65	36.36	35.70	12.33
80–90	47	313	6.65	41.66	39.06	13.79
90–100	55	317	5.76	400.00	53.75	19.22
Total	468	3,117	6.66	400.00	28.44	100.00

*The lowest observed value of per capita total consumer expenditure was Rs. 8.57 per month.

excluded from our scope. Students are classified under three heads: (i) primary (infant class to class IV), (ii) secondary (class V to X or XI), and (iii) others (colleges and other institutions conducting degree or diploma course).

Table 34.3 shows the distribution of free students by decile groups. For the purposes of this table, two half-free studentships were together taken as equivalent to one free studentship.

Table 34.4 shows the distribution of patient visits to outdoor departments of medical institutions and free-bed days spent by patients in indoor departments by decile groups of the population. Medical institutions include hospitals, charitable dispensaries, and health centres run by government and also by local bodies. It should be appreciated that only the curative side of public health services has been considered here, and the preventive side has been left out.

The money value of a free studentship is not the same for all students. Also, all students, including free students, may really be enjoying some subsidies. Similarly, outdoor services include services of physicians, distribution of medicine, operations, X-rays, and pathological tests. In the indoor department, in addition to medical treatment, the patient receives food, accommodation, and nursing care. The money value of services, etc., will vary from patient to patient and from visit to visit. The indicators chosen in this study—the number of free students,

TABLE 34.2: DISTRIBUTION OF STUDENTS BY DECILE GROUPS—LAST YEAR

Decile Group (Per cent)	Percentage of Persons	Share of Consumer Expenditure	Percentage of Students				Students as Percentage of Population			
			Primary	Secondary	Others	Total	Primary	Secondary	Others	Total
(1)	(2)	(3)	(4)	(5)	(6)	(7)	(8)	(9)	(10)	(11)
0–100	9.95	4.21	9.57	–	7.44	13.55	8.06	–	21.61	
10–20	10.04	5.80	11.62	6.08	–	8.44	16.29	7.99	–	24.28
20–30	9.95	6.82	10.25	9.49	4.00	9.56	14.51	12.58	0.65	27.74
30–40	9.88	7.80	10.02	8.52	2.00	8.89	14.28	11.36	0.32	25.97
40–50	10.04	8.73	7.74	10.46	6.00	8.89	10.86	13.74	0.96	25.56
50–60	10.07	10.07	12.53	12.41	8.00	12.22	17.52	16.24	1.27	35.03
60–70	10.04	11.23	10.48	9.73	10.00	10.11	14.69	12.78	1.60	29.07
70–80	9.82	12.33	10.25	9.98	20.00	10.67	14.71	13.40	3.26	31.37
80–90	10.04	13.79	11.16	13.38	20.00	12.67	15.65	17.58	3.19	36.42
90–100	10.17	19.22	6.38	13.86	30.00	11.11	8.83	17.89	4.73	31.54
Total	100.00	100.00	100.00	100.00	100.00	100.00	14.08	13.19	1.60	28.87
Total (Absolute Value)	3,117		439	411	50	900				

TABLE 34.3: DISTRIBUTION OF FREE STUDENTS BY DECILE GROUPS—LAST YEAR

Decile Group (Per cent)	Per cent of Persons	Share of consumer Expenditure (Per cent)	Percentage of Free Students				Free Students as Percentage of All Students				Free Students as Percentage of Population			
			Primary	Secondary	Others	Total	Primary	Secondary	Others	Total	Primary	Secondary	Others	Total
(1)	(2)	(3)	(4)	(5)	(6)	(7)	(8)	(9)	(10)	(11)	(12)	(13)	(14)	(15)
0–100	9.95	4.21	9.83	7.81	...	9.05	97.62	72.00	...	88.06	13.22	5.80	...	19.02
10–20	10.04	5.80	12.23	6.07	...	9.97	100.00	56.00	...	85.53	16.45	4.52	...	21.29
20–30	9.95	6.82	10.79	9.11	...	10.13	100.00	53.85	...	76.74	14.52	6.77	...	21.29
30–40	9.88	7.80	10.55	8.89	...	9.90	100.00	58.57	...	80.62	14.28	6.66	...	20.94
40–50	10.04	8.73	8.16	13.23	23.53	10.05	100.00	70.93	33.33	81.88	10.85	9.74	0.32	20.91
50–60	10.07	10.07	12.95	11.93	23.53	12.66	98.18	53.92	25.00	75.00	17.20	8.75	0.32	26.27
60–70	10.04	11.23	10.79	7.81	...	9.67	97.83	45.00	...	69.23	14.61	5.84	...	20.45
70–80	9.82	12.33	8.63	11.28	11.77	9.59	80.00	63.41	50.00	65.10	11.76	8.50	0.16	20.42
80–90	10.04	13.79	10.55	11.72	41.17	11.16	89.80	49.09	17.50	63.82	14.01	8.60	0.56	23.17
90–100	10.17	19.22	5.52	12.15	...	7.82	82.14	49.12	...	51.00	7.26	8.82	...	16.08
Total	100.00	100.00	100.00	100.00	100.00	100.00	94.99	56.08	28.33	72.42	13.38	7.39	0.13	20.90

TABLE 34.4: DISTRIBUTION OF OUTDOOR PATIENT VISITS AND INDOOR PATIENT FREE-BED DAYS BY DECILE GROUPS—LAST QUARTER

Decile Groups (Per cent)	Per Cent of Persons	Share of Consumer Expenditure (Per cent)	Percentage of		Per 100 of Population Per Quarter	
			Visits to Outdoor Departments of Hospitals	Days Stayed in Free Bed	Visits to Outdoor Departments of Hospitals	Days Stayed in Free Bed
(1)	(2)	(3)	(4)	(5)	(6)	(7)
0–10	9.95	4.21	16.98	4.03	64.19	7.42
10–20	10.04	5.80	17.06	10.86	63.90	19.81
20–30	9.95	6.82	16.55	19.26	62.58	35.48
30–40	9.88	7.80	13.40	2.28	50.97	4.22
40–50	10.04	8.73	6.95	16.64	24.60	30.35
50–60	10.07	10.07	4.86	5.95	18.15	10.83
60–70	10.04	11.23	6.31	3.85	23.64	7.03
70–80	9.82	12.33	5.29	...	20.26	...
80–90	10.04	13.79	5.55	33.98	20.77	61.98
90–100	10.17	19.22	7.41	3.15	27.44	5.69
Total	100.00	100.00	100.00	100.00	37.60	5.68

Note: Number of different patients: (1) visiting outdoor depts: 264, (2) staying in free bed: 26.

the number of patient-visits to outdoor departments, and the number of free-bed days spent in an indoor department—are only first approximations to the money values of benefits.

Statistical Finding

Number of students: There is a clear tendency of the number of all students increasing over the decile groups, from about 70 in the bottom decile to about 105 in the top decile. The average is 90 per decile. In terms of percentage of population, the rise is from 22 or 23 per cent to 33 or 34 per cent roughly. Average is 28 per cent. Hence the percentage share of the ten deciles in the total number of students rises from about 8 to 12. Figures for some deciles seem to be erratic; in general, one should smooth the figures before drawing inferences.

No such trend is found in the number of primary students, who constitute about 50 per cent of all students. All deciles have about 44 students (15 per cent of population). Only the top decile shows a lower figure of 28 (9 per cent of population). Each decile gets about 10 per cent of all primary students.

There is a clear tendency of the number of secondary students increasing over the decile groups, at a steeper rate than the number of all students, from about 25 in the bottom decile to 55 in the top decile, the average being 41. In terms of percentage of population these figures are 8, 18, and 13, roughly. Hence the percentage share of all secondary students rises from 6 per cent to 14 per cent over the 10 deciles.

Regarding students under the "others" category, the trend is steeper, because the number rises from 0 in the two lowest deciles to 15 in the topmost, the average being only 5. In terms of percentages of population, these figures are 0, 5, and 2, roughly. Hence the percentage share of "others" students rises from about 0 per cent to about 30 per cent over the 10 deciles.

To sum up, then, the percentage share of the ten decile groups in the total number of students is more or less the same in the primary stage, while in the secondary stage there is a rising trend from bottom to top deciles, and such a trend is steepest for the category of "others" students. A rising trend is also evident, though the rate of increase is moderate, when all students are taken together.

Number of free students: No definite trend over the deciles is evident when all students are considered. Each decile shows around 65 free students, which means just over 20 per cent of population. Each decile had about 10 per cent of all free students. If we consider the percentage of all students who are free, the percentage, however, falls from about 90 in the bottom deciles to 50 or 60 in the top deciles, the average being about 70 or 75. Free students in the primary stage form about two-thirds of all free students, and this is more prominent in bottom deciles as percentage of primary students (mostly free all over the state) to all students here is overwhelmingly large.

No definite trend is observed in the number of free primary students. Each decile shows around 40 such students, which means about 13 per cent of population. So each decile has around 10 per cent of all such students. If we consider the percentage of all primary students who are free, the percentage remains very near 100 or even reaches 100 over the seven deciles from bottom, but thereafter shows signs of some decline, reaching about 80 in the top deciles. The overall percentage is 95.

The number of free secondary students shows an increasing trend, rising from about 15 or 18 in the bottom deciles to 27 or 28 in the top deciles. Considered as percentage of population the rise is from 5 to 9 roughly, the average being 7. So the share of all free secondary students rises from 7 per cent to 12 per cent, roughly, over the ten decile groups. As regards the percentage of secondary students who are free, the overall percentage is nearly 55, but there seems to be a slight declining trend—the figures are too erratic for any definite statement—from about 65 in bottom deciles to 50 near the top.

A very negligible number of free students was observed under the "others" category, so little can be said except that since such students are rare in the lower deciles, free cases are also rare in the lower deciles.

Number of visits to outdoor departments of hospitals etc.: The number of visits shows a clear decline from nearly 200 in the three lowest deciles to about 160 in the fourth decile from the bottom and then to around 60 or 80 in the six remaining deciles. There seems to be little trend over the top six deciles. So clearly richer people avoid visits to outdoor departments of hospitals etc. Per 100 persons per quarter (the reference period was last quarter, i.e., 90 days preceding the date of survey), the number of such visits decreases from about 64 in the three bottom decile groups to 50 in the fourth and then to 20 or 25 in the six top deciles. So far as percentage of all such visits is concerned, the three bottom deciles have a share of about 17 per cent each, the fourth of about 13 per cent, and the top six of about 6 per cent.

Number of free-bed days stayed in hospitals etc.: The figures are too erratic in this case. A quarter seems to be too short a period to give reliable estimates. The numbers may be taken as fluctuating widely around an average of 57 per decile, and the figures per 100 of persons fluctuate around 19 per quarter which comes to about 75 free-bed days annually. So far as percentage share of the decile groups is concerned, very little can be said; for instance, the share is 0 for the eighth and 33 per cent in the ninth decile. Cumulative percentage shares are more stable; and they hardly show any inequality, as the bottom 50 per cent have a share of only a little over 50 per cent.

Free-studentship is more or less equitably distributed in proportion to population, if all categories of students are considered together. The same seems to be true for primary students also. In the secondary stage, the bottom deciles send fewer free students than the top deciles, the shares rising from 7 to 12 per cent. Little can be said about the "others" category; but the few free students generally fall in the upper deciles. On the whole, therefore, the higher deciles get a somewhat larger share of free educational services than the lower deciles.

Free primary education being available, almost all children seem to attend free primary schools (primary students form about 15 per cent of the population in all the ten decile groups). This is why free-studentship in the primary stage shows an egalitarian distribution. The higher deciles have a larger share of free students of "secondary" and "others" categories; but the bottom deciles send relatively few secondary students and very few students of the "others" category. As a matter of fact, the number of free secondary students seems to be roughly proportional to the number of secondary students in the ten deciles. The two considerations—economic conditions of parents and merit of the students—may have counterbalanced each other in the award of free studentship.

So far as free medical services are concerned, it is evident that the four bottom decile groups get—it is more appropriate to say "take"—a much larger share (above 15 per cent) than the top six decile groups (6 or 7 per cent), in the service rendered by outdoor departments of hospitals etc. This is apparently because the rich people try to avoid the trouble of attending hospital outdoors, while the poorer people are compelled to do so because of their economic condition. The distribution of services rendered by indoor departments of hospitals etc., may be more or less equitable, but the picture is not at all clear from this small-scale study. It is possible that acute cases, where hospital services are essential, arise equally often among all classes of population, and even the rich cannot avoid hospitals in such cases.

So far we have considered how far the distribution of these benefits is egalitarian, that is, proportional to population in the ten deciles. Perhaps it is more important to consider how far the distribution of these benefits is more egalitarian than the distribution of domestic consumer expenditure. The distribution of domestic consumer expenditure is far from egalitarian, the bottom decile getting nearly 4.3 per cent and the top decile 19 per cent (For all-India, rural or urban, the corresponding figures show even greater inequality[3]). Judged against this background, the distribution of free health and education services seems to be favouring the poorer sections considerably. In medical services rendered by outdoor departments of hospitals, the bottom deciles get more than their due share even on the population basis. In free-studentship in the primary stage, the bottom deciles get their due share on population basis and hence more than their due share on the basis of domestic consumer expenditure. The same may be said, very roughly, about services of indoor departments of hospitals. In free-studentship in secondary and "other" stages, the bottom deciles get less than 10 per cent share, but even here their share is larger than their share in domestic consumer expenditure. Hence, it is clear that the distribution of free health and education services in Madhyamgram was effectively reducing the inequality in level of living.

NOTES AND REFERENCES

[1] Previous type studies have shown that such quick methods give estimates consistently lower but highly correlated with the usual estimates of total consumer expenditure obtained through detailed family budget schedules (see N. Bhattacharya, *On the Effects of Itemisation in Family Budget Schedule*, mimeo, Studies Relating to Planning for National Development No. 273, [Calcutta: Indian Statistical Institute, 1964]). Quick estimates are sufficient for the present purposes of ranking the households by per capita total consumer expenditure. There is no point in spending three hours per household for estimating total consumer expenditure, when the main enquiry on consumption of public services required only half an hour per average household.

[2] P. C. Mahalanobis, "A Method of Fractile Graphical Analysis," *Econometrica* 28, no. 2 (April 1960), pp. 325–51.

[3] P. C. Mahalanobis, "Some Indicators for the Comparison of Level of Living over Time and Regions," *Bulletin of International Statistical Institute*, 37, 1958.

PART IX

Culture, Administration and Leadership

35

Man and Plan in India

The Background*

D. P. Mukerji

Two questions vex thinking men at the time of major social changes: what is the new society, and what is the new man? The time of questioning is seldom fixed; it may be before, during, and after the change has occurred, acquired speed, and impressed itself on the life-habits of all or most concerned. Sometimes the two questions arise separately. Intensities of the anxiety to raise them and answer them vary, in the first instance, with the quality of the change. If the change is drastic, basic, and comprehensive, that is, when "the material conditions for their (higher relations of production) existence have matured in the womb of old society" then one would expect a common concern with such questions. Marx wrote that "mankind always takes up only such problems as it is in a position to solve; for, when we look at the matter more closely, we shall always discover that the problem itself arises only when the material conditions needed for its solution are also present, or at the least are in the process of formation." Marx's "always" refers to revolutionary situations. But even when such situations are not at hand, problems about the nature of the new society and the new man disturb a few souls who formulate them under the pressure of personal responsibility towards the present and the future, and/or of acute disgust with the present. In these cases, the popularity of the issues would depend upon the prestige and the number of such souls no less than upon the extent of discontent and the means of communication.

Marxist Simplification

When these conditions conspire, there grows the envelope of the great debate in which defeat or victory is a matter of serious concern. Questions are sharpened,

* Originally published in *Economic Weekly* 5, nos. 32–34 (15 August 1953), pp. 895–900.

though the answers are not necessarily so, because they are often the replies to other questions which have not been solved. A revolutionary change, in the Marxist sense, poses sharper issues and offers clearer answers than a "natural," evolutionary change. In the usual Marxist interpretation of revolutionary change, there is, however, a tendency towards simplification in the attempt to focus the problems with all that it means in the way of serving a broad line of action, e.g., a certain narrowing of vision and the operation of a peculiar type of the sense of lightness and finality which is often akin to a puritanism of the spirit and hostile to the philosophical temper and enquiry necessary for adequate solutions. Clarity and simplicity can be synonymous, but simplification is neither simplicity nor clarity. Thus it is that revolutionary situations may throw up problems in very sharp relief but answer them in a manner that is partial. More or less clear views of the nature of society desired may emerge, but the men who formulate them are seldom full men. Probably, such is the fate of all systematic, rational, and conscious change. The impersonality of the process tends to diminish human personality in the interest of realism, action, and situation, even when the mere tempo of change and the adequate ideology would inflate it. Even utopian thinking, which has a reasoning of its own though it be not historical and which has a consciousness that is quite often undifferentiated from the awareness of traditional values, ultimately makes for a restricted society and a closed personality. Actual utopian experiments would bear witness to it.

The Ideal Indian Type

India's social change, which is both a fact and an act, has not had the benefit of a clear or a systematic theory or design of new society behind it. Nor was the outline of the new man which could be filled in by the movement towards the new society ever firmly sketched. Apart from various religious, sectarian ashrams, which could be interpreted as sort of blueprints of a desired state of society offering models of new men in the making, no pattern as such either of the new society or of the new man was envisaged by Indians before India came in contact with the West. Yet, sociologically, an "ideal type" of man in the Weberian sense could be spotted. The characteristics of such a man were the performance of customary functions and duties fixed at birth, their working out through the four defined stages to a possible state of complete non-attachment, and the resultant development of personality in the pursuit of dharma, artha, kama, and moksha. Moksha, or salvation, being the goal, the "ideal type" of man could not but be a potentially religious person with his eyes fixed beyond the world. It might have led to greater integration of personality, more poise and peace than are given to the modern man, but the problems it had to face did not spring from the dynamics of social change for the simple reason that no social change was drastic enough in the absence of any change in the modes of production.

RENUNCIATION

The impact of Islam was no doubt strong, but the resultant Hindu-Muslim culture, ideologies, and way of life, were not materially different from those of the pre-Muslim period. No marked change seems to have occurred in the nature of the "ideal" type. If anything, renunciation became a more marked trait than ever. Anti-Muslim, or anti-foreign rebels like Rana Pratap or Shivaji were not quite the new ideal types. The former was the hero of an age of chivalry and the latter was probably one of an earlier age Both were idealised by nationalist historians, but it is debatable if they were or could be identified with the ideal Kshatriya, say, like Bhishma, Arjuna, or Kama. Bhakti-cult generally centred round the perfect man-god, Krishna, or his avatar, or the founder of the sect, but in so far as he was a deity or deified, the pull of approximation which the ideal type connotes could only mean a merging, an immersion, in other words, renunciation. The glimpses of a *new* society in the literature of this period are faint. Ordinary men and women pursued their usual tenor of existence, and extraordinary men wanted a little toleration to do the same according to the traditional light. It is not strange that no utopias were built in India. (Satya-Yuga was no utopia. It was the golden age of the past.) The social urges were not strong.

DISTURBING MESSAGE FROM THE WEST

The West came with a different and a disturbing message. It shook Indian society out of its torpor. Raja Ram Mohan Roy was the first historic man to absorb it. He was steeped equally in the Hindu and the Muslim lore, and he studied Christianity with the same zeal. Probably, he had no clear vision either of the new man or the new society, but his emphasis on rationality was a new trait. This rationality was not quite the rationality of Hindu logic or of Buddhist disputations. It was more akin to the Western rationality of the eighteenth and early nineteenth century in its faith in natural laws, in reform, and the greatest good of the greatest number, and in progress to be achieved perpetually through human effort. At the same time, it was different from the rationality which was the essence of capitalism, that is, its emphasis on accounting and technology. The old Indian logic, before it became the new logic (Navya Nyaya), had always been linked with the pursuit of the Absolute or the Divine (anvikshiki vidya); and even with the Bengal logicians it did not become secularised. Ram Mohan's rationality was definitely human reason, though he never cut himself adrift from religion which he could accept only in its rationalised form. In his view, Hindu religion had acquired many excrescences which had to be removed by the application of human reason—by higher criticism, scientific scholarship, etc. This he did with marvellous learning and efficiency. There is hardly any major intellectual trait in modern India, be it in its attitude towards language or social reform, democracy, and internationalism, which cannot be traced in his writings. Above all, he was himself a full man, and not a renouncer of life. He took modern civilisation in both hands and "made" it the vital impulse of the cultural development of modern India. He did not envision a new man or a new society as such, but he introduced the new strains of rationality, of an openness of attitude, and of a certain amount of courage to face the new order, attitudes which proved to be invaluable dynamic elements in the social change that followed. No more can it be said of India that she specialises only in the production of sanyasis and mystics whose eyes are always in-turned to soul or upturned to heaven. India's self-consciousness and world-consciousness in the secular sense have gone together since the days of the Raja.

Dynamic Movement

A number of reformers and reform movements followed. Barring one, the tendency was of synthesis with a tilt towards Indian traditions. The exception was the Nava Bidhan Samaj of Kesub Chandra Sen, which leant towards Western Christianity and eclecticism. It made less headway than the Arya Samaj, the Sadharan Brahmo Samaj, and the Prarthana Samaj. The founders of each were dynamic personalities and well acquainted with the main currents of Western thought and action. Their main effort was to make them run through the Indian bed to remove its choking weeds in order that the ancient stream may flow. The Arya Samaj would have the Vedas back, and the Adi Brahmo Samaj the Upanishads instead of the Puranas and the later rituals. Yet none of them was a revivalist, and the Prarthana Samaj and the Sadharan Brahmo Samaj the least so. Each movement used *samaj* (society) for its title, though in course of time it shrank into a small community or sect. On the other hand, there was some sort of Hindu resurgence through the spread of Arya Samaj and the Theosophical Society. It was more of a general awakening than a movement. Rama Krishna cannot be said to be founder of a counter-reformist Hindu movement nor Swami Vivekananda its Loyola or Xavier. If anything, the Swami was more a Buddhist than a Hindu revivalist. His monachism and rationality, his emphasis on service and missionary zeal are more Buddhist than Hindu. Philosophically, he was a Vedantist, and actively, he followed the Geeta and the Tripitaka. His devastating criticisms of the Hindu Samaj and his missionary efforts equally appealed to the educated Indian who was unwilling to cut away from his social roots and yet felt that Hinduism needed revitalisation. Through his teachings and personality the Indian gained self-confidence. From now on the average Hindu ceased to feel that his only duty was to inform to the type of the "gentle Hindoo" whom the West had discovered. His pride would now come from the dynamic principles of Hinduism itself. Beyond this, there is no trace of Hindu revivalism in the movement of voluntary social reform and service which the Swami initiated. Other examples of Hindu resurgence are not significant from the point of view taken here. Their importance was derivative in so far as Hindu resurgence was absorbed in the larger national movement. The Muslims had always a suspicion of this element and never felt easy about it. If the British could take advantage of it to drive a wedge between the Hindus and Muslims, none can wholly blame them. The most that can therefore be said about the conceptions of society and man vaguely current in this period is this: it would be a reformed society and he would be a reformed nationalist Hindu. No social or human transmutation was necessary, and thus not conceived; it was almost inconceivable.

TAGORE'S ANALYSIS

The next important man was Tagore. He was untouched both by the fighting Hindu nationalism of Dayanand and Tilak and the anti-Westernism of revivalists. He could not also subscribe to the Westernisation that had captured the imagination of a few "England-returned" Indians. Neither the strain of rationality one noticed in Ranade or Gokhale, nor the legalism of the brilliant liberal intellectuals of Madras was prominent in his attitudes. He was too much of a poet for all that. Though he was the product of a reformed family, he was not a reformer in the usual sense. His analysis was essentially sociological. One might say that he was more interested in society than in the state, in the rural society than in the urban, and in the invigoration of the rural roots than in the grafting of the foreign notion of nationalism on the branches or the trunk. His new society was basically rural, self-growing, decentralised, and cooperative. He believed that in that process of self-growth India would easily take in all the communities that lived in India, and the universe (Visva) too. He saw no basic difficulty in a liberated and dynamic India's assimilating Western culture. For him neither science nor technology, neither secularism nor democracy was an indigestible substance. He wanted all of them to come, but, not in the protean shapes of Power. His politics was social. People called his ideas utopian, but he built no literary utopia. (Neither the origin nor the history of Shantiniketan betrays a utopian spirit.) Sociologically, he was a realist. It is this which abolishes all other distinctions between him and Gandhiji. Both knew that India lives in the villages, both wanted villages to be the growth-cones of India, both believed in decentralised economy, and both wanted self-mastery, "self-kingdom" (swaraj), before exchange took place. Negatively, too, they were similar—they both failed to point out the way of absorbing the new social forces which the West had released through science and its application to large-scale production. Tagore saw them as power uncontrolled by social sense and morality, while Gandhiji saw them as Evil, even when he considered some machines as necessary. To the sociologist the mutual admiration of the two is not strange; nor is the fact that Tagore uncannily forecast the character and technique of Gandhiji in Vairagee Dhananjaya amazing.

Gandhiji's *Hind Swaraj*

This does not mean, however, that Gandhiji's conception of the future social order was identical with Tagore's conception of *swadeshi samaj*. For one, Gandhiji's conception as formulated in his *Hind Swaraj* had a clearer outline; for another, by virtue of the later use of the words *Rama rajya*, it lost its clarity but gained a wider appeal; for a third, its blurred outline became a cloak for the mixed content. Today, many reactionaries have rallied under that nomenclature. But the basic difference was in ideas of the new man who would build and reside in the new society. For Gandhiji, he would be a moral man, ready to sacrifice his all for truth, simple, direct, and pulsating with the lowliest of the lowly. Truth, non-violence, and participation would be his nature. Tagore's new man was not the renouncer. He thought of renunciation as a means of higher enjoyment, as the Upanishad has it. Sacrifice he admired, not for its own sake, but as one excellent means of discipline. In fact, he had renounced renunciation quite early in his poetic career, and he could not recommend it to the new man or as social policy. Being the son of the Maharshi he could not minimise the importance of truth. He would want every young man to pursue truth in every way, but preferably through rationality and science whose spirit he understood better than Gandhiji. Truth or *satyam*, in his view, was one of the three eternal values of Indian thought (the other two being *advaitam* and *anantam*, that is unity and infinity, and not beauty and joy); but it was not identical with God, in the personal nature of whom he did not quite believe, say, as the Christians, the Vaishnavas, or the common Hindus do, or as Gandhi did. Yet for him, truth, in a sense, was personal, almost human. Many characters of his stories and novels object to traditional values (and party discipline) on human considerations, and Tagore sympathised with them. The strong note of dissent in the Brahmo movement (which can be traced back to earlier reformist ones, and even to the Upanishads) was evident in his treatment of human themes in prose and poetry. In regard to non-violence his position was not clear. Apart from the fact that every Hindu loves peace and is averse to conflict and hears *shanti* (peace) muttered on every important occasion, he had faith in the laws of harmony. This did not prevent him from admiring the terrorists whose courage of conviction, however misplaced, always appealed to him. His objection to them was on the score of their blind obedience to impersonal, and hence inhuman, discipline. It can therefore be said that the new type of man he liked and conjured up was an honest dissenter, emotionally rich, rational, and tough enough to die for a cause. Such a man was a fuller man than either the puritan or the one who merely accepted. He was essentially the affirmative-creative type. Unfortunately, however, the type that was immediately produced by his influence was the literary-romantic one believing more in the spontaneity of talent than in discipline, a soft and tender type, in fact effeminate. Why it thus happened is outside the scope of this essay.

The Moral Type

Gandhiji produced a different type altogether. The new man, the Congressman, was basically the moral type. His test was courage that was implied in and born out of the manner of abandonment of bourgeois caution. He was to sacrifice himself at the altar of the country in a non-violent, truthful, and simple manner. He was to be the common man (and not merely to be the one with him), self-dependent, living simply in self-sufficient villages. He would have no wants which he could not satisfy with simple, home-made implements. He need not be a thinker; simple faith in God would do. He need not be of studious habit either; the Geeta, the Ramayana, the Bible, or the Quran would suffice. But he had to be pure—primarily physically—and clean, truthful and efficient in whatever he undertook. Poetry, music, science, and learning were not relevant unless they sang the praise of God. What was wanted was moral strength, and not aesthetic or intellectual sensibility. This morality was connected with will.

Modern India has not produced a leader with greater will that was less divorced from love of power than Gandhiji. It attracted Sardar Patel to him. Gandhiji connected it with faith in God. He would want the new man to be prayerful in the first instance and to be transformed into the blessed man in the next. Like aesthetic sense, rationality was secondary. The impulse of creativity, which was a vital ingredient of Tagore's new man, was to merge in the creative love of God and service to his fellow beings. Joy as such, the joy that comes from contemplation, from creation of new art-forms, or from the disinterested pursuit of knowledge, was, if anything, a by-product of service or its handmaid. In short, the new man was to be built round the two concepts of praxis, the facts-acts of Indian life, and truth which was equivalent to God who was personal.

The relevant question is how many were true to the type made and contemplated by Gandhiji. They were more than we imagine. All sorts of people were gathered by him in the national movement. They were not of equal merit. But they were uplifted and occasionally transmuted by the moral fervour of the open movement and the moral genius of the man. In some cases the transformation was genuine, in others it was not. The strain was too much: few men could be angels: and fewer still truthful and moral, prayerful and wilful without caring for power: that is the usual explanation of the amazing fact, as a wag put it, that the white Gandhi cap has so soon become the symbol of the black market. But, probably, more plausible explanations are possible. Rama-rajya, as a concept, was wonderful, it did not demand the rigour of the society of the Hind Swaraj; it was based on plenty, though references to famine, war, untouchability, and other social crimes in the reign of Rama are not rare in the Ramayana.

Business cycles, fluctuations of employment, war contracts, economic exploitation of men, women and children, utter dependence of Indians on foreign imports, sharp contrasts of wealth, belching factories, and stinking slums were not known in Ayodhya. They were known to Indians when Gandhiji ruled their hearts. They were the basic realities of the day. So Rama-rajya only excited nostalgia. It was not a projection of the present into the future. It was not even the millennium: it was a throwback into the pre-Kali Yuga. For most Indians a vacuum intervened between the present realities and the past dreams; and no wonder that they soon ceased to dream. In other words, the type of the new society enveloped in the vulgarised notion of Rama-rajya was not only non-historical but anti-historical. But when society is what it is in India, the only hope and treasure of Indians becomes the historical sense, the acute feeling for social forces and their human direction according to laws, which may not be the laws of nature but are nonetheless the laws for all practical purposes—that is, sound hypotheses for social action. In the absence of that sense and feeling among large sections of Gandhiji's followers Rama-rajya remained an election slogan. Gandhiji intuitively realised the implications of political success. In his last testament he advised the dissolution of the Congress and wanted Congressmen to diffuse themselves in the villages for concentrated social work. The deliquescence of the hard core of the Hind Swaraj in the moist, slimy notion of Rama-rajya as a political slogan is the history of the rise and fall of the Congress movement.

Anti-Intellectual

The new man, the Congressman, who was going to be the "ideal" type, was also not the full man. Though it is true that some men of fine intellect plunged into the movement initiated and impelled by Gandhiji, it is equally true that neither they, nor the artists and scientists did so without caveat. The charge usually levelled against them is that they stood out. If they did, they did so because they felt that they had no place in the movement, that they could not find any intellectual system in it, that they could not make it fit in with any theory they knew or had read about. The movement was certainly anti-intellectual—most movements are; at the same time, the Indian intellectuals were as full of foreign ideas as they were blissfully, and often contemptuously, ignorant of Indian culture or Indian realities. Still the fact survives that the middle class had long been the most articulate class and had enjoyed social prestige by virtue of their contacts with the West, its knowledge, and ways of living, in addition to what was attached to the services and professions, which the foreign administration had fixed and done its best to limit. The hard historical core of middle class prestige and domination was their knowledge of the modern social forces, that is, science, technology, democracy, and sense of historical development, which the West stood for. The political movement which was to usher in the new society was not expected to possess this knowledge as its first requisite of success, and the new man—the Congressman, who was to be the ideal type of the new society—was not expected to utilise it. The result was a partial man, a smaller man, a shrunken man. Modern times demand a fuller person. Hence, shrunken men have shrunk further when the moral fervour, unredeemed by the sense of history and rationality, has lost its power of breath to inflate and uplift. This seems to be the basic reason of moral degradation in the ranks of the Congress.

PANDIT NEHRU

It is here that Pandit Jawaharlal comes. As he is the frankest statesman in the world, nothing more than what he has written or talked about himself can be written on him. But here his influence on the conception and making of the new society and the new man is the issue, and very little has been written on that. So what follows is tentative. He has quite a few years to go, but it is not likely that he will change his commitments. A few facts about his influence are basic. He is of the Congress and yet out of it. He does not belong to the crowd, and he does not conform to the "type," then or now. He loves the crowd whom he calls the people, and the crowd is fascinated by him. For the crowd he is the charismatic person. But he is also the idol of the middle-class educated man who knows that the world is not exhausted by India, that India must make confident strides towards the future, that willy-nilly, modern forces like nationalism for the colonies, democracy, science, and technology, have come to stay, that civilisation belongs to the city, that culture is manmade, that history halts unless it is pushed, that there is no marching back like frogs to the well, that the blind forces of nature or of social systems have to be harnessed, and that the universe has to be faced openly and squarely, without fear or favour. A part of Nehru's fascination for the middle class is snobbishness, but the rest is the conviction that he is the man of that present which enters into the future. It is this courage to recognise modern social forces, to build on them and face the future which attracts him to the educated community. He has no "party" to follow him, but he has a whole community of educated people to follow him with awakened intelligence. Where he goes they would like to go. If he moves towards a planned society, they would move as social engineers.

At long last, a social order possible to attain has been conceived and men and women are exercising themselves to achieve it. The best of Nehru is in the Plan, however vague and unsatisfactory both may be to the perfectionist. And the Plan will work India even though some Indians may not work it excitedly. Those who would do it would make up the ideal type of man for India. It is an achievement of the highest order, this transference of allegiance from Rama-rajya to a planned social order, this shifting of the axis of morality from sacrifice to planned endeavour. Gandhiji's constructive programme also demanded the highest effort and the highest sacrifice. But the programme of the Plan is for another type of society, and the typical man wanted for it is naturally also different; he should have more knowledge, more technical ability, more historical sense than his counterpart of the Sarvodaya programme; probably, he too sacrifices, but he is expected to sacrifice less. The Plan means both a change of the axis of the ideal type of man and society as well as a change of gear. Thus it is that Gandhiji's influence is reported to have disappeared. It is true in direct proportion to the reverence with which his name is held. But gone with it is his view of morality—a view which, though partial, was a genuine binder through its linkage with faith in God; and gone with it also is the faith in the spontaneity of people's creative love, however crudely it might have been held.

The Technocrat—Future Leader

From now on the ordering has to come from the engineers, social and technical, who have faith in organisation, knowledge of exact and less exact sciences, and are rational in their outlook. So they will make the ideal type for the next generation: the technocrat with imagination, the bureaucrat with the democratic touch and flexibility; in fact, a middle class know-how type. This type is going to be the norm. Voluntary village workers as envisaged in the Plan and community projects, etc., cannot but gravitate to that type. Will it be different from the modern Western counterpart? Probably not. Will it be fuller than its predecessors? In secular knowledge, yes; but in religious ethics, no. Aesthetically, it will be poor, because the cult of science and technology, this hatred of "literary" education, this mistrust of knowledge for its own sake which the hired experts, technocrats, and bureaucrats betray, can be very cramping indeed. An amount of ruthlessness is inevitable in all planning; individuals have to be sacrificed for the aggregate. So the ideal type will not always be very human either. Scope may be said to have been given to humanity and aesthetic sense in and through cottage industries and decentralised economy. But only a fool will believe that they will maintain their exclusive beauty against the vulgar invasion of large-scale state or private enterprise. The River Valley projects, the science laboratories, the state factories and services, the norms of economic pattern and knowledge, will draw them unto themselves in one mighty embrace of Hercules. There is a vague fear of it in the country; it is deeper than the fear of the unknown and more uncomfortable than the loss of the habitual. It is a spiritual nervousness before the possibilities of dehumanisation. One wonders if this be not at the back of the so-called frustration of the country. Nehru and the Plan have changed the axis and the gear; they are changing the pattern of habits; they would make young men face the unknown with courage; they would seek to modernise on the basis of knowledge of technology and historical forces. No wonder that some of them feel, with their ancient parents, that all is lost. The fact is that something is lost, and something else and more has been gained, at least, can be gained. Only the concepts of the new man and new society have not yet been clarified. For this the Indian intellectuals are to be blamed. The fault of modern Indian education does not lie in its literary, non-vocational, non-useful bias; it does lie in the lack of clarity in the concept, if it has any, of the new social order and the new man. It has so long left the ideal types to be fixed by blind forces and allowed them to slither into the average, the common, and the temporary. In fact, it has not thought about them at all. The function of universities is to fix the "ideal" types, and only incidentally and indirectly, to build character.

36

The Language Problem

A Solution*

O. L. Chavarria-Aguilar

The Indian Constitution stipulates that Hindi, in the Devanagari script, is to be the official language of the Indian Union; that Hindi shall be used for all official purposes of the Union, in place of English, from 1965, 15 years from the commencement of the Constitution itself.

Now, it is usually a rather risky business to make predictions about language, but it is highly questionable whether Hindi will indeed be able to replace English within the time limit set. Fifteen years seems hardly a reasonable and realistic period of time in which to expect Hindi to accomplish the far from easy task of replacing English, even if only in the realm of official purposes of the Union. English has been the official language of India for a good 200 years; its prestige is very great, and it cannot certainly be denied that that prestige, the use of, and the demand for English has scarcely declined since 1947—much less since 1950, the year of commencement of the Constitution. In many states Hindi has officially been adopted, while in others deliberate steps to curtail the learning of English and otherwise to impair or render of secondary importance a knowledge of English have been taken. So far this does not seem to have had much effect upon the overall position of English. On the other hand, it cannot be said that the knowledge or the prestige of Hindi has increased appreciably throughout India; certainly not to the extent that some would wish, nor to the extent that might lead even the most optimistic to regard the 1965 deadline as remotely possible of achievement.

India is still very much governed through the medium of the English language; English is today still the most important single language in India, despite all efforts to give that place to Hindi. And it is likely to remain so for a long time

* Originally published in *Economic Weekly* 6, no. 35 (28 August 1954), pp. 946–51.

to come to judge by its continued prestige and pre-eminence and by the slow progress of Hindi in its evolution toward the status of a true national language. (It is interesting to note in this connection that quite recently, a high-ranking military person, speaking on the new combined services academy at Khadakvasla, stressed the fact that the medium of instruction would be English for at least 15 or 20 years to come; and that this point was, in fact, made the basis for an appeal to Maharashtrians to join the academy for, it was stated, English is much neglected in Bombay state.)

However, rather than dwell on the probability or the improbability of Hindi replacing English within the stipulated period, I should like in this brief essay to confine myself to an examination of the concept of national language, and to a discussion of some of its corollaries. The status, the conceived roles and functions of a national language are, I think, central to the present language problems in India; it is a question that has very particular bearing on the matter of Hindi and its position among and its relation to the other regional languages. It is also of significance in the matter of Hindi versus English.

NATIONAL LANGUAGE

What is, after all, a national language? What are the properties and functions of a language so designated? What are the circumstances out of which national languages arise? And why indeed are national languages felt to be so necessary an adjunct, and even sometimes a condition, of nations? It is not easy to find wholly satisfactory answers to these questions; almost any answer that can be elicited is totally or partially inapplicable to given situations, and this is particularly true in the Indian context. Is a national language the official administrative medium of a nation, the sole language officially employed within the national boundaries? Belgium and Switzerland have no national language in this sense. Is it the language that expresses the "genius," the national character of a people? Switzerland has four, Belgium and Canada two each, and India at least 14 or 15! Or is a national language more a symbol of national identity, of the community of aims and aspirations of a number of groups who constitute themselves a nation? Again, Switzerland, Belgium, Canada, the Soviet Union, India, Pakistan, and a number of other nations have no national language in this sense.

Language in the political, social, and cultural contexts of a nation has two major functions. One is practical: the expression and intercommunication of thought; the means of conveying cultural and social items between individuals and groups of a single generation as well as from one generation to the next; the indispensable tool of political and social intercourse. The other function is symbolic: language is often the symbol of national identity, the rallying point of numerous individuals and groups, often with widely differing interests and orientations; the common denominator which serves to identify these groups, and by which these frequently identify themselves as a nation.

As we know it today and see it operating about us, this second function of language is of comparatively recent origin—though nonetheless potent a force for all that. It arose along with the modern concept of nations as rather jealous, distinct, and rigidly defined political entities, and it has come increasingly to serve as a distinguishing feature (often the sole distinguishing feature) of sovereign political states. In this context, many nations have no particular language problems. The United States, the Scandinavian countries, the nations of Latin America, and many others have but a single language—or but a single language of importance. In such nations there is little or no conflict of language ideologies or of language loyalties; the practical and symbolic functions of language are served by a single language. Other nations, bi- or multilingual, have evolved in such fashion historically as to render language differences within the national boundaries of less than secondary importance. Here the symbolic functions which elsewhere attach to language are embodied in some other common aspect of cultural or even of political heritage. Switzerland is perhaps the best example of this, while Canada is another.

Purpose and Function of Hindi

Many language problems arise in the Indian context—where the picture is, it must be admitted, much more complicated than anywhere else in the world—because there seems to be no clear conception of the two distinct primary functions of language. And this is particularly true as regards the status, present and future, of Hindi and the purpose which this language is to serve in India. Among other things this gives rise to a good deal of antagonism against Hindi in many quarters, for it is felt that attempts are being made to give to Hindi a scape much broader than that to which its position of official language entitles it. This antagonism, in turn, becomes a barrier to the spread and acceptance of Hindi even in its rightful domain.

What role is Hindi intended to serve in India? Is it to be the language of purely administrative convenience, simply a handy tool to facilitate inter-provincial and centre–province communication? Or is a somewhat wider, more all-embracing role, a more symbolic function being sought for it? Is Hindi to be simply, as the Constitution of India has it, the language for official purposes of the Union? Or is it rather to be conceived of as the symbol of Indian nationality, a device syntonising the community of purpose, the oneness, of the many varying groups that make up the Indian Union?

A national language such as the Indian Constitution seems to call for is not only possible, it is, in addition, a highly necessary and desirable tool for the nation.

A symbolic national language for India—as Gaelic is, for example, the national language of Eire—is not only impractical, if not impossible, it is hardly desirable, for it cannot but give rise to conflicts, having no other basis than a difference in language, where no conflicts existed before. Any attempts to give this status to the national language of India will only increase linguistic self-consciousness and make for stronger, more fanatic, linguistic and regional chauvinism. And while the Constitution is, it seems to me, quite clear as to the function of the official language, the numerous partisans of Hindi—the government not excluded—evidence nothing but confusion on the issue and, if anything, carry on as if Hindi were to become the sole language of India. There is a widespread notion that Hindi is to become the national language, both practical and symbolic—the language not only of Union administration, but of literature, of science, and of everyday intercourse, of bazaar and ministry, from Cape Comorin to the Himalayas, and from the Punjab to Assam.

Limitations of Hindi

Hindi simply cannot fulfil the symbolic functions of a national language in a nation linguistically so varied; nor can it be expected to be the culture language of more than those who claim it as their mother tongue, their regional language. India as a whole has many significant features of common cultural heritage which might better serve as the symbols of the unity, the Indianism, for the many groups that make up the nation. To ask Hindi to fulfil this function is a disservice to it and a slight to the other regional languages. Hindi may eventually become the full-fledged language of inter-provincial communication, official and non-official, but it would be foolish to expect almost 30 crores of people whose mother tongue is other than Hindi to identify themselves with the official language and to display it proudly as the symbol of their Indian nationality. If clothes do not indeed make the man, much less is Hindi going to make the Indian.

The function of Hindi as national language (for it must not be forgotten that Hindi is also an important regional language) must be conceived of solely in terms of inter-provincial communication, for official purposes of the Union. The spread and the development of Hindi, whether spontaneous or consciously guided by its speakers, in other spheres of activity should be considered apart from its status as official language—though, of course, in this capacity, Hindi is bound to benefit. The efforts of the government to extend the use and knowledge of Hindi, to gain its greater acceptance, must be limited to Hindi as the tool of governmental convenience. Otherwise the task before the government, far from easy as it is, becomes immeasurably and unnecessarily complicated, and will give rise to evermore serious language conflicts. Much of the antagonism that exists against Hindi today is the result, not of the work of the numerous Hindi Prachar

Samitis, Sabhas, Parishads, and what have you, but of the conflicting attitudes, the vague, inconsistent policies of government as the apostle of Hindi. The apprehension with regard to the future status of Hindi is not without justification. For many the national language has assumed the guise and the fearsomeness of an ogre, out to gobble up all the regional languages and to reign in India, not as primus inter pares, but as the sole Indian language. An exaggerated notion, no doubt, but the feeling is nevertheless there and there is some substance to it. And so long as it persists, the task of spreading Hindi will be made more difficult for there is always bound to be resistance to it.

Hindi and English

The biggest single hurdle that Hindi has to get over is, of course, the English language. So long as English continues to occupy the privileged position that, it cannot be denied, it occupies today in India, Hindi will make relatively little headway. Hindi is not at present in a class with English; it does not have as much to offer, intellectually or economically, as does a knowledge of English. Any language, Hindi included, can have its development guided towards equal effectiveness with a rival. But there must be clear-cut aims in view—there must be no equivocation as to what exactly is expected of the language. One simply cannot legislate the matter, as should be more than evident from the little relative progress that Hindi has thus far made and at present seems to be making. The ambivalent attitude toward Hindi current today is in large measure responsible for this slow progress. No one seems to know quite what is expected of Hindi, and too many have taken for granted that everything is to be expected of it.

Hindi as the expression of the thought of a certain segment of the Indian population can be expected to develop, in its own milieu, as the expanding and increasing needs of its speakers require, in those spheres in which the language is employed. This is the history of language development. The point to consider is, of course, the extent to which Hindi and, in fact, all the regional languages, are indeed employed. The Indian languages have suffered in the past, have had their growth arrested or impaired, because for the last 200 years or so English has been almost the sole linguistic key to success in India. A knowledge of English in British India (and indeed today) could be expected to take an individual much farther up the ladder of success than any single one of the Indian languages. This was particularly true in Government and in education, both of which were carried on in English above the primary stages. It was also true, though perhaps to a lesser degree, in commerce and industry. Almost everywhere, above the taluka level, English was an essential to individual advancement, so that the regional languages, including Hindi, were neglected in favour of English and their development thus held back. Now that Hindi is to replace English, if only for official purposes of the Union, there is a definite fear in many quarters that the regional languages will soon be as much at the mercy of Hindi as Hindi and they have so far been at a disadvantage because of the preferred status of English.

This fear is not without foundation —and it is certainly kept alive by the antics of many of the more fanatic Hindi protagonists. Furthermore, government policies, both state and central, subject as they are to confusion and lacking any concise notion as to the proper function and properties of the national language, only add to the fear that Hindi is indeed out to usurp the domains that are felt to belong rightly to the regional languages. Certain recent policies of the Government of Bombay state have certainly given a good deal of substance to this fear. While it is unlikely that Hindi will ever completely supplant the other regional languages (nor do I think that the Government and the saner pro-Hindi element intend that it should do so), it is certainly true that the fear of this arouses a good deal of anti-Hindi sentiment, thus hindering the development of Hindi even in what we might consider its proper sphere. Furthermore, the possibility is quite real that, given its ability to displace English (a not undebatable proposition), the future status of Hindi as the national language and any overemphasis as to its importance in the national scene are quite likely to affect adversely the development of the other regional languages, as all the Indian languages have up to now been affected by the pre-eminence of and the great emphasis upon English.

RELATIVE PRESTIGE OF THE NATIONAL LANGUAGE

Now it is very difficult to see how, if Hindi is indeed to become the *de facto* as well as the *de jure* national language of India, the regional languages can be expected to be on a completely equal footing with it. As the national language (as defined by the Constitution and not as a symbolic device) Hindi will offer and enjoy advantages that the other Indian languages will not. A knowledge of Hindi will certainly offer possibilities of employment, if nothing else, that the regional languages cannot hope to match. In the nature of things, the situation being hardly avoidable, this somewhat enhanced position of Hindi will simply have to be taken with as good grace as can be mustered.

The relative prestige of Hindi and the disadvantages that might be the lot of the regional languages can, however, be considerably minimised—or equalised—in many spheres. Hindi will, of course, have a preferred place in education, for example—though to attempt to make it the medium of instruction in non-Hindi areas, where it is still a foreign language despite its being Indian, seems a very perverse and short-sighted measure indeed. Unless, however, every effort is made to see to it that the importance of Hindi is not unduly emphasised, we shall have much the same situation as we have today with regard to English and the Indian languages, only it will be Hindi which will prosper at the expense of the other regional languages.

If Hindi is given preference in every field over the regional languages the development of these latter will continue to languish as it did when English was the official language of India. In the field of Union Public Service, where the position of English is possibly the strongest, the relative importance of Hindi, when it eventually displaces English, can easily be stabilised with respect to the regional languages, and it is, in fact, precisely here where some equalisation will be most required and where it can most readily be effected. All that is needed is a constructive and realistic attitude on the part of Government, and a clear understanding of the functions of the national language and of the limits of its proper domain.

Hindi in Government

Hindi need not, indeed should not, be made the "open sesame" to Union Public Service as was English during the British Raj. In all fairness to the inhabitants of non-Hindi regions and, in fact, in fairness to the nation itself, since she should be able without discrimination to draw on the entire population for service, Hindi should not only not be made a prerequisite to service in the Central Government service, but should not even be given any consideration for such service.

Consider that if Hindi is made compulsory for application for government service, as English certainly is today, many otherwise capable individuals might easily be excluded in favour of others whose only qualification is a knowledge of Hindi. There is no doubt that in British days this sort of situation was not uncommon, the British assuming that a knowledge of English made an individual *ipso facto* more like themselves—namely, better. Unless we assume that a knowledge of Hindi makes one a better veterinary surgeon, say, than one could possibly be without that knowledge, we must forgo completely considerations of Hindi competence in the selection of applicants for government—Central Government—service. Hindi does not, I think we can agree, make X a better veterinary surgeon than Y who happens to speak only Telugu. Why then should Government deprive itself of the potentially better services of Y, simply because his Hindi is not up to Lucknow or Allahabad standards? Each applicant should be judged solely on his merits as an individual and on his competence as an engineer, a chemist, a pilot, or a night watchman, regardless of his competence, or lack thereof, in Hindi.

To take such a view of things—and I cannot think of a more impartial view to take—will mean (1) that the qualifying examinations for government service, where required, must be given in the major regional languages, in order to afford every single applicant, regardless of his place of origin or his mother tongue, an equal opportunity, and (2) that the Government of India will perforce find itself in the language teaching business.

Qualifying examinations in the regional languages should then be limited to the testing of general aptitudes and knowledge, and of the special requirements for specific posts; questions of language competence—particularly of competence in the national language—should be rigidly excluded except, of course, in the case of posts for language teachers or, in general, wherever competence in a given language is a necessary special qualification for employment. Once selection on this basis has been made, language competence examinations, specifically competence in Hindi, can be given. Selected candidates can then be sent for whatever language training it is deemed necessary they acquire. And this type of training should be given with the individual on full pay and allowances for his post, in order that there may be, even here, no discrimination between Hindi and non-Hindi speakers. At this time too, by the way, speakers of Hindi can be sent for training, as required, in one or another of the regional languages. This measure would seem to be much more realistic than to attempt to force the burden of a second Indian language on secondary school students in Hindi regions, as has been frequently suggested. How many students who complete their secondary education ever feel the need of a second Indian language? Suggestions to require a second Indian language of Hindi speaking students are not based on the need of students, but are the product of spite, pure and simple, of a desire to penalize students whose mother tongue is Hindi, simply because theirs happens to also be the national language. Learning a language, a second language, even to read it passably, is a serious and lengthy process and one that should be undertaken from choice and never from compulsion. To require a language other than the mother tongue is well enough, but to restrict the choice of a second language simply from narrow provincial considerations is of questionable value.

The Union Government can readily accomplish its task as teacher of languages in one (or both) of two ways: either Government establishes its own school of language training, or else it sends its selected candidates to the various regional universities for that training. Even in the latter event, however, it is most likely that Government will find itself directly committed, for it will undoubtedly have to subsidise in some way the appropriate language training programmes. I do not think that there is as yet a university in India properly equipped to offer intensive and scientifically balanced courses in language.

Regardless of how Government decides to go about its job of language teacher, however, the scheme will in the long run pay handsome dividends. It is, for one, the only way of ensuring that candidates for Union Public Service will be selected on their knowledge and competence, general and specialised, without regard to their ability to handle the national language. The nation will thus be potentially assured of being able to draw on the best-qualified individuals for the services required, and not be restricted more or less to those who possess a knowledge, fortuitous or otherwise, of Hindi. There seems, moreover, to be no real alternative if the disabilities are to be minimised under which the regional languages would otherwise be compelled to labour. This will serve too, to lessen the possibility (indeed, the probability) of giving undue emphasis to Hindi as the key to success in government service: it will certainly lessen the antagonism against the national language and, by making Hindi less of a competitor with the other regional languages, or of equalising the terms of competition, enhance the opportunities and incentives for the rapid and more even development of the latter.

Development of the National Language

Finally, Government, as teacher of languages, whether directly or indirectly, will be in a much better position to undertake still another important task prescribed for it by the Constitution: the proper development of the national language. Here there must be absolute certainty on the part of Government as to the function and status, the true role, of the national language. At present this seems not to be a striking feature of official language policies.

Provided we understand clearly the functions and properties of Hindi as the national language, I should like respectfully to submit that it is incumbent upon Government to attempt the development of Hindi solely within the frame of reference provided by the Constitution, namely, for official purposes of the Indian Union. The proper function of Government, in connection with the development of the national language is, it seems to me, limited to Hindi as the tool of Union administration and no more. It is not the function of Government to concern itself with the development of Hindi as a literary vehicle, nor along any other lines with which Government is itself not directly concerned. Government's concern with Hindi exists only insofar as this is a necessary tool for more efficient national administration. For the Government of India to extend its interest beyond this limit can lead only to eventual overemphasis on Hindi, which would be to the detriment of the other regional languages. It will lead, in effect, to placing Hindi on the pedestal at present occupied by English—a situation which, in view of the effects that the emphasis upon English has had on the development of all the Indian languages, Government would do well to avoid.

The development of Hindi as the means of literary, cultural, and scientific expression of the people whose mother tongue it is, the development, in short, of Hindi as a regional language is the proper function of those people who claim it as their mother tongue. And I am sure that these will not be wanting in zeal.

Unless it is fully intended to make of Hindi the symbolic as well as the practical national language of India, the symbol of the unity of aspirations, goals, and interests of 365 millions of people speaking many, often widely differing, languages—and it should be obvious that this is manifestly an impossible role for any language in India—the Union Government must make very clear its linguistic impartiality. The activities of the Union Government in the linguistic field should be limited to Hindi as the practical tool of more efficient central administration. Otherwise the cries of "Hindi imperialism" will continue to be raised, and not without justification. For if Government, especially, insists on overemphasising the importance of Hindi, the other regional languages will soon find themselves in a subordinate position—and their development adversely affected—in much the same way that all the Indian languages have for the past 200 years been subordinate to English.

37

English, Hindi and the Regional Languages*

I. P. Desai

I entirely agree with the conclusion of your correspondent in his Letter from South in the Annual Number, February 1965, that "The only way for Hindi is first and foremost an emphasis on the regional languages, carefully worked out plan for their rapid take over from English."

I also agree with the reasoning by which he arrives at this conclusion and I endorse the social realism behind it. Your correspondent observes correctly, "India has still largely a pseudo-self and "what has not happened is the creation of Indian nation." He comes to the point which touches the sociologist when he says that "this must rank as one of the biggest failures of middle class in history." The important question, therefore, is what is the character of the middle class? What are the social groups from which this class comes, and what are the values and attitudes that it possesses at this particular point of time in the history of the nation?

Changed Role of English

The identification by your correspondent is simple and workable. He refers to the class of persons educated under the system of education introduced by the British, particularly the class which has taken education up to graduation and above. "In the early phase this intelligentsia drawn from the landlord class or from one or another comprador occupations came to English as a means of westernisation which they felt was the only way forward to the modern regeneration of their country." A point needs to be added here. These were also the people settled in

* Originally published in *Economic Weekly* 17, no. 10 (6 March 1965), pp. 441–45.

the urban areas, the big towns of those days, and they came from one or two higher castes in each linguistic region.

To these nineteenth century proponents of English, the English language was the language of culture. The role of English today has changed and it has become the means of earning the livelihood and of achieving social status. The position of English in the hierarchy of values has come down to more immediate ends than to distant ends in the minds of the mass of population, which is taking to education in numbers much larger than at any time in the past. And what is more important, it will continue to grow larger. This means that the social base of the college and university educated is becoming broader and will continue to do so. Education is growing among the lower-income groups of the higher castes and higher-income groups of the so-called lower castes in urban and rural areas respectively. Their traditions and the contemporary experience of life are different from the traditions of the nineteenth century educated class. Consequently, the large mass of the recently educated and uneducated class has different values and its attitude towards English, as we have said, is of a more functional nature, and there is a hiatus between the values of the policy makers and of those influential in policy-making and the values and attitudes of the large number of newly educated people.

The Stumbling Block

These policy makers and influential persons do not see or probably do not like to see the changed role of English. They cannot get rid of the heritage of the nineteenth century intelligentsia which was clear and honest about the Indian society of the future—the westernised India. Westernisation was the openly accepted creed with them. Their contemporary inheritors are not in a position to stand by them in their creed, probably because they do not have the conviction and perspective of the nineteenth century Indian Westerniser. That is why the defenders of English always begin by agreeing that the regional language is the proper media of instruction and administration in the states. But in the same breath they start advocating caution, gradualness, preparation, etc., so that ultimately the changeover to regional language never materialises. They know that English just does not work in the colleges and universities but they cling to it. They know very well that the large mass of students do not have the environments, either at home or in the educational institutions, congenial to English as a medium of instruction. They run away from this reality and try to save English by advocating the restriction of admissions and by proposing increase in papers, hours, and years of teaching English. But the command of the students over English does not increase. Yet English is continued as the medium of instruction. The same students go out as assistants in offices and teachers in schools and colleges. Hence, again, the complaint of their poor standard of English. They just fail to realise that the regional language is the most effective means of communication for the spread of science and scientific attitude. Not to introduce, therefore, the regional language as the medium of instruction is to hamper the spread of science and scientific attitude. The advocates of English in this sense are becoming the stumbling block in all that is new and desirable. In effect, they are playing the role of conservatives and reactionaries however progressive they may like to appear.

Role of Intelligentsia

Is the intelligentsia not intelligent enough to realise this? The intelligentsia is, though the class of influential persons may not be. Here it is necessary to point out a new development in the composition of the intelligentsia. With the growth of university education an academic intelligentsia is growing as specialists in their subjects. It is not of any significant size but it is a qualitative difference which will grow. These are the persons with ability to see things, but they are cut off from the social currents because they are interested in solving their own academic problems. Their intellectual honesty is not questioned here but their awareness of their social responsibility is perhaps not based on sufficient observation and thought, just because they dislike being disturbed in their pursuits. Yet they have opinions based on their contact with their "society" of policy-makers and the influential who use them for their own purposes. Also, they are cut off from the large mass of teachers who handle the large mass of students in undergraduate colleges and postgraduate students in places other than the metropolitan cities. If they had either first-hand experience or contact with those in touch with the large mass of students, they would very probably hold different opinions.

So, the effective supporters of English are the policy makers and the influential. Who are they? Among the policy makers are included the secretaries—joint, additional, deputy, assistant, and under—and advisers. We designate them as government intelligentsia. Then there are the ministers of various statuses at the Centre and in the States. They are directly related to the influential in their political party as also the members of legislatures at the Centre and in the States belonging to the non-government parties. These have their supporters in their parties and outside it in the society who may not be the members of any political party.

The Policy Makers

The social characteristics of these policy makers and the influential, their values and attitudes enter into policy making and in the execution of the language policy and in the reactions of the people to the policy.

The government intelligentsia comes from the upper castes, upper income groups, and urban areas or from the urban-influenced sections of rural areas, but in small numbers. They are all degree holders and also probably specialists in some branches of knowledge. They obey and respect the ministers as a matter of routine. But they like or dislike the minister according to his social origin, his academic achievements, experience, and ability. Being what they are, they have to execute the policy. But they can influence the ministers by putting up a weak case strongly or a strong case weakly. The declared policy can be delayed, hastened, or twisted in practice. The dependence of the ministers or the government on these persons is an established fact all over the world. Thus, their social base, their values, and attitudes play an important role in policy making and its execution. It is not that they consciously ally with the particular stratum from which they come. The stratum strongly conditions a man's outlook and he normally acts according to its standards. Hence we find that persons from a given upper strata are against their own regional language or at least they are not enthusiastic for their regional language.

DIFFERENCE IN OUTLOOK

The government intelligentsia do not find much difficulty in their daily work because the politicians who are the principal policy makers are as a rule English knowing, at least those who are put in ministerial position. But among politicians the heterogeneity in terms of the university degree, knowledge of English, occupation, income, and rural or urban origin and outlook and caste is more pronounced than in the case of government intelligentsia. In all the political parties at the leadership level in the parliamentary groups the ministers are either degree holders or English knowing but the members of the legislative parties are not always. Yet the proportions of rural agriculture-based persons, having not much knowledge of English, do not have dominating influence in the parliamentary parties at the centre. The urban-based working class members are still rare, but their number and the number of agriculture-based members are growing in the State legislatures. The result is that the difference in the outlook of the leadership and of their immediate supporters is growing in all the political parties.

But the difference between the top leaders and the electorate is still wider. It is true that in any State a political party can come to power only on the agricultural vote. At least this is true in the case of the present ruling party. Nearly 70 per cent of the Indian voters are illiterate, i.e., innocent of even the alphabets of their regional language. Yet it is this voter who puts a party in power. They live in rural areas and earn their living by agriculture and occupations dependent on it. But the top level leadership comes rarely from this group and even the second rank leadership, which is nearer to this group, physically and socially, is yet not of that group.

By the very nature of the political activity this is bound to happen, and there will always be some distance between the various levels of leadership and their supporters through whom they gain positions of power. This gulf is generally narrowed by the growth of specialists in political activity, the professional politician. He generally represents the interest group in wider society. Until, therefore, the interest groups are organised, this hiatus continues to be glaring. As interest consciousness grows, the distance between leadership and its following narrows down. This is probably what is happening at this level in India.

Urban Interests in Rural Areas

The rural areas in India are not the same today as they were in the pre-Independence era. Of course, the changes have not been to the same extent in all the states, and that makes a difference. The main difference is of the penetration of the urban occupational interests and the outlook corelated to it in the rural areas. The small towns, with population ranging from, say, 30,000 to 1 lakh, are growing in number and importance and the metropolitan urban interests have their footholds there. Their agents there set a standard for the style of living and aspirations. These agents are the lawyers, doctors, businessmen, government officers, branch managers of banks, and such other concerns. All these groups have their associations with the bigger cities of the area and the importance of the individuals in these groups in their local setting depends on this contact with the luminaries of their interests in the bigger cities and, in the final analysis, in the capital city. The Rotary, the Lions Clubs, and the Junior Chambers provide them with the contact places. The well-to-do agriculturist and the shopkeeper in the interior are their last posts in the rural area. The leadership comes from these interests or their nominees. They are the proponents and supporters of English in rural areas, and they are the vocal groups, and when it is said that even the rural people want English, these are the rural people, the vocal groups. The social base of English is thus widened and its spread has gone into the rural areas—nearer to the villages.

A development which the proponents and supporters of English deplore is that the strata which formerly remained untouched by education now show a strong desire for it and are sending their children to schools and colleges. The social composition of primary and secondary school pupils and of college students in rural areas is changing. Though the higher caste students may be larger in proportion to their caste population, the absolute number of other castes is increasing. These are also the lower income groups. For them education is not only a means of earning a livelihood, it is also a means of raising their own status in their groups and of their groups in relation with the traditionally higher groups.

The whole mass of rural students and that section coming from lower income groups of all castes in urban areas suffer the most from the handicap of the English medium. Compared to the size of these groups it is to the insignificantly small group in society that English medium affords an advantage in addition to the social and economic advantages that they already have. Large number of school and college teachers come from this latter section and their views are generally consistent with their position in the hierarchy. There is some modification in their position when they are guided by linguistic chauvinism and by the considerations of job opportunities for men from their own region.

English and Mobility

The usual argument in favour of English as promoting mobility is a further illustration of the interests of the small group that English serves. From every region two types of persons migrate: the educated and the illiterate. The educated communicate in English with the English-knowing persons of the other regions. But do the large numbers of engineering, textile, and building workers from other regions communicate with the local people in English? They manage with some sort of Hindi. Do the proponents of English visualise a day when all such migrants will be communicating in English? This is moonshine in view of the fact that only 35 per cent of the population is literate and 2 per cent know English. Even so, English is shown as the language promoting mobility. It does, but whose? Of the minor groups of two or three higher castes and the new well-to-do of the lower castes. The reference group of the proponents of English is that small group from which they come.

English medium is thus thoroughly inconsistent with the advocacy of democracy and socialism. Yet what has been the position of the parties professing these? The position of the Swatantra Party is easily understandable. Their vision of the future Indian democracy is that of the nineteenth century British society. But have the communists and the PSP unequivocally and wholeheartedly proposed and propagated for the regional language as the medium of instruction at all levels of education? It is possible that in particular plans and in particular situations they might have paid lip service to regional language because it suited their immediate political aims. Otherwise, they have been more faithful to the strata from which their leadership comes than to their rank and file on whose votes they win their elections.

The real conflict regarding the place of English, Hindi, and the regional languages is in the Congress Party. At the states level, the consensus is on the regional language as the medium of administration. But there is division regarding the medium of instruction at the university level. Even regarding the administration, the judiciary at the top level is conservative.

Language and the Civil Service

In administration the resistance to the regional language comes from what we have called the government intelligentsia and the high-ranking officials, many of whom might belong to the central services. In some regions which were slow in catching up with the spread of education, there are many persons from other linguistic regions. But in others there are few persons from other linguistic regions in that cadre. A powerful chief minister of a state was reported to have said that he would not have central service men coming from a different linguistic region. The distribution of regional and non-region men in every state, in Central and the higher services of the state will be quite revealing. It would reveal that mobility means mobility in one direction only and it is not interregional mobility. This will be true even in regard to secondary and university teachers. Thus the personnel of the services in one factor in the resistance to the regional language. When the personnel are from the same region, the resistance to the regional language is largely due to their class position. The resistance to Hindi as the official language of the union is due to the expected competition to existing groups from other regional groups. The members of the central services who are working hard against monopolies in the economic field are working equally hard to maintain their monopoly in their own field.

This situation is largely due to the unequal development of different regions in economic and educational fields. But it has given a sense of inherent quality to certain regional groups in regard to certain types of administrative and technical jobs. Side by side with the channelisation of ambitions of the educated section of that region in that direction comes the belief in the inherent incompetence of the people of other regions in that field. The other groups do not admit that claim. Consequently, there are tensions. These sorts of tensions are not peculiar to India, but they exist in all countries wherever similar situations obtain, including Europe and America. They are eased when development reaches a comparable level in all regions. But the intensity of the tensions becomes greater while development is taking place and also probably when the rate of development is faster or slower in different regions. The political policy makers have to devise mechanisms to manage these tensions and not wait till the crisis overtakes them. If the tensions are not managed now, they will hamper the development process. Therefore, it is necessary to face the problem and not postpone it. The ostrich-like policy of the last 17 years has aggravated the tensions and not eased them.

Regional Languages Neglected

The clever policy of giving support to English, Hindi, and regional languages has not satisfied anyone, and by administrative manoeuvres, English or Hindi has been pushed forth and back at the cost of regional languages. In each State attention and energy have been diverted to the Hindi-English controversy and the State administrations continued to operate in English and not in the regional language. Not only that, but the conflict between Hindi and regional languages was aggravated, thanks to the cleverness of the proponents of English and the folly of some Hindi speaking proponents of Hindi. The latter did not declare their full-throated support to the regional language in State administration and as the medium of instruction. They thought that more officers and teachers from Hindi speaking areas would automatically strengthen Hindi in other regions. The behaviour of these officers and teachers was also repugnant to the local people. They not only brought the clerks but also the peons from the Hindi speaking areas (for example, in the oil projects in Gujarat). The standards of efficiency of the local peons fell much below the standards inherited by the officers and their wives from the feudal landlordism. If the peons do not come up to that standard of efficiency, need anything be said of clerks and lecturers from that region? If such was not the situation, the Maharashtra chief minister would not have to plead while inaugurating some project that local people should also be given opportunities of employment in that project. Thus the suspicion of Hindi imperialism becomes stronger. The English enthusiast asks the peon if he knows English. Whether or not he knows cooking and table service is inquired by both Hindi and English enthusiasts. As a matter of policy in all the central projects the smaller posts must be filled by the local people. This will not affect efficiency at all, because we complain of inefficiency all over India. An inefficient man does not become efficient in another region. And further, as our aim is to reduce tension, a little difference in efficiency should be tolerated in favour of the local man. The higher posts have to be filled keeping the requirements of the post in view and not the region of the candidate or his mastery over English or Hindi. And whatever the language of the union may be, government officers must be required to know the language of the region in which they work. A good deal of the edge of interregional mistrust will be eased off if this is done.

But who will make the rules we ask for? The services will depend on the political policy makers. In the Congress Party with which we are concerned now, the urban interests which have penetrated into the rural areas from the social base are the proponents of English. We have described their character. A section of them, particularly in the bigger cities and towns, and even agriculturists support the Swatantra Party openly. The Swatantra Party relies on the English-supporting interests as their fifth column in the Congress Party. As against these interests in Congress and outside, there are the supporters of Hindi and the regional languages. Their main source of strength is in the rural areas. In terms of interests, the PSP members who have recently joined Congress have more things in common with them. But the social roots of their leaders and their urban nurture fosters in them a "modernistic" mentality and they cannot easily join hands with the leadership of the pro-Hindi pro-regional language group. Also, tactically they would not like to toe the line easily. But if they do not unite with them they will be as ineffective in the Congress as they were when they were outside it. The realisation of this position and corresponding action requires political maturity and vision which may be wanting. The probability is that they might act more as individuals rather than as a group or they might act as sub-groups among themselves. What the actual outcome of their union will be also depends on the sections of the Swatantra and anti-Swatantra or rural-based group in Congress. Anyway, the present position is that PSP group in Congress, though it is nearer to the rural group, does not support them wholeheartedly in their pro-Hindi pro-regional language policy. Among the leaders, some are rootless and some are still rooted in Swatantra social base.

Thus within the Congress there is rivalry and conflict between pro-Swatantra interests and what we have now called the rural interests. The strengthening or weakening of these interests within the Congress will decide the language issue.

The Communists, if they remained true to their ideology, cannot but support the pro-Hindi pro-regional language groups. But who can say what they are and what they will do. For an immediate tactical gain, they may do quite the opposite of what their philosophical position would require them to do.

The question of medium of instruction and the medium of administration are thus closely linked with the "interests" in society and the political action of the parties according to the interests that they serve. It may happen that the actions of political groups such as the Swatantra section among the leaders and the influential in the Congress or some PSP leaders and the communists may go against the interests of the masses for which their parties profess to stand. But that does not divert the language from its political and social linkage. It happens because of the social characteristics of these leaders.

Conflicting Interests

The proponents of English lack the conviction and therefore the courage of conviction because their idea of nineteenth century British society and the polished Indian Englishman does not cut ice with the large masses. The masses want to know English not for the love of it but because they know that it has some use for them and there it ends. Their attitude towards English is like that of a tenant towards the hired house in which he lives. Consequently, the command over English of the large mass of students and teachers, lecturers, and of clerks and officers is not of that standard expected by the minority coming from higher castes, higher income groups, and prestige educational institutions. Each group has the feeling of separateness or estrangement from the other. The only consequence can be inefficiency. Yet English helps the top people as a means of showing and retaining their superiority. Thus they have become a vested interest.

The proponents of Hindi fear the growth of regional languages. Their fear was and is that if the regional languages become the medium of instruction and administration, it will be difficult to dislodge them and the state administration and education will not be in Hindi. That is why, without specifying whether it was English or Hindi, they emphasise the need for a common language for the whole of India whenever the question of medium of instruction and administration comes up. The result has been that the regional languages have not been encouraged and English has remained entrenched in its position. None of the accredited associations of Hindi has wholeheartedly and unequivocally declared itself in favour of regional language as the medium of instruction and administration in the States. Supporters of English were naturally glad. Thus English and Hindi supporters have been for some time partners, though strange partners, against the regional languages. When the Official Language Act came into force on 26 January 1965 the proponents of English naturally thought that Hindi was scoring a point and therefore regional chauvinism was commissioned into the service of English. If the regional languages had by now come into their own what happened in Madras would not have happened. The natural course for Hindi is to come via the regional languages. The Hindi expansionists are pressed by the growth of the new educated class in Hindi-speaking areas which in part were lagging behind in the economic and educational race. They find the Bengali and the South Indian English-speaking people entrenched in their own regions. They want to shove them off and export their surplus to other areas. Education in the Hindi-speaking areas is still confined to upper income and upper caste strata there. They press for standard Hindi of their stratum and their attitude towards Hindi speakers of other regions is the same as those who complain of poor English of the new English-speaking stratum. Consequently, the Hindi speaking man from the standard Hindi-speaking area is to be preferred to Hindi speakers from the non-Hindi speaking area for jobs. This is encouraging Hindi provincialism in non-Hindi regions and the regions which are not opposed to Hindi also begin to be apathetic to Hindi. The genuine fear of Hindi imperialism is aroused and the creation of a new-Hindi herrenvolk in addition to the English herrenvolk is threatened. If the regional languages are freely entrenched in their regions looking to the growth of education among the masses in every region, inevitably poor command over English will naturally lead to Hindi being accepted as the link language. But the reasoning of the Hindi herrenvolk is the reasoning of the feudal-based expansionist.

The growth of the national language will come through the growth of the regional language and not vice versa as some Hindi protagonists think.

38

Administrative Institutions of Government*

Rajni Kothari

The organisation of government in a democracy calls for constant reconciliation of conflicting elements. The principles of democracy are not always conducive to administrative efficiency. The preservation of democratic forms might necessitate a continuity of tradition and a piecemeal approach to problems of change, while a revolution in administrative methods may be necessary to secure efficiency. The attractiveness of political office in a democracy might draw talent away from administration. Accountability to popular opinion may make for timidity and lack of drive. Administrative efficiency calls for a simple line of command, but popular government leads to complexity of administration. Administrative departments multiply according to exigencies of the moment. Finally, the administration has to be constantly wary of "what the public will not stand."

Tradition versus Change

These difficulties are aggravated in countries where the expansion of the functions of government has not been a gradual process but has come almost at one stroke with political independence. The dilemma that these countries face is real though it does not always appear on the surface. On the one hand, sweeping changes in organisation might affect the delicate balance of constitutional government. On the other hand, excessive reverence for traditional forms and failure to carry out much-needed reform may lead to much frustration.

It is in this context that the conflict between tradition and change within the machinery of government in India has to be seen. In what follows, an attempt

* Originally published in *Economic Weekly* 13, no. 21 (27 May 1961), pp. 819–26.

is made to examine the assumptions on which a democratic administration is based. These assumptions govern the place of administrative departments in the scheme of government. They also deal with such matters as the relation between ministers and civil servants and between civil servants and the general public. Then the departures from these assumptions in actual practice in India and their bearing on the nature of the government will be studied.

Traditional political science distributes the functions of the state between the legislature, the executive, and the judiciary. Government departments thus fall entirety under the purview of the executive; they have no separate existence of their own in constitutional theory.

CENTRAL POSITION OF BUREAUCRACY

Such a view of administration in the scheme of government finds support in the theory of ministerial responsibility, according to which the individual minister is to be left free to organise his department as it suits him so that he is fully answerable to parliament. Ministerial responsibility to parliament involves ministerial sovereignty in administration.

Such a view of the functions of government may be attractive but is not real. It ignores the bureaucracy, oversimplifies the line of responsibility, and draws a sharp distinction between the making and carrying out of policy. In practice, however, large bureaucratic establishments have come to occupy so central a position in government that their constitutional importance can no longer be ignored. They constitute a fourth organ of government, alongside the three traditional organs.[1]

Recognition of the pivotal position of administrative departments in modern government has led some people to hold a point of view which though diametrically opposed to the traditional view, is no less misleading. Known as the "realist" view of public administration, it makes government a purely technical undertaking and considers the administrative secretariat as much a part of the machinery of government as the executive and the parliament without making any qualitative distinction. While traditional theory denies any distinction between the executive and the administration by including the latter in the former, the new school does the same by conceiving of the former as part of the latter. Evidently, this is an "operational" view of government;[2] it fuses together the executive and the administration and conceives of the former in non-political terms, as the latter. In bringing down the barriers between the ministerial and the bureaucratic wings of government, it erects a bigger barrier between administration and politics. It assumes that the administration of government can be considered apart from the politics of government.[3] It ignores the overriding fact that a cabinet is more than a mere bundle of executives; it is a team of politicians tied together by common loyalties, depending for its survival more on political ingenuity than on its administrative record. The important point is that the bureaucracy, the executive, and the political party are all part of a single continuum, and the business of government is the business of all of them. Any distinction drawn between them is more to facilitate analysis than to represent the actual state of affairs.

Artificial Division

The old dichotomy between politics and administration must now be rejected. Even the creation and maintenance of a career service is more a question of political values than of administrative necessity.[4] Administration has become a major political process, and organisational theory is ultimately a part of political strategy, and public accountability and popular control turn administration into a problem for political theory.[5] Both the traditional and the modern theories fail to take account of this immense change in the character of public administration that has taken place in recent times.[6]

The gap between theory and practice becomes all the more vivid in a country like India. Administration and politics in such a country interact with each other to a very large extent, and their respective areas of competence have yet to be specified.[7] Nevertheless both administrators and politicians continue to indulge in their own private games, resenting the "interference" or "high-handedness" of the other.

A study of the actual development of the machinery of government in India reveals the extent to which politics and administration are intertwined.[8] The lack of reliable facts makes such a study difficult. The government's tendency is to shroud public acts in secrecy and such information as percolates through the veil in the form of "revelations" by men who have fallen from public grace is unreliable. The lack of adequate channels of communication between the world of politics and that of scholarship accounts for much of our ignorance of public administration. Some general observations may, however, be possible from what is known.

Administration: Bulwark of Stability

The period immediately following Independence was one of great confusion. It was a question of sheer survival. Under such conditions, the administrative apparatus became the bulwark of stability. It provided a nucleus around which a national government could consolidate its position in a country torn by violence and disaffection. The administration became the basis of political authority. The experience required for new and challenging tasks could come only from the public services. Politicians were untutored in the arts of government. The mantle of responsibility passed to the services who continued to dominate the political process in the first phase of development.

That the predominance of the services was allowed to continue may seem surprising. During the Independence movement, resentment against the personnel of the Indian Civil Service was widespread. Civil servants were much maligned. It was also believed that the administrative structure evolved under the British was alien and unsuited to free India's needs; it was a servile order. It would have been quite within expectations, therefore, if the new inheritors of power in their first flush of victory, had proceeded to dismantle the administrative apparatus with a view to building it up again on the basis of new political objectives. This did not happen because the tasks that faced the country were urgent and because of the common sense of Sardar Patel, whose ability as an organiser was equal to that of any in the world of administration. The power he wielded over the civil servants was not simply a reflection of his "iron will"; it was more a measure of the confidence that existed between him and the services, for creating which he was largely responsible. His contribution to the political stability of India by canalising the loyalties of a band of outstanding and exceptional men in the task of national reconstruction is without parallel.

Those who rightly give credit to Nehru for India's stability should not forget the pivotal role of Sardar Patel in consolidating and strengthening the infant state. Far more important than the unification of the country by the absorption of the princely states was the manner in which he dealt with the law and order situation and consolidated the administrative structure by imparting a sense of security to the services.

EXPANSION OF ADMINISTRATIVE STRUCTURE

The result was that the political process developed initially within the rigidity of an administrative framework. The next stage of political development was conditioned by a similar framework of political authority. Shortly after the proclamation of the Republic, a largescale programme of social and economic change was launched. There followed an unprecedented expansion of the administrative structure. The result was a great dilution of standards of efficiency and integrity in administration. The fact that the whole programme was conceived within the traditional framework led to the persistence of an ethos not conducive to development effort. Even new types of administration that were set up—such as the machinery of planning, the Community Development Administration, or the new institutions of local government—came to be conditioned by the structure and ideology of the old set-up. Consequently, frustration with a large part of the process has set in. The old methods were employed in carrying out new tasks. The nature of the state was sought to be transformed within the confines of the old bureaucracy.

But the political process had also its own dynamics which conditioned the development of the administration. The interaction between politics and administration took place at two levels. There was first, the interaction between the ruling party and the bureaucracy. Alongside an administration which enjoyed virtual monopoly of power for so long, a new power now emerged: the politician. The conflict between the civil servant, hardened by experience and cynicism, and the politician full of ideas and impatient for power assumed many forms, not the least of which were opportunistic alliances between utterly incompatible elements. The other development took place within the party, in the relations between its organisational and government wings. The process was one-sided for a long time, the governmental wing providing leadership and patronage while the party machinery was used to sustain it in power. Slowly, however, with the waning of the popularity of the Congress governments and the growing power conflicts within the party, the trend has reversed: the government is under constant criticism and challenge from the organisational wing of the party which does not hesitate to take the conflict on to the floor of the legislature and to the council room of the cabinet. The strength of the ruling party is increasing not only vis-à-vis opposition groups but also vis-à-vis the administration. This political conditioning of the administrative process is at least as important as the administrative conditioning of political policies and programmes.

The Ministerial Hierarchy

The organisation of government has been conditioned by interplay of the two processes. In the process, the accepted principles of constitutional and administrative theory have been modified. The expansion of the functions of government has brought out the conflict between the principle of ministerial responsibility inherent in the constitution of parliamentary government and that of collective responsibility which developed as a convention of cabinet government. Collective responsibility, to be effective, necessitates a small and compact team of ministers. Ministerial responsibility, on the other hand, limits the size and number of administrative units under a single minister, thus increasing the total number of ministers. As a result, the ministry and the Cabinet could not obviously be the same. Distinctions set in and the hierarchical organisation of the bureaucracy was also projected into the ministerial structure.

The position was complicated by the fine and delicate sense of honour that led to much political semantics. Some ministers not included in the cabinet were, however, to be called ministers of cabinet rank and the substantive hierarchy of powers was overlaid by a formal equality of status. Considerations of prestige led to much confusion. A minister of cabinet rank could be provided with an appropriate designation if he could be in charge of specific functions grouped under specific departments (such as the minister of heavy industries). This was not always possible and that led to such designations as minister in the Ministry of External Affairs. More logical was the designation of ministers of state for all subordinate ministers. The conflict between logic and honour led to change from one designation to another four times in the 10 years between 1948 and 1957. The practice is still not uniform. The position was further complicated by the practice of having some ministers of state in charge of independent portfolios while others occupied a subordinate position under a cabinet minister.

Deputy ministers and (in certain cases) parliamentary secretaries occupy the lower tiers in the hierarchy. The category of deputy ministers was created with the specific purpose of giving experience to younger men and to train them for ministerial position. In practice, however, elderly politicians are accommodated as deputy ministers. Also accommodated in these positions are politically turbulent persons like members of the Congress "ginger group." All of this shows how personal and political influences interfere with considerations of administrative efficiency.

MULTIPLICATION OF PORTFOLIOS

The overlapping of functions of, for example, the deputy minister, the parliamentary secretary, and the permanent secretary; the consequent dilution of the line of responsibility; and the wide gulf between a ministerial council charged by the Constitution to be collectively responsible to parliament, but which never even meets as a group, and the actual cabinet which meets and decides issues often beyond the competence of those who attend such meetings—all these create a peculiar situation. Of course, the development of the cabinet secretariat and the system of memoranda bring some order to the situation but it falls far short of giving a cabinet government to the country.

The multiplication of portfolios during the last 14 years shows similar influences at work. Here the unfortunate impression is often created that these adjustments are made either to suit the convenience of ministerial changes or to widen the avenues of advancement of secretariat personnel.[9] Thus, on the death of Sardar Patel in December 1950 the portfolios of States and Home were separated even though by then the former had ceased to be an exacting undertaking. The Ministry of Food and Agriculture was bifurcated in October 1956 as it was felt that the importance of preventing food prices from rising necessitated that food administration be placed under a "whole-time secretary." The same minister held the two portfolios but the new arrangement could accommodate two permanent secretaries. In April 1957 the two ministries were once again united. The death of Maulana Azad led to a protracted conflict of personalities, resulting in separation of Scientific Research from Education, each being placed under a minister of state. As a result, such an important subject as education remains unrepresented in the cabinet. The same is the case with the Ministry of Law, which was downgraded in the ministerial hierarchy in 1957 and was placed under the charge of a minister of state; the personality of the law minister then was not strong enough to secure for him a seat in the Cabinet. The Health Ministry also suffered the same fate. On the other hand, the powerful personality of the Railway Minister prevented the integration of transport and communication in April 1957 from affecting the railways, which with other modes of transport should have logically been placed under one ministry. Planning, labour, and now the vice-chairmanship of the Planning Commission are in the charge of Shri Gulzarilal Nanda. They make a motley combination.

Case of Ministry of Production

The classic example of personal considerations frustrating efficient administrative development is provided by the short-lived Ministry of Production. Keeping in view the needs of planning, it was decided in June 1952 to set up two new ministries, one of production and another of irrigation and power. Powerful resistance to the former came from the Ministry of Commerce and Industry, which was in no mood to part with its control over the steel industry. The control over iron and steel was retained by it for the time being. The dilemma was ultimately resolved by a compromise: an altogether new Ministry of Iron and Steel was set up[10] to look after the steel plants, at first only those in the public sector, but with another reorganisation, those in both the private and public sectors. The new ministry, however, continued to be under the charge of the Minister of Commerce and Industry and not of the Ministry of Production; the power of the latter was greatly circumscribed.

This was not all. When Shri T. T. Krishnamachari left the Ministry of Commerce and Industry to become the finance minister in August 1956, he took the iron and steel portfolio with him. In fact, when he left the Ministry of Commerce and Industry, the latter was split into two separate ministries of (i) commerce and consumer industry and (ii) heavy industry.[11] Shri T. T. Krishnamachari had hitherto represented in the Cabinet the Ministry of Production and the Ministry of Iron and Steel apart from the Commerce and Industry Ministry. Now, when he became finance minister, he continued to represent Iron and Steel. One anomaly led to another: the home minister was asked to look after the interests of the Ministry of Heavy Industry in the Cabinet. Finance and Steel, Home and Heavy Industries—one cannot imagine more curious combinations. At last, in the 1957 reorganisation, the two ministries of Commerce and Consumer Industries and Heavy Industry were once again merged into a Ministry of Commerce and Industry. The Production Ministry, set up with so much fuss, was also finally wound up.[12]

Cabinet Committees

It is not suggested here that political considerations are irrelevant to the development of the machinery of government. Two points, however, emerge from the above analysis. One is that when political and personal considerations are carried too far they render the administration liable to such confusion and instability as to defeat their political objectives. Secondly—and this is the focus of our analysis—the substantive process that emerges deviates from the expected pattern to a very significant extent.

Deviation from more fundamental constitutional principles also can be seen in practice. Thus, the collective responsibility of a council of ministers that never meets has more the character of a coalition than a unified team, is divided into several layers of hierarchy, and allocates functions on a basis of drift and stop-gap arrangements, can neither be collective nor responsible. The cabinet committees seek to coordinate the functioning of the various ministries. It has been found in practice, however, that most of these committees share the top-heavy structure of the cabinet; in fact, they are more top-heavy than the cabinet. The prime minister is the chairman of nine out of ten standing committees, the home minister presiding over the tenth. In fact, the prime minister, the home minister, the finance minister, and one or two other ministers dominate the deliberations of these committees. "Appointments to these Committees have been made more on personal considerations than on the consideration of bringing only ministers concerned together in relevant committees."[13] The concentration of decision-making power in the "inner Cabinet" is also reflected in the working of the committees. In any case, it hardly makes for collective responsibility of the ministry as a whole. The result in practice is that the principle has been flouted on a number of occasions, though perhaps never seriously enough to jeopardise the Constitution. The emergence of the Planning Commission as a semi-political, semi-administrative arm of the governmental machinery, without really becoming an integral part of it, has also added to the general vagueness of the decision-making process. All this modifies the working of cabinet government considerably.

The principle of ministerial responsibility has also been subjected to considerable strain. The question will be taken up below in dealing with the relations between the minister and the civil servants. Suffice it to say here that the fact that a number of important aspects of the administration in the fields of planning, development, and social welfare remain unrepresented in parliament affects the working of the principle. The view that for every act of government some minister is answerable to parliament has not been fully accepted in this country. Also, the ministers feel that their responsibility is more to the prime minister or the chief minister than to the elected legislature. The general result is a ministry more of the presidential type where neither collective responsibility nor ministerial responsibility is constitutionally important. But the analogy should not be stretched too far. Actually, the structure conforms neither to the cabinet model (although its formal requirements are usually complied with) nor to the single executive model (although much of its practice can be discerned in actual working). It is a structure which is in some senses unique and without parallel in other democracies.

The Substantive Pattern

The substantive pattern that has emerged is made up of three layers of organisation. There are the bureaucratic departments which provide the structural framework within which the governmental machinery has expanded and functioned. They constitute an elaborate structure from the centre down to the district level. It has its own rules, procedures, jurisdictions, and lines of command. Overlaid on this structure is the development of an intricate network of planning and development administration. This is a newer type of organisation with its own jurisdictions and work techniques, independent authority and specified functions. The Planning Commission commands a huge staff organisation that provides leadership in research and evaluation, direction for action programmes, advice on specific policies, and acts as a clearing house of information on diverse issues. It shapes a large part of the government's programmes both at the Centre and in the States and, although acting in an advisory capacity, makes its weight felt. It has ensured in a manner which has no precedent in modern administrative systems that investigation and appraisal should go hand in hand with the implementation of programmes.[14] It has maintained a close contact with the Cabinet by having a common membership, the same secretary, joint deliberations, and continuous informal contacts. Indeed, the Planning Commission is more political than professional in its character. The prime minister is its chairman as he is the chairman of the National Development Council. The finance minister and two other cabinet ministers are its members. All the other official members of the commission enjoy the status of ministers of cabinet rank. Its members attend all meetings of the Economic Committee of the cabinet and meetings of the cabinet whenever economic questions come up for discussion. The recent appointment of the minister of planning as the vice-chairman of the commission has completed the process of identification. The commission is thus, in many ways, "a small edition of government itself."[15]

Planning Apparatus

It is not often realised in assessing the mammoth growth of the extra-constitutional apparatus of the Planning Commission and its auxiliaries that quite apart from carrying out their special purpose in the field of development, the latter have also performed a more general role in the country's administration. In the period after Independence the administration was in the danger of breaking up into so many parts, each jealous to preserve its local identity and to carve out their respective areas of influence. Against the background of virulent parochialism in the country as a whole, this would have spelled disaster. (Even today the danger is not wholly absent). The development of various planning authorities cutting across the existing pattern of administration both horizontally and vertically with the clear purpose of carrying out defined tasks has provided a unity of outlook and a sense of direction to the machinery of government as a whole. The Planning Commission, the National Development Council, the Committee on Plan Projects, the Research Programmes Committee, the Programme Evaluation Organisation, even the Statistical Institute, the Panel of Economists, and the various institutes of public administration—these and other institutions have succeeded to a marked degree in instilling a sense of common purpose. There is, of course, the danger of too much uniformity and conformism in such a system. This must be guarded against. But the primary need in this country is to develop a common consciousness among the people, transcending their diverse identities without completely destroying them. And this is being done in some measure by the new administrative pattern that is emerging in this country. At a time when the governmental structure is suffering from divisive tendencies, the administration imparts some unity and continuity to the political process.

The other important element making for such unity of effort is the political party which is the third "layer" of the substantive pattern. Enveloping the administrative and developmental structures is the large network of the Congress Party, stretching in depth as well as breadth, and touching all levels of governmental organisation. Its personnel man most of the district development boards, provide information to government officials and actively collaborate (at times in spite of the resistance of entrenched officialdom) in solving local problems. It is especially effective in spreading "plan consciousness" among the people. There is also an attempt at evolving a machinery of consultation and communication at the *pradesh* and district levels in various States, while coordination of effort between the Congress Party and the community development blocks and extension services is even more marked. Very often non-official but nonetheless officially sustained organisations like the Bharat Sevak Samaj serve as useful links in such collaboration. Other and more informal methods are also employed. The techniques of collaboration between the party and the government are wide and varied. The result is immensely useful in the present phase of political development. Of course, much tension is generated in the process and personal rivalries and opportunism often get more than their due spill. There is also the danger of the administration virtually becoming an arm of the ruling party. The overall effect, nevertheless, is to provide a type of organisation and leadership which would not have been otherwise available.

Force of Tradition

The pattern that emerges is largely the creation of the last decade or so in which the same men have provided the leadership of the various key organisations and served as links between them. On the other hand, it is a pattern that has evolved within the framework of the old bureaucracy. And it is this that has created a number of problems. The exercise of power resides with the traditional departments and collectorates; only lately inroads are being made into their power, largely without success. The results are disappointing. When it comes to the actual execution of plans and programmes, inertia and vested interests together frustrate the attempts. A remarkable feature of administration is the wide gap in enthusiasm and initiative between its higher and lower levels. The lower down you go, the farther you feel you are removed from the vitality you found at the top. The administration thus provides a classic case of "apoplexy at the centre and anaemia at the circumference." The result is waste and frustration. Targets remain unfulfilled, policies remain on paper, consultations (for example, between the block development officers and the district authorities) are rendered fruitless by mutual jealousy, statistics are unreliable, and administrative waste and corruption rampant. Red tape becomes a technique of self-preservation and reverence for traditional forms is matched only by attachment to strict routine and an unwholesome preoccupation with questions of accountability. Concentration of decision-making powers and reluctance to grant discretionary authority to the men on the spot reflect the same mentality. The conservatism of habit and thought and suspicion of experiments disparage the whole process of change and distort it.

All Staff, No Line

The fact that much of the administrative structure of the Planning Commission and even the Central Government is all "staff" and little, if any, "line" adds to the problem. There is no way of ensuring that the implementation of policies in the districts advances the goals laid down. There is no way of checking on the progress reports, the statistics, and other information supplied from below. The findings based on such data tend to be unreliable and lead to faulty policy conclusions. More important is the fact that lack of experience in a "line" organisation lends unreality to the process of deliberation and policy-making: the important maxim of modern public administration that it is ultimately the executors who should make policy is neglected. Similarly, while the insistence on investigation as a preliminary to policy-making[16] is laudable in itself, lack of communication in administration leads to the fruits of research being accumulated without making their impact on action programmes; the two proceed apace, unrelated and uncoordinated. The result is that a large part of the directives and advice received from above appear like so many sermons which have little relevance to the actual problems of administration and are generally scoffed at by the "realists" in the field. The process is aggravated by the fact that the party men at the bottom do not share the zeal and idealism of their counterparts in the middle and upper ranks and often conspire with the administrators to share the spoils and consolidate their political control over the locality.

Concentration of Power

Lack of flexibility and creative enthusiasm, a chronic preoccupation with rules and precedents, and low morale at the lower levels of administration have been noted by many observers.[17] Much of the rigidity springs from concentration of authority at the top and from an "inherited disinclination to delegate, to consider administration as literal execution of orders and to think of decision-making as issuing orders, to confine subordinates by too many and too precise rules, and to limit both inter-organisational and public communication to a few as empowered to 'commit government.'"[18] Even the emphasis on "coordination" is often wrongly placed: attempts at coordination take place even before action has started, the smallest case is "referred," there are successive verifications and re-verifications, and inquiries, commentaries and reports constantly pile up, the net result being delay, inaction, lack of initiative, and dilution of responsibility. Even the *esprit de corps* is confined to one's own unit of work, thus giving rise to not one but several bureaucracies. Lack of an efficient communication system between different levels of authority results directly from an insufficient "line" organisation. The coordination that occurs is largely one that takes place in the higher regions of government. It is coordination "between peers and between different hierarchies, not within unified hierarchies."[19] In fact, the structural inadequacies of the machinery of government in India derive not from too much hierarchy as is often alleged, but from an *irregular* hierarchy, a hierarchy that is not well filled-in, that is not truly pyramidal. Coupled with the tendency to concentrate authority at the top, this leads to lack of flexibility, impedes communication, and encourages isolated behaviour among bureaucrats who are neither sure of their own abilities nor of the confidence of their superiors.

Ministers and Civil Servants

Ministers also tend to concentrate decision-making power in themselves and to interfere unduly with the administrative process. A reaction seems to have set in to the earlier practice when most of the substantive decisions were taken by the civil servants. The results are sometimes unhappy.[20] In their zeal to exercise initiative and take their own decisions, ministers often adopt questionable methods. They tend to rely too much on reports from outside, especially from party men. Although popular opinion often sets a corrective to departmental orthodoxy, the former is not always correctly represented by the minister's informants. The tendency among ministers to take particular decisions instead of confining to general policy leads to irresponsibility and evasion lower down in the hierarchy.[21] When we remember that ministers also shift responsibility to their subordinates by declaring to have acted "on the best available advice," the extent to which confusion can spread in the administrative process can be imagined. Weak in their grasp of governmental processes, the ministers rely far too much on civil servants. Cashing in on the principle of anonymity of the civil servant, they naturally get the credit for the department's performance. This is as it should be. When subjected to criticism, however, the ministers are equally quick to shift responsibility to the civil servant.

On the other hand, the "favourites" among the civil servants are almost full-fledged politicians, often neglecting their official duties. The odium of the whole arrangement is experienced by those who feel left out of the network of patronage. Ministers wield considerable patronage and influence in the administration. There is a growing number of posts to which direct recruitment is made. Even in recruitment to the regular posts, the Public Service Commission's authority has sometimes been limited by withdrawing some categories of appointments from their competence by invoking Article 320 (3) of the Constitution. All this makes for significant departures in practice from the accepted relationship between the political and administrative parts of the machinery of government.

Where the political party and the bureaucracy form the twin pillars of government, the interlinking of political and administrative processes becomes inevitable. The development of healthy practices would depend here on the quality of political and administrative leadership. It would also depend on the extent to which the leadership can build up and rationalise a hierarchy and delegate power to it and thus vitalise administration all the way down and provide it with a unified outlook and a sense of oneness. The efficiency and ability of an administrative system can ultimately be judged by the extent to which it furthers the political objectives it is designed to serve. In India, the public's attitude to bureaucracy is very often prejudiced. Experience with an alien regime has left in the popular mind an unhappy image of the administrator. Bureaucracy appears to be antithetical to democracy, and the picture of an officialdom fighting to enslave the people has not died.

Public's Antipathy for Bureaucracy

But the public antipathy for the bureaucracy cannot be entirely explained away as a hangover of the past. The rigidity of the administrative structure noted above results in a rigidity in the approach to the public. The preoccupation with rules and precedents leads to an undue insistence on forms and procedures that do not fail to annoy; the insistence on formal correctness leads to excessive red tape; the concentration of discretion at the top leads to a shirking of responsibility, leaving the citizen in doubt about whom to approach to get his work done; above all, the bureaucratic norms of impersonal treatment, supplemented by a tendency to "categorise" persons into "cases," results in much irritation at the point of contact with the public. The impression of officialdom as arrogant, indifferent, and inhuman leaves a deep mark and opens up a wide chasm between the administration and the general public.

In a sense, what is clear from the above analysis is that an authoritarian structure of administration cannot go hand in hand with a democratic polity; the former defeats the latter. Concentration of decision-making powers is as bad for administrative efficiency as it is for political organisation. Similarly, a static and rigid model of administration ill serves a dynamic society that must find new flexible avenues of effecting change. Above all, a system that has not devised the principal need of modern administration, namely, an efficient system of communication with the general public, fails to provide the psychological context from which the mechanics of political democracy finds its chief sustenance.

Putting Administration in Its Place

Unless we cut the administration down to its proper size and assign to it its due place in the scheme of democratic government, we would slip imperceptibly into an "administrative state." Efficiency in administration is not always the first objective in a democracy; indeed, an inefficient bureaucracy may provide opportunities for the exercise of capacities which a highly efficient system would have streamlined into standardised behaviour. What is more important is flexibility, scope for initiative for all, and the readiness to submit traditional forms to scrutiny and change them when they are found unsuited. Democracy survives only in an atmosphere of open dealings and incessant questioning of forms and beliefs.

The machinery of government in India displays two marked characteristics. There is, in the first place, a subtle and intricate interplay of politics and administration at all levels, giving rise to complex forms and multiple structures. Second, there is a very wide gulf in the quality, vigour, and outlook, of the elite and the laity in each of these structures. While the cross-conditioning of the political party and administrative bureaucracy has modified the accepted relationship between the two, the development was both inevitable and desirable and can, properly directed, lead to the growth of healthy and sound conventions in the long run. Much would depend, however, on the extent to which the process of nullification, distortion of policies at the point of implementation, is arrested. It is suggested here that this would depend on three factors: flexibility and dispersal of the power to use discretion, the filling-in of the administrative hierarchy by rationalising its "line," and the building up of an active system of communication both within the administration and between the administration and the general public. These are no obiter dicta. They follow logically from the analysis of the substantive process of government.

Notes and References

[1] W. F. Willoughby, *Principles of Legislative Organisation and Administration* (Washington, DC: The Brookings Institution, 1934).

[2] For the classic expression of such a view, see Frank Goodnow, *Politics and Administration* (New York: Macmillan, 1900), p. 9.

[3] The first systematic steps towards such rejection were taken by Fritz Morstein Marx (ed.), *Elements of Public Administration*; Paul Appleby, *Policy and Administration* (Alabama: University of Alabama Press, 1949).

[4] This is shown very well in the monumental study of Philip Selznick, *TVA and the Grass Roots: A Study of Politics and Organisation*. See, however, Herbert Simon, *Administrative Behaviour*, where the dichotomy between value and policy continues to be maintained.

[5] Dwight Waldo, *The Administrative State* (New York: Ronald Press, 1948).

[6] A. D. Gorwala, *Report on Public Administration* (Delhi: Government of India, 1960). See also M. Venkatarangaiya, "The Pattern of Public Administration in the Five-Year Plan," *Indian Journal of Political Science* 14, no. 3 (July 1953), pp. 210–29.

[7] Asoka Chanda, *Indian Administration* (London: George Allen and Unwin, 1958), pp. 61, 78.

[8] N. Gopalaswami Ayyangar, *Report on Reorganisation of the Machinery of Government*, pp. 20–22.

[9] Chanda, *Indian Administration*, p. 82.

[10] The Indian Institute of Public Administration, *The Organisation of the Government of India*, p. 119.

[11] Ibid., p. 95.

[12] For further details on the development of portfolios, see Shriram Maheshwari, "Evolution of Portfolios in the Central Government since Independence," *The Modern Review* 108 (December 1960).

[13] Chanda, *Indian Administration*, p. 91.

[14] Merrill R. Poodall, "Organisation of Administrative Leadership in the Five Year Plans," in *Leadership and Political Institutions in India*, ed. Richard Park and Irene Tinker (Princeton: Princeton University Press, 1959), pp. 318, 328.

[15] Paul Appleby, *Re-examination of Administrative System: Report of a Survey* (Government of India, 1956).

[16] For an early and forceful expression of the principle, see *Report of the (Haldone) Committee on the Machinery of Government* (Government of Great Britain, 1918).

[17] Paul Appleby, *Public Administration in India: Report of a Survey* (New Delhi: Government of India, 1953). See also Appleby's article "Morale at Subordinate Levels," *Indian Journal of Public Administration* 111, no. 2.

[18] Paul Appleby, "History and Precedent Versus Reform," *Indian Journal of Public Administration* 1, no. 4 (1 October 1955), pp. 304–5.

[19] Appleby, *Public Administration in India*, p. 11.

[20] On the whole question of the relations between ministers and civil servants in India, see Gorwala, *Report on Public Administration*. See also R. Duarkadas, *Role of the Higher Civil Service in India* (Bombay: Popular Book Depot, 1958).

[21] Paul Appleby, "Concerning Ministers," *Indian Journal of Public Administration* 1, no. 2 (1 April 1955), p. 90.

39

Generalists versus Specialists in Indian Administration—I*

Asoke Mohan Roy

In order to understand the issues in the debate on generalists versus specialists in the Indian administrative system one has to be clear about the definition of the terms. A generalist is one who has knowledge of the technique of the processes involved in a factory or a technical undertaking or in administration, but he is not an expert. A specialist or an expert is a man whose special training makes him an authority in a particular field. Whereas the concern of the expert is with the "particular," the distinguishing feature of an administrator is the element of "generality." The expert is a specialist in knowledge and in action; the administrator must be a generalist in knowledge and in action.

The problems of defining the respective roles of the specialist and the generalist in an administrative system become acute at or near the top of the hierarchy, deepen as the functions of government expand, and become crucial in a government committed to direct participation in securing rapid economic growth.

The Two Models

The British administrative class and the ICS have truly embodied the principle of the generalist in governmental administration. The instrument of a laissez-faire government at home and a colonial administration in the Empire, the administrative generalist was both a product of and suited to the objectives of a law and order, revenue-collecting government. By education, training, and experience he was deliberately made non-specialised. His functions were to limit the role of government, to promote stability by minimising change, to

* Originally published in *Economic Weekly* 16, no. 26 (13 June 1964), pp. 1059–64.

coordinate the activities of government. His major administrative tasks were the "rules" and the "files."

The use of the specialist in government finds its most vigorous expression in the American Civil Service. The skills needed to administer a vast continent, to develop its natural resources, and to promote social and economic growth were specialised skills. The staff of governmental agencies were accordingly recruited as specialists, each group highly committed to the importance and relevance of specialisation. These agencies were led by specialist administrators. No class of generalist administrators was interposed between the specialist and the "political" executives and the legislators who supervised them. Coordination was achieved by statute, by budgets, by Presidential supervision and by Congressional vigilance; in essence, coordination by "rules and files" was subordinated as a goal to the preferred objectives of experiment, competition among specialists, and innovation in policy and procedure.

The preceding observations are brief and oversimplified. Each of these systems, of course, makes some efforts to accommodate the rival claims of the generalist and the specialist. The specialists in the British system have made some notable recent gains in science agencies, in public enterprise agencies, in the welfare agencies. In the US the generalists struggle for greater recognition and have gained a little. A generalist service recruited by competitive examination and known as the Junior Management Service has been created. All other administrators are recruited departmentally. The recommendation of the Hoover Commission for the creation of a small senior civil service cadre has not been accepted. "But the fundamental contrast remains; in Britain the generalist administrator is on top, the specialist is on tap to the generalist, while in the US the specialist is on top while the generalist is on his tap."[1]

The suitability of each of these models in the context of the Indian administrative system will be discussed in this paper. Before that we will analyse the developments which have led to the debate on the specialist versus the generalist in administration in advanced countries and in the developing economy of India.

Changed Character of the State

The bureaucracies of the twentieth century differ from those of the eighteenth and nineteenth centuries largely because the character of the state and of government problems has changed. Large-scale industry, division of labour, the headlong pace of development of applied science, the concentration of economic power, and the increasing recognition of the responsibility of the state towards the underprivileged have all contributed to determine the character of the modern administrative system. The above developments have led to a conflict between "line" and "staff," especially technical staff agencies.

The traditional concept of staff is aid to the executive. This is to be done without disturbing the formal command relationships in hierarchy. Increasing specialisation in the organisation and growing pressure on the top executive have complicated this initially simple concept greatly. Secondly, the watertight division between staff and line looks unreal. Authority is now believed to be more a matter of influence than of command. The staff, like the specialists, now exercise authority, control, and command over the line authorities like the generalists. Staff agencies like planning, personnel, budget and finance, organisation and methods, etc., wield coercive power over the line agencies. The staff work is performed by persons of high intellectual attainments and specialised training. The fact that they are near the chief executive invests their work with extraordinary importance.

Indian Context

The generalist versus specialist debate in the Indian administrative system has assumed much importance since the launching of planning. India has combined planning for a socialist economy with democracy. She has launched an ambitious programme of industrial development to diversify the economy. Side by side there are the objectives of reducing inequalities in income and promoting the welfare of the greatest number of the population. In fact, India is a welfare state with a socialist pattern of society as its basic objective. This means the expansion of state activities to realise these objectives. Due to the extension of the functions of the state and change in the conception of the state the specialists as staff agencies are not content with their advisory functions. They do not like to be placed in line hierarchy. They interfere in the work of line authority.

It is against this background that one has to consider the arguments advanced in favour of the specialist and the generalist in India.

It is argued that administration in the context of a developing economy should place less reliance on procedures, rules, and regulations and more on speedy work based on expert knowledge in various fields of development. A dynamic situation created by the need for speedy, multi-sided development of a country, it is said, requires a change in the principles and methods of administration in such a way that the natural allies of the development process, namely technology and science, get their due. This, it is remarked, is not possible so long as those who head the administrative machine are themselves semi-literates in so far as knowledge of science, technology, economics, etc., is concerned. It has been contended that in the present era of rapidly advancing technology, a non-technical civil servant is generally incapable of informed judgement on technical matters. It is said that there is no person more dangerous than a layman with pet ideas. In fact, in the modern world the administration of engineering enterprises can only be done by technical generalists.

This point has been supported by Dr. K. L. Rao. He has analysed the administrative working of DVC and pointed out that non-technical administrative men were put at the head of this project. The DVC had no chief engineer for years. Foreign consultants were imported to advise the non-technical administrators at the top. Work was done at a higher cost than if indigenous sources had been tapped. According to Dr Rao, the most important lesson one could draw from the DVC venture is that for engineering projects it is most essential to start the work under technical control. To avoid faulty implementation in the plan it is necessary for fully qualified technical personnel to be entrusted with erecting the engineering works. In most of the projects, materials account for 60–70 per cent of the total cost and labour for about 10–15 per cent. A saving on materials by proper selection will lead to a large saving and this obviously can be done by an engineer. It is only the technical men placed at the top who can assume responsibility with authority.

Too Many Non-Experts

It is contended next that with persons drawn from generalised service as heads of departments concerned with development, planned development suffers. It is the view of Prof. V. K. N. Menon[2] that a generalist head of department is likely to view things from the point of view of generalist administration of the Secretariat rather than the technical work of the department. In the context of a welfare state, a generalist as head of department is undesirable. This system results in a non-expert minister assisted usually by a non-expert secretary to whom a non-expert head of department is adviser. There is thus a solid non-expert top and many technical people feel that it is a hopeless situation. Senior engineers have to waste a good deal of their time in educating civil servants in the intricacies of the department's work and in writing minutes on simple technical matters, on which they could easily have given final orders if they had the authority. Another anomaly is that the responsibility for efficient performance of the department rests entirely on the head of the department. Its progress depends entirely on his initiative, whereas a Secretary who has the power to overrule him bears no responsibility for giving effect to technical or departmental proposals. Hence there is the pattern where there is authority without responsibility and responsibility without authority. Moreover, the present system involves frequent transfer of officers from one department to another. These transfers lead to a confusion in the department and continuity is lost. One takes time to become proficient in his departmental matters. Before one has learnt his job, he is transferred.

Less Bureaucratic

In a developing economy specialists such as doctors, engineers, physicists and economists should be right at the top in the line authority rather than thrown somewhere in a staff-cell attached to the generalist line authority. As an incidental advantage of adopting this system, it is claimed that government would become less bureaucratic, more programme-oriented, and committed and better suited to create an environment of respect for science and knowledge in the community.

It is also advocated that experts understand each other better because they speak in a common language and know each other's difficulties sufficiently well to appreciate and understand each other's problems. The generalist administrator usually does not develop a sustained interest in any particular field of activity. Even in exceptional cases when he does develop such an interest, this becomes infructuous because by the time he has learnt the job he is transferred to some other job.

Another line of thinking is that there should be differentiation and specialisation in different types of administrative work. It is argued by H. K. Paranjape[3] that in the face of the changed character of a considerable proportion of government operation, it is essential to break up the generalist administrative cadres into more and more specialised ones.

The crux of the whole argument in favour of the specialist in the Indian administrative system, especially at the top level, is that the management and the administration should be well-trained in the know-how of the enterprises that they manage. The emphasis should shift from mere theoretical, bureaucratical control to a self-contained knowledgeable set-up. This would impact scientific and practical orientation to the formulation of plans and their implementation.

The generalist admits that the requirements of administration in a planned developing economy are different from those in a laissez-faire economy. He accepts the thesis of the specialist that science and technology are the allies of progress and routine, and that precedent and rigid adherence to hierarchical formalities inhibit progress. He confesses that answers to all the complexities have not been found. But he argues that these are problems of long-term adjustment and not of mere orderly transition. His view may be summarised as follows.

Enforcing the General Point of View

(1) Administration is politics in action. It cannot, therefore, be divorced from the political process. According to Paul H. Appleby,[4] "government is the primary, indispensable institution capable of maintaining an advancing state of balance in a condition of advancing complexity. It is charged with the extraordinary function of making general sense out of a dynamic

proliferation of special occupations and preoccupations." The very quality of administration is derived from the fact that as the divergent points of view get coordinated, filtered, and ultimately crystallised into decisions, compromises are affected all along the line in such a manner that an overall general view emerges in the shape of policy. No matter how specialised in training and interests a civil servant administrator may have been initially, each promotion upward constitutes a vesting in him of successively larger responsibility for enforcing the general point of view of his minister and his government. If the thesis of the specialist were accepted, decisions should be weighed in favour of specialisation in such a way that while the specialist view would, of course, get the place of prominence, the entire nature of administrative decision, being ultimately a generalist one, would undergo an undesirable change. As Appleby has argued "as one's knowledge increases in a specialised way, by study or situation and assignment, one's general ignorance increases disproportionately. The price of specialisation of every kind is parochialism."[5]

(2) Top management job requires a general understanding. It requires a view of the whole. It demands tested ability for independent command and the willingness to assume the responsibility for a decision. It asks for detachment, patience, and the ability to take a long view. This function can be discharged adequately by a generalist administrator.

(3) The more the specialists get involved in administration, the less they will be able to develop in their own fields of specialisation. Two results would follow from this.
   (a) they will lose touch with their subjects and therefore suffer loss of their special utility to government; and,
   (b) their other colleagues, who are less fortunate in terms of opportunity and authority but have more time to devote to their subjects, will lose respect for the knowledge of their specialist bosses.

(4) Government through specialists may be a luxury for highly developed countries but in the initial stage of development of nascent democracies like ours where articulating the feelings and desires of a vast mass of illiterate people is of vital importance, it may even be dangerous to place specialists at the level of secretaries.

NARROW APPROACH

(5) A general mind is far more important today when the entire character of the state is undergoing radical and revolutionary change. In such a context a specialised mind and a narrow approach are a hindrance rather than a help. A person who knows much in a small field cannot have the vision and

foresight which is required for the administration of a modern state. In the words of N. V. Gadgil, "We should have the general mind in preference to a specialised mind. What really is needed is not the knowledge in a detailed way but the right approach, the right perspective with which the man analyses the problem."[6]

(6) The chief function of the administration is generalisation. The more the specialisation, the more the need for generalisation to put technical knowledge in a form and in a manner which would facilitate the formulation of policies. Appleby argues that with "the increase in technical character of government activities, the need for generalist personnel who can sensibly relate different aspects of matters will increase both in importance and in numbers at geometric ratio."[7] A generalist at the top becomes a specialist in generalisation.

(7) Many of the grievances of the specialist are in the nature of charges against the generalist. It is bad if specialists are arrogantly treated or insufficiently respected by the generalist. Perhaps some civil servants may be guilty of this. The hangover from the past is partly responsible for this. The remedy, however, is not necessarily that the specialist should replace the generalist. A system of cooperative working and right of directly approaching the minister in case of disagreement, perhaps may provide better answers.

Difficulty in Communication

(8) Most specialists usually employ an esoteric language to convey their ideas. In administration it leads to difficulty in communication between the eminently non-expert minister and the highly specialised expert secretaries. This difficulty is not limited only to minister–secretary relationship but becomes worse in interdepartmental communication. In this connection the extreme example given by Appleby of the Manhattan Project, where an English professor was brought in as interpreter among various specialists, is relevant. A lot of capacity for expression in elegant and diplomatic language is required to get the departmental point of view accepted. It is doubtful whether in this game, the specialist, by virtue of his knowledge will be able to measure up to the task.

(9) No generalist is a downright generalist in the sense that he knows nothing of anything else. In fact, the advantage of a generalist is that as he goes to the top be brings to bear on the job an intelligent awareness of a vast variety of knowledge with capacity to articulate in meaningful overall terms.

(10) Today if specialists are not at the top in many cases, they are not necessarily at the tap. They are in fact found at all levels from the top to the tap according as they are needed. With the change in the nature of the functions of the

government, there has been evidence in India of a growing diversification in the composition of the public services by the employment of more and more specialists, technicians, and experts. The Report of the Second Central Pay Commission (1960) reveals that one-third of the total number of the employees in 1957 were specialists.

(11) It is said that generalists are prisoners of rules, regulations, and precedents and there is too much stress on continuity, caution, and red tape. There is no doubt some truth in this statement. But there is no proof that when specialists are at the top they do not suffer equally or even more from the same maladies.

We shall now attempt to analyse the impact of this debate in three spheres of the Indian administrative system—at the district level, the secretariat level, and in the public enterprises.

NOTES AND REFERENCES

[1] Wallace S. Sayre, "Some Problems of Public Administration in a Developing Economy," *Indian Journal of Public Administration* 8, no. 2 (April–June 1962), pp. 137–52.

[2] V. K. N. Menon, *Planning in India* (Indian Institute of Public Administration, August 1959).

[3] Report of First Annual Conference on Recruitment and Training for Public Services held in the Indian Institute of Public Administration, New Delhi, on 6–7 April 1957, p. 15.

[4] Paul H. Appleby, *Public Administration for a Welfare State* (New Delhi: Asia Publishing House, 1961), p. 50.

[5] Ibid., p. 49.

[6] N. V. Gadgil, "The New Administrator," *Indian Journal of Public Administration* 5, no. 1 (January–March 1959), pp. 48–55.

[7] Paul H. Appleby, "Meeting Future Personnel Needs," *Indian Journal of Public Administration* 2, no. 1 (January–March 1956), pp. 7–11.

40

Generalists versus Specialists in Indian Administration—II*

Asoke Mohan Roy

The district as a vital unit of administration has been one of the fundamental aspects of our administrative system and the district magistrate and collector has always been a key government functionary. The district officer is a generalist administrator; this position should be continued. By virtue of his influence as magistrate and collector, the district officer is best equipped to enlist the active support of the people in the successful implementation of any major programme of development. He can effectively coordinate the development and welfare activities of different departments. The state governments have, therefore, decided that all development and welfare duties should be entrusted to the district officer.

Role of Coordinator

The Grow More Food Enquiry Committee stated that development activities should be united under the collector as extension officer, assisted by the specialist officers. The First and the Second Plans envisaged the position of the collector as the head of the district: with the district officers of the development departments working with him as a team. The Third Plan charges the district officer with the responsibility of ensuring coordination at the district level between the Zila Parishad and the technical officers in different fields. In the context of the Community Development and National Extension Service Programme, the collector is invested with powers of coordination and supervision over the district heads of technical departments, besides being made entirely responsible for the execution of development plans in the district.

* Originally published in *Economic Weekly* 16, no. 27 (4 July 1964), pp. 1095–98.

According to S. P. Bapat[1] this role of the district officer as generalist administrator and coordinator fulfills the need of coordination to prevent conflicts, competition, duplication, and waste and differences in approach and treatment. This point has also been forcefully urged in the report of the Bengal Administration Enquiry Committee (1944–45):

> We are satisfied that the time has come in Bengal, and we do not doubt in other provinces as well, to coordinate all the district development activities under a single administrative head. When the objective in geographical area like a district is the welfare of his people, separate activities are merely means to a single end and each cannot be considered in isolation from the rest. Moreover, specialisation is itself a disruptive force.

METHOD OF CONTROL

The district officer's control over development and welfare activities in the district takes the following pattern: While the organisational and professional or technical control over development officers of district rank is that of the departmental superiors, the functional control in non-technical matters is exercised, within certain limits, by the district officer.[2]

This method of control is based on the theory of dual hierarchy which has been credited with being "the best method of solving the problem of coordination." It rests on a dichotomy between the specialist and the generalist and assumes a dual line of supervision and control from the top down and a dual set of loyalties from the bottom up. "The crux of the problem," according to Dimock and Dimock, "is that certain officers must be administratively responsible to one superior, and technically responsible to another."[3] The District Officer embodies the principle of organisation by area and the principle of general administration. The role of the district officer as coordinator and area administrator is very crucial in the system of integrated field administration.

Chapman has justified this type of field structure on two grounds: firstly,

> unless there is a single state authority on the spot with a general responsibility and recognised superiority over other state officials ... cooperation must either consist in informal arrangements between the local heads of services or be imposed by decisions taken at the centre by the ministries. The second justification is that decisions and activities can be controlled locally and not by remote control by central officials unaware of local circumstances and sentiments.[4]

The need for this dual supervision arises out of the peculiar circumstances of the district which requires the district officer to be a generalist. A. W. MacMahon has given a few illustrations to substantiate this point:

> If a bridge is being considered, the design and estimates of cost as well as the preferred location are technical decisions, but it is properly an administrative judgment to take account of public protest about the inconvenience of the proposed location and to approve a different though practicable site even at an increased cost ... The award of loans is technical but the question of leniency if they are not repaid involves factors that call for an administrative decision. In a different sense, it is an administrative question, to be decided in the light of the total situation, whether a particular employee should be allowed to take leave at a particular time in accordance with the routines of his department. In such a situation it is the general administrator's duty to protect a programme in which a number of agencies and individuals are involved.[5]

Advantage of the Generalist

In the execution of development schemes something more is required than the specific expertise of the canal engineer, the agriculture scientist, the animal husbandry expert, or the engineer concerned with roadbuilding. The district officer's task consists of coordination and unified execution, for he alone among all the development officers has the opportunity to see the process and effect of development in its totality, which the unifunctional preoccupation and responsibility of the different experts prevents them from doing.

It appears, therefore, that the generalist administrator at the district level is best suited to the task of coordinating and supervising development and welfare activities. What is necessary is some sort of reorientation of policy regarding education and training of civil servants. What is important is not merely some general pre-entry knowledge about the structure of working of the economic system, but also systematic and adequate post-entry and mid-career training. Post-entry and mid-career training are particularly important for promoting in the administrator the capacity to integrate diverse specialised knowledge.

The above observations equally apply in the case of the block development officer, who is conceived of essentially as a generalist administrator at the block level. His functions are those of a generalist administrator and, in the context of panchayati raj, it will be useful if the BDO remains as a generalist. The BDO has to perform the functions of a coordinating authority at the block level, to take overall responsibility for formulation of an integrated working plan for the block, and to guide and supervise the work of other functionaries in the block. The Third Plan has also emphasised this role of the BDO in the administrative set-up at the block level (pp. 339–40) in the following words:

> The manner in which the block extension team, comprising the BDO and extension officers in different fields of development functions, is of the highest importance for the success of panchayati raj. To assist the Panchayat Samiti effectively, these officials

> must continue to function as a team, the BDO providing the necessary coordination and leadership and extension officers in different fields participating actively in formulating programmes and schemes for the consideration of the panchayat samiti and its standing committees, executing them impartially in accordance with the rules and ensuring that the supplies and services needed are organised efficiently.

At the Secretariat Level

Both at the centre and in the states the general practice is to have a secretary of the ICS or the IAS cadre, drawn from the general line. The secretary looks at the matters from the point of view of the government as a whole.

The adoption of a federal constitution in India, coupled with the present centralisation of planning, has made it imperative that the Central Government should have the benefit of a pool of diverse, practical experience of field administration brought to it by the "deputationists" from the states, so that it can be closely advised as to the manner in which its development policies influence the lives of the people it serves. On the political plane the task of advising the ministers is performed by party organisations and elected legislators and parliamentarians; on the administrative plane, the function is discharged by the permanent civil servant who, besides being detached and objective, has the advantage of bringing to the counsels of policy making diverse field experience continually refreshed and renewed.

Conflicting Views

The experts argue, on the other hand, that the development of science in such fields as transport and communications, electronics, and power, as well as in the field of social and economic engineering has contributed to the growth of the tribe of specialist public servants. Experts and their supporters deny that the intensive preoccupation of an expert with a narrow field of activity comes in the way of sound administrative judgment. They criticise the practice of channelling expert advice to the political executive through the lay generalist. They complain of interference by general administration in the internal working of specialist departments.

The Second Pay Commission (1957–59) has also considered this question and its recommendations are well worth considering:

> Where the work of a department at the headquarters of the Government of India is mainly technical, it is desirable, in our view, that the Secretary should be a person who, while possessing administrative ability and capable of taking a broad government-wide view of matters, has a technical background in the particular field. In a department which has a considerable amount of technical as well as administrative work, the Secretary may be either a technical officer with proved

> administrative capacity or a generalist administrator. Technical officers should not be excluded from the field of choice, on a priori considerations but should be considered on merits. Further, the top technical advisers or heads of departments should have full opportunity to have their views considered by the Minister, along with any views which the Secretary of the Department may have; for which a suitable arrangement may be a joint discussion with the Minister, whenever there is unresolved difference of opinion between the technical head and the Secretary. The basic idea governing the relationship must be in the recognition that the former should have an effective share in the framing of policies and programmes at the highest official levels.[6]

In this context the recommendation of V. T. Krishnamachari[7] to put the technical men at the top of the agricultural and animal husbandry services may be given due consideration in view of the importance of agriculture and allied activities in the Third Plan.

In spite of sympathetic considerations of the views of experts by the Second Pay Commission and V. T. Krishnamachari in the sphere of policy formulation, the consensus in India is in favour of the general administrator. A. K. Chanda[8] has pointed out that in the higher levels of departmental organisation, general administrative experience, a wider outlook, and a common-sense approach are more important than specialised knowledge. It is argued that a general administrator is more appreciative of social necessity. He specialises in coordination. One important judgment which he has to make is whether the proposed programme is such as can be easily put into action for the benefit of society.

Public Enterprises

The debate centres on whether a generalist or a specialist should be at the head of public enterprises. There is one school of thought which is of the view that technical personnel cannot make good administrators or managers. The other school holds that except at the level of the man at the machine or bench, a technologist has to carry out managerial tasks side by side with technological ones and the higher the position that he occupies even in his own technical line of work, the larger would be the managerial element in his total work. To decide in advance that a technologist is incapable of occupying positions requiring general management ability is unfair both to the persons concerned and to the organisation which is employing them. The organisation is deprived of one important source from which it could draw persons with a potential ability to manage it at the highest levels. The individual also should not, in fairness to him, be deprived of the possibility of reaching the highest positions. Using a technically qualified man for general management work which can be carried out by a person without such qualifications is no doubt wasteful in a country where there is such shortage of technical personnel. Hence the suggestion of this school is that those who like only technical work and those who are only suited for such work should not occupy managerial positions. But those who are considered suitable for higher management positions and who would like to take up such work should not be denied that opportunity.

No satisfactory answer has been so far found to the question of the proper relationship between the generalist and the specialist in public enterprises. Although the general trend has been to have a generalist as a manager, the claim of the specialist should not be totally ignored, especially in engineering or technical enterprises.

CONCLUSION

In underdeveloped countries like India the progress towards specialisation must be gradual and adjusted to the rate of economic and cultural development. Reorientation and training of civil servants to enable them to adjust themselves to the new task of coordinating and integrating the innumerable administrative activities connected with development has already started, and it will grow as development gains momentum. In a developing economy the technicians and the generalist administrators have a complementary role. As development proceeds and specialisation advances, the service structure will adjust itself and become differentiated rather than unified except at the topmost level.

The present controversy in India stems largely from the differences in scales of pay and in position or power between the generalist and the specialist. While it may be true that a generalist secretary of a department is necessary to guide ministers properly as the man who takes into account larger public interests, the specialist should not be denied the opportunity to occupy such position at the top if he is deemed to be fit. In the words of D. V. Kulkarni,

> suffice it to say that an administrator can be a social worker and a social worker can also prove to be an administrator by years of experience and training. No category either of the administrator or the specialist should claim a superiority over the other. It is only by accepting this position that both these categories can help each other and help together the common cause.[9]

This point has also been urged by Sir James Dunnet in a lecture delivered at Royal Institute of Public Administration (London) on 10 April 1961:

> The higher the expert rises in his profession, the more he in turn becomes an administrator. Moreover, the higher the level at which problems must be considered, the more they become matters for general judgment ... Thus the relationship between, say, the permanent Secretary of the Ministry and his chief engineer is essentially a partnership. In fact, it seems to me, that the relationship is essentially one of trust and mutual respect between the various parties concerned.[10]

The real solution to the problem, therefore, lies in the growth of proper understanding between the specialist and the administrator, and ultimately

> it is a matter of personalities rather than of organisation. If the administrative class are to have at all levels the last word it must be tactfully and understandingly said. No administrator could deny the importance of technical considerations; therefore, no administrator who is any good should deny the expert his say. Conversely, no specialist who is any good should assume that his administrative colleague is an ignorant bigot. Where the attitude is one of mutual understanding the public service benefits greatly.[11]

Staff, i.e., the specialist, and line, i.e., the generalist, are, therefore, operating not in a hierarchical relation but on a horizontal plane of authority and responsibility under the chief executive.

Notes and References

[1] S. P. Bapat, "Thoughts on Coordination," in *Indian Journal of Public Administration* 2, no. 3 (July–September 1956), p. 262.

[2] Letter No. 1/CI-102/55A (Part) 6828, dated 1-9-55, from the Chief Secretary, Govt. of Bihar to all departments.

[3] Marshall E. Dimock and Gladys O. Dimock, *Public Administration* (1964), p. 331.

[4] Brian Chapman, *The Profession of Government: The Public Service in Europe* (London: Allen and Unwin, 1954), p. 70.

[5] Arthur W. MacMahon, *Delegation and Autonomy* (Bombay: Asia Publishing House, 1961), p. 42.

[6] *Report of the Commission of Enquiry on Emoluments and Conditions of Service of Central Government Employees, 1957–59* (Government of India Press, 1959), p. 111.

[7] V. T. Krishnamachari, *Report on Indian and State Administrative Services and Problems of District Administration* (Delhi, 1962), p. 52.

[8] A. K. Chanda , "Indian Administration," p. 113.

[9] D. V. Kulkarni, "Organisation and Administration of Social Work," in *History and Philosophy of Social Work in India*, p. 491.

[10] James Dunnett, "Civil Service Administrator and the Expert," *Public Administration* 39, no. 3 (September 1961).

[11] Bosworth Monck, *How the Civil Service Works* (London, 1952), p. 39.

41

Generalists versus Specialists in Indian Administration

A Comment*

Deepak Lal

Ashoke Mohan Roy's two long articles[1] are more in the nature of a restatement and survey of old positions and battlegrounds in the generalist-specialist controversy, and do not add anything new to the debate. This comment seeks to redress this by focusing attention on some crucial distinctions and clarifying some vague terms whose continual use has obscured the really important points in the debate. Finally, an attempt will be made to outline a possible solution for this rather unnecessary cleavage.

The first important distinction to be noted is that between policy *formulation* and policy *implementation*. As most often the same governmental organisation is involved in both these aspects of government, there is a natural tendency to slur over this distinction. This is best exemplified by the indiscriminate use of that emotive word "coordination." The generalist administrator's chief virtue is that he is the coordinator *par excellence*. Once, however, it is remembered that coordination is an administrative function of the operational or implementational kind, it becomes clear that it is connected with the policy-implementing rather than the policy-formulating role of the administrator.

Let us examine this term coordination a little more closely, for its loose use has been responsible for a great deal of confusion in the generalist-specialist debate.

To talk of an administrator exercising the coordinative function in the decision making process sounds, to say the least, a bit odd. For "coordination" normally implies the coordination of activities, seldom if ever, of ideas or theories. One

*Originally published in *Economic Weekly* 16, no. 28 (8 August 1964), pp. 1355–58.

can "synthesise" or "reconcile" the latter, but one can hardly talk of coordinating these ideas or theories. Thus, common language makes a distinction between the coordination of decisions and the synthesising of ideas and theories which go to make these decisions.

Coordination is, therefore, a function which is concerned with the part of government which is concerned with the performance of various activities, namely, implementation of policy. It is, moreover, related to activities which are complementary or interdependent and cannot be applied to areas which are completely unconnected with each other. This function moreover does not require any specialist expertise but is the most important part of the generalist art of managing people. Therefore, a very important conclusion of our discussion at this stage is that in the policy implementing stage there is the need for the exercise of a very important function, that of coordination, which is pre-eminently a generalist function.

What is Coordination?

If someone, however, does speak of "coordination" at the policy formulating stage, what could he mean? What he means is, clearly, the reconciliation of divergent viewpoints at the policy formulating stage, and this is not coordination, but the *reconciliation of divergent viewpoints*. It is important to put the above point in this tautologous form, for it is sought to be emphasised that there is no need to twist the ordinary meaning of words to assimilate statements which can be stated quite adequately in terms of ordinary language in their own right.

There is, moreover, a grave danger in trying to dilute the fairly clear-cut meaning of words to make them fit different descriptions. For, by using the same word to describe two distinct kinds of functions one is tempted to assimilate one in the other. This, in fact, is what seems to have happened in much of the writing on the generalist-specialist debate. Take Roy's statements, for instance. Here is an extract:

> It is argued that a general administrator is more appreciative of social necessity. *He specialises in coordination.* One important judgment which he has to make is whether the proposed programme is such as can be easily put into action for the benefit of society.[2]

Here we have three statements. From the first and the last it is clear that what is being discussed is the role of the generalist administrator in the formulation of policies, and yet sandwiched between the two is the statement in italics about coordination, which we have identified as a policy-implementing function. Clearly Roy doesn't appreciate the policy-formulating, policy-implementing distinction and the role of coordination in the latter. By this illegitimate slurring over of these crucial points persuasive content is given to the argument for having generalists in the policy formulating stage by quietly slipping in the term coordination, which everyone recognises to be an exclusively generalist virtue.

Apart from the above methodological points, the question "What are the specifically generalist functions in the decision-making process?" still remains. The first and last sentences in the passage quoted above illustrate the point that the distinctive role of the non-specialist in the decision making process is in introducing what I will call "extra-disciplinary" value judgments. Whereas the mere specialist is likely to be myopic as regards value judgments which do not directly impinge on his discipline, or his value judgments may not take cognisance fully of "social reality" or "necessity,"[3] the generalist, it is assumed, will not suffer from any of these disabilities, and his value judgments are likely to conform more to the needs of the "general welfare" of the citizens. For, the non-specialist administrator has "the advantage of bringing to the counsels of policy-making diverse held experience continually refreshed and renewed."[4] This enables him to work with value judgments which are tied more closely to "social necessity" than the specialist's. In fact it can be maintained that the administrator's generalist role in the policy formulating process is largely, if not only, that of applying the necessary normative constraints on the specialist's recommendations.[5] This is all that oft-repeated phrases "looking at matters from the point of view of the government as a whole," "a wider outlook and a commonsense approach," "not detailed knowledge, but the right approach, the right perspective with which the man analyses the problem"[6] can really be reduced if they are to have any meaning at all.

Value Judgments

Granted that the role of the generalist in the decision-making process is that of introducing extra-disciplinary value constraints, two questions arise. The first one is: Isn't the introduction of value judgments the exclusive role, and right, of the political executive? The answer to this is, not entirely. Apart from the normative question of whether it *ought* not to be, there is the contingent fact that the value constraints are given as a result of joint debate amongst the policy makers, namely, the political and permanent executive. But even within the value sphere there are value judgments of differing kinds and of differing degrees of importance. Hence the second question: The supplying of what form of value judgment, if any, is the exclusive prerogative of the bureaucracy? To find an answer to this question we may approach it by asking: In the case of conflicting value-judgments is there any particular sort of judgment which the political executive would find very difficult to override? Clearly, in the case of most value judgments, given the constitutional superiority of the political executive, any conflict, if it arises between, say, a minister and his secretary will be resolved by the overriding authority of the political boss. There is, however, one class of subjective evaluations where the political boss may find it difficult, if not impossible, to override the judgment of the bureaucrat. This is in the sphere of judgments regarding the feasibility of a particular policy or programme. This is a judgment of administrative feasibility, not technical feasibility (which is the specialist's area), and it is here that the wide administrative experience of the generalist administrator in implementing particular and diverse policies is likely to be so important. It is important to note that it is his experience as a *policy implementor* which enables him to introduce this specifically generalist value judgment into the policy-making process. Furthermore, it is the relative permanency of the bureaucracy vis-à-vis the political executive, and the consequent existence of a "departmental memory," which gives the bureaucracy its overriding influence in judgments of feasibility which are a very important part of any decision-making process.[7]

We thus find that we can delineate two broad generalist functions of the administrator. Firstly, the coordinative function, which is part of the policy-implementing aspect of his job. Secondly, the function of introducing normative extra-disciplinary constraints, chiefly in the form of judgments of feasibility, which is part of the policy-formulating aspect of his job.[8]

What, then, of specialist functions within government? Clearly in the actual implementation of many programmes exclusively specialist skills are called for—for example, in building a dam. These may be called the "engineering" aspects of implementation, and would clearly be a specialist monopoly, just as the other important aspect of implementation, coordination, it has been argued, is a generalist preserve.

This takes us to the sphere of decision making. With the increasing role of government in the socio-economic life of the community, the problems faced by government have become more complex, more technical, and more far-reaching in their impact. At the same time, planning necessitates positive decisions which involve choosing and allocating between different ends and resources. Very often the latter task involves the evolution, understanding, and application of fairly technical criteria. Furthermore, planning is always being done within the constraint of the time factor. Quick technical decisions are called for.

These considerations bring us to the heart of the shortcomings of the pure generalist in the contemporary decision-making process—the problem of being adequately informed. The decisions which the administrator has to make, or help to make, must be informed, and if a precondition of the success of the necessary information being understood is some technical knowledge, clearly, specialist knowledge will be required by the administrator. This specialised knowledge can be looked upon more as familiarity with a particular language of discourse, or the ability to maintain a discussion in a particular idiom. This language or idiom must necessarily be that of the specialist, firstly, because of the time constraint noted earlier—constant translation into a language the administrator understands would be inefficient—and secondly, because the conclusions of the specialist will flow from the particular and peculiar logic of his own specialised language. In order to carry on a meaningful discourse with him, which would be purposeful in the sense of either finding fault with the logic of his argument, or the illegitimacy of his conclusions and/or assumptions (implicit and explicit), or of trying to grope towards an alternative formulation, the administrator will require knowledge of and training in, the specialist's idiom. Translation would be inadequate as the conceptual framework of the particular discipline, which alone gives meaning to disparate elements of fact and judgment, is likely to become hazy and loose in the process of translation, with all the concomitant dangers regarding the "correctness" of the administrator's decisions. And considering the far-reaching implications of even the most minor decision taken by government—in terms of people affected—even small mistakes would be socially costly, and hence have to be avoided.

Clearly, therefore, mere generalist capacities of "having one's heart in the right place"—in other words, feeding in the socially desirable value judgments—will not be sufficient and are certainly inefficient in performing the tasks of government in a welfare state. Lacking specialised knowledge—in the sense we have outlined—the administrator will become either redundant, just accepting the recommendations of the specialist departments, or else he will take a decision which, being uniformed, may be completely arbitrary and unjustified. This is especially so in the case of economic decisions. These can involve highly technical concepts and theory, whose complexity increases with the growth and sophistication of the economy. "Dr Beeching's example shows what happens when a distinguished metallurgist begins to dabble in welfare economics without prior training."[9]

TRAINING THE ADMINISTRATOR

This raises the question of the content of the specialised "prior-training" for the "would-be" administrator. Here again, there are a number of confusions all connected with the term "specialisation." One general misconception is that specialisation is connected in some very close manner with the degree of rigour of a discipline. On this view a more specialised knowledge of a subject is merely a more rigorous knowledge, and hence what the administrator needs is a less rigorous treatment of a subject. This is the assumption behind the current training scheme for Indian administrators. That this assumption is false can be demonstrated in the following manner. Take two students of a particular discipline, of equal brilliance and competence in their subject. At the end of their degree course one of them decides to specialise in the subject, whilst the other decides to enter the bureaucracy. Clearly, before the choice of their respective careers both students had the same degree of rigorous mastery over their subject—given our homogeneity assumption. What, then, does the decision of one of these students to specialise imply? I would suggest that it implies two things. Firstly, it implies a decision to devote one's working time to that particular discipline, and this has got nothing to do with increasing rigour (assuming that both the students already have a rigorous mastery over the subject) and, secondly, it implies an undertaking to be at the frontier of advance of his particular area of study, in the sense of both assimilating and adding to advances. Specialisation can, therefore, be looked upon as a commitment to continue practising and using the skills and tools of a particular discipline. Specialised knowledge, on the other hand, would imply knowledge of, and proficiency in the skills and tools of a particular discipline, without any commitment towards using these tools and skills to make further advances in that area of study. From this it seems reasonable to conclude that when specialisation is talked about, what is normally meant is not the intensifying rigour of the discipline, but greater devotion of time and energy to a particular discipline. In mastering a particular subject with or without the intention of specialising in it, the rigour of the discipline is indivisible, and the absence of rigour merely marks off the bad student from the good one.

Thus it is most important to remember that in imparting specialist knowledge to administrators, for the reasons we have outlined, it is imperative that the fallacy of considering the providing of specialised knowledge for the administrator as merely diluting the discipline, be avoided. To attain specialised knowledge, the particular discipline must be mastered, irrespective of whether or not one is going to specialise in it later on. In this context a study of the French system of training administrators may prove very useful. The French give their administrators a thorough grounding in specialised disciplines in the social sciences, and they perhaps approximate closest to the ideal administrator in a modern welfare state whose features will be delineated in the last paragraph of this article. The contemporary French bureaucrat is both a specialist and a generalist, and his superiority over the traditional dilettantish English bureaucrat is proved by the Brussels negotiations where "in the negotiations with the French technocrats, the sole British representative to stand up to the challenge was a war time re-emit from a University."[10]

We are thus led to our general conclusion that much of the generalist-specialist cleavage is spurious, and certainly as traditionally presented, confusing. The modern administrator needs *both* specialist and generalist qualifications. There is the need for, to coin a phrase, 'specialist-generalists." As Appelby points out,[11] generalist and specialist are relative terms. There should not be any question of an "either-or" type answer. In fact, from our analysis we have discovered that the modern administrator needs both these qualifications for his efficient functioning. In the policy-implementing aspect of his job he needs to be a coordinator, which is a very important generalist function. At the policy-formulating stage, he needs to be a generalist in the sense of feeding in extra-disciplinary value-judgments, culled from his wide administrative experience, into the decision-making process. The most important of these judgments is with regard to feasibility. But at the same time, in policy formulation, he requires mastery over certain specialised techniques, or languages of discourse, in order to facilitate the taking of informed decisions. This specialised knowledge is unfortunately lacking in most of our administrators, whilst attempts to impart this to fresh recruits are misplaced because of a misunderstanding of the nature of specialised knowledge required—a misunderstanding we have traced to the "specialisation" fallacy. Until our administrators are given a rigorous training in certain social sciences they will not be able to fulfill one of their most important functions within the decision making process—the taking of informed decisions. We must therefore bid farewell to the ICS and usher in the age of the "specialist-generalist" administrator, or more simply of the technocrat.

NOTES AND REFERENCES

[1] Reprinted as Chs. 40 and 41 in this volume. Originally published in *Economic Weekly* 16, nos. 26 and 27 (27 June and 4 July 1964).

[2] Roy, "Generalists vs. Specialists in Indian Administration—II," p. 1097.

[3] Both the terms *social reality* and *social necessity* are by no means clear cut in their meaning, but we will for the purposes of this article abstract from the difficulties inherent in clarifying them.

[4] Roy, "Generalists vs. Specialists in Indian Administration—II," p. 1097.

[5] I shall be using the term normative in a wider sense than it is normally used. I shall use it to mean any subjective evaluation.

[6] Roy, "Generalists vs. Specialists in Indian Administration—II," p. 1097; N. V. Gadgil, quoted in Roy, "Generalists vs. Specialists in Indian Administration—I," p. 1063.

[7] It may also be noted that in the decision-making process the bureaucrat is generally presenting a departmental view point in cases where the decision involves a number of departments, and as such, phrase like "point of view of the Government as a whole" are certainly false if not meaningless. To give them any sort of operational significance some analysis of the sort outlined above seems necessary.

[8] Another very important distinction between interdepartmental and intradepartmental policy formulation has to be borne in mind. This has been slurred over in this article for reasons of space and emphasis. Using this distinction, one needs to emphasise the role of the bureaucrat in reconciling divergent interests *within* his department at the policy formulation stage. Interdepartmental reconciliation is the task mainly of the political executive. But it must be emphasised that the reconciliation of divergent viewpoints will be made impossible if the reconciliator lacks specialised knowledge which maybe a precondition of these viewpoints being understood. See the later sections of this article.

[9] Thomas Balogh, "Planning for Progress" (Fabian pamphlet, 1963), footnote 2, p. 31. Also see his "The Apotheosis of the Dilettante," in *The Establishment: A Symposium*, ed. Hugh Thomas.

[10] Balogh, "Planning for Progress," p. 31.

[11] Paul H. Appelby, "Generalist and Specialist," in *Public Administration for a Welfare State* (New York: Asia Publishing House, 1961).

42

The Meaning of Jawaharlal Nehru*

Rajni Kothari

Nehru's role in the development of a national consensus has been rather complex. He both embodied its spirit and worked for its substance. The former aspect has attracted more attention than the latter, his "charismatic" power more than his role as a nation-builder. Now, no one can deny the great unifying role of a powerful personality in the difficult period of transition and institutional fluidity. Such a personality symbolises a new age, quickens the pace of history, and drives and presses diverse elements into a single stream. Nehru did all this and thereby consolidated the more subtle bases of the Indian polity. But he did more. He gave to it a more durable foundation by incorporating his life's work—and the work of all his distinguished forbears—into a framework of rules, institutions, and conventions.

Beginning, Not End

Nehru doggedly allowed free scope to parliamentary government, was the chief operator of its mechanism of power, and through his long tenure legitimised its institutions and working principles. He was himself not too confident of this aspect of his work and often held too exaggerated a view of his own personality in holding the country together, and of the possible danger of disintegration after him. But here he reflected the empty mood and naiveté of the Indian intelligentsia[1] who projected him as their chief showboy rather than his own achievements as a politician and a man of affairs. It was in his social engineering capacities rather than his neat ideological formulations that Nehru's lasting contribution lies.

* Originally published in *Economic Weekly* 16, special number (18 July 1964), pp. 1203–07.

We have been told that with the passing away of Nehru an era has come to an end, but the fact is that the era of which Nehru laid the foundations through his long and uninterrupted leadership is only now beginning to take root. Nothing has ended with the passing away of Nehru: everything of value he left behind is going to last. Indeed, from all indications, things may take a turn for the better.

PROOF OF MATURITY

The ease with which the succession issue—for long a bogey of both Western and Westernised intellectuals—has been settled is a testimony to the maturity to which this country's institutions have arrived. In many ways we have now entered a period which is more fruitful and one with greater developmental potential than the one we have been through. Every developing society has to go through an integrative stage before it can think of building its productive powers and its national strength on an organised basis, or of even formulating a policy to this end. It cannot be different with India. Those who have so often lamented at the failing of the Indian political system have done so because they have put their fingers on the wrong problems and because they lack a perspective on national development. What the country has achieved under its first prime minister is no mean achievement by any standards. And it is not just the achievement of one man.

Several factors have contributed to this maturing of the nation's institutional growth under Nehru's leadership. The first biggest factor no doubt was the work done and the legacy left behind by the nationalist movement led by the Congress under the leadership of Mahatma Gandhi. A proper appreciation of the role of the nationalist movement in India's nation-building has not been made by academic historians. Working simultaneously on so many fronts and adopting a strategy remarkable in its unifying character, the "movement" took the Indian people to a new level of self-awareness. The legacies it left behind have also served us for a pretty long time. Firstly, there was the organisational legacy, a structure around which men and institutions could function at various levels, channelise their loyalties, and draw upon the loyalties of others. It was, secondly, a leadership legacy, the availability of tall men the like of whom has not been found in any newly independent country after the United States. It is true that both these legacies have, with the passage of time, thinned out, the organisation has been weakened, and the men have been demoralised under the strain of more exacting tasks. And this has its problems. Meanwhile, however, other structures have been created and these are likely to take root.

AT THE GRASSROOTS

Secondly, building on the legacy of the nationalist movement, there has been the penetration of the country by new institutional developments, especially at the lower tiers of the nation. In this, the system of patronage to which the Congress has given rise in the states and the districts is of great importance. It has enabled the spreading of distributive benefits and the involvement of traditional elites and entrenched social interests in the political-competitive processes of Indian democracy. The great drive of the Congress to either capture or neutralise labour and peasant organisations, to set up ancillary agencies in the cooperative, community development and local government sectors, and to penetrate caste and community organisations, has led to an integration into the national mainstream of critical subsections of the public. Finally, there is the new multi-tier system of Panchayati Raj which has led to a further penetration into society of democratic institutions adopted by the modernist leadership at the national level.

The third factor that contributed positively to India's institutional growth is the result of the legislative-deliberative process. It consists in the removal of major sources of cleavage and disaffection from the Indian polity. The end of feudalism and landlordism removed the biggest single source of antagonism from the Indian countryside. The reorganisation of the states on linguistic basis removed a major source of cleavage from the political elite. Legislation dealing with labour disputes and providing protection and welfare to workmen contained, and brought contentment to, this potentially volatile section of the public. Laws dealing with property and inheritance rights, as well as with compensation for forfeiture of inherited rights, removed gross inequalities in the treatment of different classes and legitimised a more rational system of economic relations. And, finally, the partial success in handling the communal problem has helped contain the forces of disruption. Such a policy of neutralising social fissures has made obsolete the "class conflict" model of development in the Indian case. This is one important reason why stability has been made possible.[2] Together with the institutional growth factors mentioned above, these measures have provided us with a remarkable consolidation of our independence.

Amorphous with a Purpose

Fourthly, and providing the framework to these other factors, has been India's—and primarily Nehru's—faith in the values and institutions of democracy; and sincere and sustained efforts to put these into practice through the general elections. There is no doubt that without this last factor, all the other factors mentioned above would not have resulted in the present national consensus which is Nehru's greatest legacy. Even the mechanics employed by Nehru, which were the object of frequent criticism, such as the "balancing" of political groups and the consequent "amorphousness" of the political structure, had a role to play in the integrative stage of our development. It ensured that no single element in the constitution of the nation was carried too far, lest this may disrupt the entire nation-building enterprise. It is true that at times Nehru carried his apprehension of disruptive forces a little too far and this often inhibited a free competition between opposing points of new. But the logic of his approach is quite clear. It is also true that Nehru's preoccupation with the maintenance of his own personal power and ascendancy often led to acute political factionalism and the need for political scapegoats from time to time. This affected morale and gave rise to bitterness. On the other hand, by basing political power on self-interest (thus going against the cannons of India's political tradition), Nehru gave rise to a pragmatic orientation to politics, taught Indian leaders the art of managing men and institutions, and based political solidarity on the complex mechanics of secular relationships rather than on neat notions of sacrifice and transcendental nationalism. Nehru's role (often unconsciously played) was both to hold groups together under him and to tie them into a competitive web of relationships which would crystallise into more normal channels once his own personal weight was lifted.

Gift from China

There are also negative factors which have contributed to our stability and institutional development. Thus a substantial dose of political realism was injected in this nation through the Chinese aggression. By stirring the nation to its depths, the Chinese action forced us to come face to face with our strengths and weaknesses, destroyed our illusions and even managed in distributing the all-too-comforting symbol provided by the late prime minister. The results have in the long run been salutory. The Chinese would never have expected the constructive and integrative impact of their action on this country. Secondly, the bitter struggle for power that ended in the implementation of the "Kamaraj Plan" crystallised forces whose effects are only now being realised. The remarkable instrument of power and discipline called the Congress High Command that was forged by Mahatma Gandhi, and which was allowed to be overshadowed by the personality of Jawaharlal Nehru for some time, has again reasserted itself and is likely to hold power for a pretty long time. Thirdly, even the prime minister's illness in Bhubaneswar and in Delhi thereafter led to a crystalisation of individuals and positions which accounts for the ease with which the transition to the new collective has been made possible. It is this smooth transition, after a brief period of open confrontation and trial of strength, that has given a stamp of legitimacy and competence to the institutional development that has been described above.

Path Clear for the Centrists

As said in the beginning, we have arrived at a stage which may be more fruitful and exciting for the country's development. There are many reasons to support this point. For one thing, the wholly artificial left-right dichotomy in our politics will now lose much of its force. For all practical purposes, the "Left" in the Congress was both an unnecessary usurpation from the opposition and an unseemly assertion against the traditional leadership of the Congress Party. It now seems that this leadership will find the crystalisation which was not possible under the shadow of Jawaharlal Nehru. After nearly 15 years, the traditional Congressmen will again come into their own. It should be realised that these are powerful men, that the small and weak men who had found shelter for so long will have to go, and that a powerful and homogeneous group will emerge.

More important—and without this such a pragmatic group could not have emerged—is the fact that there has crystallised over the last few years an ideological consensus in this country, a consensus that has been ably summed up in the "Democracy and Socialism" resolution of the Congress Party. Academic critics of the resolution have characteristically missed the substance in it which consists in the compromise and consensus that it represents. It is a consensus to the making of which Nehru's life work was devoted. Significantly, the new leadership has emphasised this very aspect: Prime Minister Shastri, in his first broadcast to the Indian nation on 11 June, described the task ahead as the building of a "socialist democracy."

Finally, and providing a framework to all these, is the crystalisation of the party system of India. It is a party system which is in many ways without parallel. It can be characterised as a one party dominance system which, while it is open and competitive, assigns rather special roles to the opposition parties on the one hand and the state and national factions within the ruling party on the other.[3] Again, the passing away of Nehru has brought into bold relief the clear features of this party system—the importance of the Congress High Command as a collective, the complex relationship between the High Command, the Parliamentary Party, and regional Congress chiefs, and the crucial role of the party organisation in critical decision-making, and of party discipline in cementing differences. At any rate, single personalities will now play a lesser role in the party system than was the case so far. And the articulation and further crystalisation of the political consensus will be based on a more complicated inter-group structure than was the case so far, and on ideas and policies which are more the product of compromise and bargaining and less of theoretical or administrative rationale.

Genesis of the Consensus

Observers of Indian affairs have often criticised the "consensual" approach to politics and have traced it to conformist trends in Indian tradition.[4] What these writers overlook is the vital fact that every society must find its way to forming a consensus, and that a modernising society has to do so even more assiduously, especially where a colonial interlude has shaken traditional structures and values without replacing them with anything more durable. It is true that traditions of social and ritualistic conformism have left a deep mark on contemporary India, although contrary traditions can also be traced. It is also true that such conformist trends often militate against competitive politics and inhibit organisations built around the competitive principle. It is important to realise, however, that there is more than meets the eye here—that the emphasis on consensus and integration reflects an important problem of contemporary nation-building and is not just a carry-over from the past, that the democracy we study here is democracy at a particular stage of development, and that at this stage of development the competitive component in it is not the only or even the most important component to attend to. It is imperative at this stage to maintain order in the midst of change, to hold the temper of political struggle low, and to maintain a balance between competitive and consensual elements in the operation of democratic institutions.

At the same time, as seen above, the consensus that has been developing in India is not any single product of social conformism but the result of an involved process of interactions, in which force of personality, organisational discipline, penetration of political forms in society, political and factional struggle, and a drive for the removal of major sources of dissension have played their respective parts. The result is an increasingly pragmatic orientation of politics, a political culture that manages to be consensal by being accommodative and flexible, and a complicated structure of political decision-making. It would be a mistake to view the consensual forms in which Indian politics operates out of both the historical and the situational contexts that I have mentioned here. The best and most recent example is the "consensual" form in which Shri Kamaraj announced his party's decision on the question of the succession to Prime Minister Nehru.

My attempt in this article has been to describe more than to assess. Consequently, it perhaps leaves more of an impression of optimism than I had intended. However, this does not mean that I undervalue the tasks that lie ahead. The tasks are many and in some ways overpowering. They can be divided under two broad heads. The first are the consolidation tasks. The work of consolidation and integration is not yet over. The task is to meet the impending critical problems with equanimity, to keep the ideological temper low, and to put down with a strong hand the forces of disruption whenever they raise their ugly head. (It should be remembered that the communal problem has only been partially tackled in the past and it still remains largely unsolved. It can again be triggered off by either an internal or an external event.) This also brings out the critical importance of our external relations. More thought needs to be given to this than was done under Prime Minister Nehru.

Crucial Tasks

Secondly, there are what may be called the developmental tasks. Having achieved a degree of consolidation and integration, and having brought about an element of consensus in the nation, the leadership should look beyond, towards the productive functions of nation-building. The critical areas which require a determined approach are the reorganisation of the administrative structure and personnel in the country (the real blind spot in the nation), the building up of the military infrastructure of Indian democracy (necessarily a part of the developmental effort), and the pushing ahead with the programme of economic development through a greater concern for encouraging and mobilising voluntary effort and people's willing participation, with or without the help of the bureaucracy. These are tasks that may require substantial rethinking on some of our pet theories and models. Knowingly or unknowingly, Prime Minister Nehru had often permitted a simplistic view of things to prevail in his government. Himself, however, he had always shown a readiness to change outdated ideas and theories that had become dysfunctional to the tasks in hand. Preoccupied with his integrative role, he did not have enough time to implement this outlook in the realm of policy. There can be no better memorial to him than a continuous search for building further on the foundations he left behind and, wherever necessary, improving upon them.

Notes and References

[1] Sisir K. Gupta has expressed the view that Nehru provided the only symbol of unification in India. See his "Some Aspects of the Problem of National Integration in India, Pakistan and Ceylon," *Parliamentary Studies* 8, nos. 1 and 2. For a more naive presentation of the problem of disintegration, see Selig S. Harrison, *India: the Most Dangerous Decades* (Princeton: Princeton University Press, 1960). Harrison, who subtitles his book, "Can the Nation Hold Together?" found a very receptive audience among Indian intellectuals.

[2] For another view on the reasons for India's stability, see Sisir Gupta, "Indian Democracy: What Gives It Stability?," *The Economic Weekly* 12, special number (4 June 1960), pp. 843–45.

[3] For a more elaborate discussion of the one-party dominance system, see Rajni Kothari, "Party System," *The Economic Weekly* 13, no. 22; and Rajni Kothari, "Developing Political Pattern," *Seminar* (February 1962).

[4] A large number of western observers take such a position. See, especially, S. H. Rudolph, "Consensus and Conflict in Indian Politics," *World Politics* 13, no. 3 (April 1961), pp. 385–99. See also Myron Weiner, *The Politics of Scarcity* (Chicago and London: University of Chicago Press, 1962; and Bombay: Asia Publishing House, 1962).

43

Economic Ideology of Jawaharlal Nehru*

M. L. Dantwala

India's economic policy since Independence has a fairly clear vision of the ultimate goal, its social and economic colour and content, and the broad path to be followed in reaching it, though every street is not named. It is well-known that it was mainly because of Nehru's insistence that the ultimate goal of the socialist pattern of society has been adopted. It may be contended that this itself is a proof of Pandit Nehru's doctrinaire predilection. Such a view would, however, be unfair and quite erroneous. It would be tiresome to hunt out a string of apposite quotations to justify this verdict. But there is enough evidence in Pandit Nehru's speeches and writings to show that his image of socialism was anything but doctrinaire. In fact, he has often been chided by petty critics for the vagueness of his ideas. Pandit Nehru's socialism was born out of a deep attachment to the values of ethics and social justice. He had no intellectual commitment whatsoever to its mechanics as prescribed in the Marxist textbooks. While Pandit Nehru had great respect for many of the abiding insights of Marxist thought, he did not subscribe uncritically to any of its dogmas. The people around Nehru had perhaps a stronger attachment to the orthodox Marxist remedy. That their influence was not greater than what was occasionally reflected in his thinking, clearly shows that Nehru had an imaginative and not an imitative approach to socialism.

Divergence within Cabinet

Nehru has been often accused of harbouring in his Cabinet men with not only divergent but conflicting views and also those whose faith in socialism was at best

* Originally published in *Economic Weekly* 16, special number (18 July 1964), pp. 1209–11.

lukewarm. Was this an evidence of economic indecision or of political sagacity? Perhaps he was compensating for the lack of effective outside opposition by providing for it from within his own party! More seriously, was there at each stage in the course of development, an economic consensus about the one and the only right line of action, which Nehru and his well-knit Cabinet ought to have followed? Assuming there was, can we name the team retrospectively since 1947—which could have been selected or rejected—for doing the job and see whether we succeed where Nehru failed? In spite of his tolerance of doubtful socialists and transparent free-enterprisers perhaps as a countervailing force to disguised fellow-travellers at the highest level of policy-making, on certain basic aspect of the policy he was quite firm.

Biggest Contribution—Planning

Nehru's biggest contribution to economic strategy was in committing the nation to a policy of planned economic development. This was by no means the easiest thing to do. Within the country, he had to contend with his Gandhian colleagues who saw in this imposition of centralised statism, while they were emotionally committed to village self-sufficiency. Planning was equally an anathema to Western democracies whose financial aid was a critical factor in the task of development. (Soviet Russia was yet to adopt economic aid as an instrument of foreign policy). Whatever one's opinion may be on the functioning of the Planning Commission, there is no doubt that its very constitution, with the prime minister as its chairman, was an important landmark in the economic policy and development of the country.

Another equally important, though somewhat controversial, element of our economic policy, which but for Nehru's support would not have passed muster, is the launching of the modern type of industrialisation with its emphasis on heavy industries. This was interpreted by interested political groups as leading the country on the Soviet path, and by implication, towards totalitarianism. There was another section—well-meaning and sincere—in the country which felt that such a pattern of industrialisation was wholly contrary to what Gandhiji would have wished. The emphasis on heavy industries has been variously presented as tantamount to neglect of agriculture, the death-knell of khadi and village industries, and callousness towards the problem of unemployment. This is not the place to controvert this contention. Not only is such interpretation not true of Pandit Nehru's concept of economic development, support for it cannot be derived even from the Planning Commission's documents on Five Year Plans. As is being increasingly realised, the antithesis sought to be drawn between the development of industries and that of agriculture is totally false.

FLEXIBILITY, THE SAVING GRACE

It has been said that Nehru had a fascination—to which many political leaders are prone—for the big and the grandiose: the steel mills and the giant multi-purpose river-valley projects. Perhaps he had. It can also be said that he rarely went beyond the broad idea and did not bother to examine its manifold implications. How much of this blame should attach to him or to his advisers and administrators is perhaps a debatable issue. But then, there was always the saving grace of non-insistence and flexibility.

A classic example is the Nagpur Resolution on the future pattern of the agrarian structure. The resolution had categorically stated that the future agrarian pattern should be that of cooperative joint farming, in which land will be pooled. The reference was presumably to all land and not to the land only of the small uneconomic cultivator. At that moment, and for a considerable time thereafter, Nehru was convinced that this was the right stand. Later, partly because of the successful misrepresentation of this policy as confiscatory and anti-peasant and partly because of the practical difficulties in implementing it, the Nagpur Resolution was allowed to fade away.

There is another notable example in which he did not shirk the odium and embarrassment of reversing an accepted policy. This was in respect of the policy on the character and composition of Primary Cooperative Societies. The Committee of Direction of the Reserve Bank's Rural Credit Survey had recommended the formation of state-sponsored, large-sized, viable units of primary cooperative credit societies; and this was accepted by the Government of India. While, by and large, the recommendation was sound, in its implementation, several distortions took place. The idea of state-partnership led, in some places, to the dominance of government officials; and in launching large-sized societies, the element of mutual cooperation was relegated to the background. The prime minister reacted rather sharply. While inaugurating the Third Indian Co-operative Congress he said: "The government was quite wrong in accepting some of the decisions of the Rural Credit Survey Committee—not all. There was a tendency on the part of that committee to think that they (the people) are not competent enough, they cannot do a job by themselves; therefore, government officials must come in and help. Government money should push them up. If government money comes, that money is followed by government officials."

Later, when the National Development Council considered this question, the indiscriminate establishment of large-sized societies was stopped and renewed emphasis was placed on the cooperative element in the formation of primary societies. Apart from whether such a sharp reaction was justified or not, the episode illustrates how averse Pandit Nehru was to unnecessary extension of state interference in economic activities.

Basic Economic Policies Sound

The one significant test of the soundness of the basic economic policies adopted by the country under Nehru's leadership is their almost universal acceptance within the country as well as outside by all those who have taken an intelligent interest in the question. To quote a fairly recent and competent testimony, Prof. John Lewis in his *Quiet Crisis in India* states: "As a piece of macroeconomic calculus, the strategy that is incorporated in the Second and the Third Five-Year Plans (and presumably will be also in their successors) is basically sound and fairly well spelled out in its details."

He has also observed that among all the Indian groups concerned with national policy issues, there are only two that are fundamentally opposed to the kind of developmental effort the government is trying to lead: the neo-Gandhians and the ultra-laissez-faireists. I shall not mention his characterisation of these two groups. But unless some sort of Goldwaterian retrogression takes place, the economic philosophy of neither group is likely to enlist any significant following.

Whether this country is thrust to the brink of the Most Dangerous Decade and the Quiet Crisis or gathers speed on the runway for a graceful take-off will depend not on the adoption of any brand new economic strategy, but on the success or failure in the implementation of the strategy to which Pandit Nehru got the country committed, and which has come to stay. Marginal adjustments will no doubt be necessary, but the very fact that these would have to be only marginal, speaks a great deal of Nehru's economic statesmanship.

Notes on the Editors and Contributors

F. G. Bailey is Professor Emeritus of Anthropology, University of California, San Diego.

Pranab Bardhan is Professor Emeritus of Economics, University of California, Berkeley.

André Béteille is National Research Professor and Professor Emeritus of Sociology, University of Delhi.

Krishna K. Bharadwaj held the Chair of the Economics at the Jawaharlal Nehru University, New Delhi and worked at the University of Cambridge and the MIT Center for International Studies.

N. Bhattacharya was a Professor at the Economics Research Unit at Indian Statistical Institute, Kolkata.

Nirmal Kumar Bose was former director of the Anthropological Survey of India, and editor of the anthropological journal, *Man in India*.

S. Chakravarti was a distinguished Professor at the Delhi School of Economics. He was also a member of the Planning Commission.

O. L. Chavarria-Aguilar was Professor of Linguistics at the University of Michigan, Ann Arbor.

Bernard S. Cohn was Professor Emeritus in Anthropology at the University of Chicago, and former chairman of anthropology at the University of Rochester.

V. M. Dandekar was former director and then Professor Emeritus at the Gokhale Institute of Politics and Economics, Pune.

M. L. Dantwala served as the director of the department of Economics at Mumbai University and was founder-chairperson of the Centre for Development Alternatives.

A. K. Dasgupta was one of the pioneers of theoretical economics in India, and had taught at Dhaka and Banaras Hindu University, and was the director of the A. N. Sinha Institute at Patna. He was closely associated with the *Economic Weekly* and the *Economic & Political Weekly*.

Amlan Datta was former Vice-Chancellor of Visva-Bharati University and the University of North Bengal, and was director at the Gandhian Institute of Studies.

Bhabatosh Datta was Emeritus Professor of Economics at Presidency College, Kolkata and former chief of the South Asia division of the International Monetary Fund.

I. P. Desai was founder-director of the Centre for Social Studies, Surat and served as president of the Indian Sociological Society.

B. Dey was at the Indian Statistical Institute, Kolkata.

R. K. Eckaus is the Ford Foundation International Professor of Economics Emeritus at the Massachusetts Institute of Technology, Massachusetts, United States.

D. R. Gadgil was founder-director of the Gokhale Institute of Politics and Economics, Pune and served as Vice Chairman to the Planning Commission of India.

Ranjit Gupta was a Professor at the Indian Institute of Management, Ahmedabad and was Research Director of the Institute of Social Studies Trust, New Delhi.

Nicholas Kaldor was Professor of Economics at the University of Cambridge.

Iravati Karve was head of the Department of Sociology and Anthropology, Deccan College, Pune and founded the Department of Anthropology at the University of Pune.

D. V. Kelkar was a contributor to the *Economic Weekly*.

Rajni Kothari was founding director of the Centre for the Study of Developing Societies, New Delhi.

Raj Krishna taught at the Delhi School of Economics and the University of Rajasthan, Jaipur, and was a member of the Seventh Finance Commission.

Deepak Lal is a Professor of Economics at University of California, Los Angeles.

W. Arthur Lewis was a Nobel Laureate in Economics and served as University Professor, Princeton University.

McKim Marriott is Professor Emeritus of Anthropology and of Social Sciences in the College, University of Chicago.

D. P. Mukherjee was Head of the Department of Sociology at Lucknow University and held the Chair of Economics at the University of Aligarh.

Sudipto Mundle is Distinguished Fellow, National Council of Applied Economic Research and has worked as a director at the Asian Development Bank. He has also served as a member of the Fourteenth Finance Commission.

K. N. Raj was Professor of Economics at Delhi University, and founded the Centre for Development Studies in Kerala.

V. K. R. V. Rao was a National Professor, Government of India and established the Delhi School of Economics, the Institute of Economic Growth, New Delhi and the Institute for Social and Economic Change, Bengaluru.

Joan Robinson was a famous Professor of Economics at the University of Cambridge.

Asoke Mohan Roy was a contributor to the *Economic Weekly*.

George Rosen was Professor Emeritus of Economics at the University of Illinois at Chicago.

Paul N. Rosenstein-Rodan was Professor of Economics at the Massachusetts Institute of Technology, and also held positions at the World Bank, the London School of Economics, and University College, London.

Ashok Rudra had taught at the Indian Statistical Institute and Visva-Bharati, Santiniketan.

J. C. Sandesara is Professor Emeritus and former Professor of Industrial Economics at the University of Mumbai.

Amartya Sen is a Nobel Laureate in Economics and the Thomas W. Lamont University Professor, and Professor of Economics and Philosophy at Harvard University.

A. M. Shah is former Professor of Sociology, Delhi School of Economics, University of Delhi.

Ghanshyam Shah is former Professor, Jawaharlal Nehru University, Delhi and Centre for Social Studies, Surat.

Rohini Somanathan is Professor of Economics at the Delhi School of Economics, University of Delhi.

M. N. Srinivas was perhaps India's best-known sociologist. He established departments of Sociology at the Universities of Baroda and Delhi, and was a faculty member at the Institute of Social and Economic Change and the National Institute of Advanced Studies, Bengaluru.

Daniel Thorner in his 10 years of early career in India was closely associated with *Economic Weekly*; he then left India to take up an academic appointment at Sorbonne, Paris.

Jan Tinbergen was a Nobel Laureate who was founder-director of the Bureau for Economic Policy Analysis and founding trustee of Economists for Peace and Security. He was also former Professor at the Netherlands School of Economics, Rotterdam.